Shinobi Life

Vol. 7

Created by
Shoko Conami

HAMBURG // LONDON // LOS ANGELES // TOKYO

Shinobi Life 7
Created by Shoko Conami

Translation - Lori Riser
English Adaptation - Ysabet Reinhardt MacFarlane
Retouch and Lettering - Star Print Brokers
Production Artist - Star Print Brokers
Cover Designer - Amy Martin

Editor - Lillian Diaz-Przybyl
Print Production Manager - Lucas Rivera
Managing Editor - Vy Nguyen
Senior Designer - Louis Csontos
Director of Sales and Manufacturing - Allyson De Simone
Senior Vice President - Mike Kiley
President and C.O.O. - John Parker
C.E.O. and Chief Creative Officer - Stu Levy

A **TOKYOPOP** Manga

TOKYOPOP and 🐸 are trademarks or registered trademarks of TOKYOPOP Inc.

TOKYOPOP Inc.
5900 Wilshire Blvd. Suite 2000
Los Angeles, CA 90036

E-mail: info@TOKYOPOP.com
Come visit us online at www.TOKYOPOP.com

ISBN: 978-1-4278-1847-8

First TOKYOPOP printing: April 2011
10 9 8 7 6 5 4 3 2 1
Printed in the USA

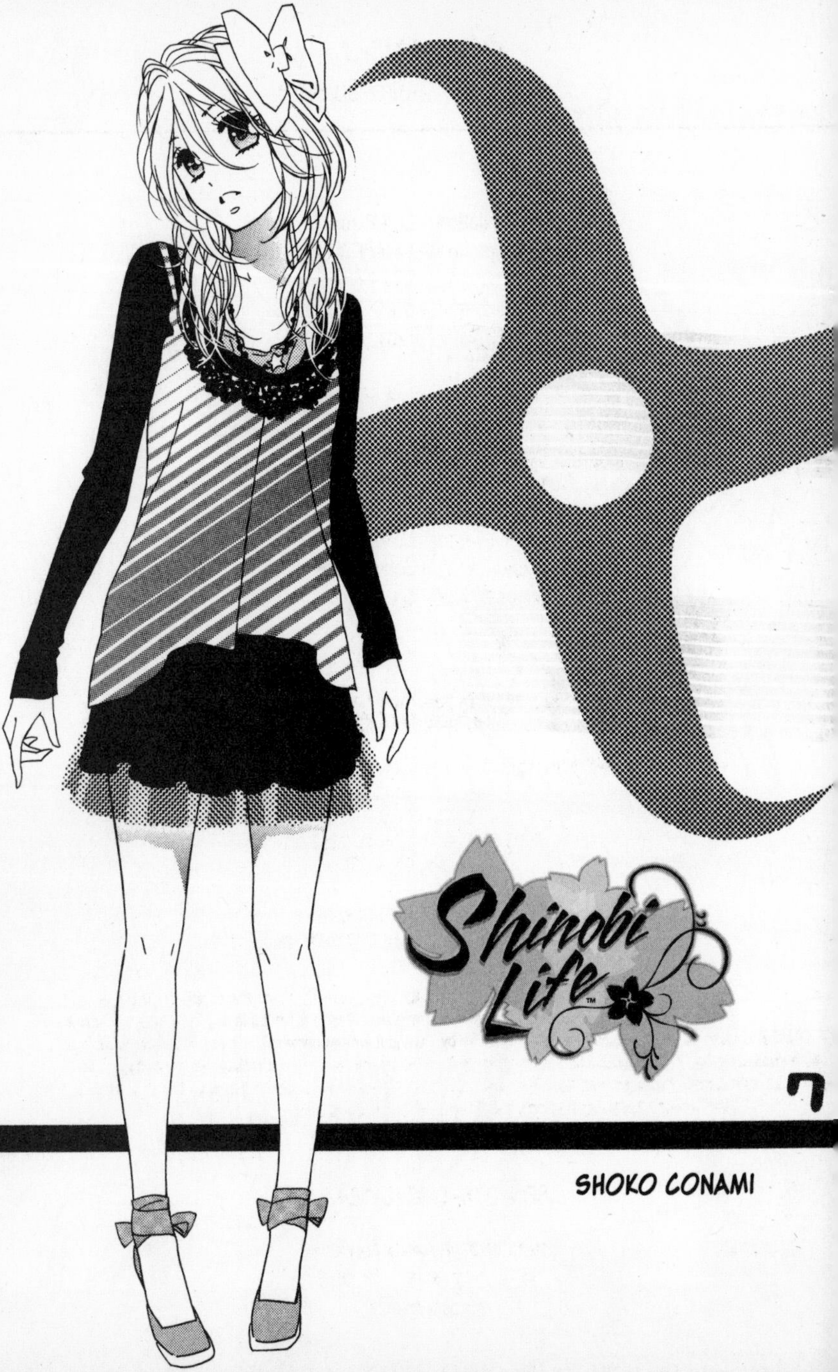

Shinobi Life™

7

SHOKO CONAMI

haracter Introduction

YOUNG KAGETORA

KAGETORA

A NINJA FROM THE PAST. HE'S DECIDED
TO LIVE IN THE PRESENT WITH BENI.

BENI FUJIWARA

A HIGH SCHOOL GIRL WHO'S FALLEN
IN LOVE WITH KAGETORA (?!).

YOUNG HITAKI

HITAKI

KAGETORA'S NINJA COMRADE. HE'S
OUT TO DESTROY KAGETORA'S LIFE.

RIHITO IWATSURU

BENI'S CLASSMATE AND FIANCÉ

✦ BENI, A HIGH SCHOOL STUDENT, AND KAGETORA, A NINJA WHO TIME-TRAVELED FROM THE PAST, FELL IN LOVE AFTER THEIR FATES (LITERALLY) COLLIDED. THEY'VE HAD THEIR UPS AND DOWNS, AND RIGHT NOW THEIR RELATIONSHIP'S FUTURE DOESN'T LOOK SO BRIGHT.

✦ BENI AND KAGETORA FLEE HER FATHER'S HOUSE TO ESCAPE HIS CONTROL AND RIHITO'S AGGRESSION. WHEN HITAKI CORNERS THEM ON A ROOFTOP, THEY DECIDE TO ESCAPE TO THE PAST...BUT ALONG THE WAY, THEY'RE SEPARATED. ALONE IN THE PAST, BENI ENCOUNTERS KAGETORA—A 14-YEAR-OLD KAGETORA WHO DOESN'T KNOW HER *OR* BENI HIME! SHE SOON MEETS HITAKI'S YOUNGER SELF AS WELL.

✦ MEANWHILE, KAGETORA HAS BEEN TRAVELING BACK AND FORTH BETWEEN THE PAST AND PRESENT, TRYING TO FIND BENI, BUT HAS HAD NO SUCCESS. AS HE VENTURES INTO THE PAST ONCE AGAIN, HITAKI AND RIHITO FOLLOW HIM.

✦ IN THE PAST, A MENACING AIR HANGS OVER THE VILLAGE OF THE SHINOBI. ONE AFTER ANOTHER, NINJAS ARE DYING WHILE CARRYING OUT THEIR MISSIONS. MANY PEOPLE SUSPECT RENKAKU, WHO HAS THE POWER TO SEE THROUGH LIES, BUT THE TRUE TRAITOR IS HITAKI'S GUARDIAN, HACHIKUMA—WHO IS ACTUALLY HITAKI'S LONG-LOST OLDER BROTHER, TOUKICHI, IN DISGUISE! TOUKICHI'S MISSION IS TO OBLITERATE THE INUI CLAN, BUT HE STRUGGLES WITH WHAT HE MUST DO...

RENKAKU

KAGETORA AND HITAKI'S GUARDIAN IN THE PAST.

HACHIKUMA

HITAKI'S GUARDIAN IN THE PAST.

TOUKICHI (SHIROUSA)

CONTENTS

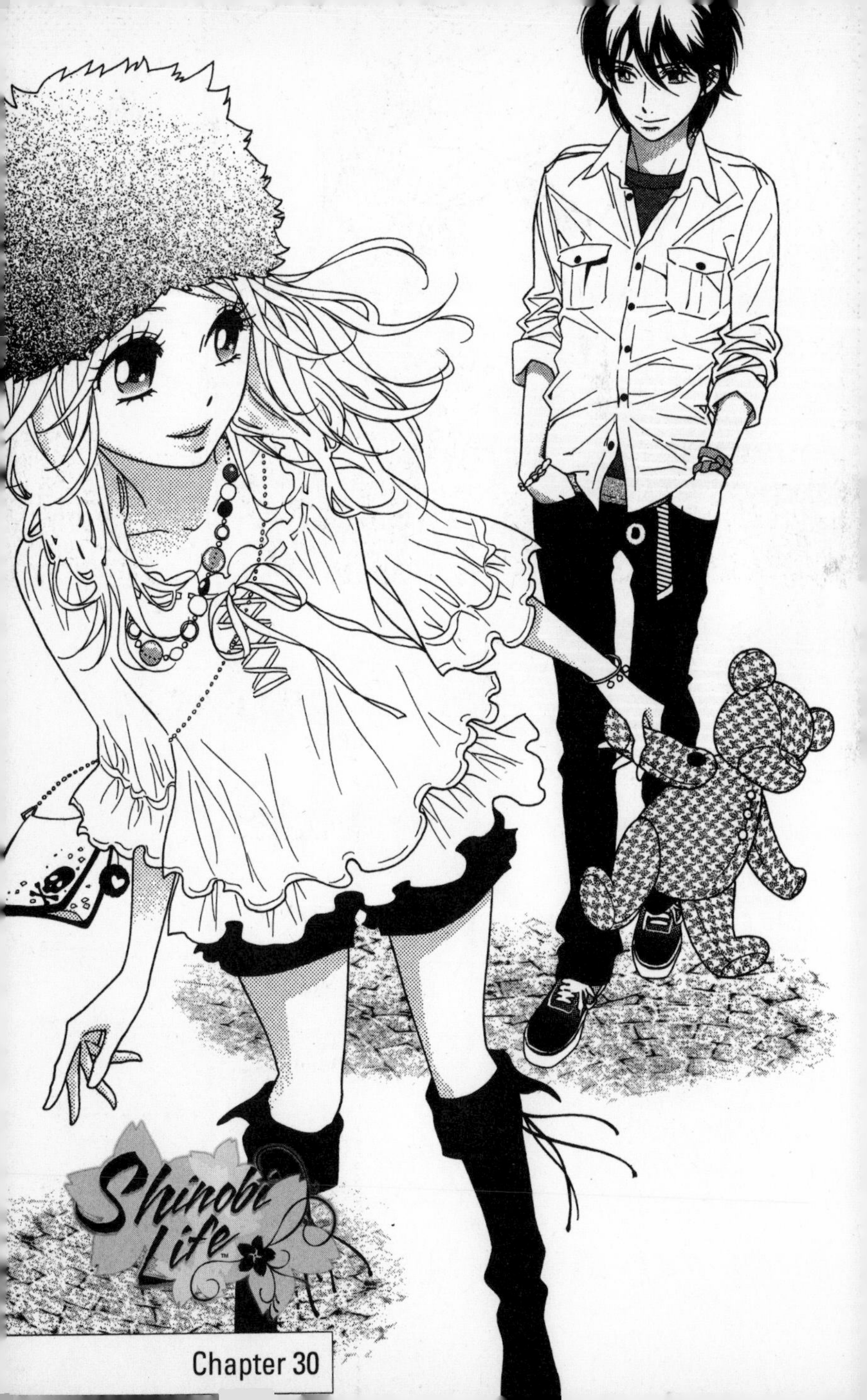
Shinobi Life™
Chapter 30

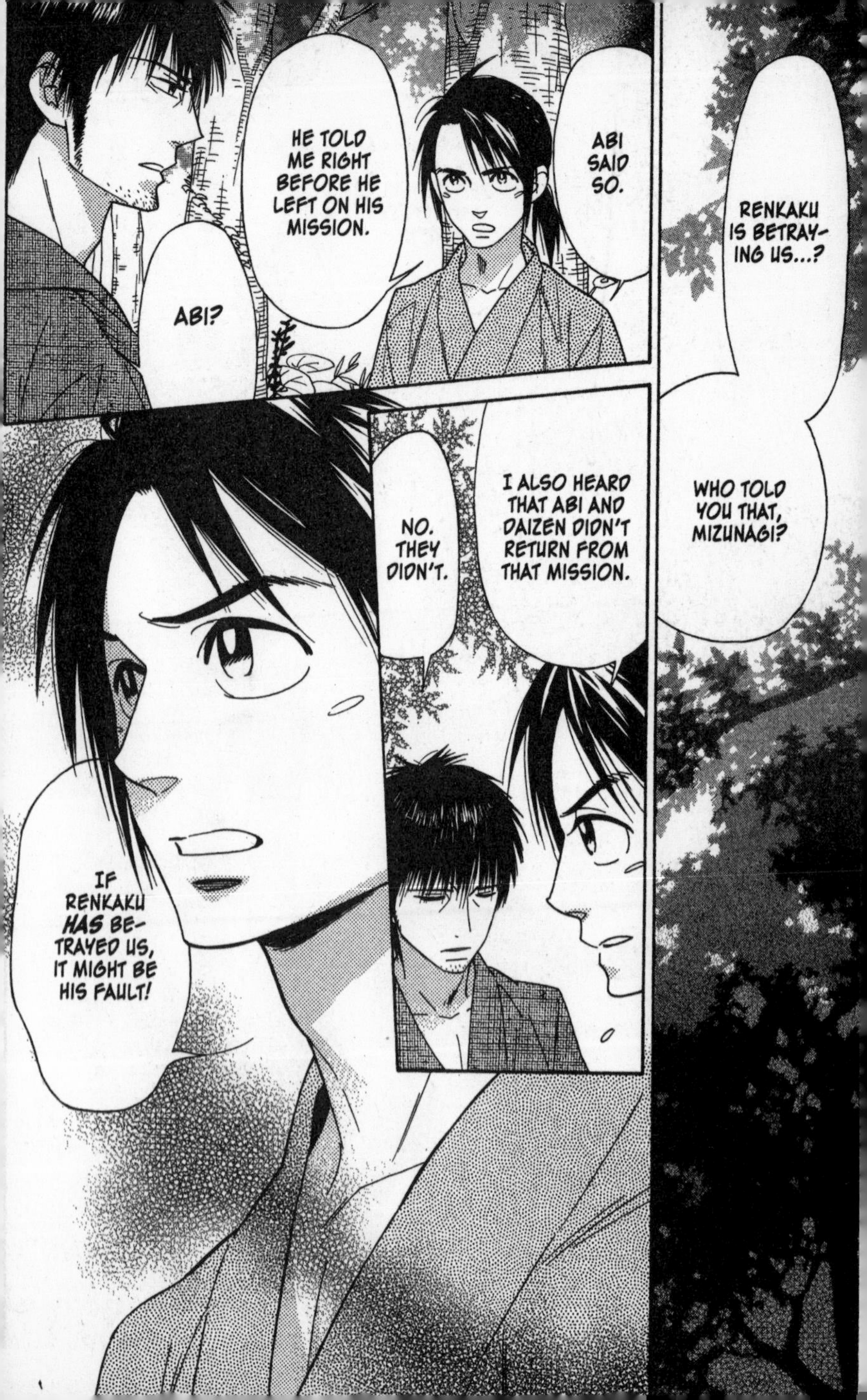
RENKAKU IS BETRAYING US...?
WHO TOLD YOU THAT, MIZUNAGI?
ABI SAID SO.
HE TOLD ME RIGHT BEFORE HE LEFT ON HIS MISSION.
ABI?
I ALSO HEARD THAT ABI AND DAIZEN DIDN'T RETURN FROM THAT MISSION.
NO. THEY DIDN'T.
IF RENKAKU ***HAS*** BETRAYED US, IT MIGHT BE HIS FAULT!

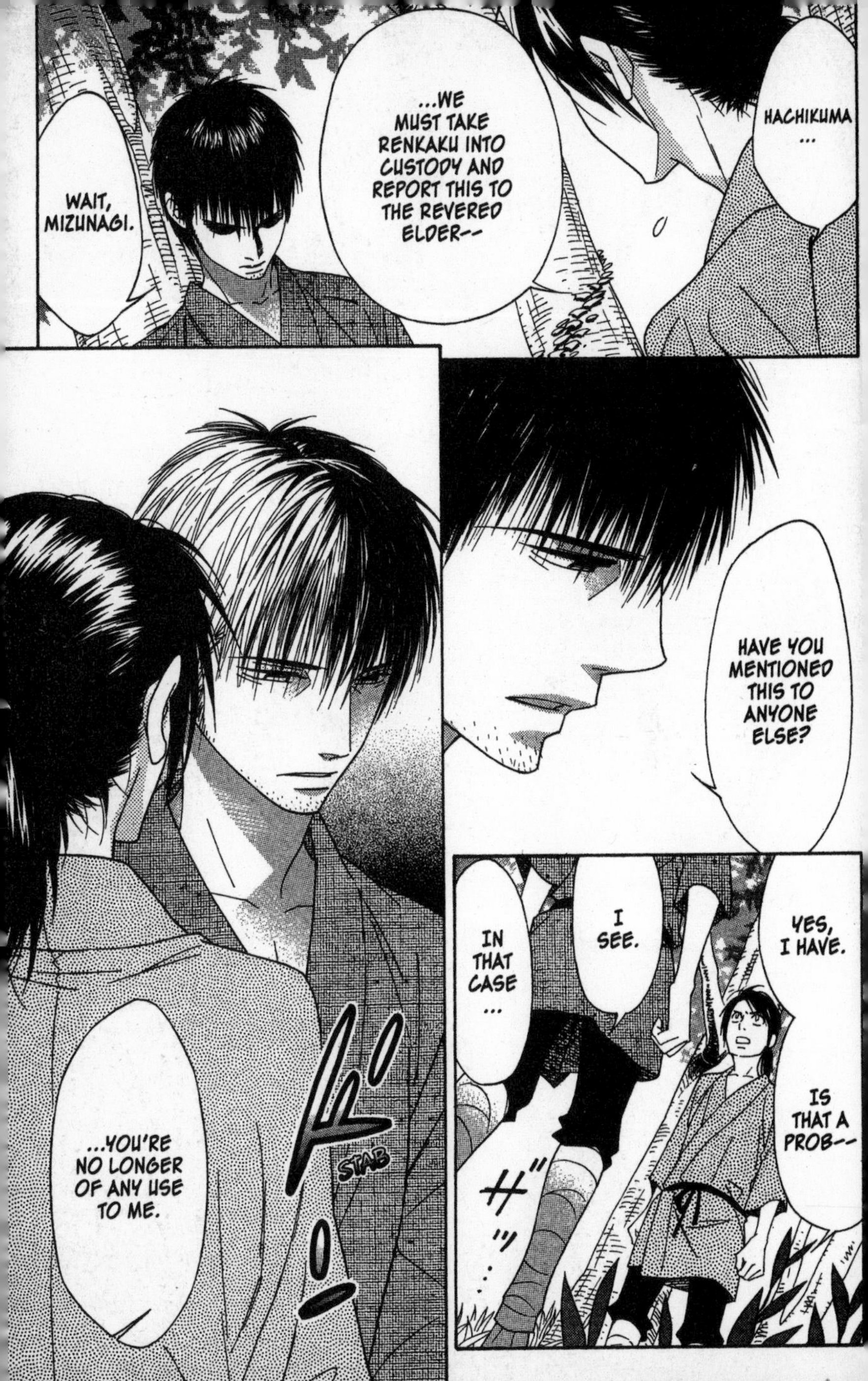
HACHIKUMA...
...WE MUST TAKE RENKAKU INTO CUSTODY AND REPORT THIS TO THE REVERED ELDER--
WAIT, MIZUNAGI.
HAVE YOU MENTIONED THIS TO ANYONE ELSE?
YES, I HAVE.
IS THAT A PROB--
I SEE.
IN THAT CASE...
...YOU'RE NO LONGER OF ANY USE TO ME.
STAB

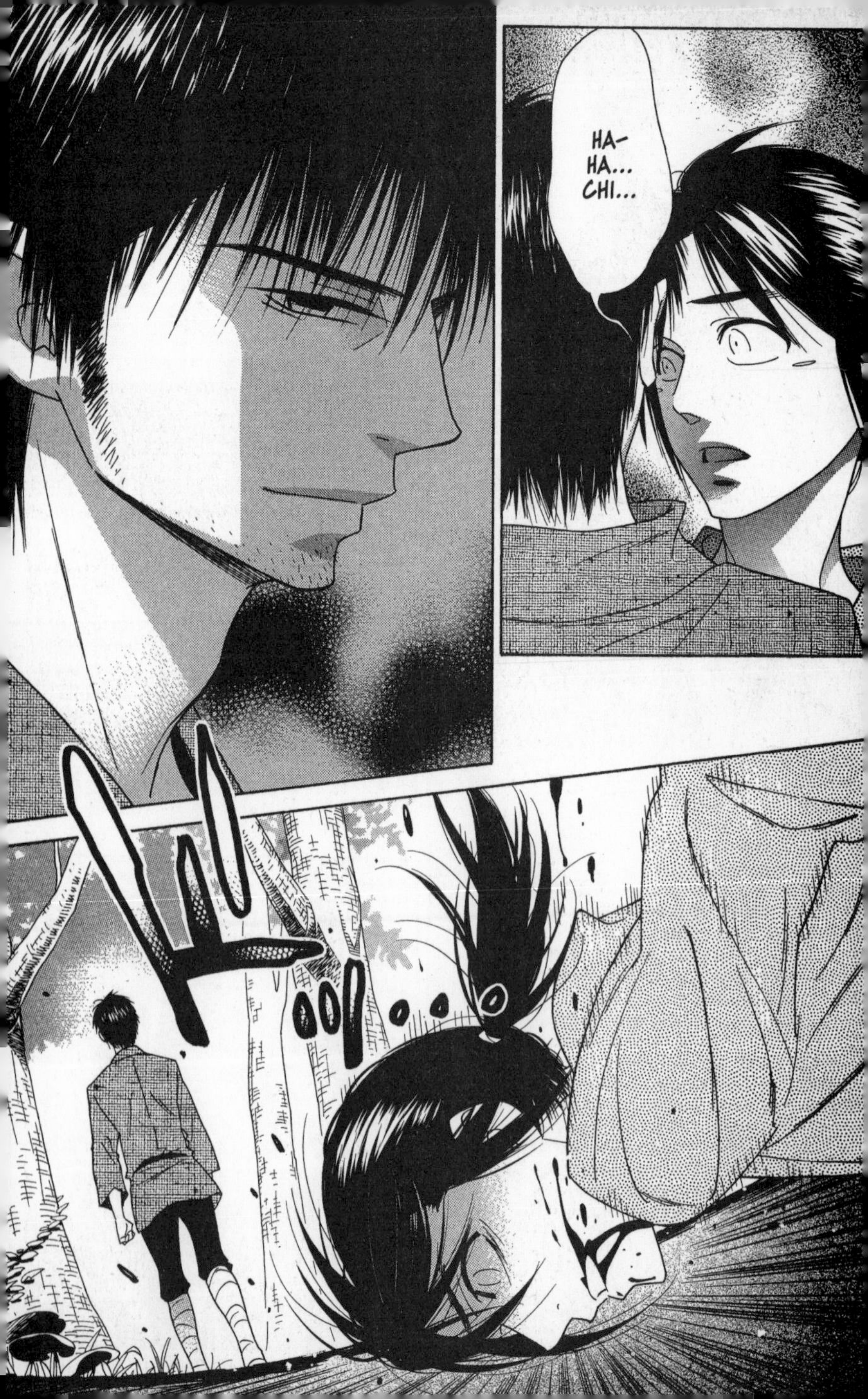
HA-HA... CHI...

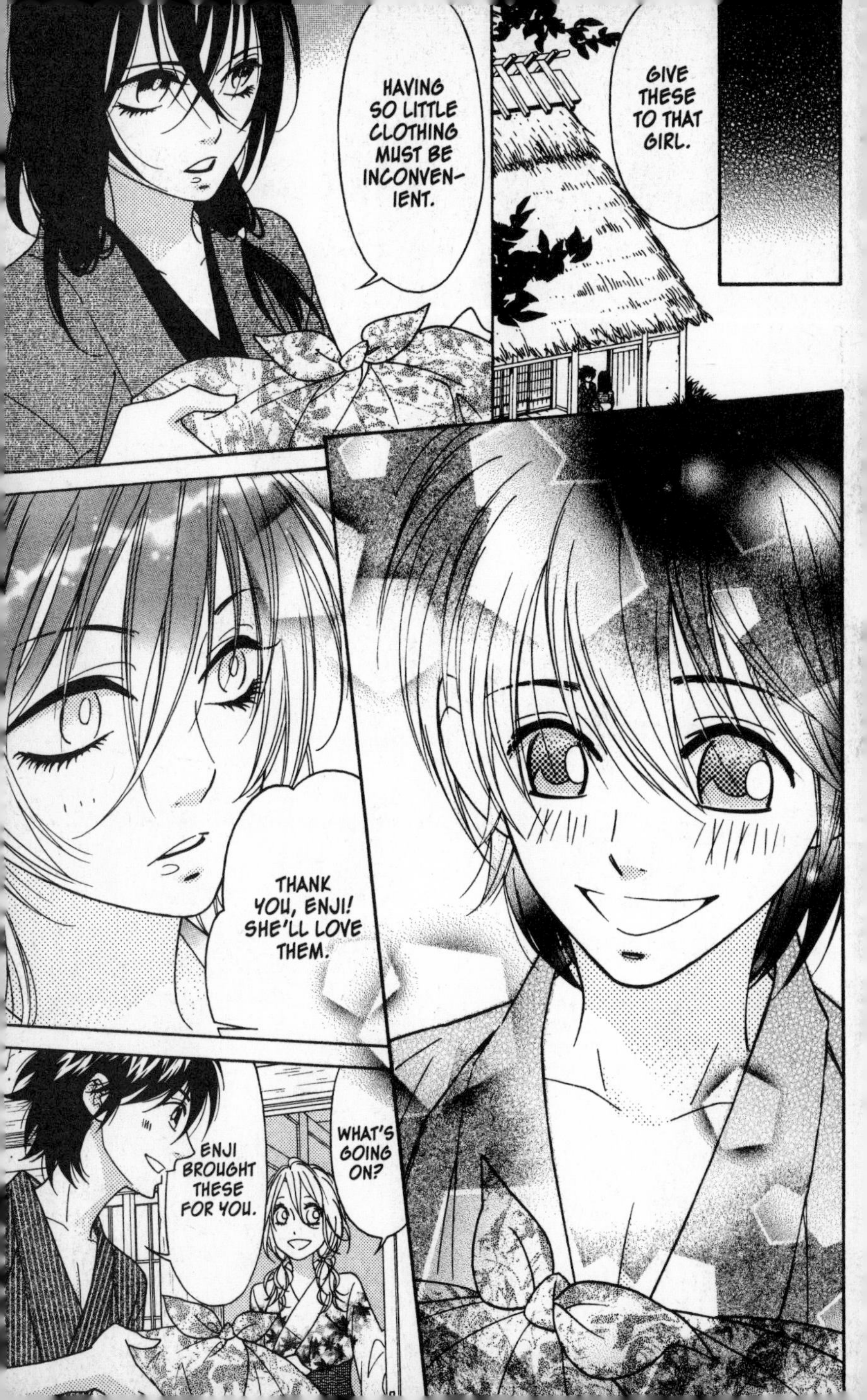
GIVE THESE TO THAT GIRL.
HAVING SO LITTLE CLOTHING MUST BE INCONVEN-IENT.
THANK YOU, ENJI! SHE'LL LOVE THEM.
WHAT'S GOING ON?
ENJI BROUGHT THESE FOR YOU.

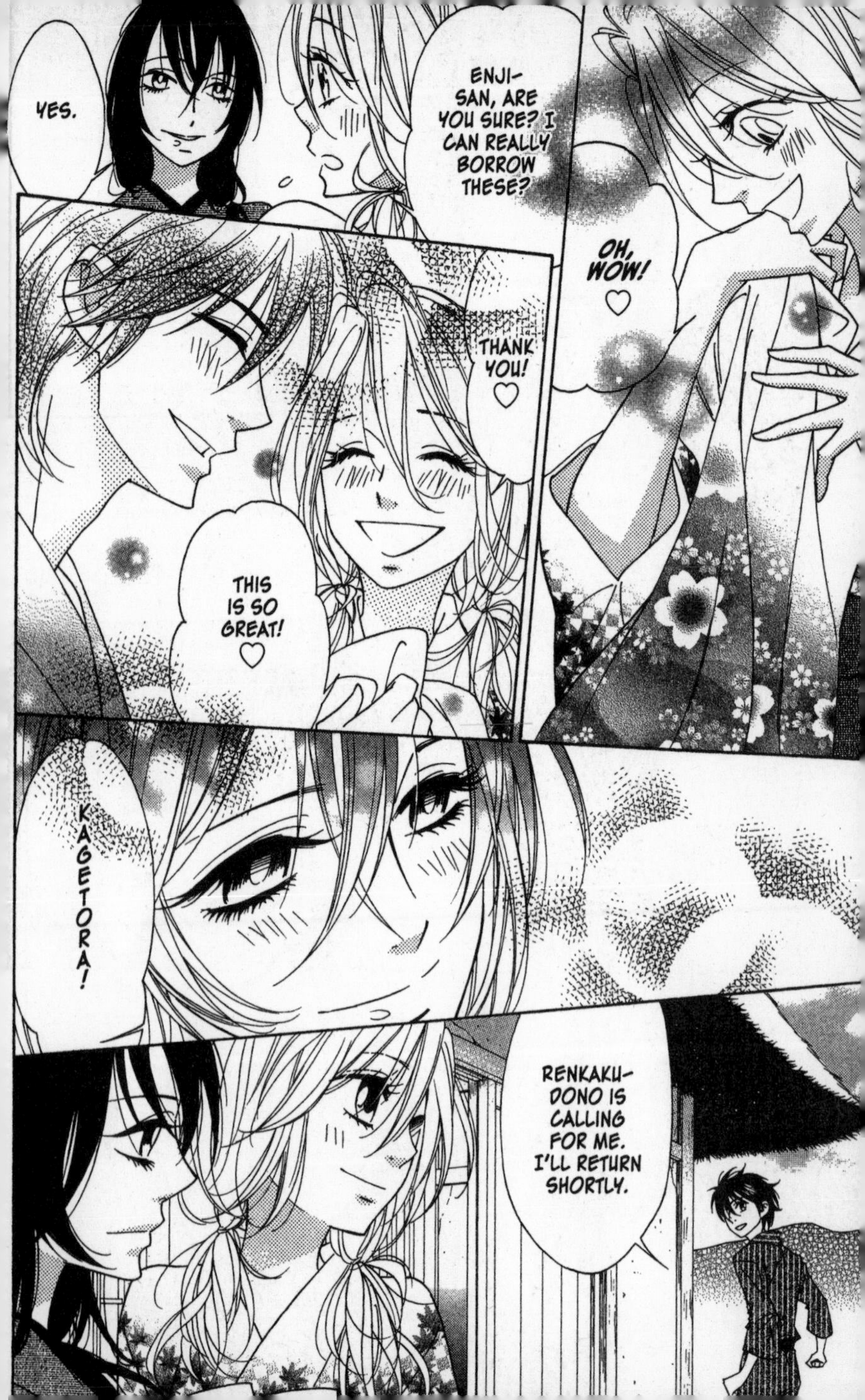
OH, WOW! ♡
ENJI-SAN, ARE YOU SURE? I CAN REALLY BORROW THESE?
YES.
THANK YOU! ♡
THIS IS SO GREAT! ♡
KAGETORA!
RENKAKU-DONO IS CALLING FOR ME. I'LL RETURN SHORTLY.

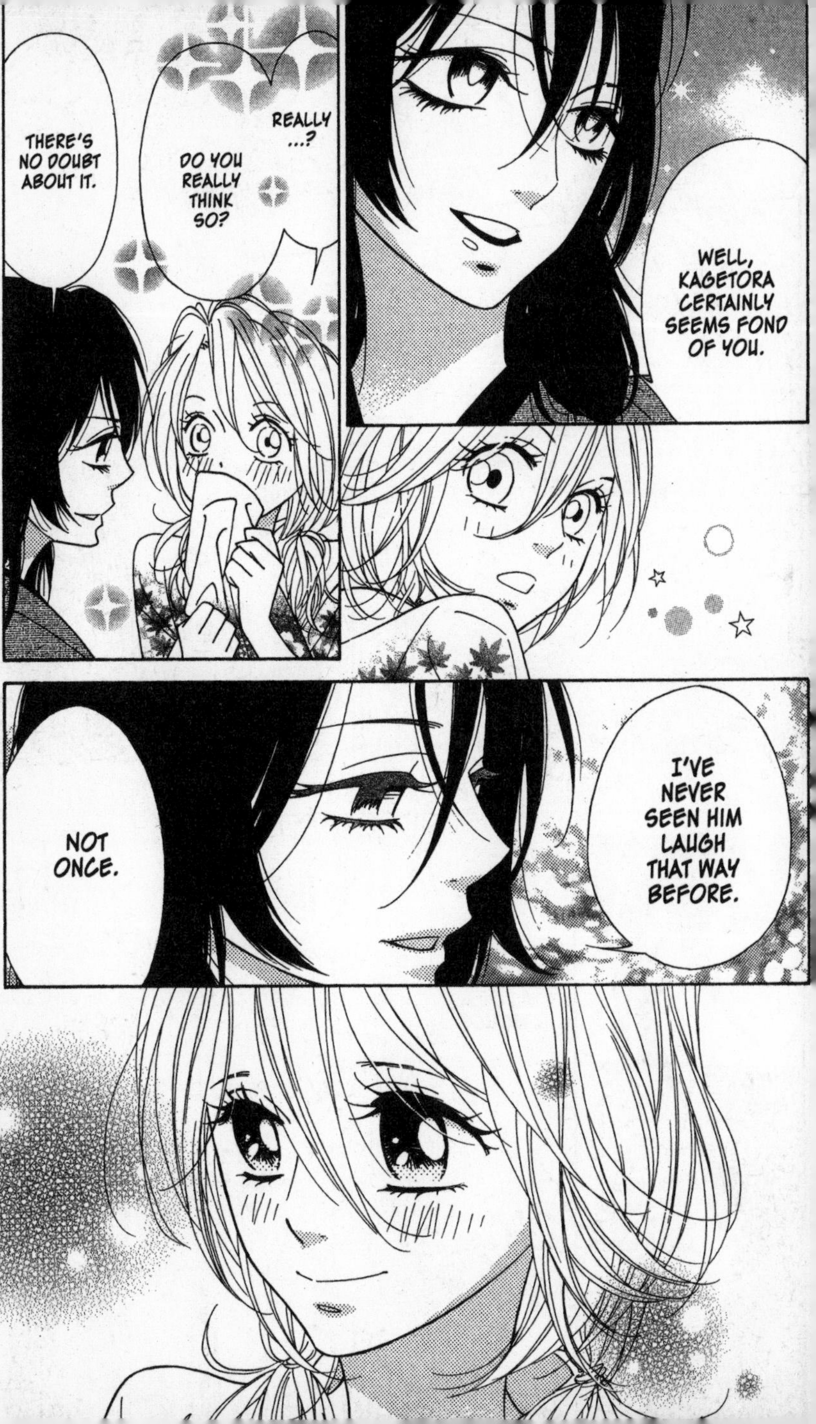
WELL, KAGETORA CERTAINLY SEEMS FOND OF YOU.
REALLY ...?
DO YOU REALLY THINK SO?
THERE'S NO DOUBT ABOUT IT.
I'VE NEVER SEEN HIM LAUGH THAT WAY BEFORE.
NOT ONCE.

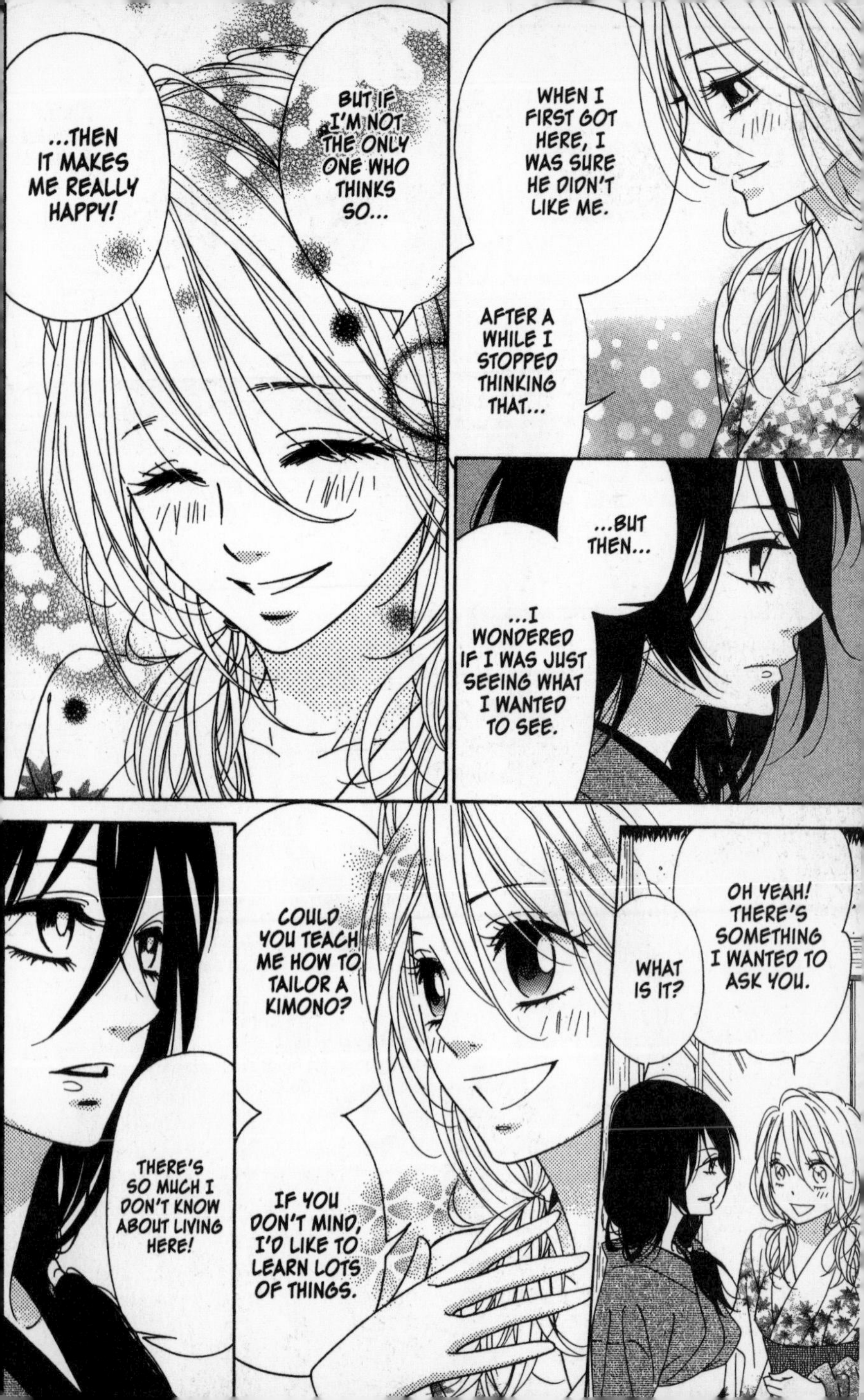
WHEN I FIRST GOT HERE, I WAS SURE HE DIDN'T LIKE ME.
AFTER A WHILE I STOPPED THINKING THAT...
...BUT THEN...
...I WONDERED IF I WAS JUST SEEING WHAT I WANTED TO SEE.
BUT IF I'M NOT THE ONLY ONE WHO THINKS SO...
...THEN IT MAKES ME REALLY HAPPY!
OH YEAH! THERE'S SOMETHING I WANTED TO ASK YOU.
WHAT IS IT?
COULD YOU TEACH ME HOW TO TAILOR A KIMONO?
IF YOU DON'T MIND, I'D LIKE TO LEARN LOTS OF THINGS.
THERE'S SO MUCH I DON'T KNOW ABOUT LIVING HERE!

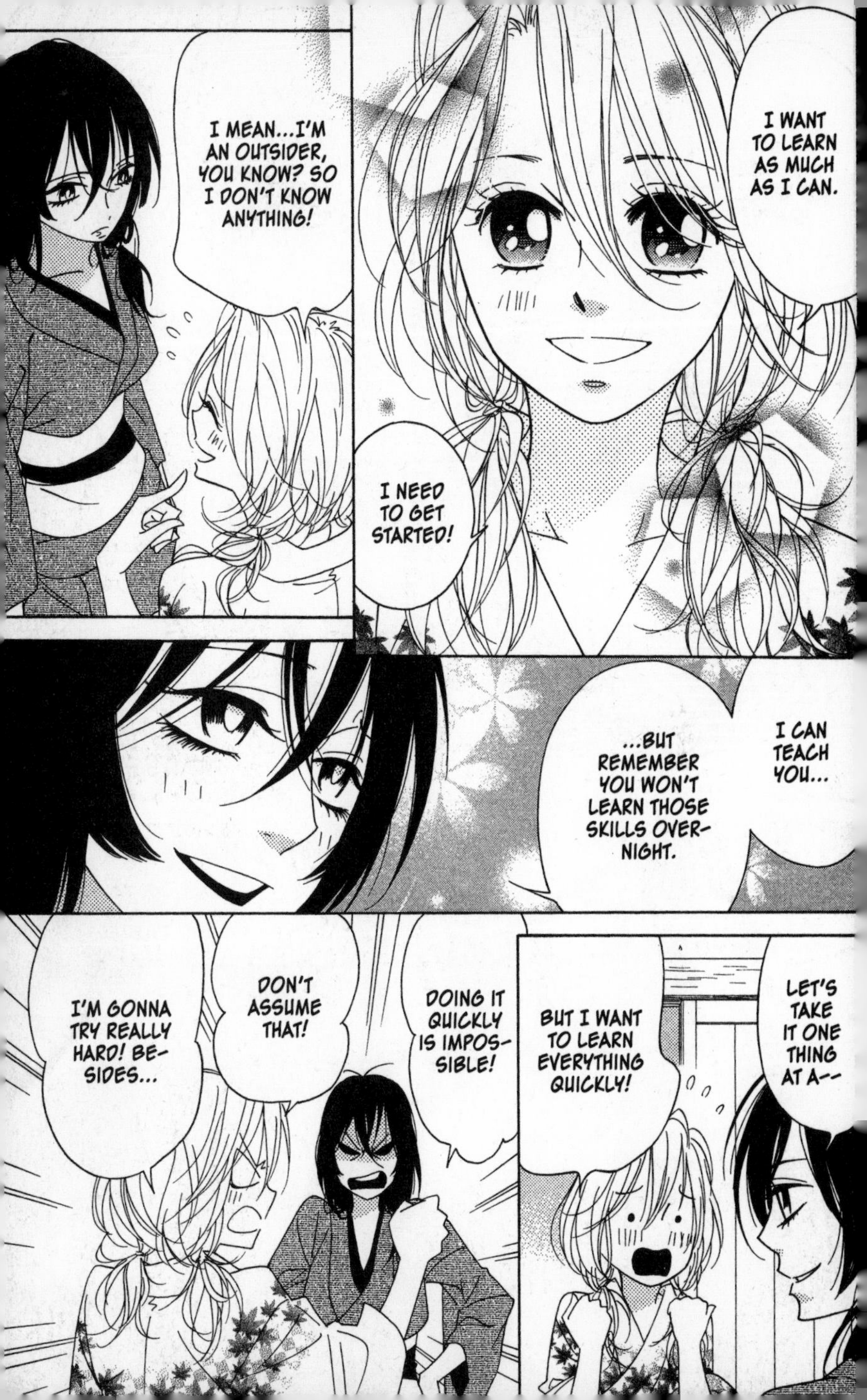
I WANT TO LEARN AS MUCH AS I CAN.
I NEED TO GET STARTED!
I MEAN...I'M AN OUTSIDER, YOU KNOW? SO I DON'T KNOW ANYTHING!
I CAN TEACH YOU...
...BUT REMEMBER YOU WON'T LEARN THOSE SKILLS OVER-NIGHT.
LET'S TAKE IT ONE THING AT A--
BUT I WANT TO LEARN EVERYTHING QUICKLY!
DOING IT QUICKLY IS IMPOS-SIBLE!
DON'T ASSUME THAT!
I'M GONNA TRY REALLY HARD! BE-SIDES...

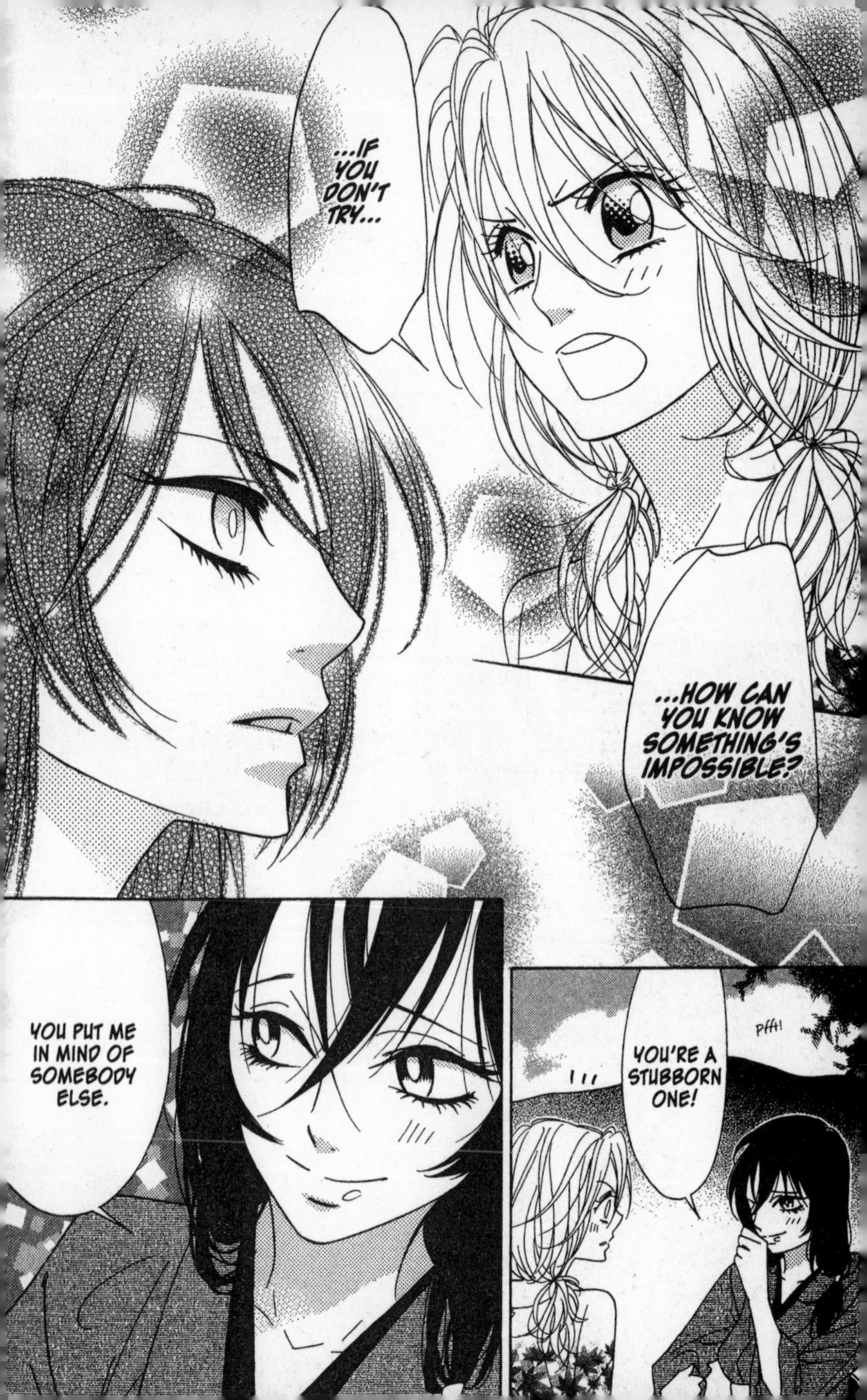
...IF YOU DON'T TRY...
...HOW CAN YOU KNOW SOMETHING'S IMPOSSIBLE?
pfft!
YOU'RE A STUBBORN ONE!
YOU PUT ME IN MIND OF SOMEBODY ELSE.

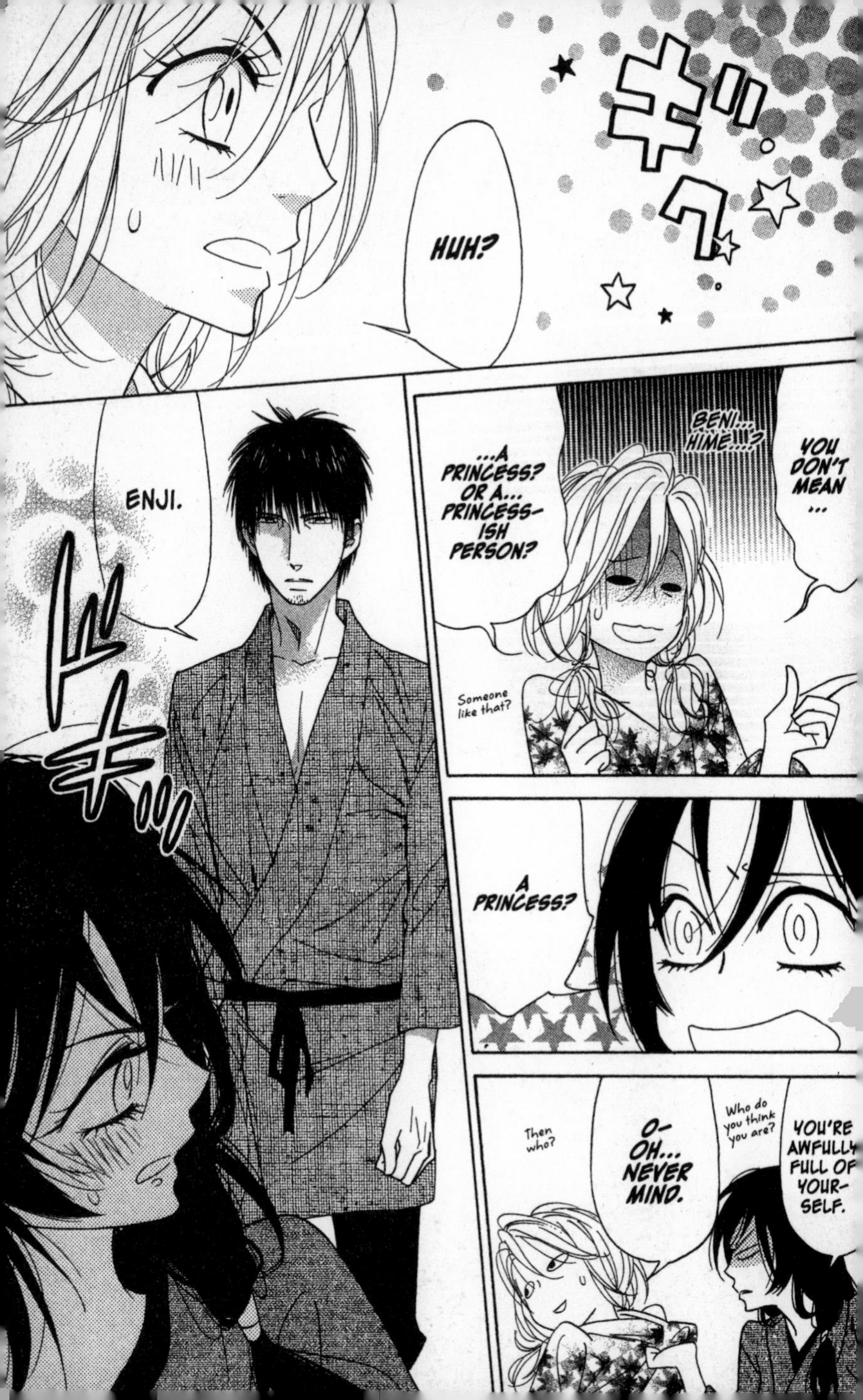
HUH?
YOU DON'T MEAN ...
BENI... HIME...?
...A PRINCESS? OR A... PRINCESS-ISH PERSON?
Someone like that?
A PRINCESS?
YOU'RE AWFULLY FULL OF YOURSELF.
Who do you think you are?
O-OH... NEVER MIND.
Then who?
ENJI.

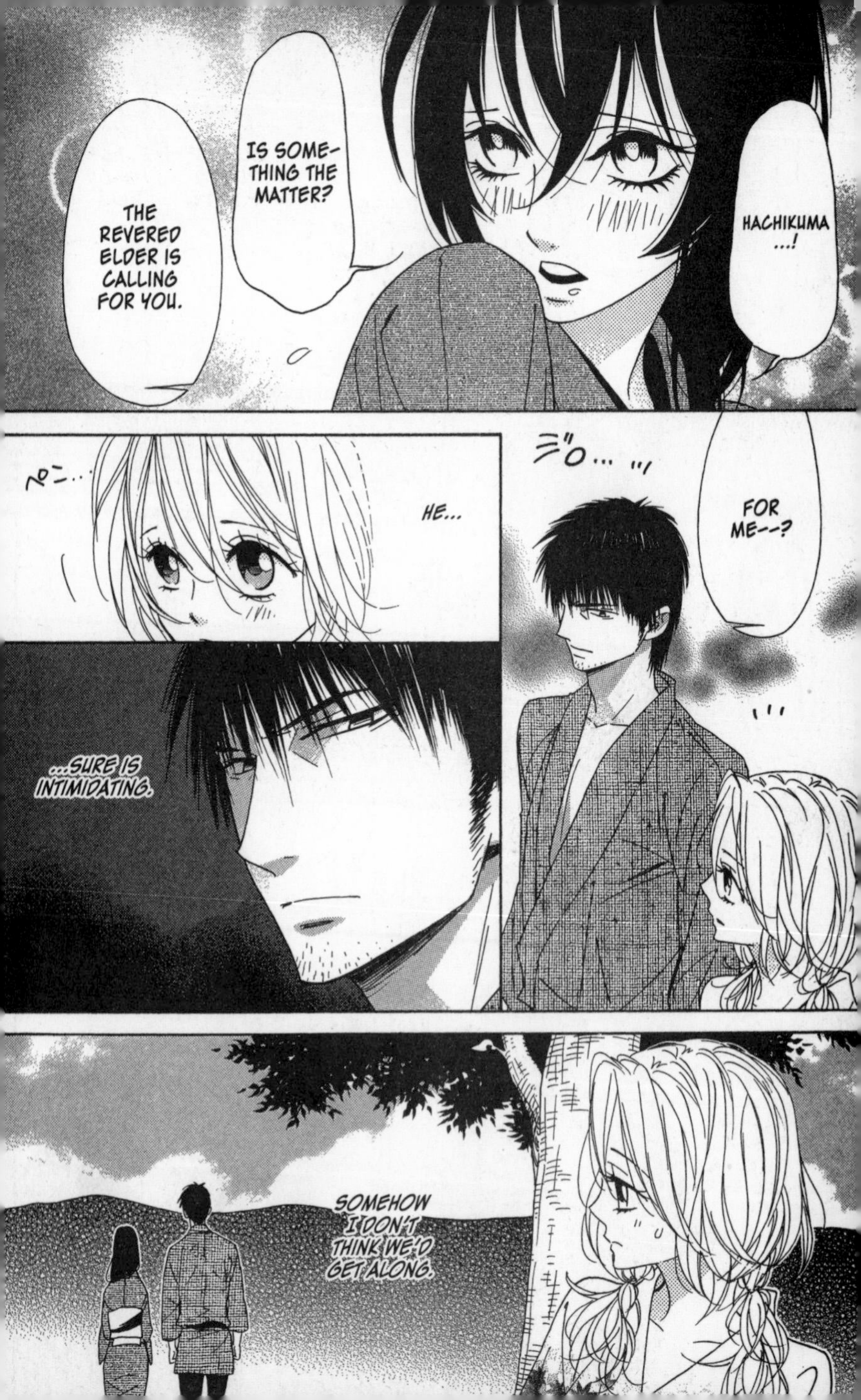
HACHIKUMA ...!
IS SOME-THING THE MATTER?
THE REVERED ELDER IS CALLING FOR YOU.
ジロ…
FOR ME--?
ぺこ…
HE...
...SURE IS INTIMIDATING.
SOMEHOW I DON'T THINK WE'D GET ALONG.

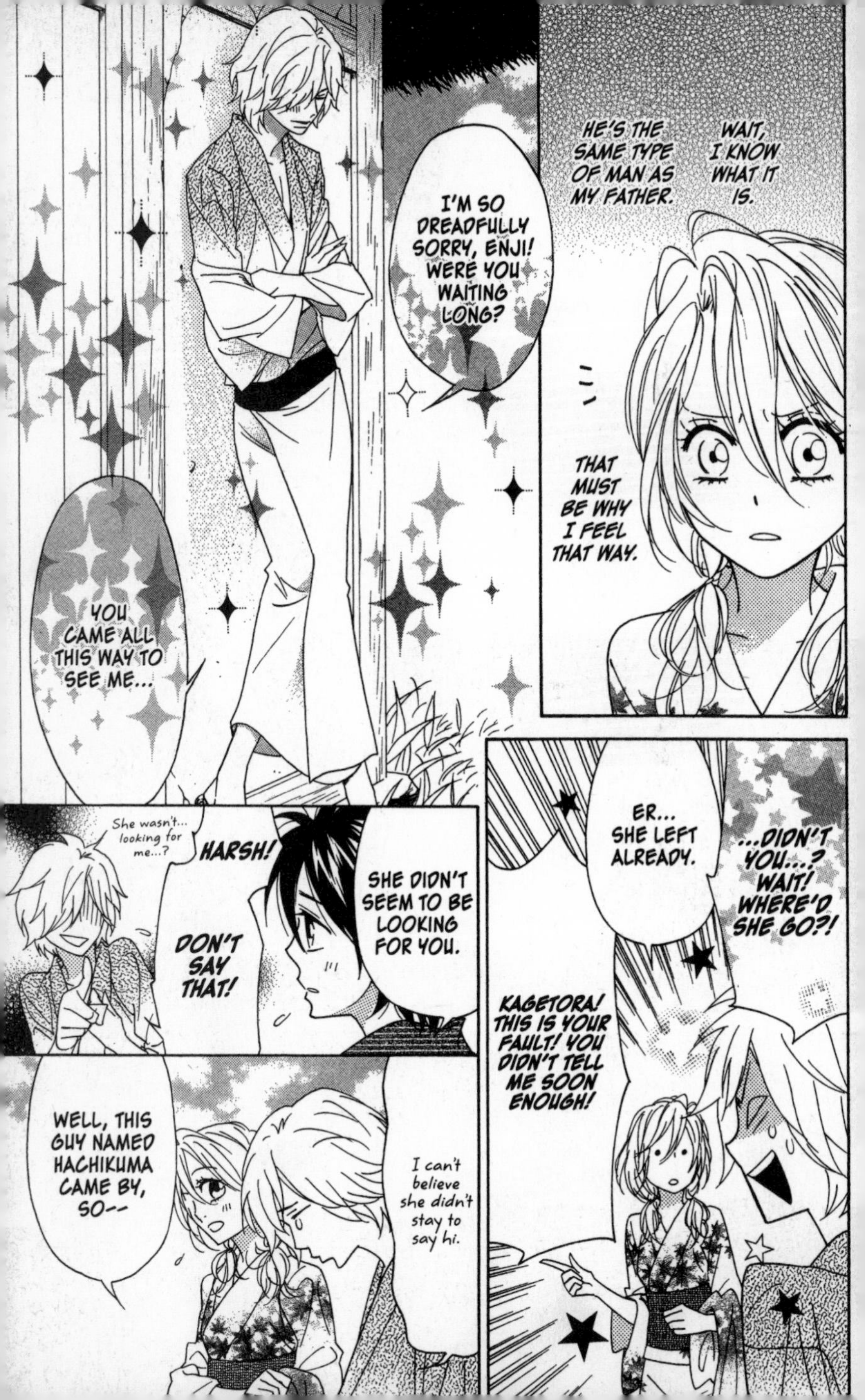
WAIT, I KNOW WHAT IT IS.
HE'S THE SAME TYPE OF MAN AS MY FATHER.
THAT MUST BE WHY I FEEL THAT WAY.
I'M SO DREADFULLY SORRY, ENJI! WERE YOU WAITING LONG?
YOU CAME ALL THIS WAY TO SEE ME...
ER... SHE LEFT ALREADY.
...DIDN'T YOU...? WAIT! WHERE'D SHE GO?!
KAGETORA! THIS IS YOUR FAULT! YOU DIDN'T TELL ME SOON ENOUGH!
SHE DIDN'T SEEM TO BE LOOKING FOR YOU.
HARSH!
DON'T SAY THAT!
She wasn't... looking for me...?
I can't believe she didn't stay to say hi.
WELL, THIS GUY NAMED HACHIKUMA CAME BY, SO--

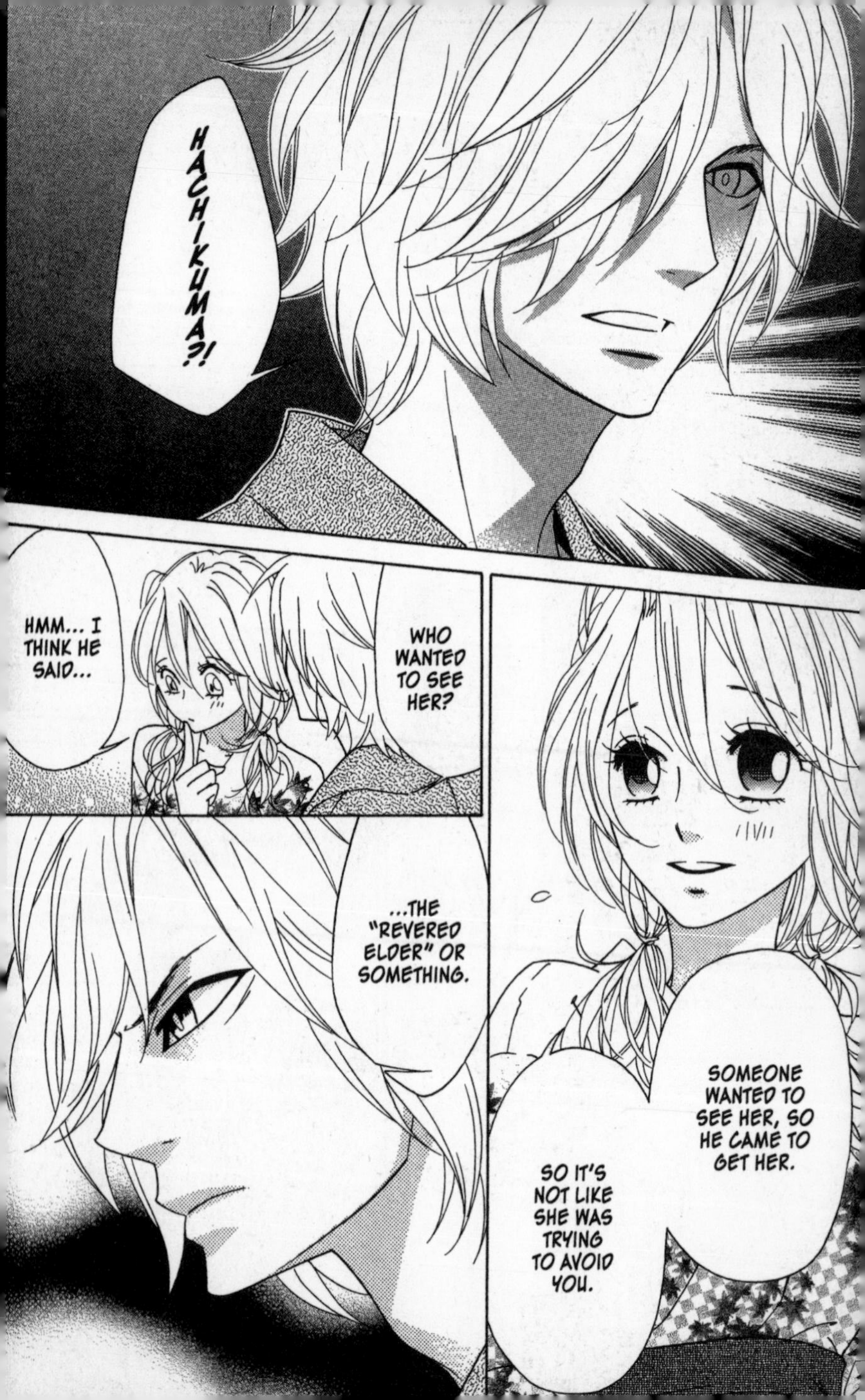
HACHIKUMA?!
SOMEONE WANTED TO SEE HER, SO HE CAME TO GET HER.
SO IT'S NOT LIKE SHE WAS TRYING TO AVOID YOU.
WHO WANTED TO SEE HER?
HMM... I THINK HE SAID...
...THE "REVERED ELDER" OR SOMETHING.

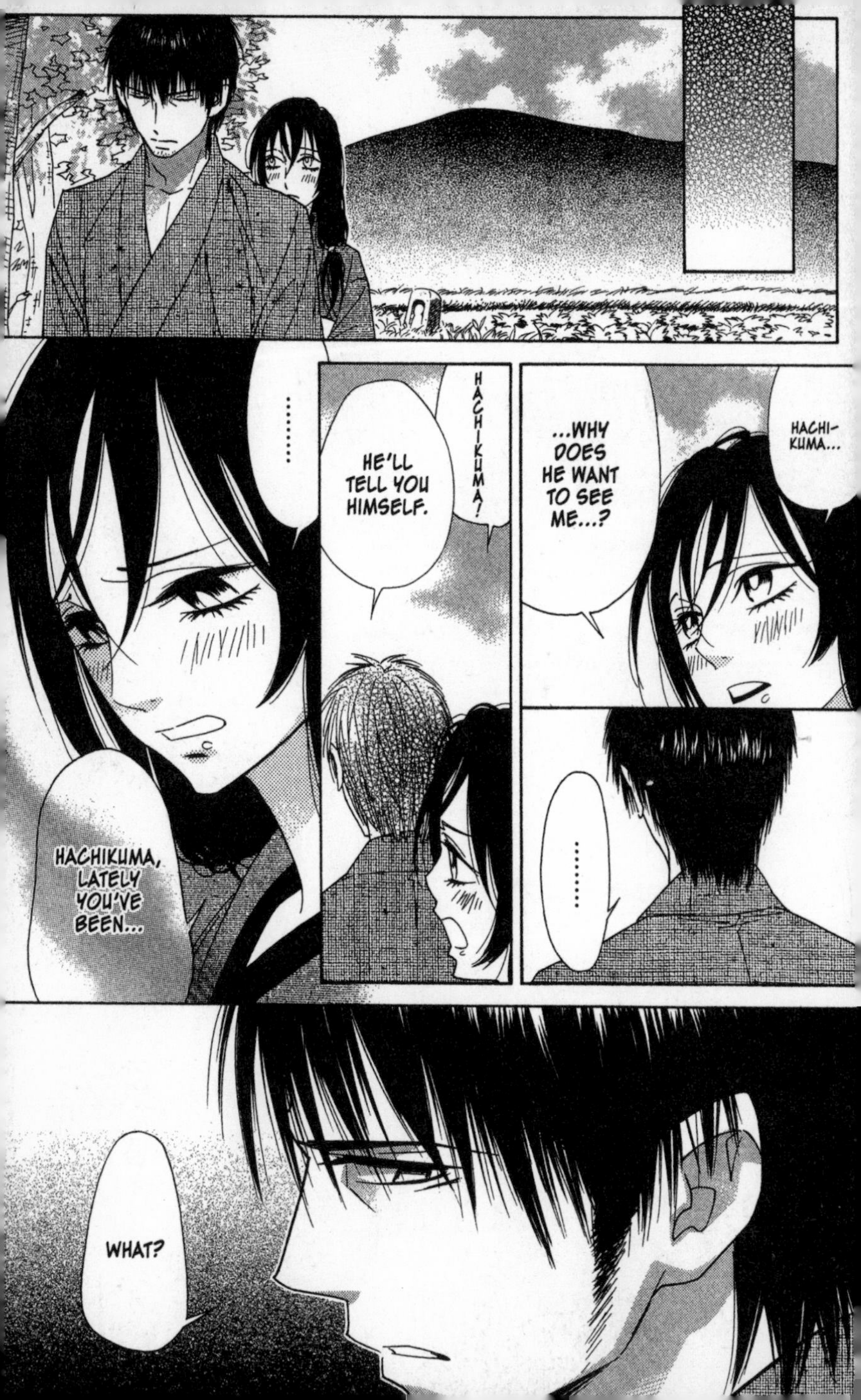
HACHI-KUMA...
...WHY DOES HE WANT TO SEE ME...?
....
HACHIKUMA!
HE'LL TELL YOU HIMSELF.
....
HACHIKUMA, LATELY YOU'VE BEEN...
WHAT?

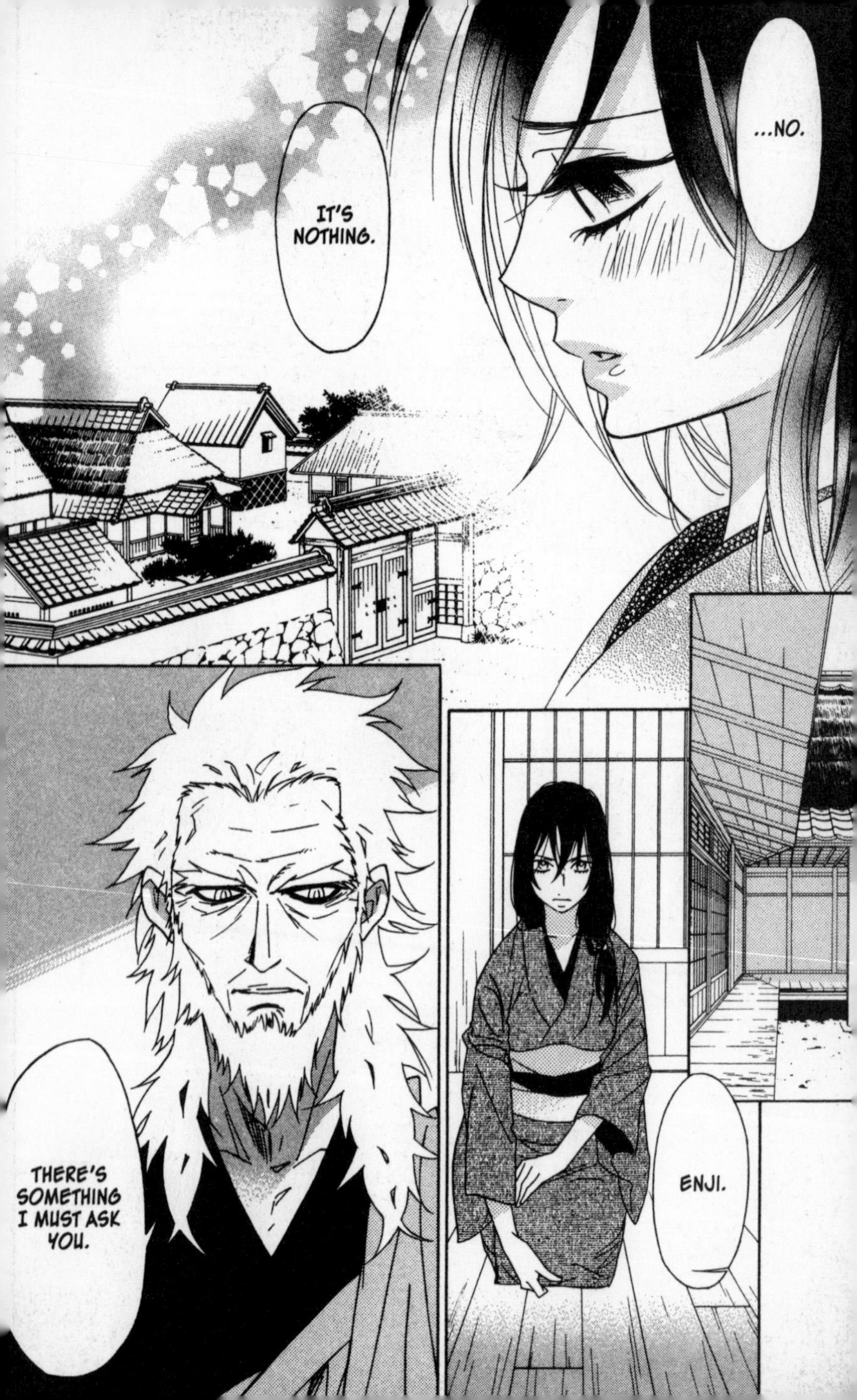
...NO.
IT'S NOTHING.
ENJI.
THERE'S SOMETHING I MUST ASK YOU.

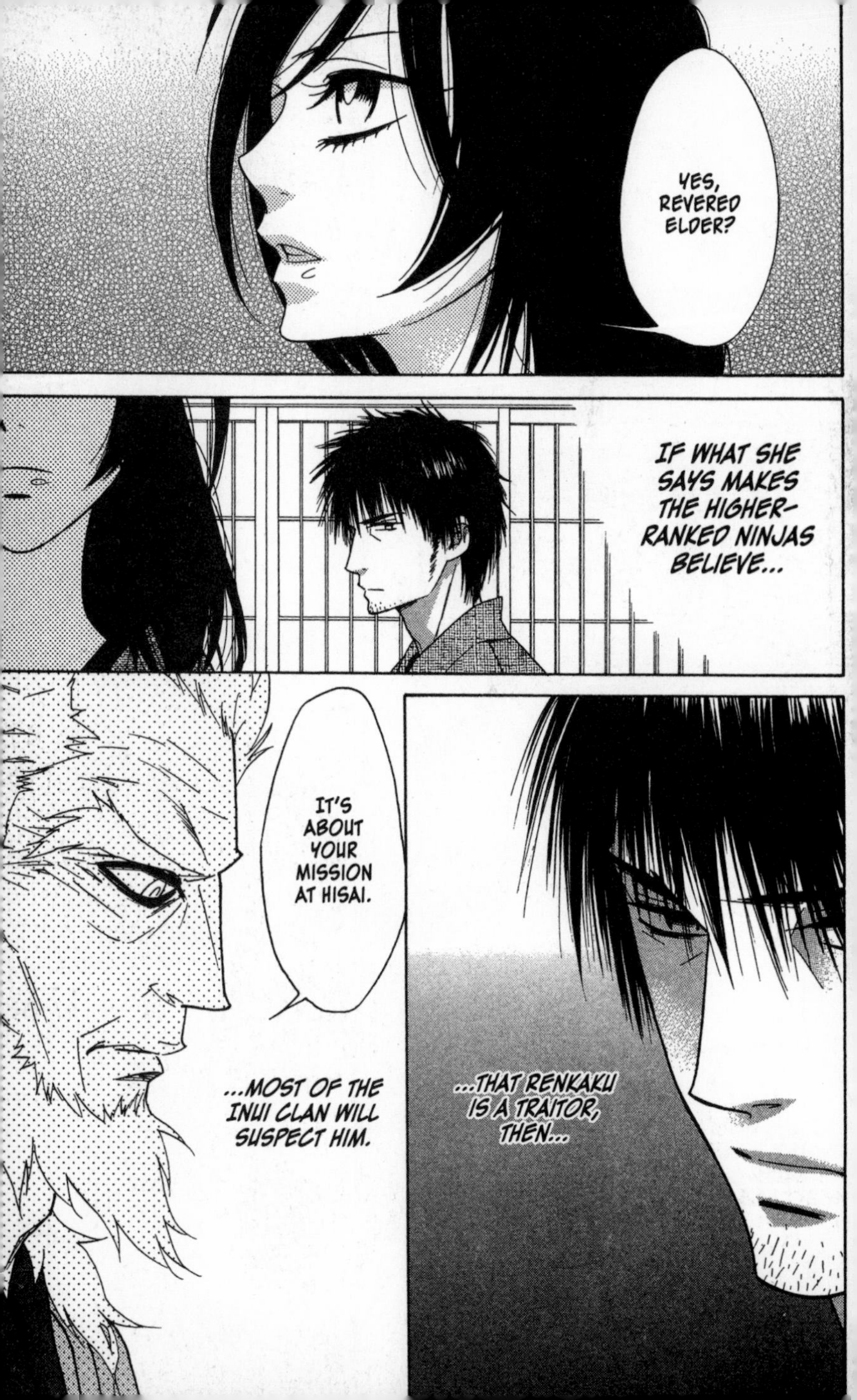
YES, REVERED ELDER?
IF WHAT SHE SAYS MAKES THE HIGHER-RANKED NINJAS BELIEVE...
...THAT RENKAKU IS A TRAITOR, THEN...
IT'S ABOUT YOUR MISSION AT HISAI.
...MOST OF THE INUI CLAN WILL SUSPECT HIM.

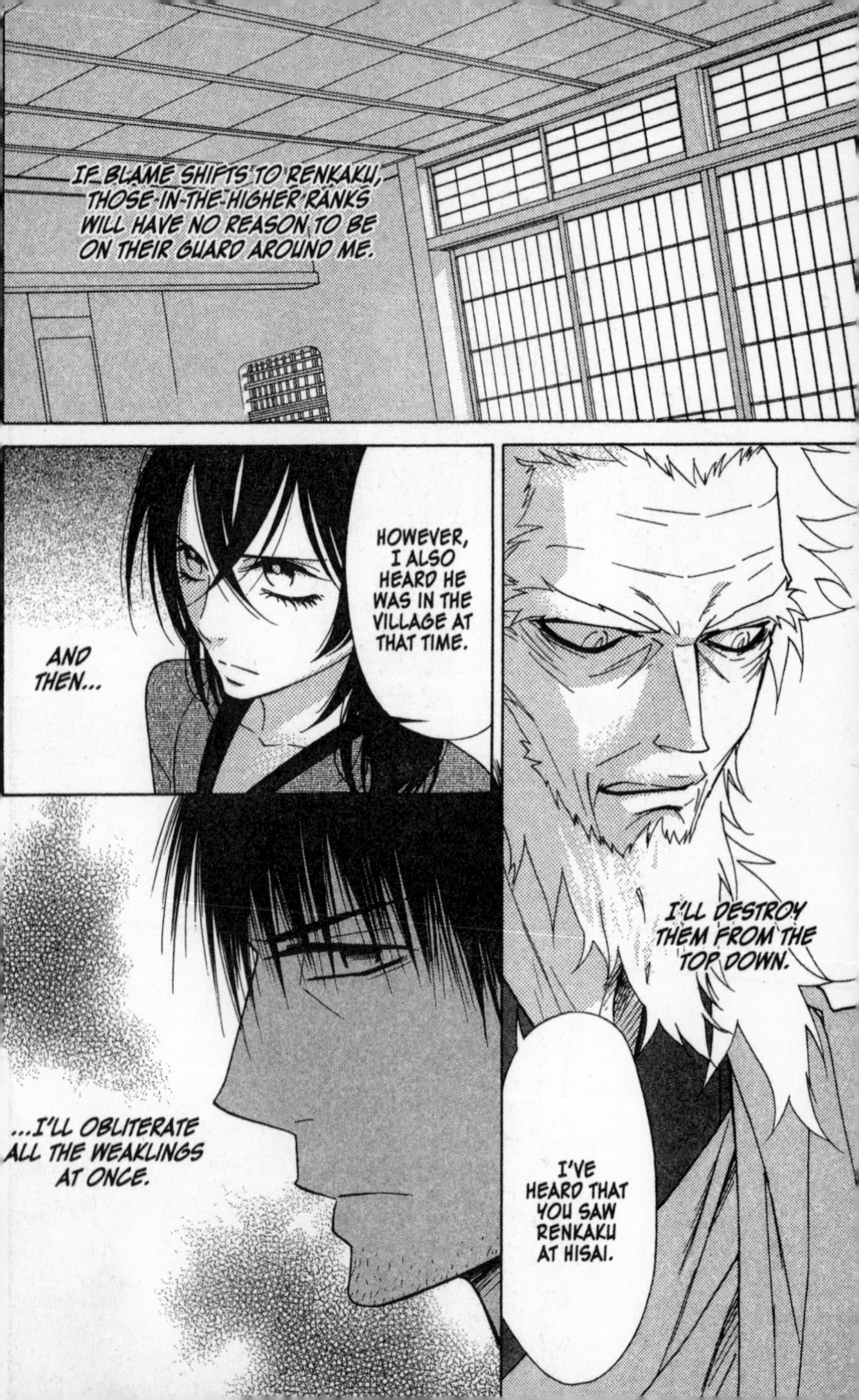
IF BLAME SHIFTS TO RENKAKU, THOSE IN THE HIGHER RANKS WILL HAVE NO REASON TO BE ON THEIR GUARD AROUND ME.
I'LL DESTROY THEM FROM THE TOP DOWN.
I'VE HEARD THAT YOU SAW RENKAKU AT HISAI.
HOWEVER, I ALSO HEARD HE WAS IN THE VILLAGE AT THAT TIME.
AND THEN...
...I'LL OBLITERATE ALL THE WEAKLINGS AT ONCE.

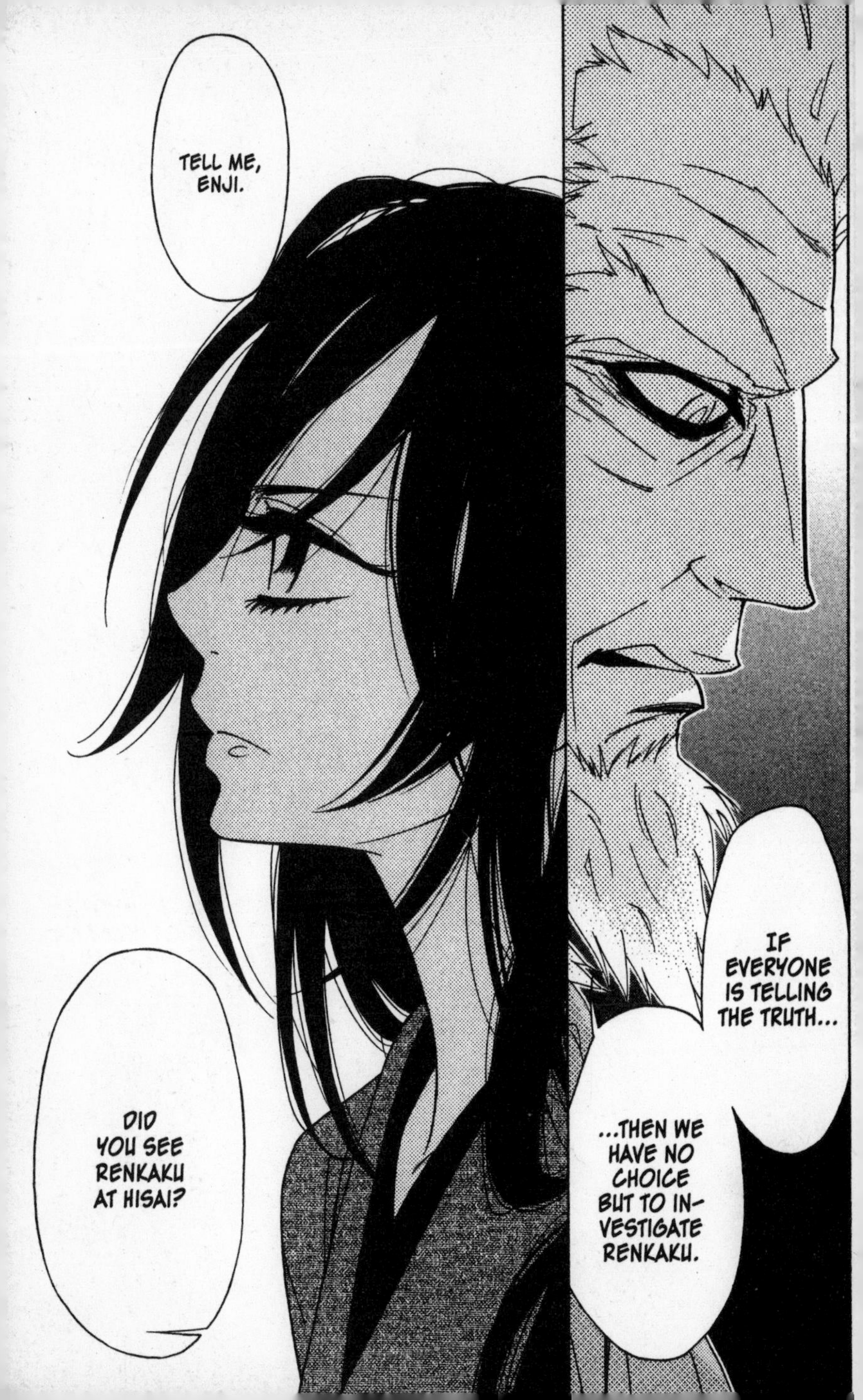
IF EVERYONE IS TELLING THE TRUTH...
...THEN WE HAVE NO CHOICE BUT TO IN-VESTIGATE RENKAKU.
TELL ME, ENJI.
DID YOU SEE RENKAKU AT HISAI?

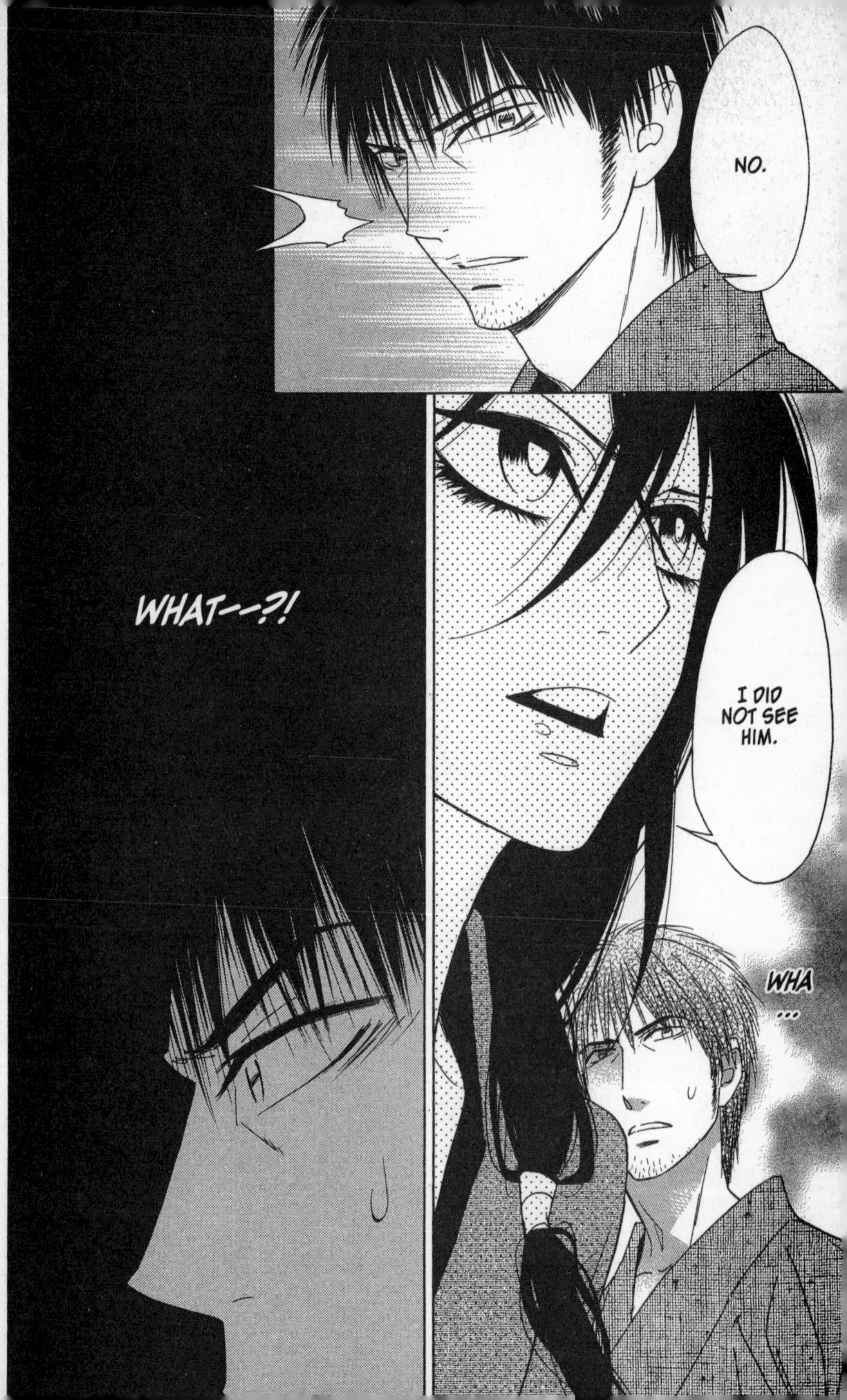
NO.
I DID NOT SEE HIM.
WHA...
WHAT--?!

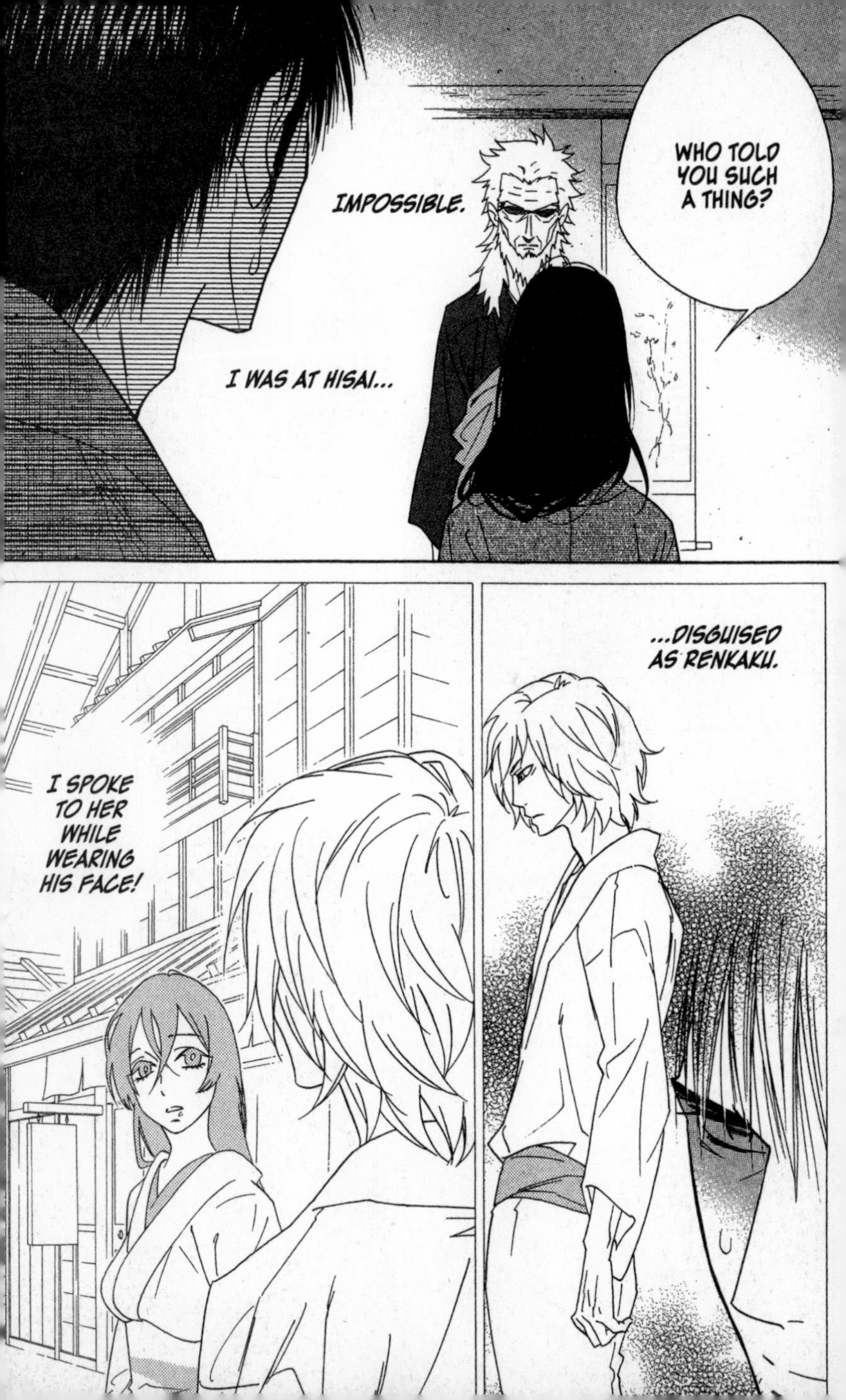
WHO TOLD YOU SUCH A THING?
IMPOSSIBLE.
I WAS AT HISAI...
...DISGUISED AS RENKAKU.
I SPOKE TO HER WHILE WEARING HIS FACE!

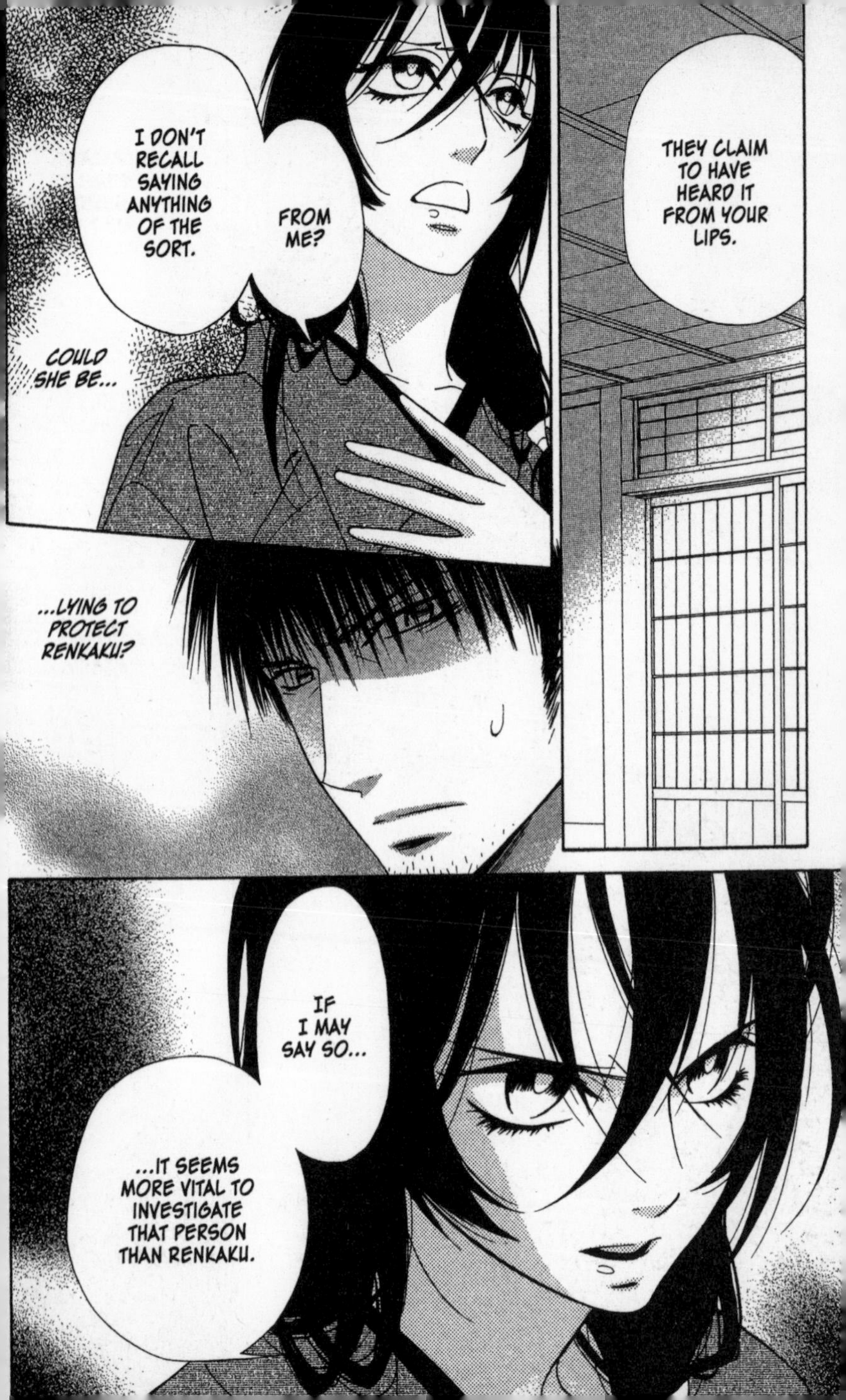
THEY CLAIM TO HAVE HEARD IT FROM YOUR LIPS.
FROM ME?
I DON'T RECALL SAYING ANYTHING OF THE SORT.
COULD SHE BE...
...LYING TO PROTECT RENKAKU?
IF I MAY SAY SO...
...IT SEEMS MORE VITAL TO INVESTIGATE THAT PERSON THAN RENKAKU.

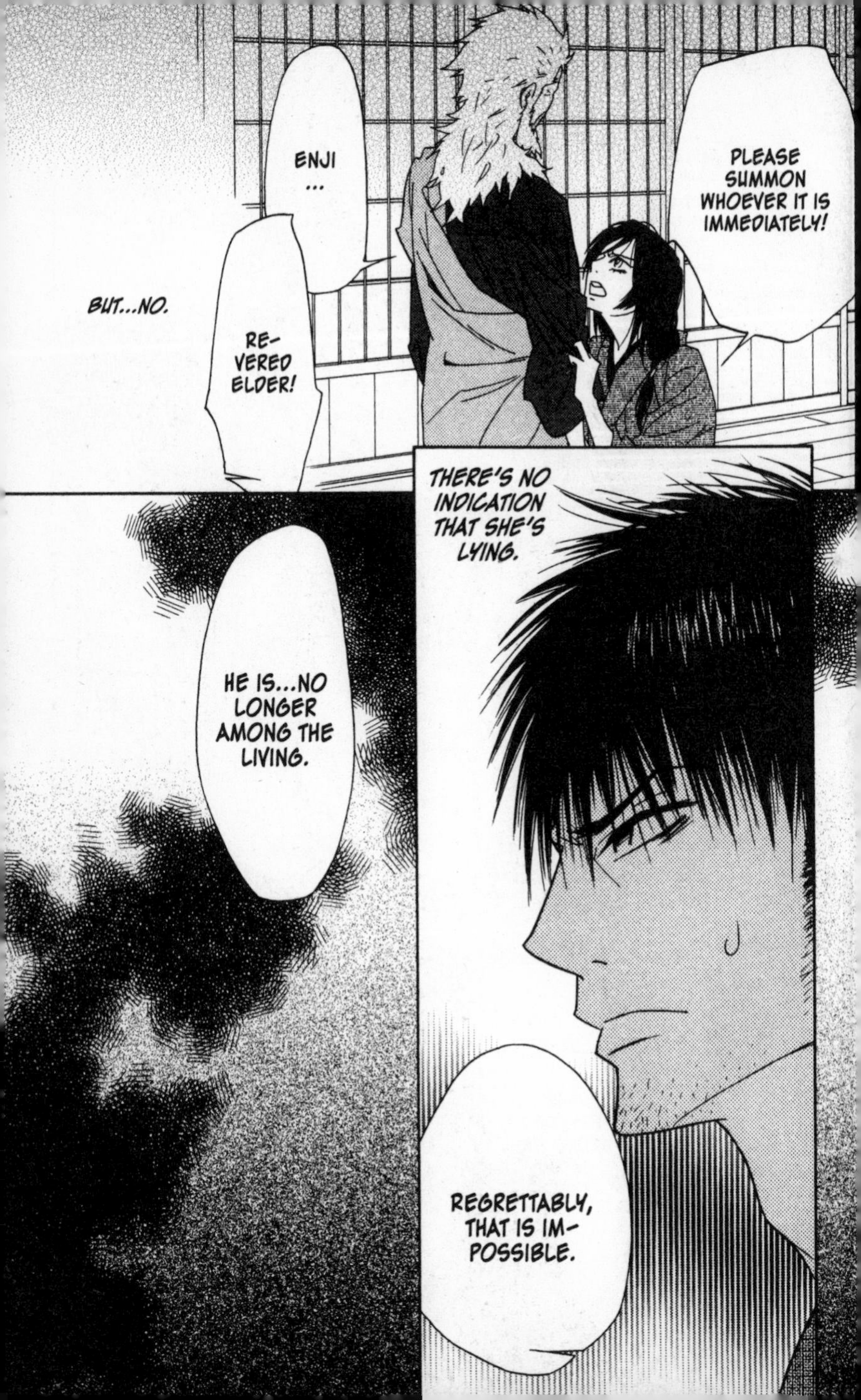
PLEASE SUMMON WHOEVER IT IS IMMEDIATELY!
ENJI ...
RE-VERED ELDER!
BUT...NO.
THERE'S NO INDICATION THAT SHE'S LYING.
REGRETTABLY, THAT IS IM-POSSIBLE.
HE IS...NO LONGER AMONG THE LIVING.

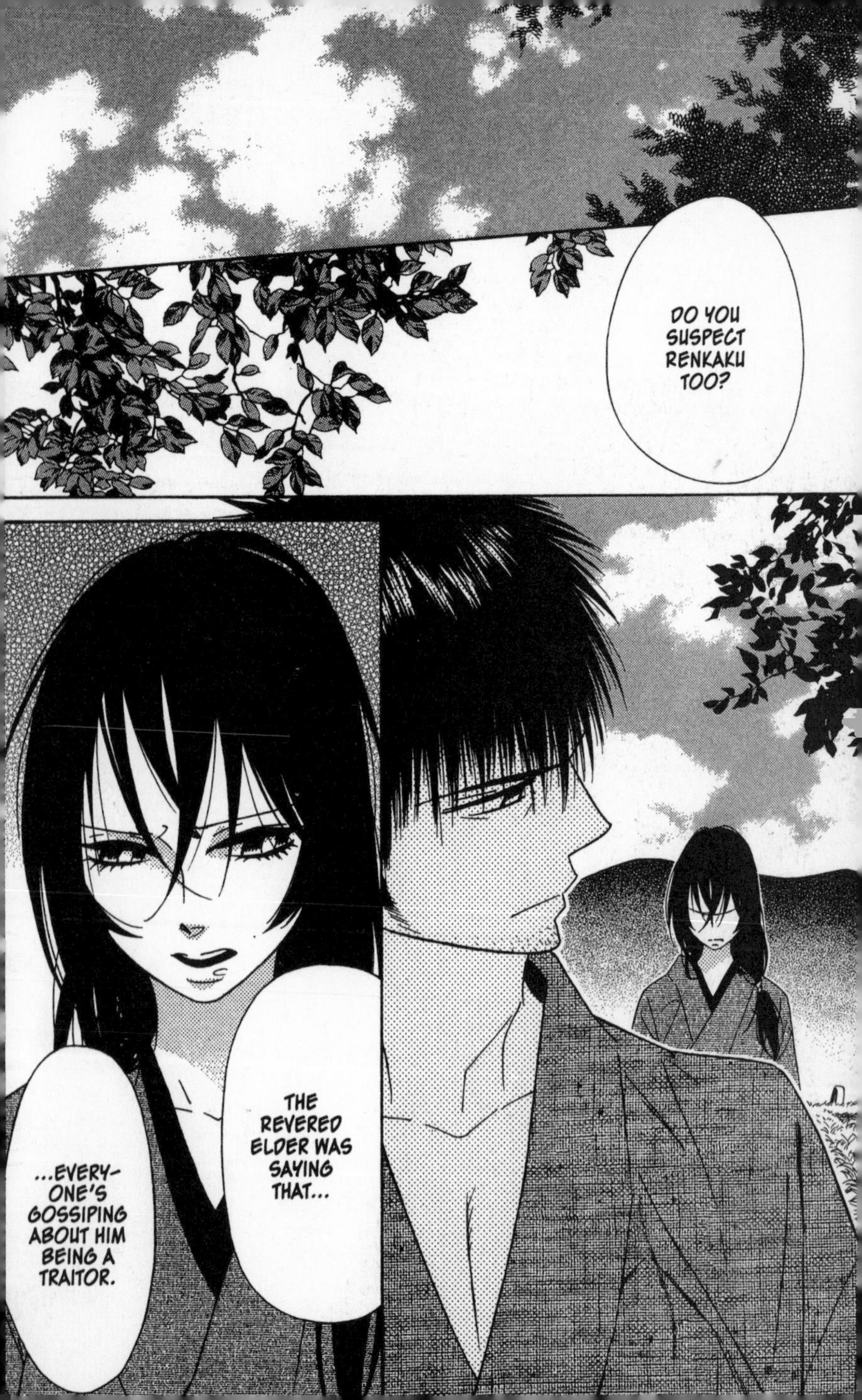
DO YOU SUSPECT RENKAKU TOO?
THE REVERED ELDER WAS SAYING THAT...
...EVERY-ONE'S GOSSIPING ABOUT HIM BEING A TRAITOR.

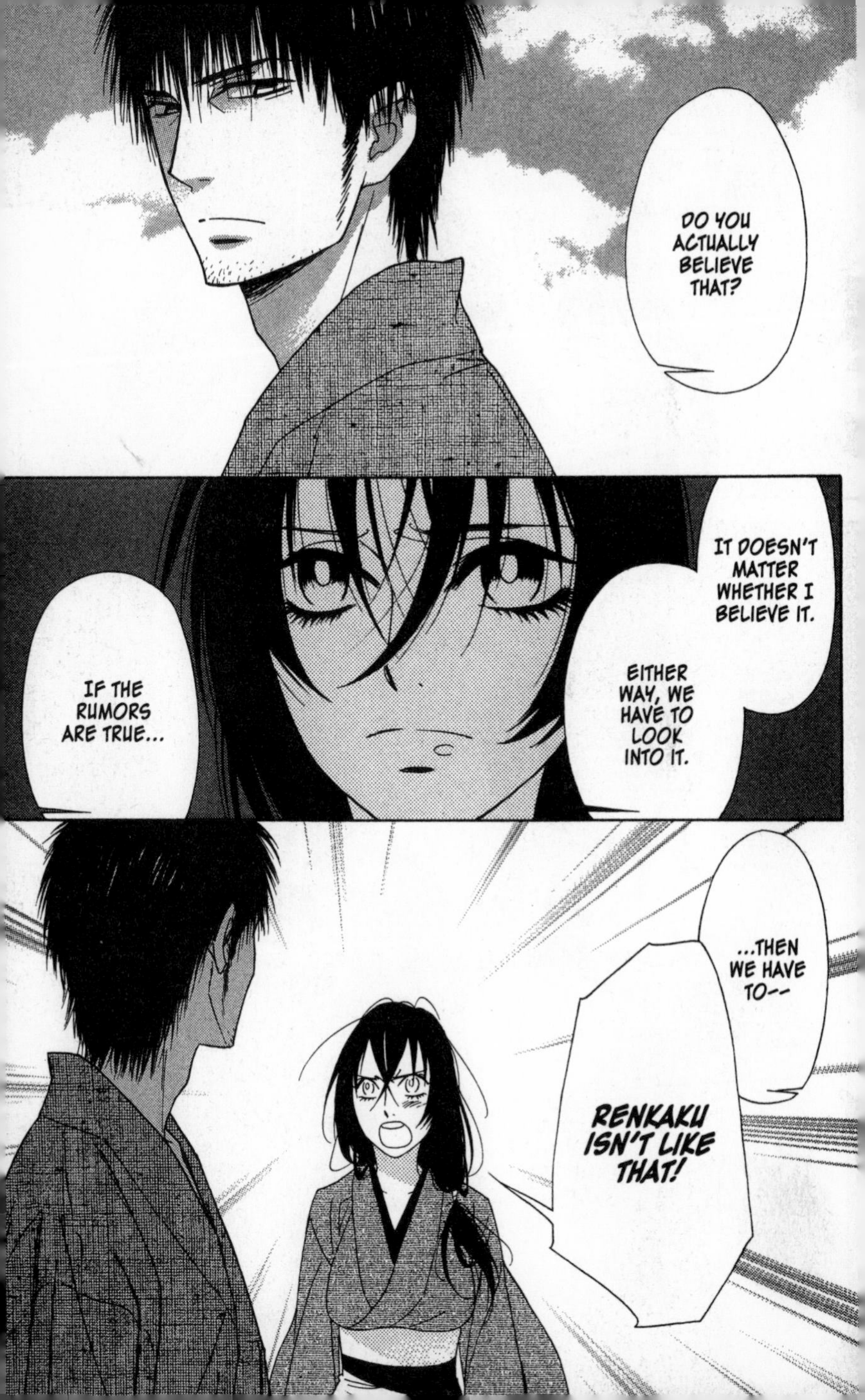
DO YOU ACTUALLY BELIEVE THAT?
IT DOESN'T MATTER WHETHER I BELIEVE IT.
EITHER WAY, WE HAVE TO LOOK INTO IT.
IF THE RUMORS ARE TRUE...
...THEN WE HAVE TO--
RENKAKU ISN'T LIKE THAT!

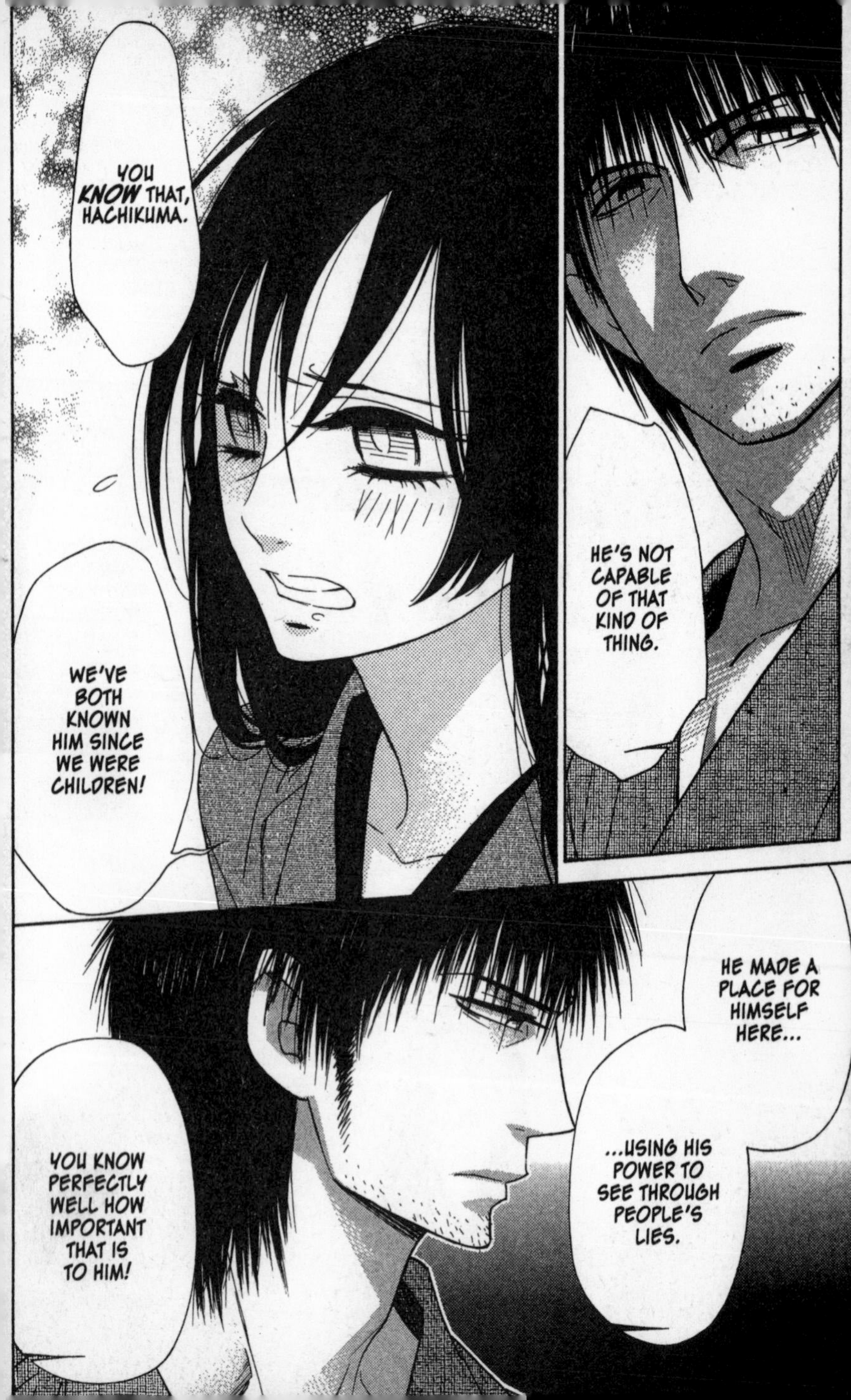
HE'S NOT CAPABLE OF THAT KIND OF THING.
YOU *KNOW* THAT, HACHIKUMA.
WE'VE BOTH KNOWN HIM SINCE WE WERE CHILDREN!
HE MADE A PLACE FOR HIMSELF HERE...
...USING HIS POWER TO SEE THROUGH PEOPLE'S LIES.
YOU KNOW PERFECTLY WELL HOW IMPORTANT THAT IS TO HIM!

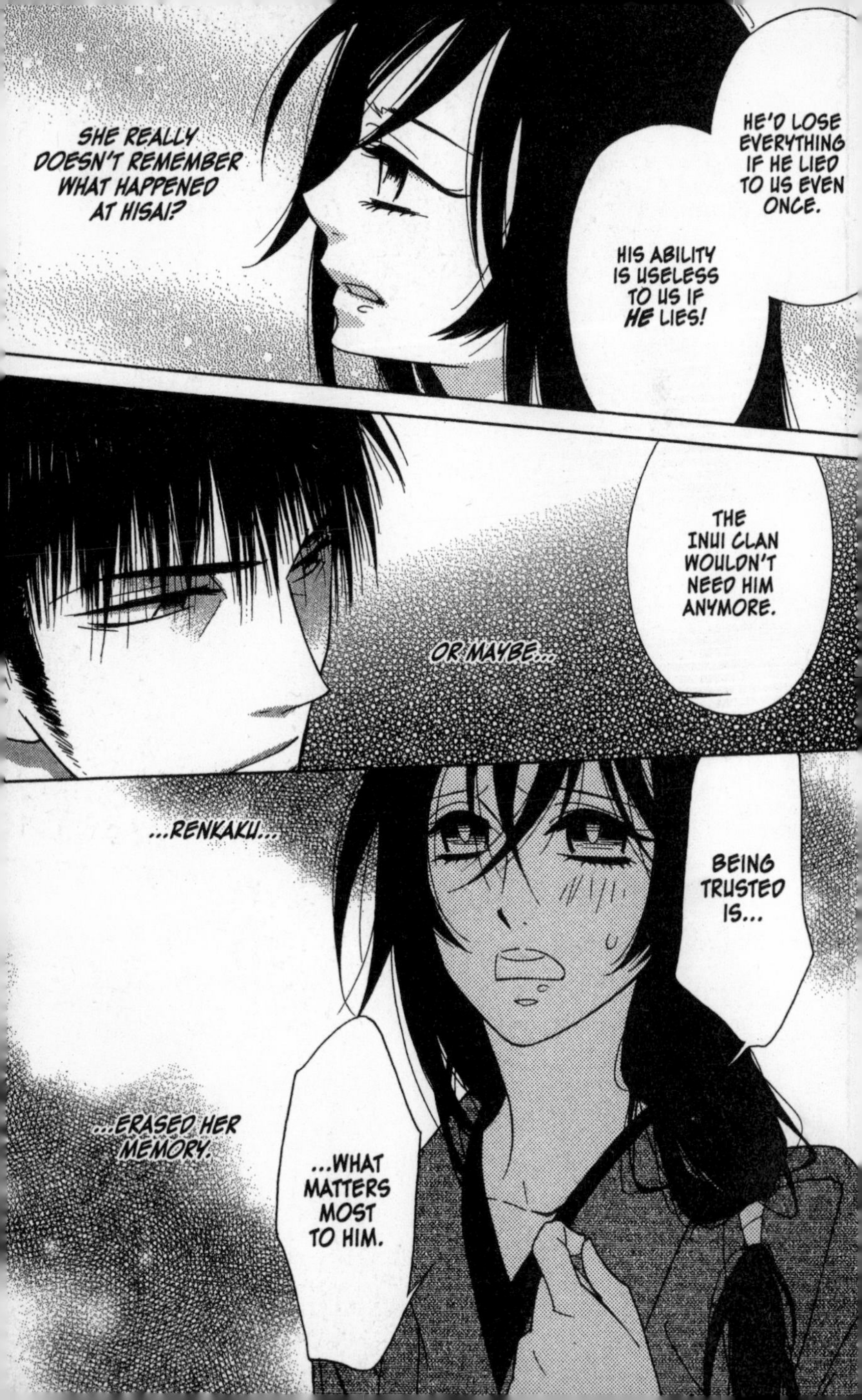
HE'D LOSE EVERYTHING IF HE LIED TO US EVEN ONCE.
HIS ABILITY IS USELESS TO US IF *HE* LIES!
SHE REALLY DOESN'T REMEMBER WHAT HAPPENED AT HISAI?
THE INUI CLAN WOULDN'T NEED HIM ANYMORE.
OR MAYBE...
BEING TRUSTED IS...
...WHAT MATTERS MOST TO HIM.
...RENKAKU...
...ERASED HER MEMORY.

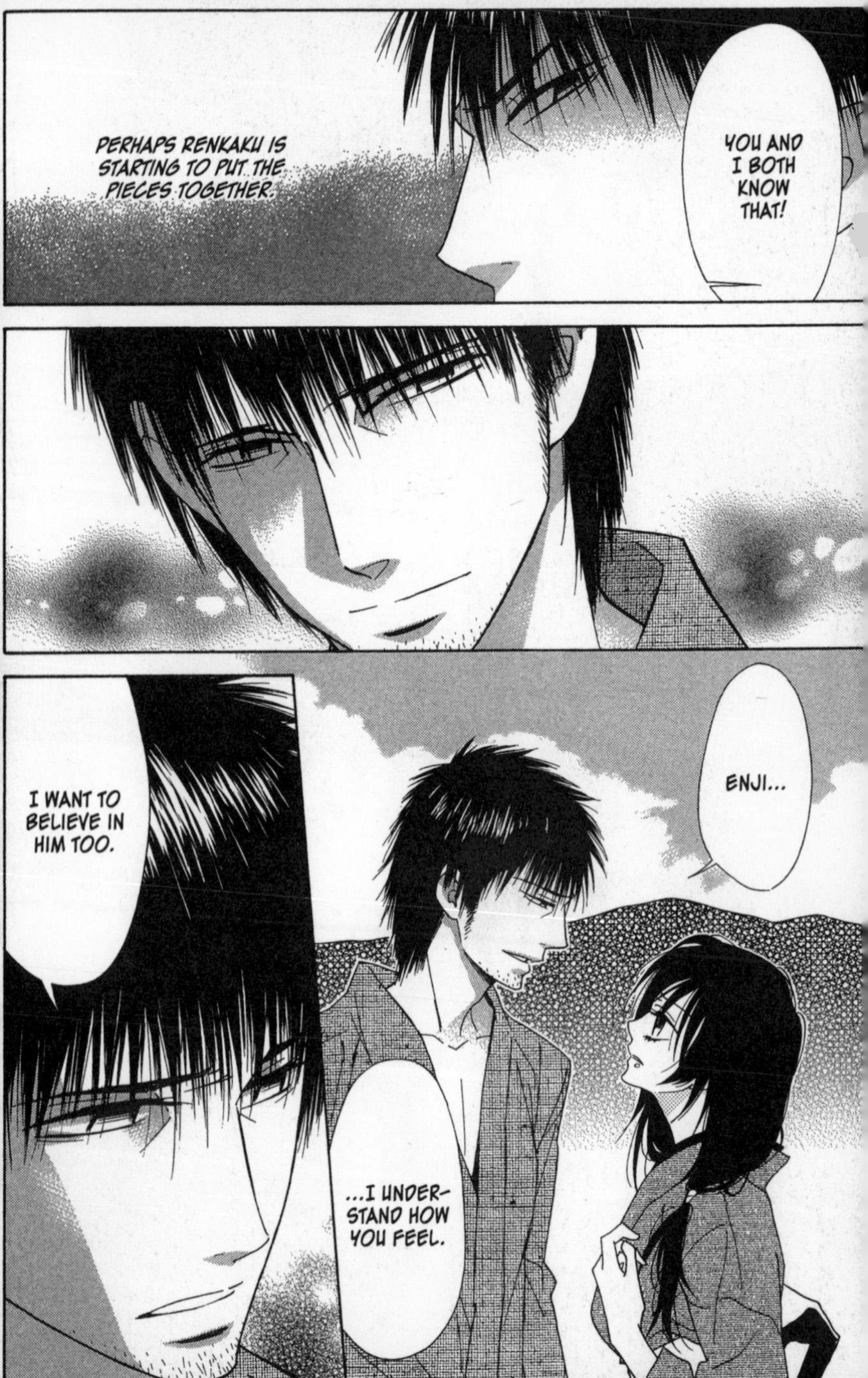
YOU AND I BOTH KNOW THAT!
PERHAPS RENKAKU IS STARTING TO PUT THE PIECES TOGETHER.
ENJI...
...I UNDER-STAND HOW YOU FEEL.
I WANT TO BELIEVE IN HIM TOO.

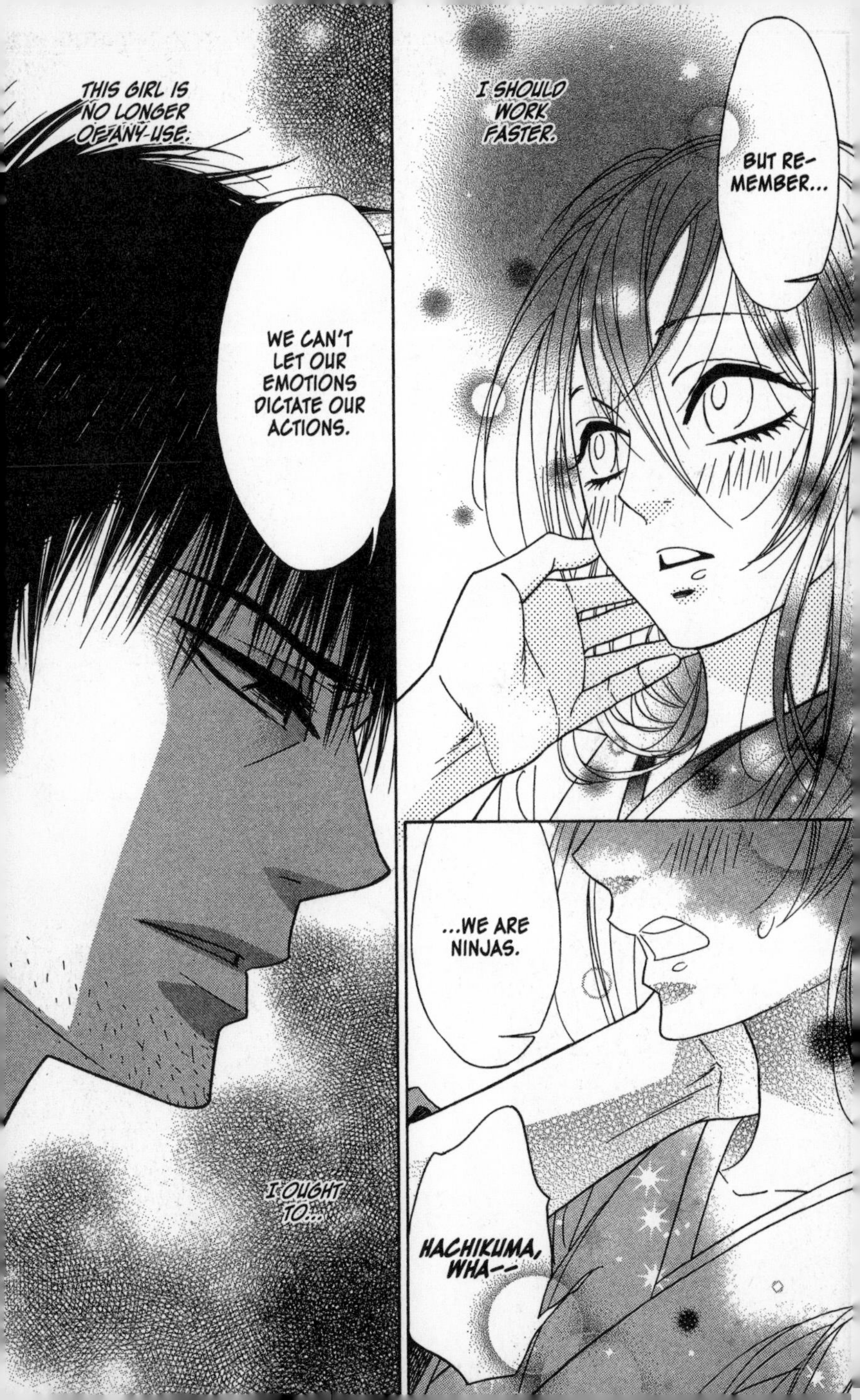
BUT RE-MEMBER...
I SHOULD WORK FASTER.
...WE ARE NINJAS.
HACHIKUMA, WHA--
THIS GIRL IS NO LONGER OF ANY USE.
WE CAN'T LET OUR EMOTIONS DICTATE OUR ACTIONS.
I OUGHT TO...

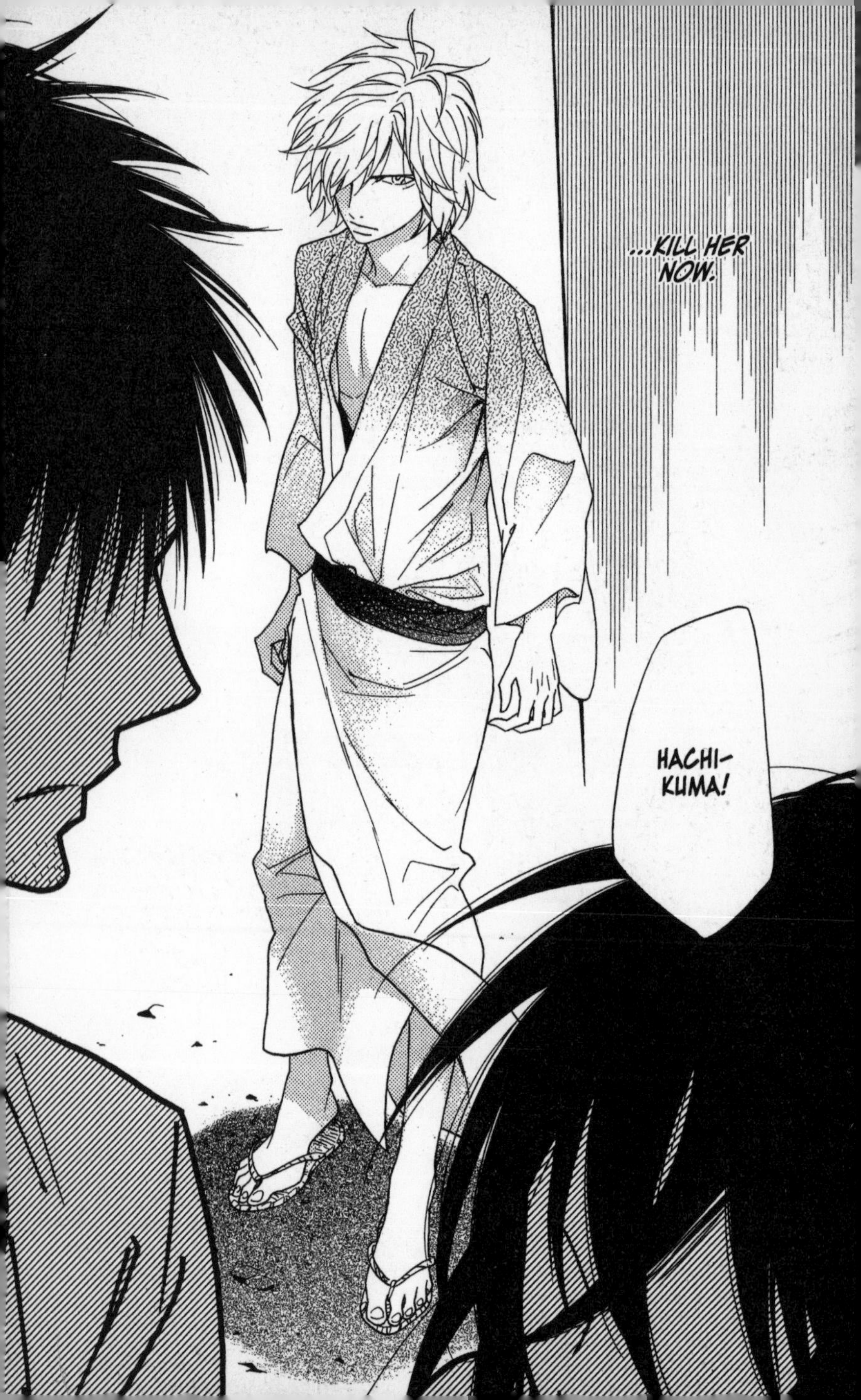
...KILL HER NOW.
HACHI-KUMA!

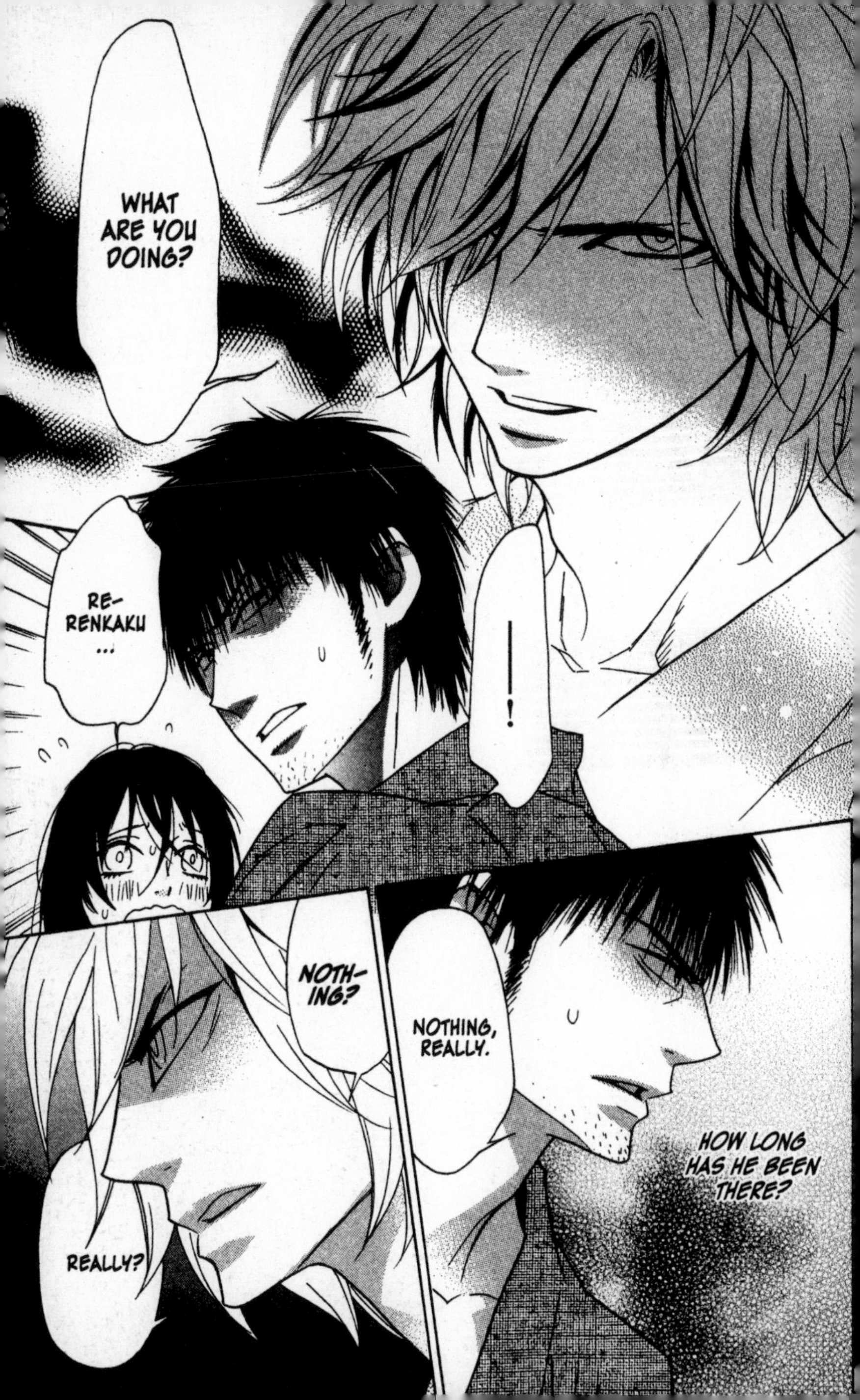
WHAT ARE YOU DOING?
—!
RE-RENKAKU...
NOTHING, REALLY.
HOW LONG HAS HE BEEN THERE?
NOTH-ING?
REALLY?

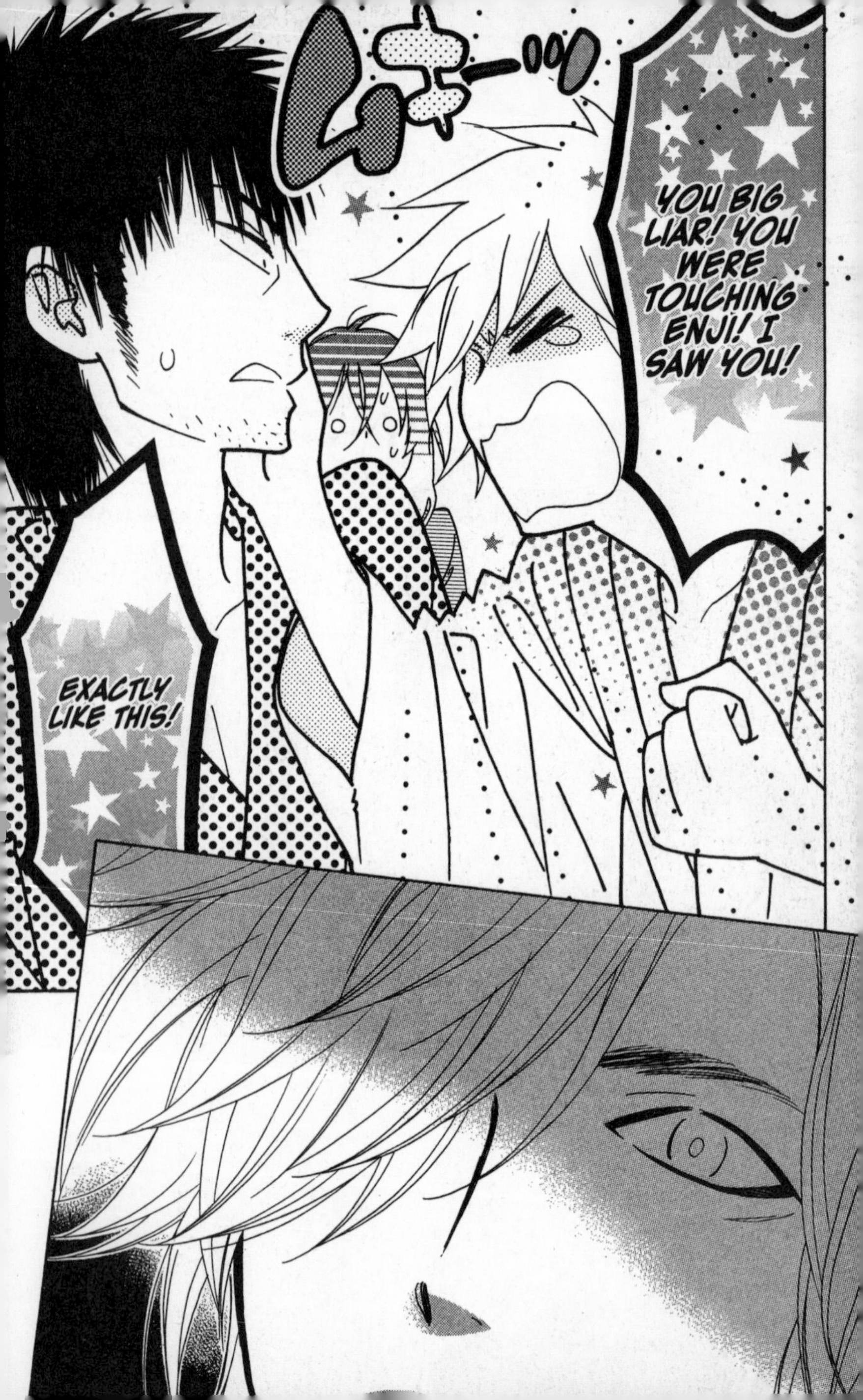
YOU BIG LIAR! YOU WERE TOUCHING ENJI! I SAW YOU!
EXACTLY LIKE THIS!

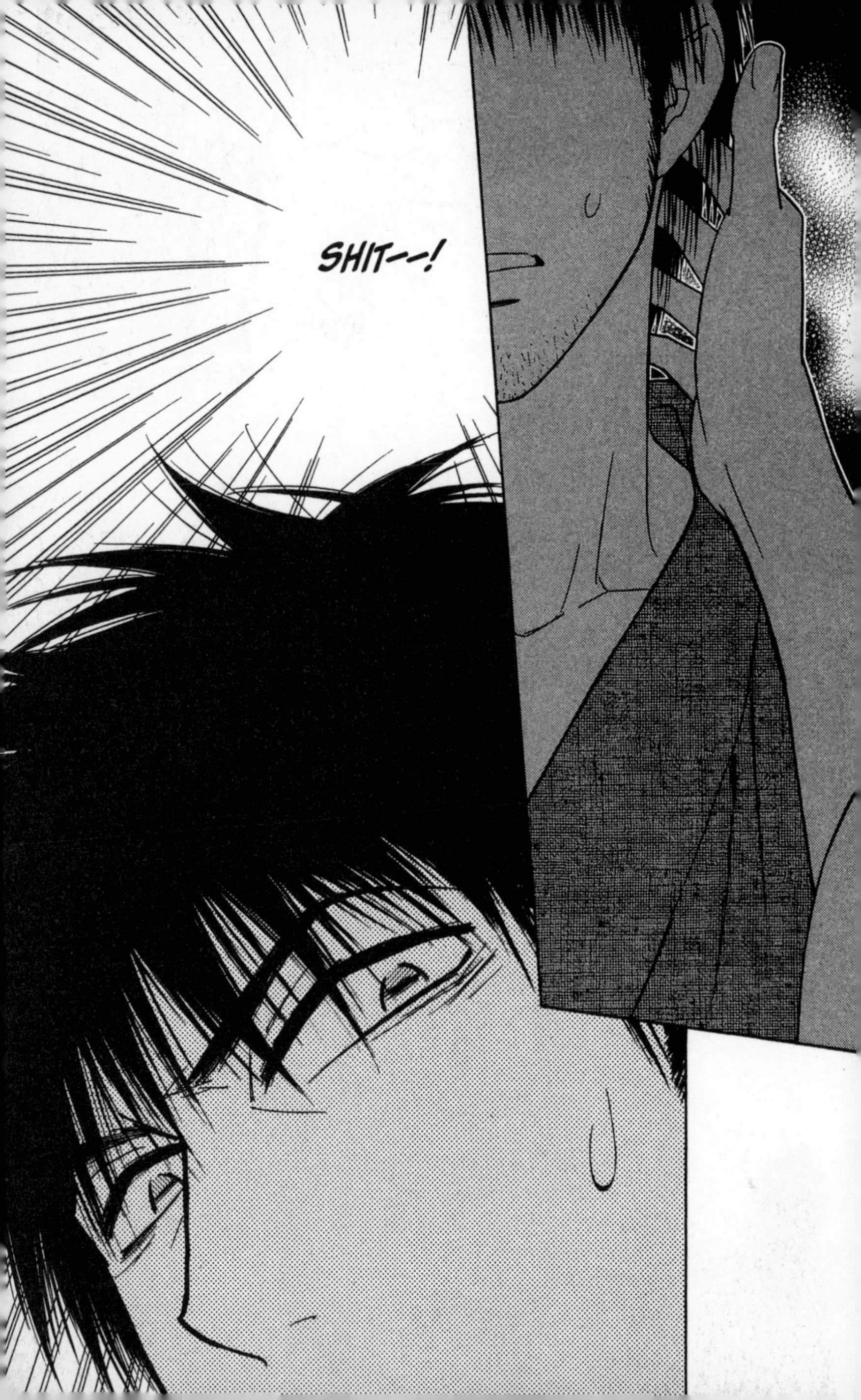
SHIT--!

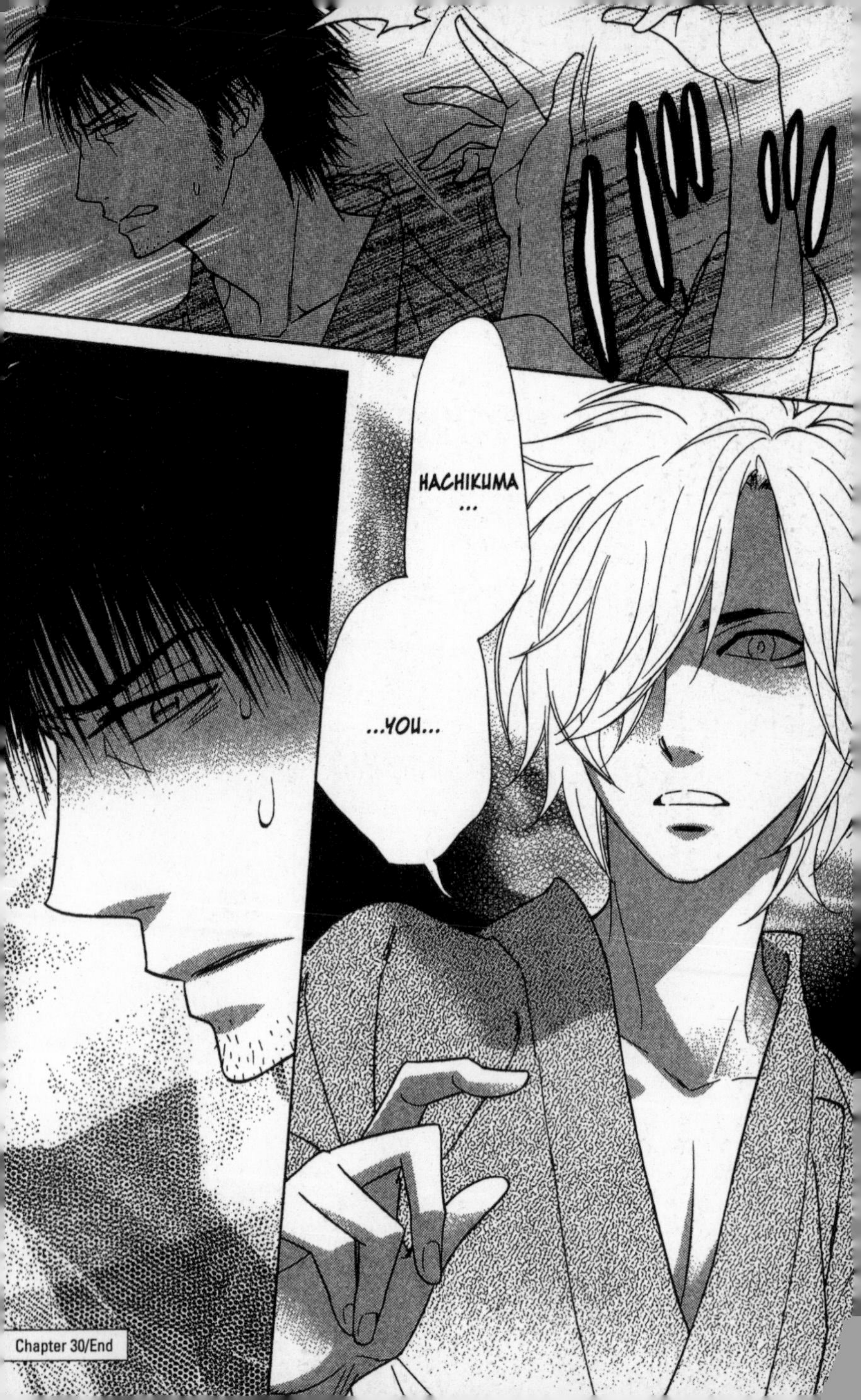
HACHIKUMA ...
...YOU...

Chapter 30/End

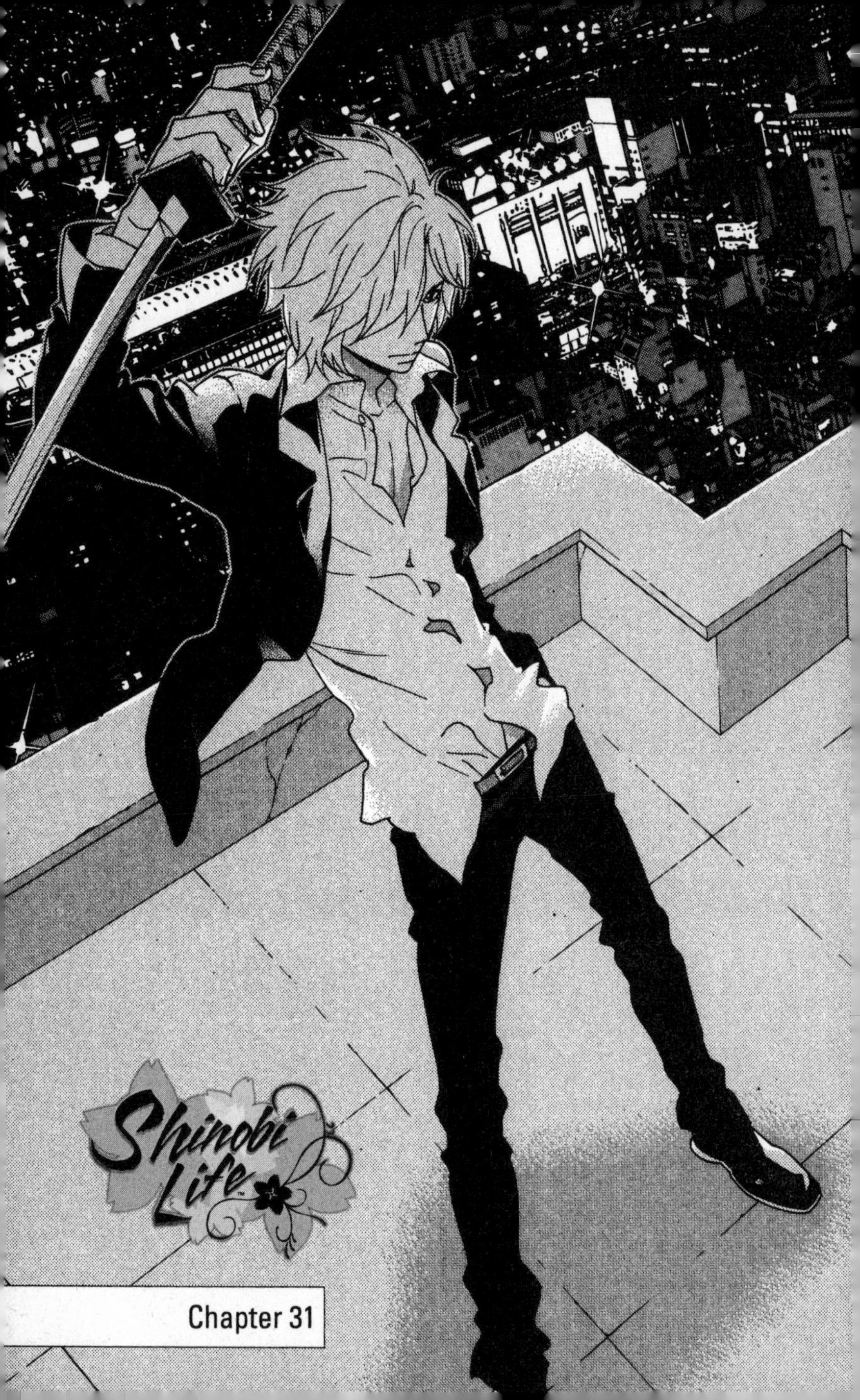
Shinobi Life
Chapter 31

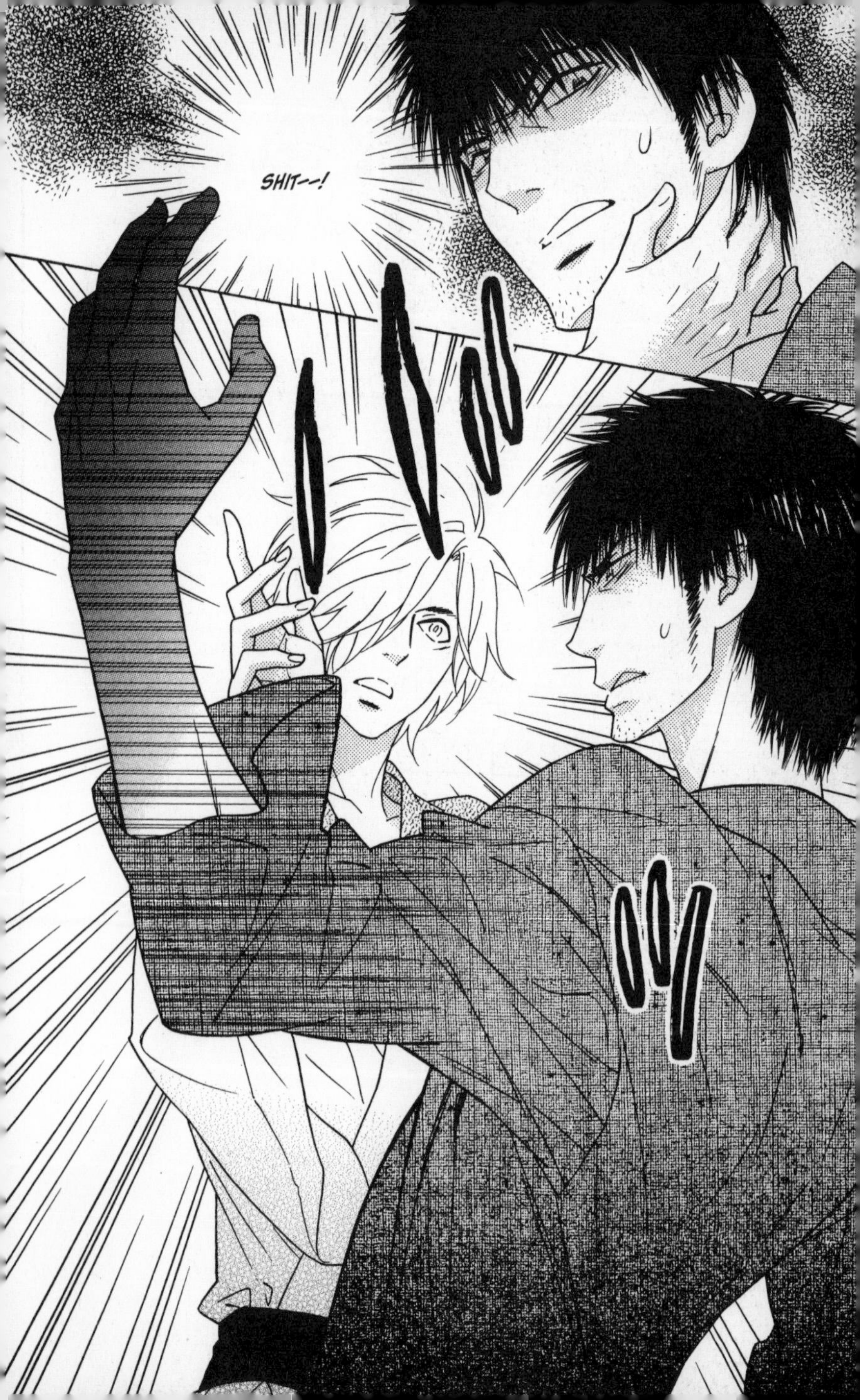
SHIT--!

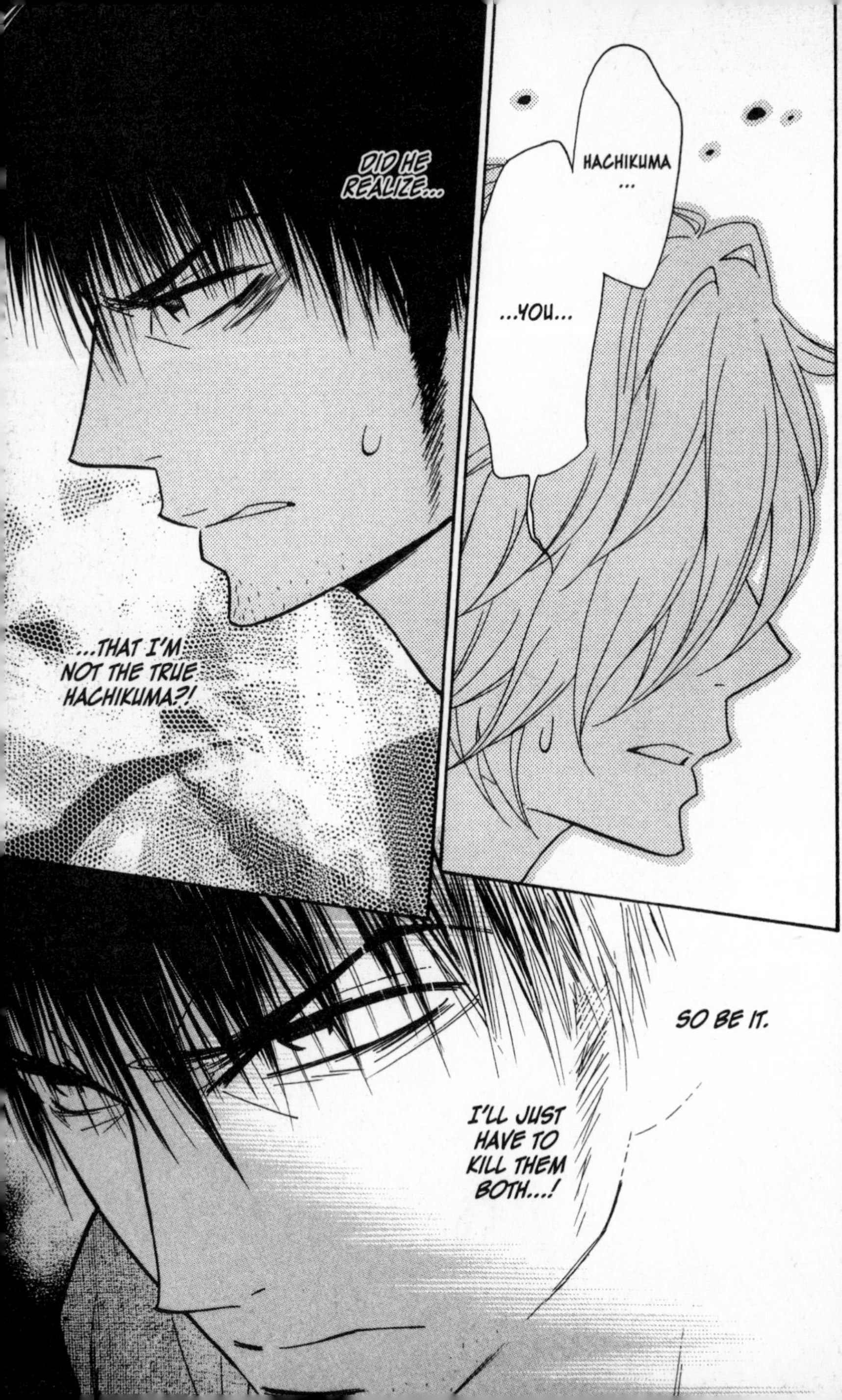
HACHIKUMA...
...YOU...
DID HE REALIZE...
...THAT I'M NOT THE TRUE HACHIKUMA?!
SO BE IT.
I'LL JUST HAVE TO KILL THEM BOTH...!

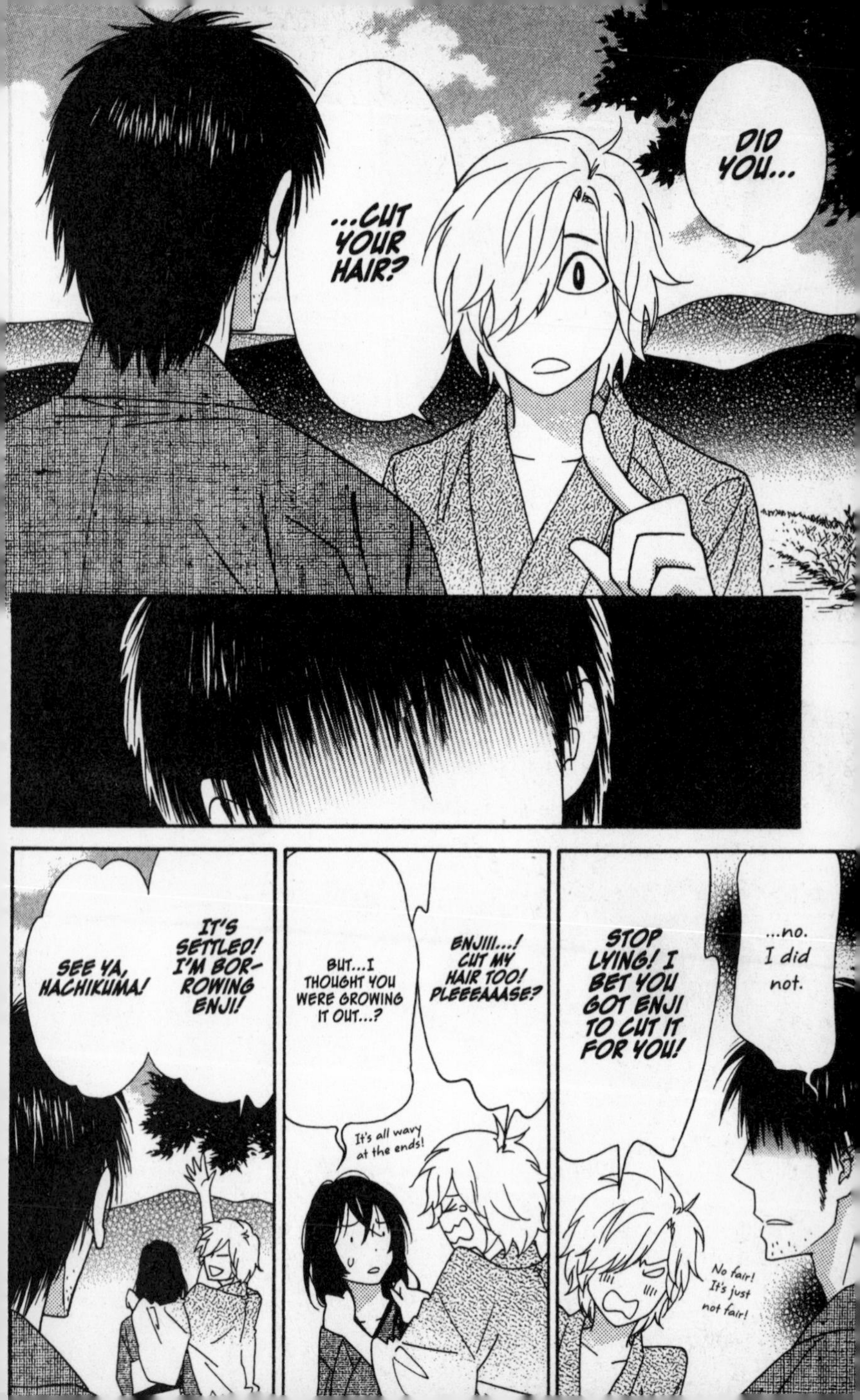
DID YOU...
...CUT YOUR HAIR?
...no. I did not.
STOP LYING! I BET YOU GOT ENJI TO CUT IT FOR YOU!
No fair! It's just not fair!
ENJIII...! CUT MY HAIR TOO! PLEEEAAASE?
BUT...I THOUGHT YOU WERE GROWING IT OUT...?
It's all wavy at the ends!
IT'S SETTLED! I'M BOR-ROWING ENJI!
SEE YA, HACHIKUMA!

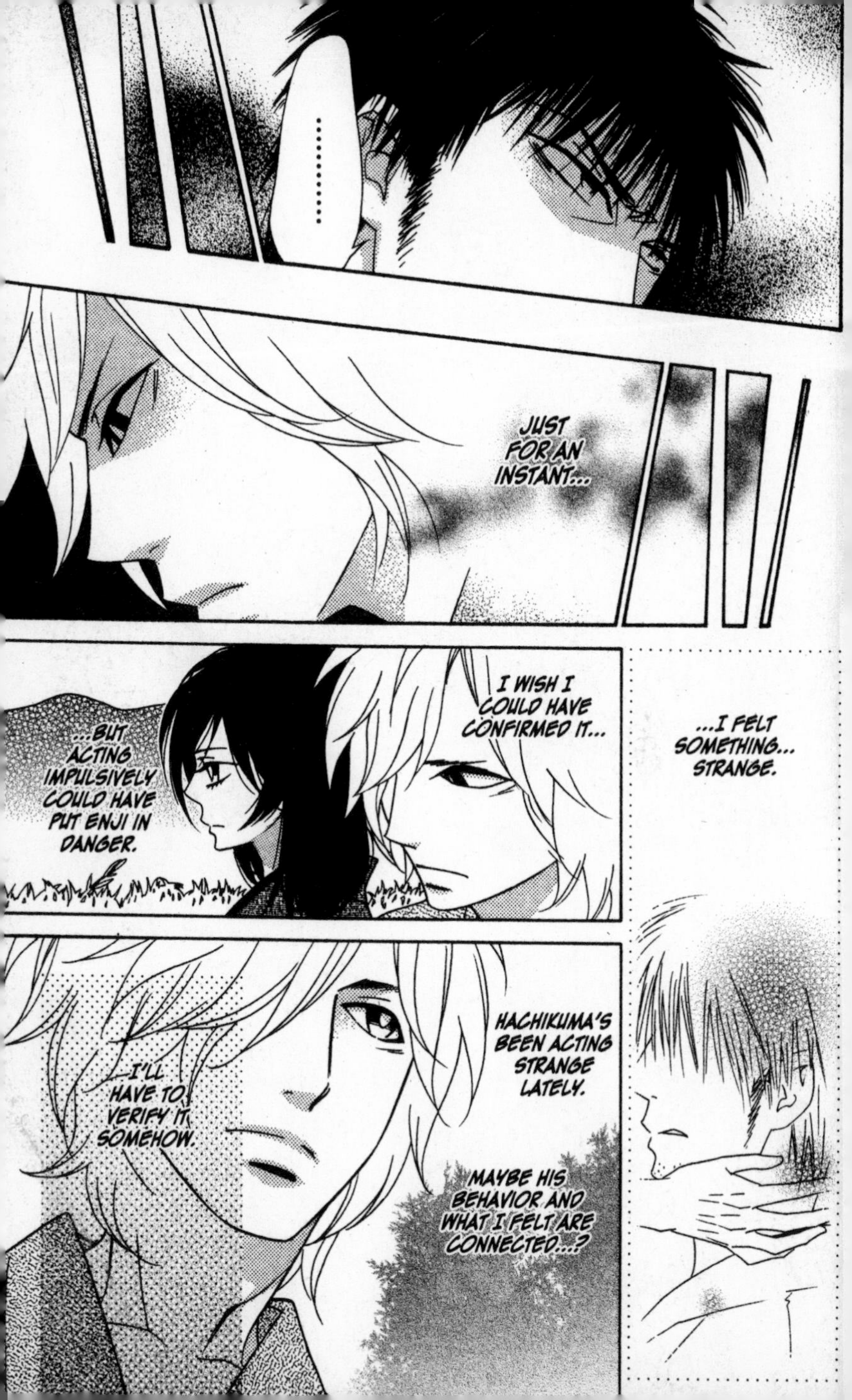
......
JUST FOR AN INSTANT...
...I FELT SOMETHING... STRANGE.
I WISH I COULD HAVE CONFIRMED IT...
...BUT ACTING IMPULSIVELY COULD HAVE PUT ENJI IN DANGER.
HACHIKUMA'S BEEN ACTING STRANGE LATELY.
MAYBE HIS BEHAVIOR AND WHAT I FELT ARE CONNECTED...?
I'LL HAVE TO VERIFY IT SOMEHOW.

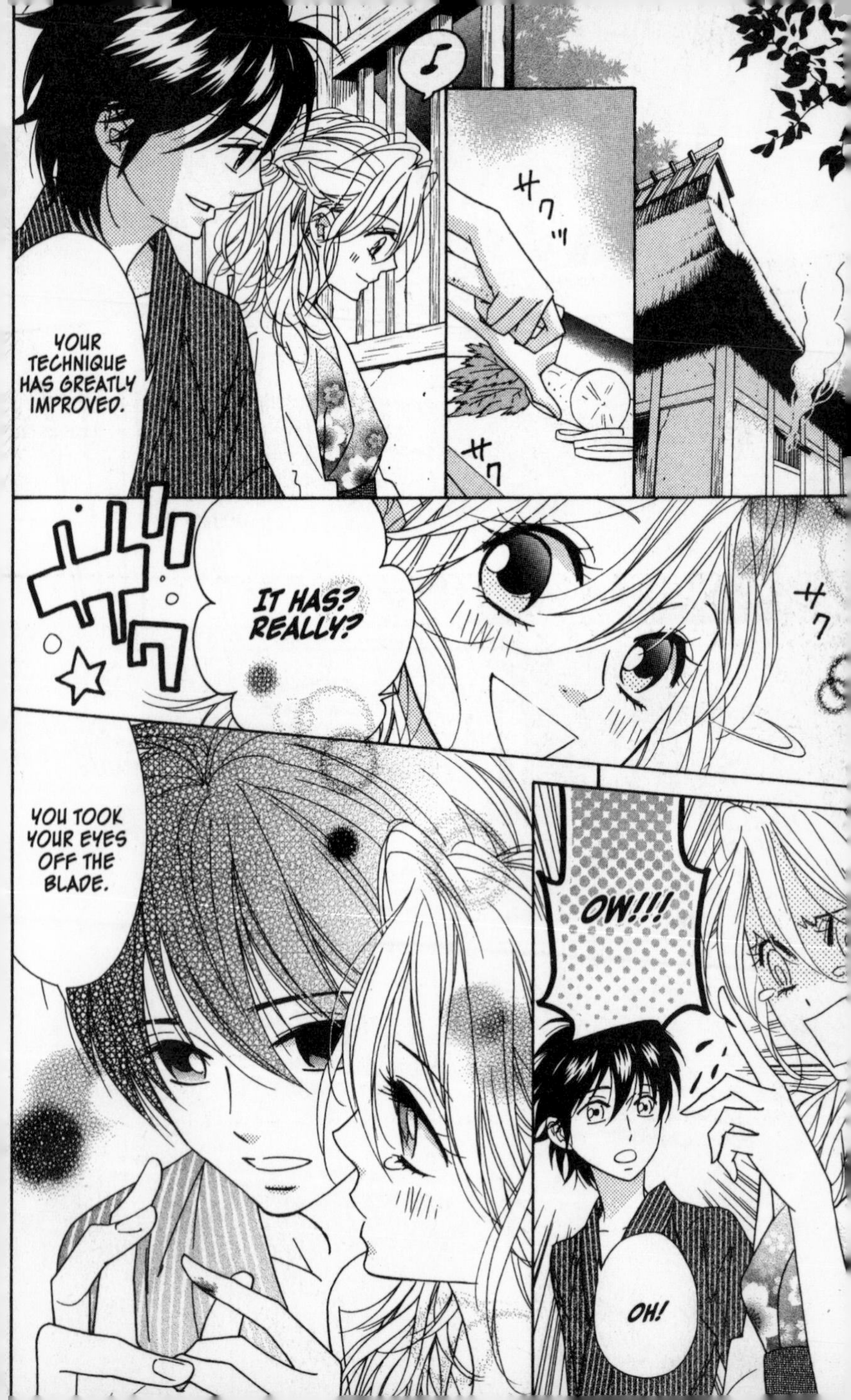
サクッ
サク
♪
YOUR TECHNIQUE HAS GREATLY IMPROVED.
サク
IT HAS? REALLY?
OW!!!
OH!
YOU TOOK YOUR EYES OFF THE BLADE.

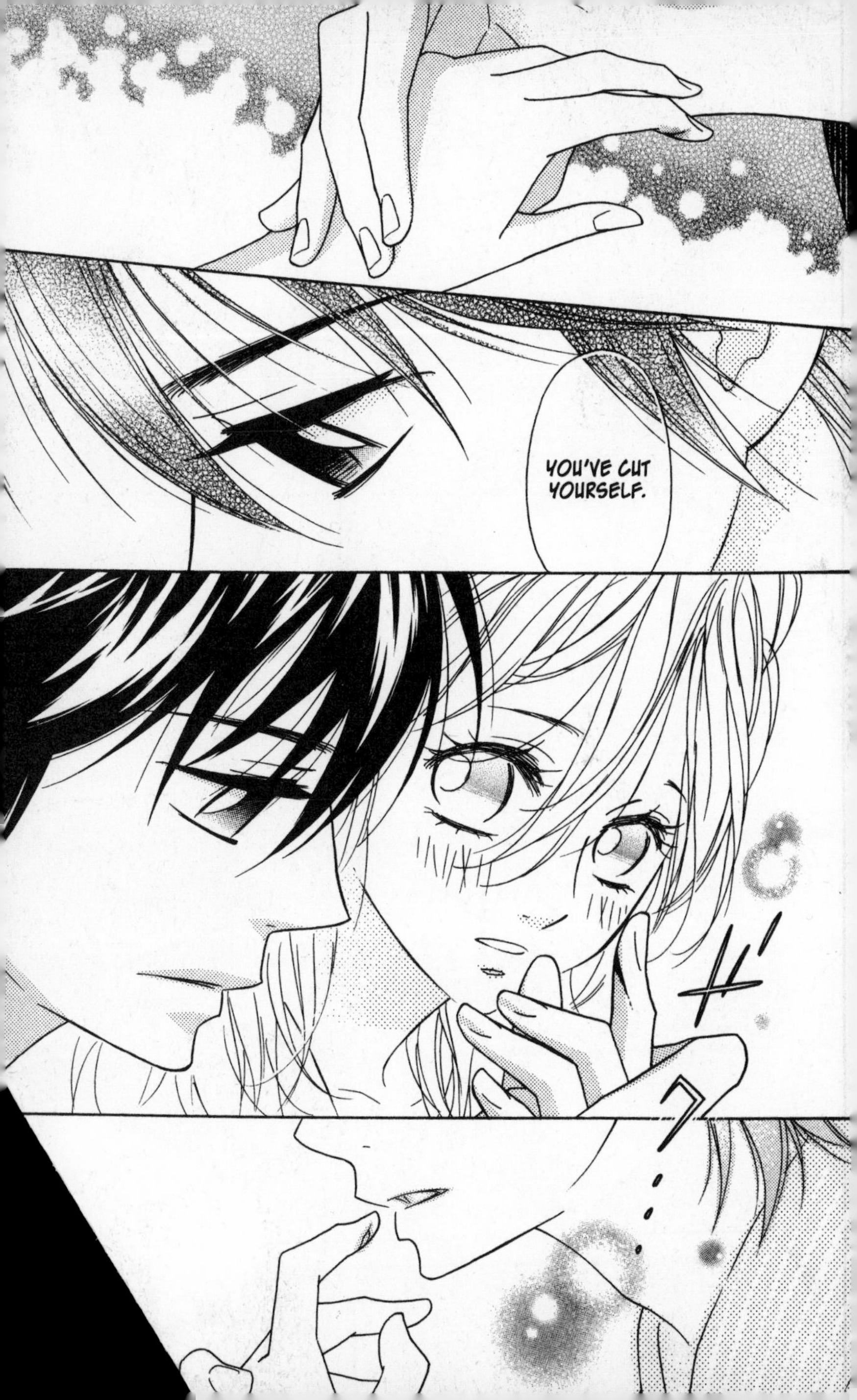
YOU'VE CUT YOURSELF.

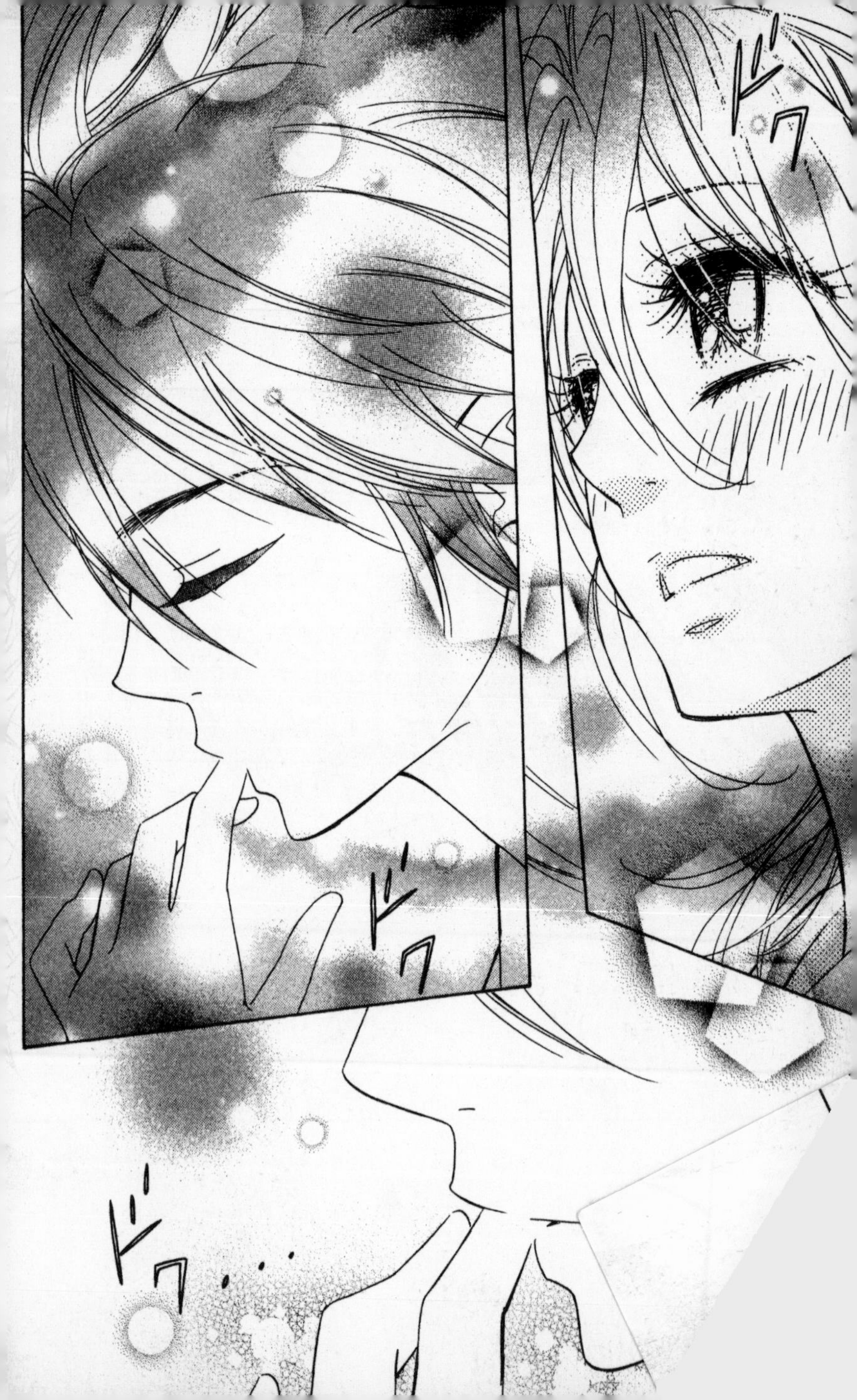
ドク
ドク
ドク…

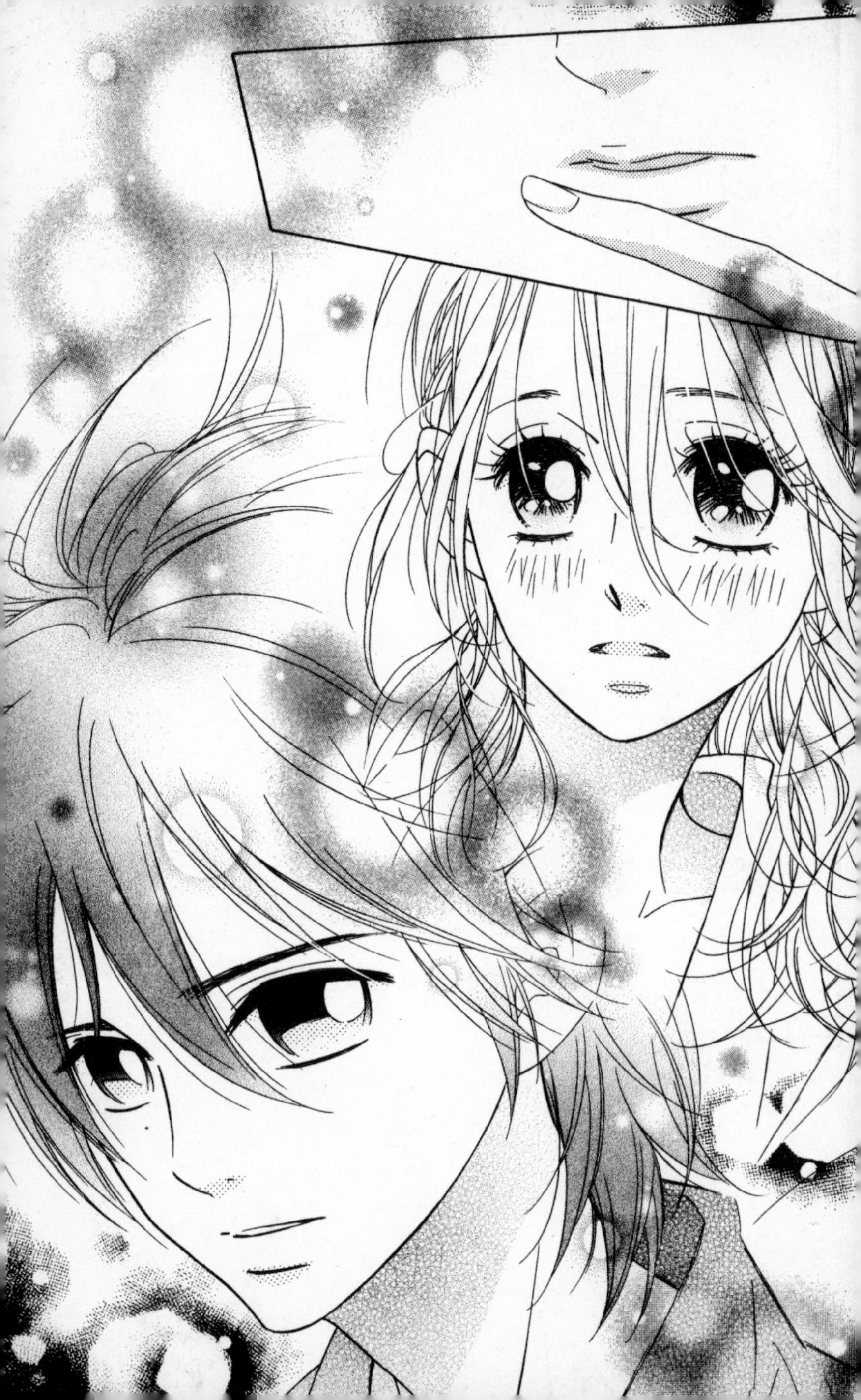

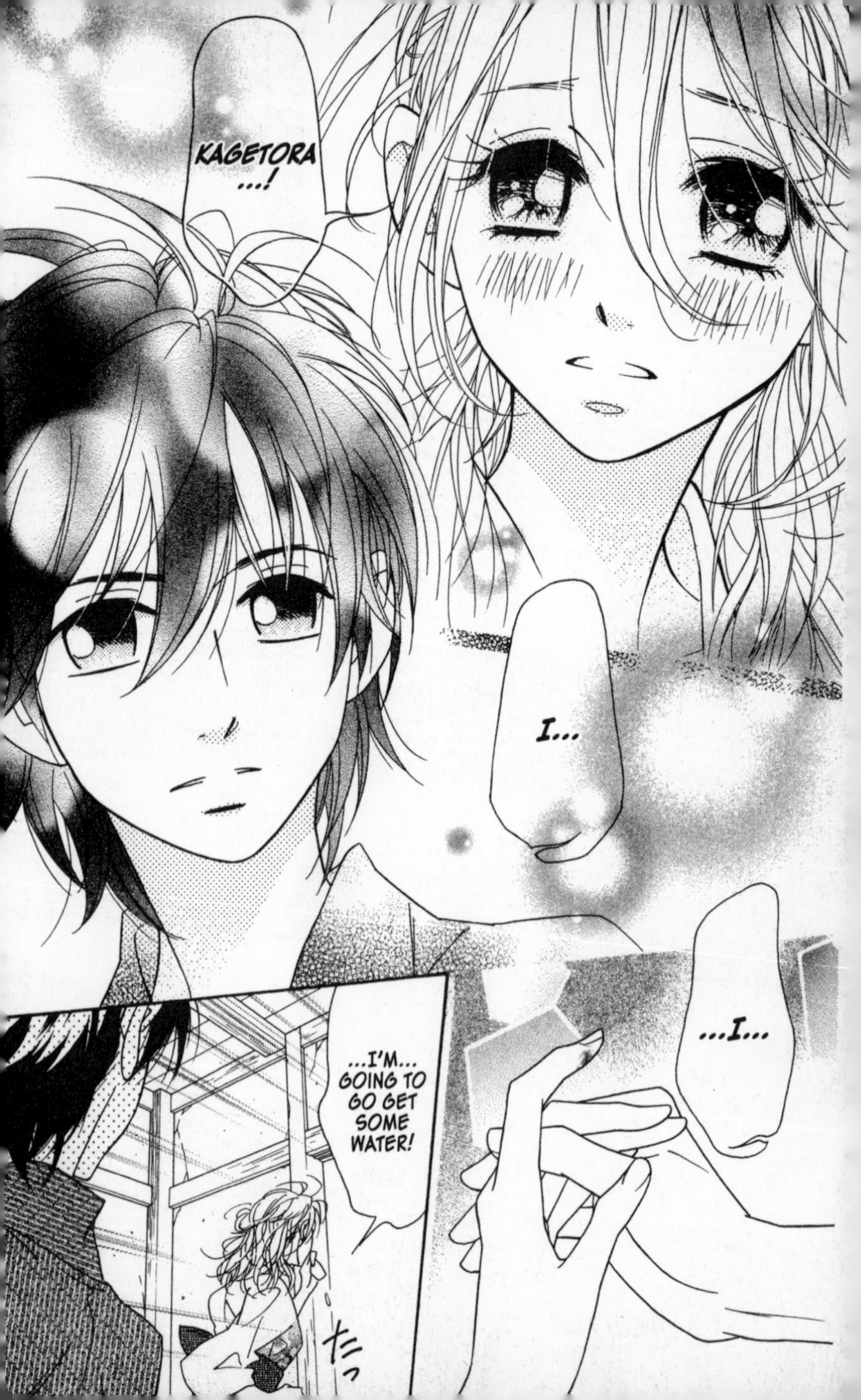
KAGETORA ...!
I...
...I...
...I'M... GOING TO GO GET SOME WATER!

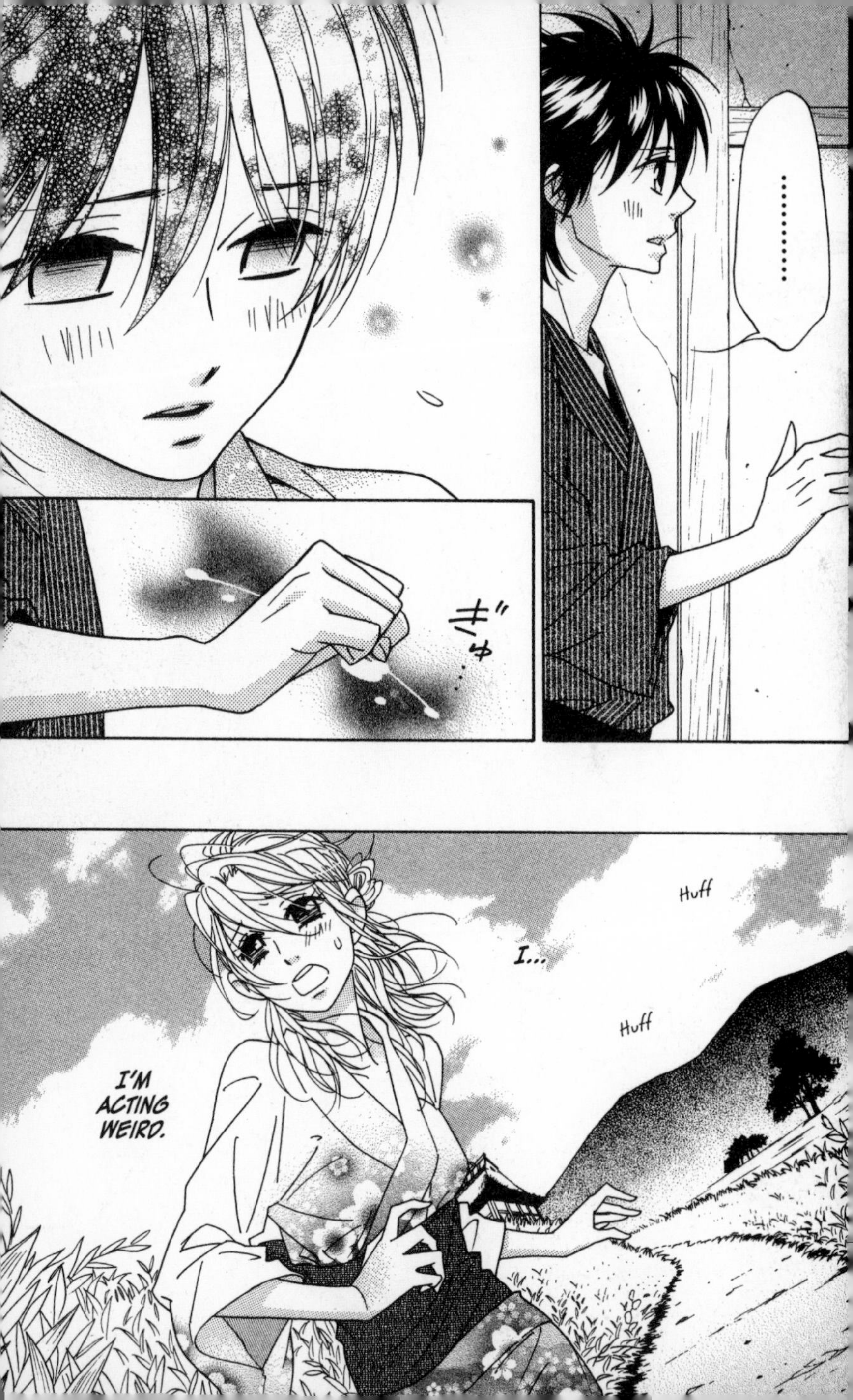
......
ぎゅ…
Huff
I...
Huff
I'M ACTING WEIRD.

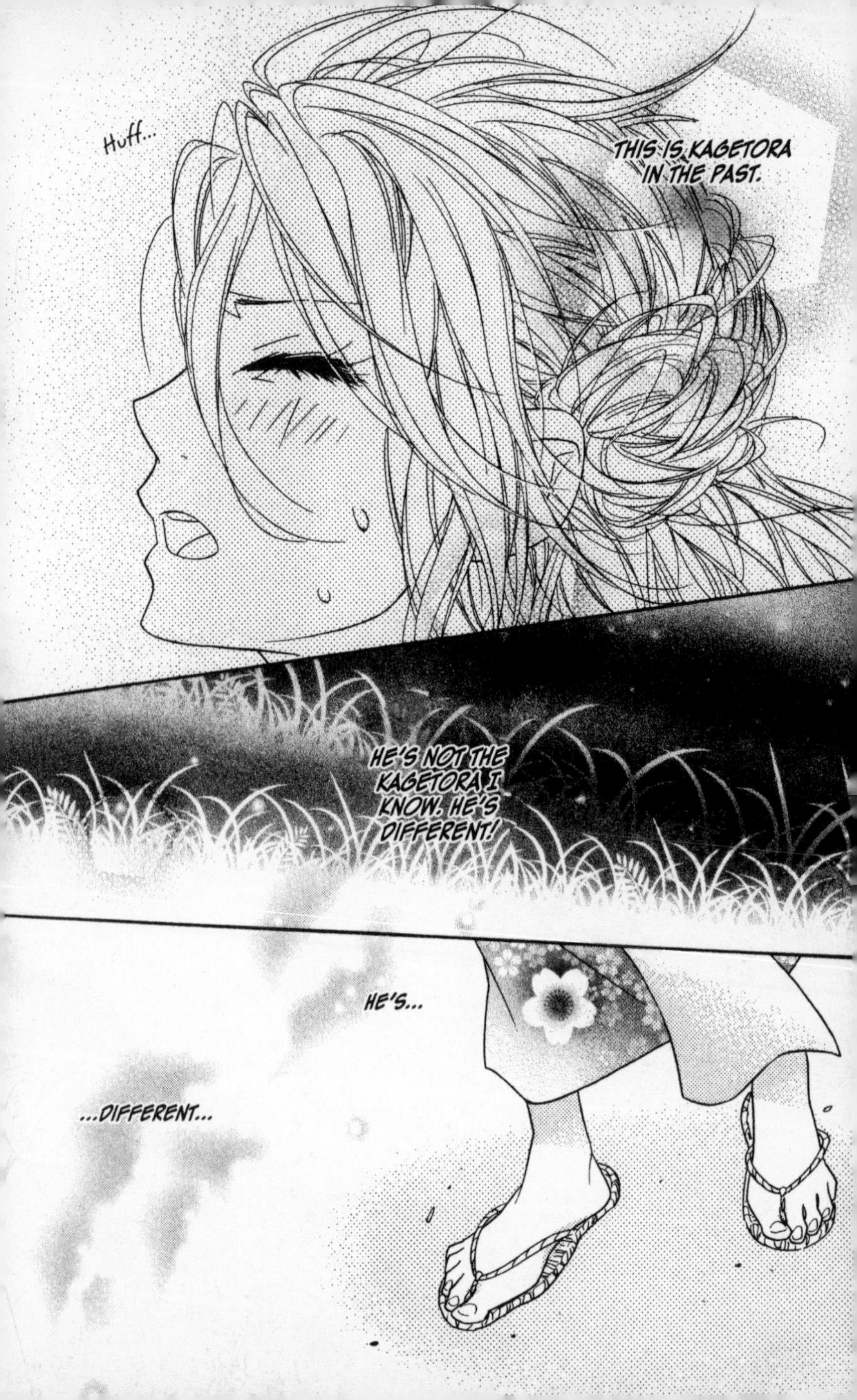
THIS IS KAGETORA IN THE PAST.
Huff...
HE'S NOT THE KAGETORA I KNOW. HE'S DIFFERENT!
HE'S...
...DIFFERENT...

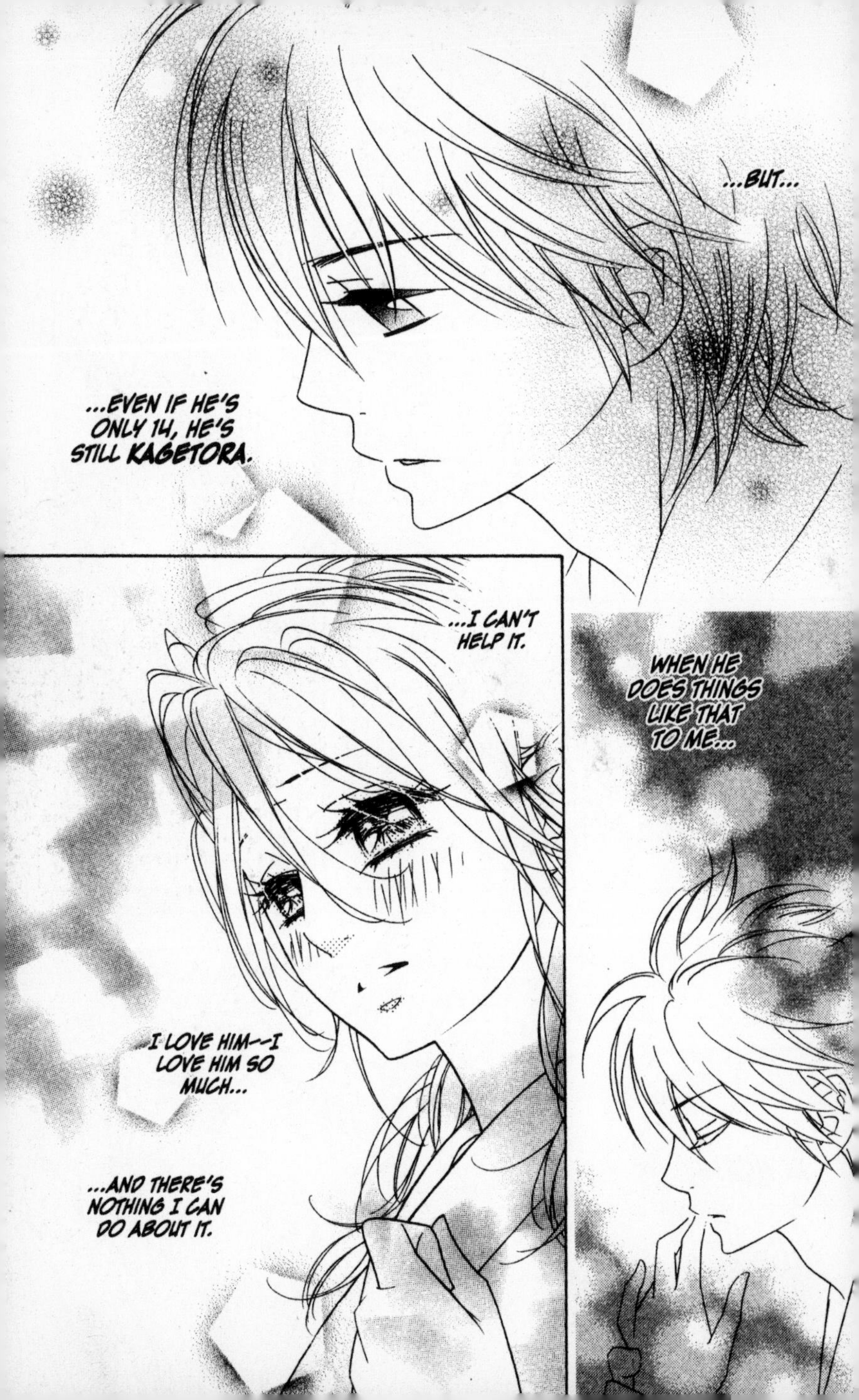
...BUT...
...EVEN IF HE'S ONLY 14, HE'S STILL KAGETORA.
WHEN HE DOES THINGS LIKE THAT TO ME...
...I CAN'T HELP IT.
I LOVE HIM--I LOVE HIM SO MUCH...
...AND THERE'S NOTHING I CAN DO ABOUT IT.

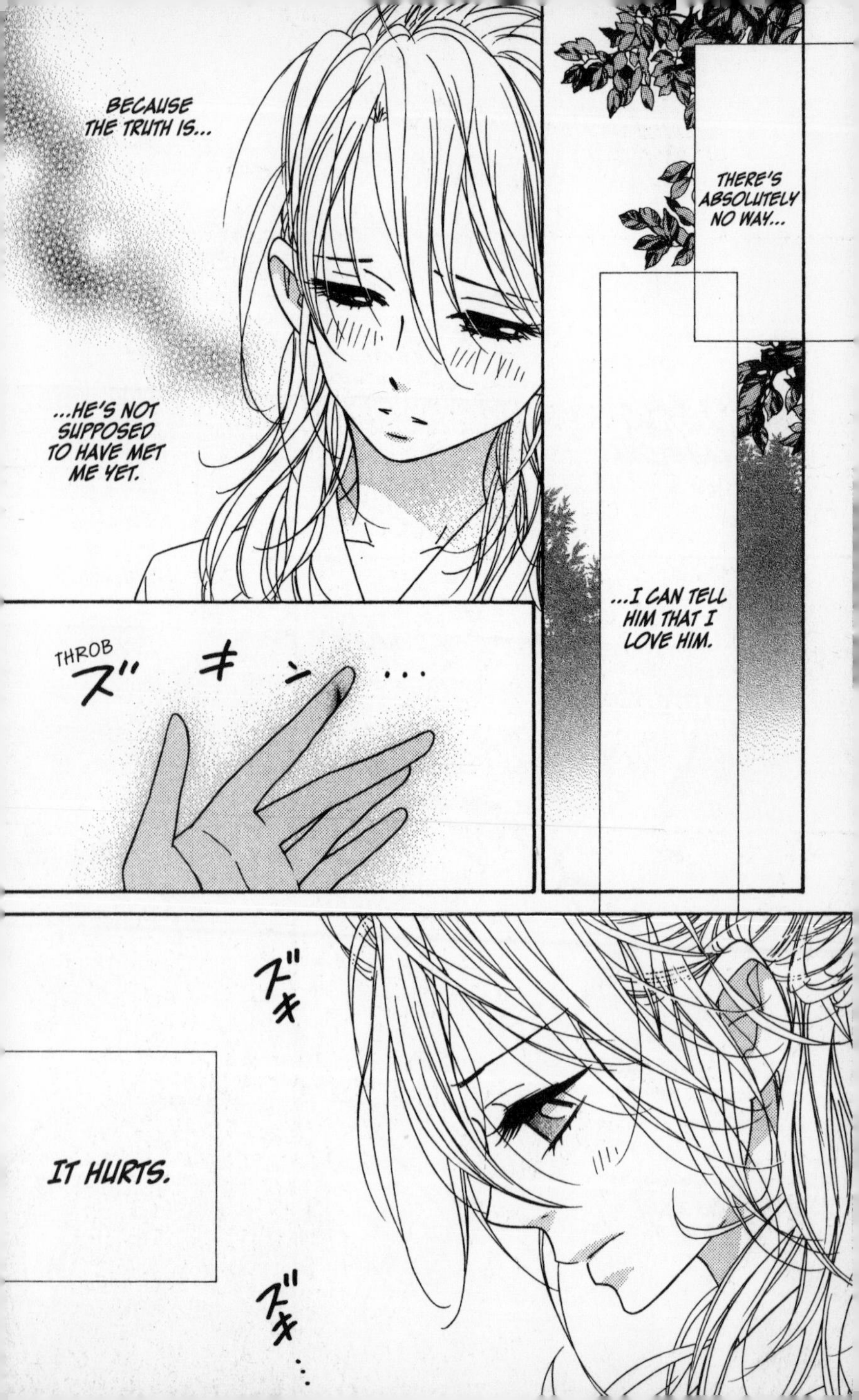
THERE'S ABSOLUTELY NO WAY...
...I CAN TELL HIM THAT I LOVE HIM.
BECAUSE THE TRUTH IS...
...HE'S NOT SUPPOSED TO HAVE MET ME YET.
THROB
ズキン...
ズキ
IT HURTS.
ズキ...

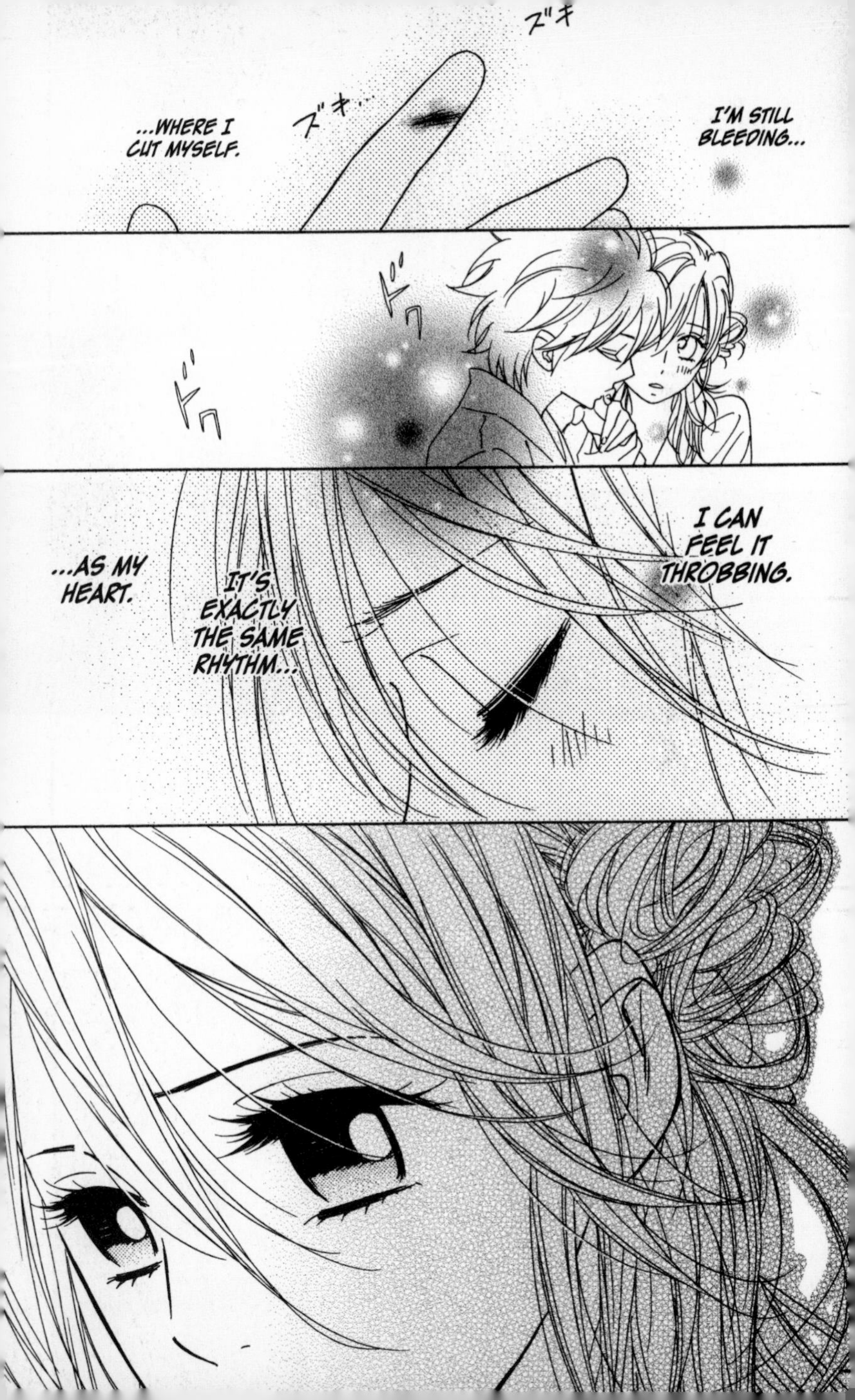
ズキ
I'M STILL BLEEDING...
ズキ...
...WHERE I CUT MYSELF.
ドク
ドク
I CAN FEEL IT THROBBING.
IT'S EXACTLY THE SAME RHYTHM...
...AS MY HEART.

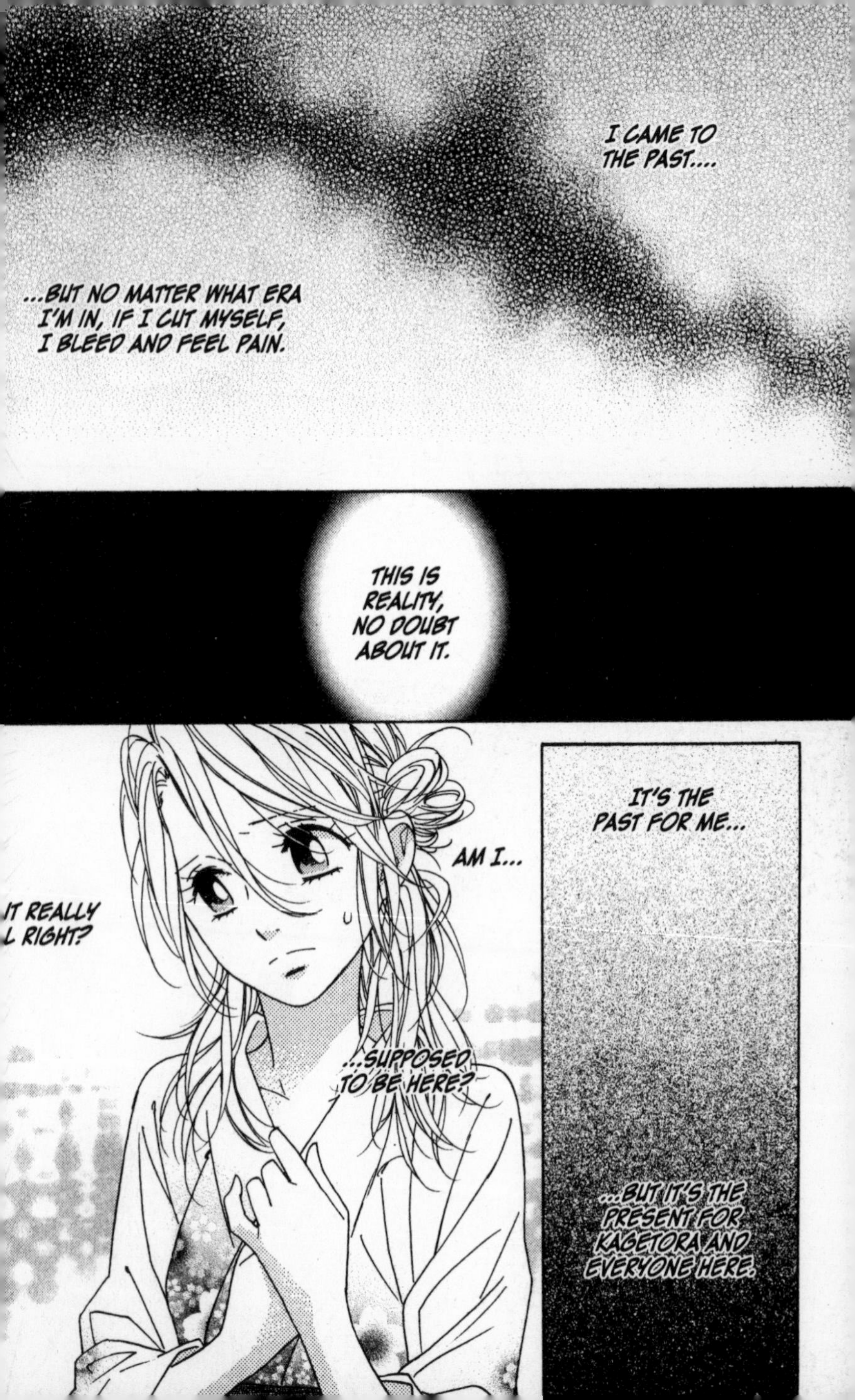
I CAME TO THE PAST....
...BUT NO MATTER WHAT ERA I'M IN, IF I CUT MYSELF, I BLEED AND FEEL PAIN.
THIS IS REALITY, NO DOUBT ABOUT IT.
IT'S THE PAST FOR ME...
...BUT IT'S THE PRESENT FOR KAGETORA AND EVERYONE HERE.
AM I...
...SUPPOSED TO BE HERE?
IT REALLY L RIGHT?

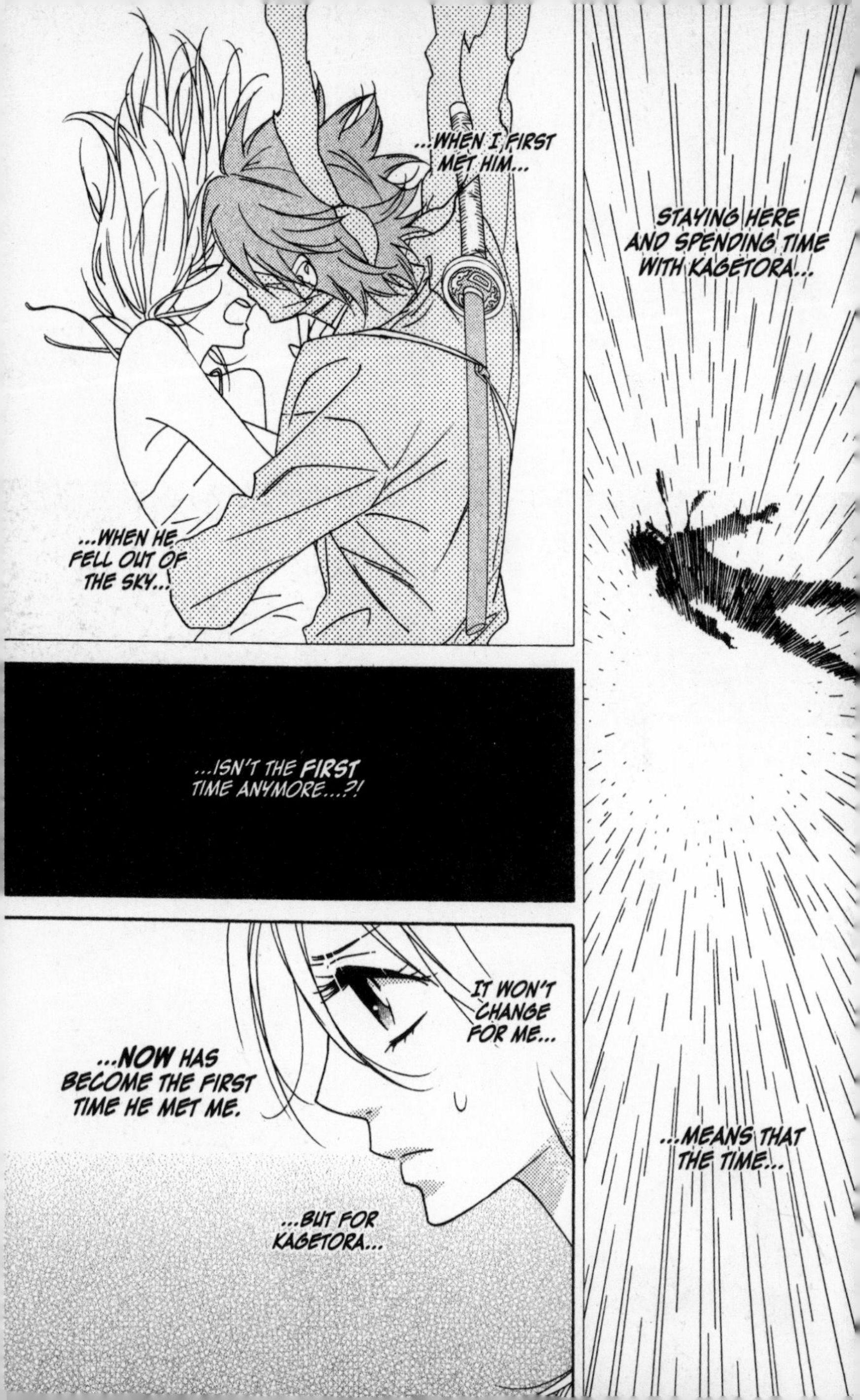

STAYING HERE AND SPENDING TIME WITH KAGETORA...
...MEANS THAT THE TIME...
...WHEN I FIRST MET HIM...
...WHEN HE FELL OUT OF THE SKY...
...ISN'T THE FIRST TIME ANYMORE...?!
IT WON'T CHANGE FOR ME...
...BUT FOR KAGETORA...
...NOW HAS BECOME THE FIRST TIME HE MET ME.

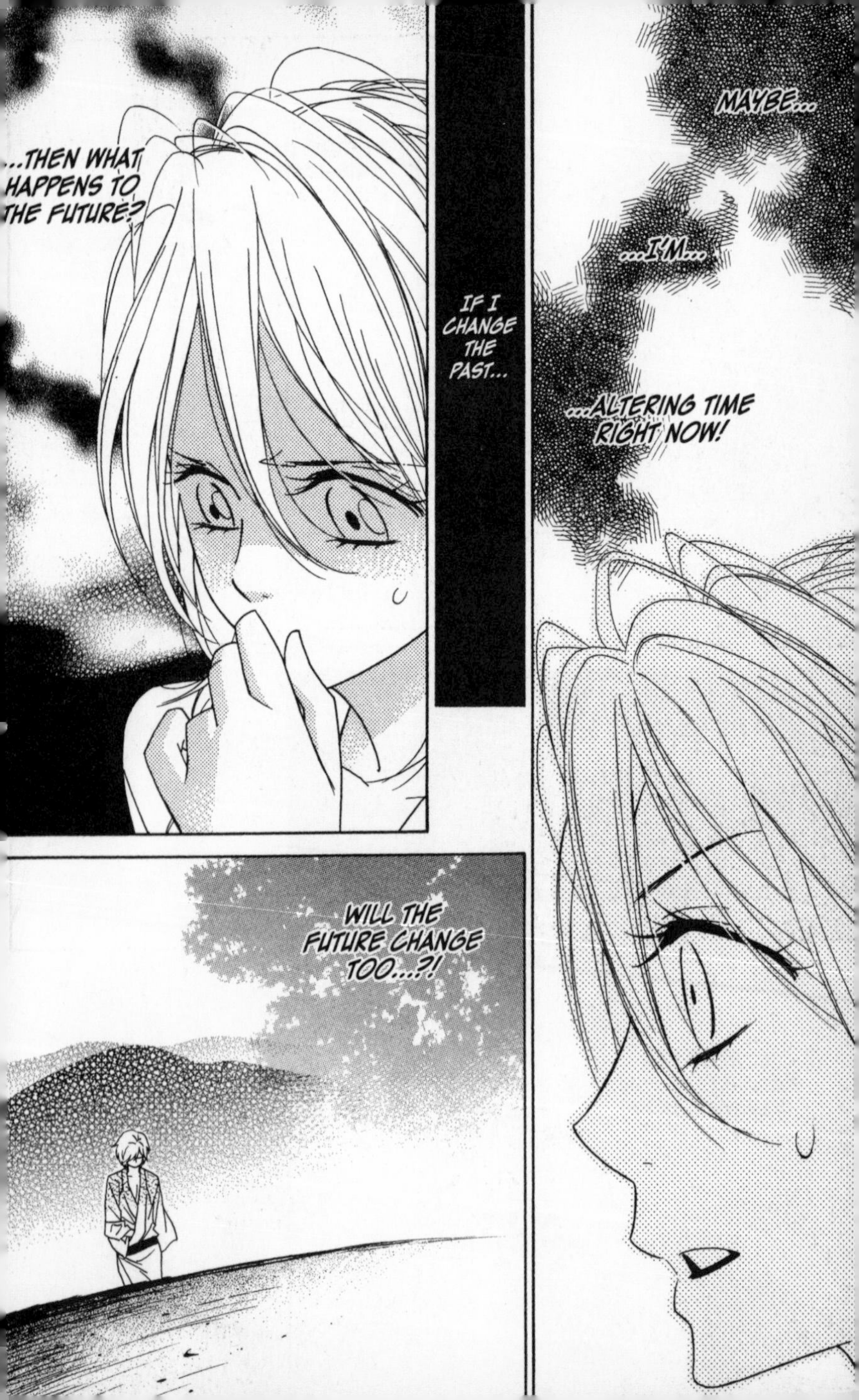
MAYBE...
...I'M...
...ALTERING TIME RIGHT NOW!
IF I CHANGE THE PAST...
...THEN WHAT HAPPENS TO THE FUTURE?
WILL THE FUTURE CHANGE TOO...?!

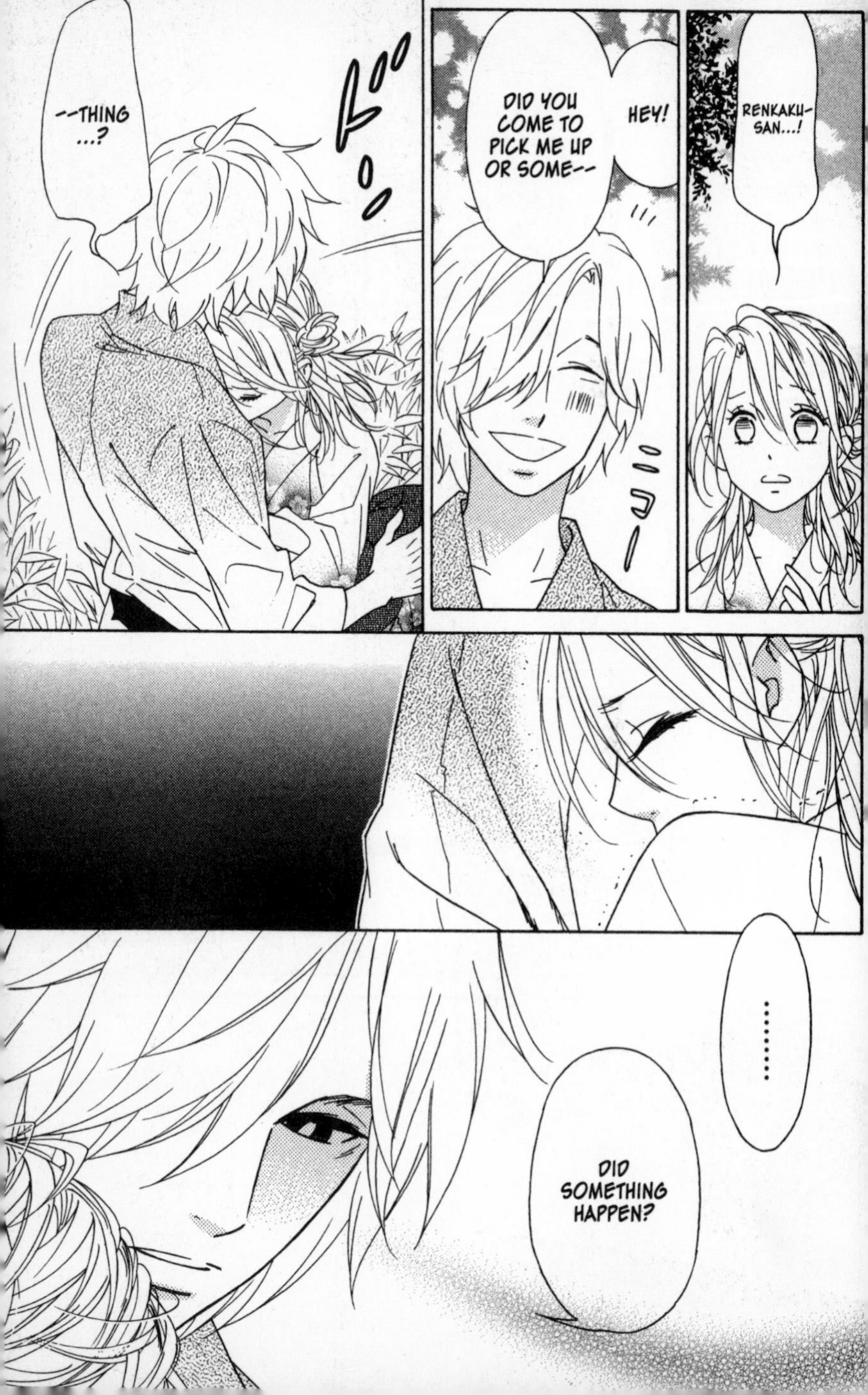
RENKAKU-SAN...!
HEY!
DID YOU COME TO PICK ME UP OR SOME--
--THING ...?
......
DID SOMETHING HAPPEN?

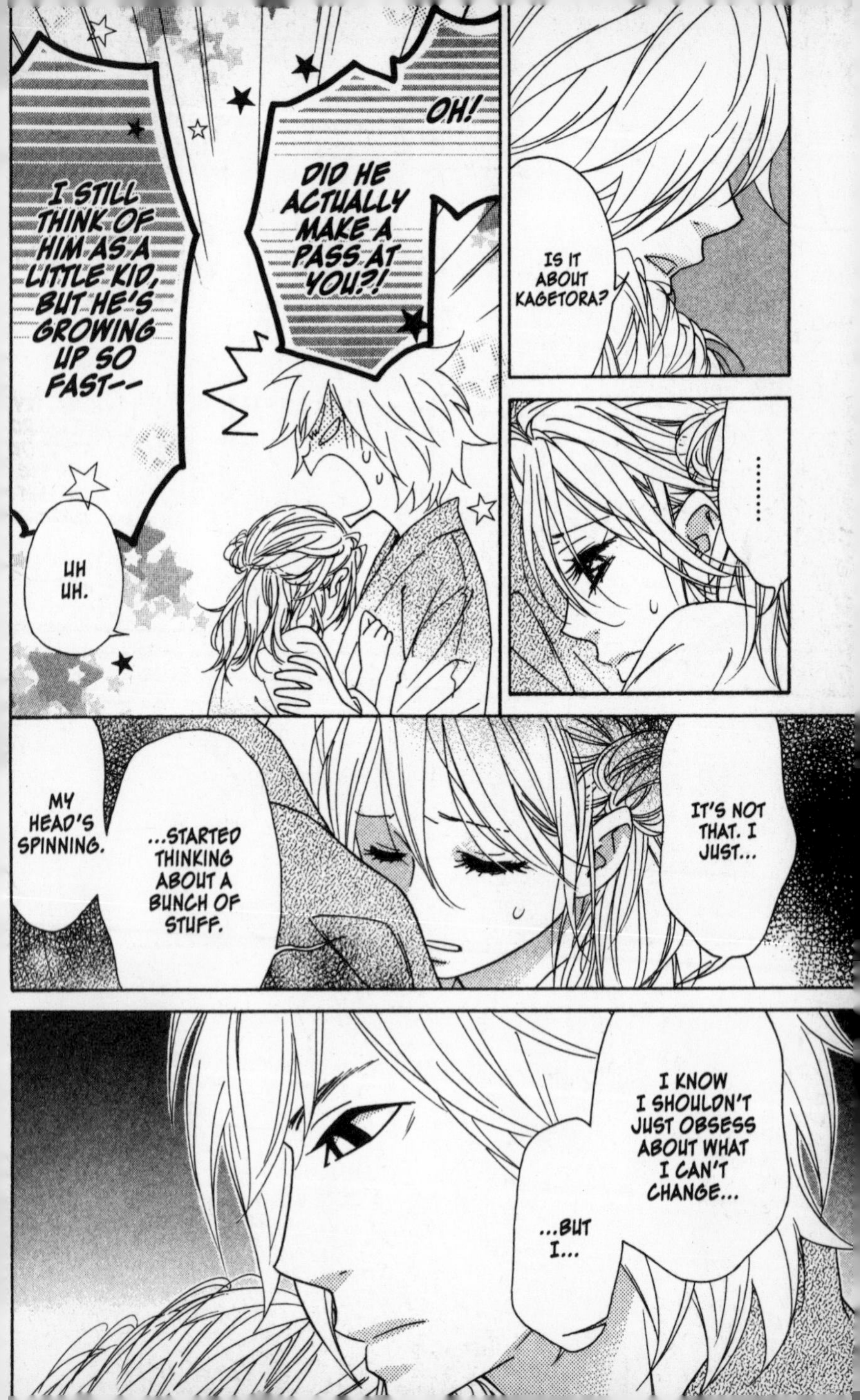
IS IT ABOUT KAGETORA?
......
OH!
DID HE ACTUALLY MAKE A PASS AT YOU?!
I STILL THINK OF HIM AS A LITTLE KID, BUT HE'S GROWING UP SO FAST--
UH UH.
IT'S NOT THAT. I JUST...
...STARTED THINKING ABOUT A BUNCH OF STUFF.
MY HEAD'S SPINNING.
I KNOW I SHOULDN'T JUST OBSESS ABOUT WHAT I CAN'T CHANGE...
...BUT I...

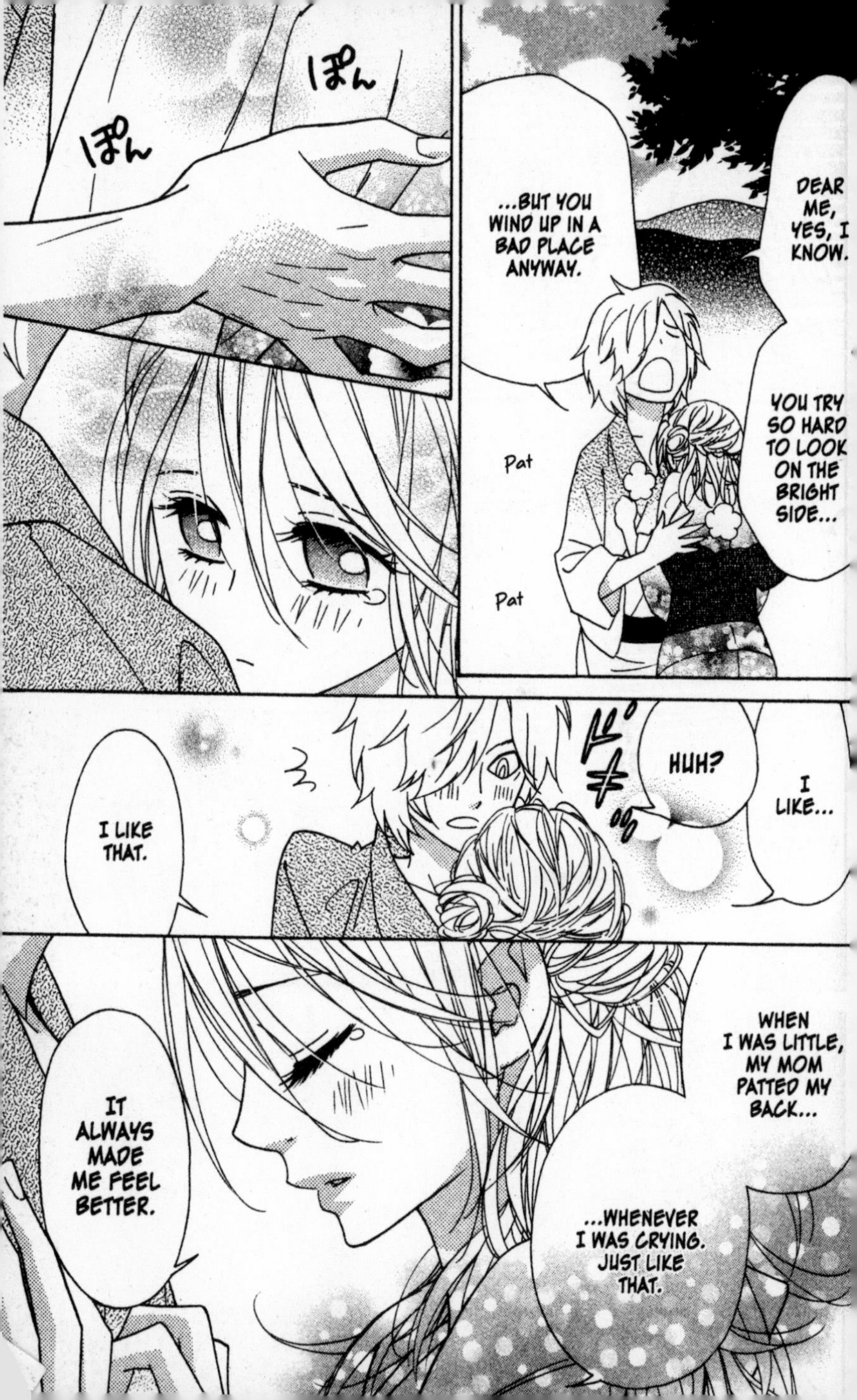
DEAR ME, YES, I KNOW.
YOU TRY SO HARD TO LOOK ON THE BRIGHT SIDE...
...BUT YOU WIND UP IN A BAD PLACE ANYWAY.
Pat
Pat
ぽん
ぽん
I LIKE...
HUH?
I LIKE THAT.
WHEN I WAS LITTLE, MY MOM PATTED MY BACK...
...WHENEVER I WAS CRYING. JUST LIKE THAT.
IT ALWAYS MADE ME FEEL BETTER.

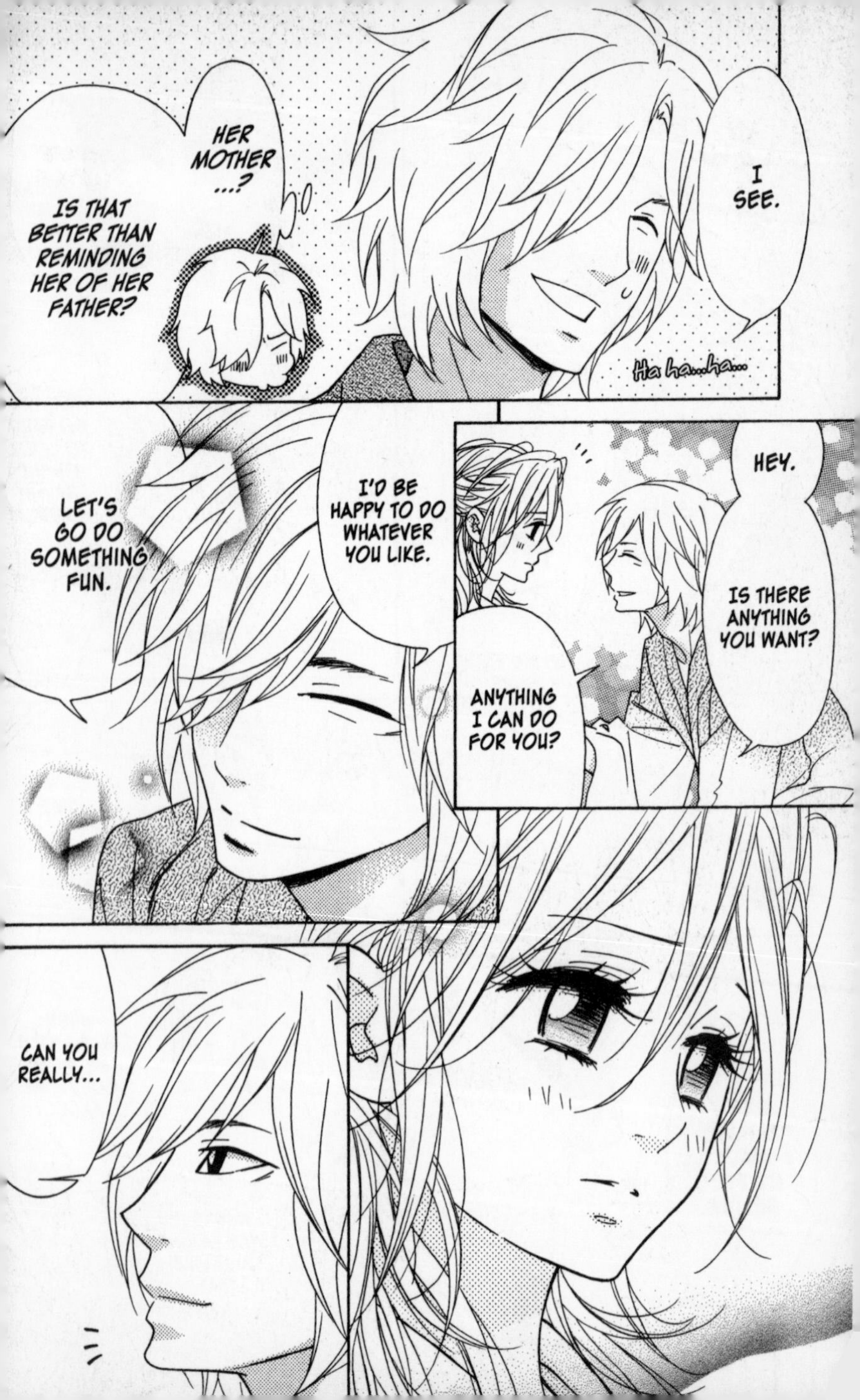
I SEE.
Ha ha...ha...
HER MOTHER ...?
IS THAT BETTER THAN REMINDING HER OF HER FATHER?
HEY.
IS THERE ANYTHING YOU WANT?
ANYTHING I CAN DO FOR YOU?
I'D BE HAPPY TO DO WHATEVER YOU LIKE.
LET'S GO DO SOMETHING FUN.
CAN YOU REALLY...

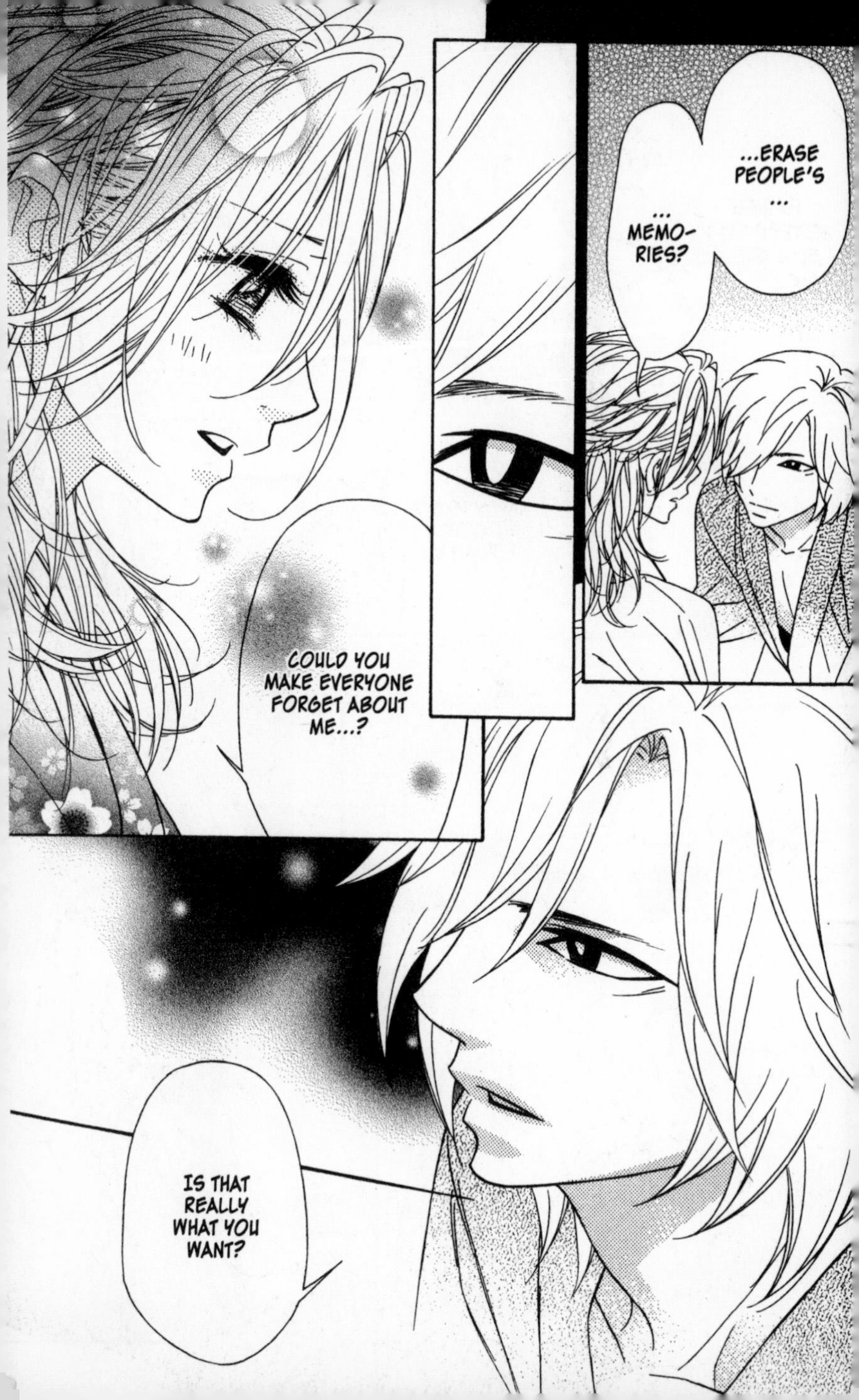
...ERASE PEOPLE'S ... ... MEMORIES?
COULD YOU MAKE EVERYONE FORGET ABOUT ME...?
IS THAT REALLY WHAT YOU WANT?

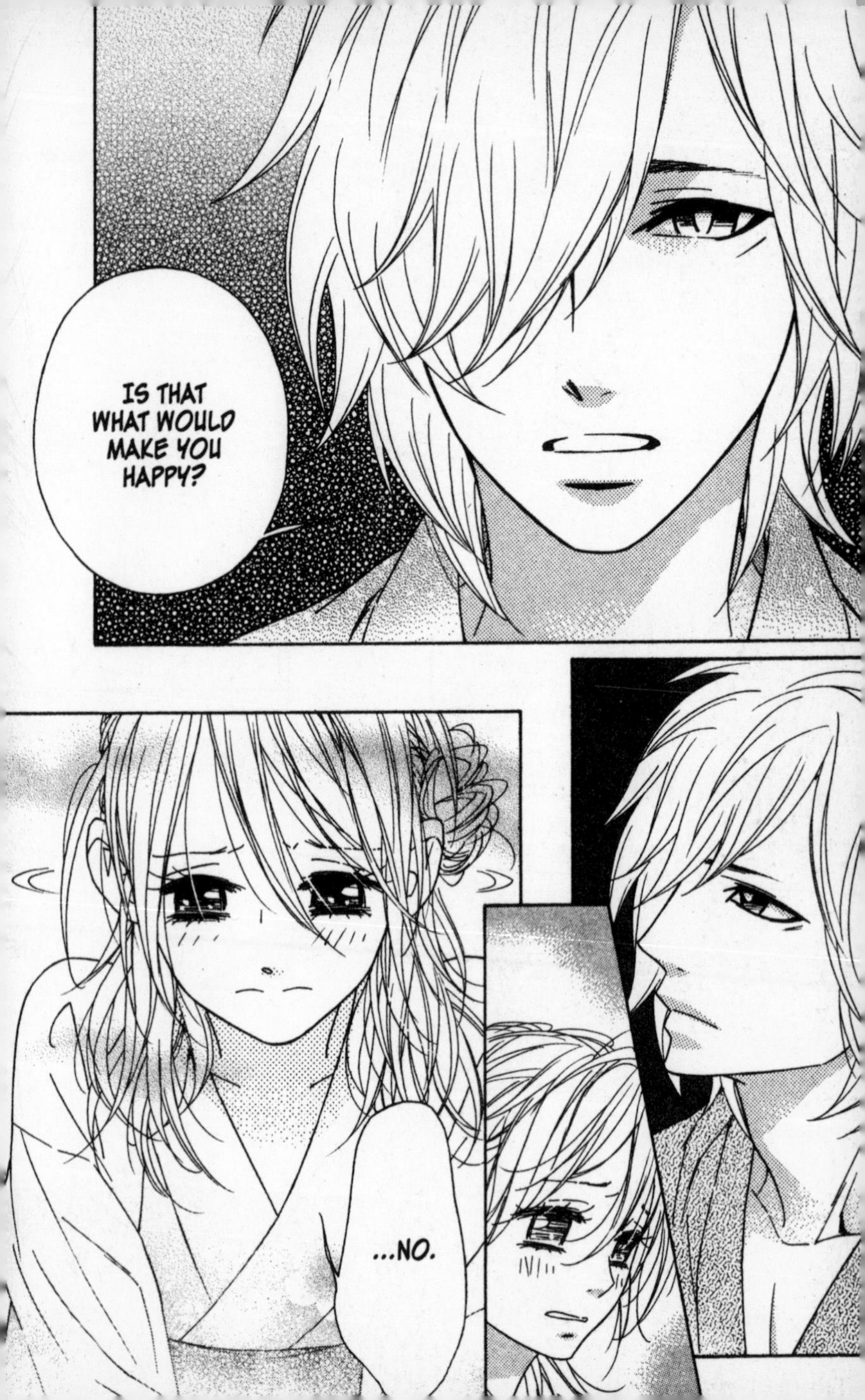
IS THAT WHAT WOULD MAKE YOU HAPPY?
...NO.

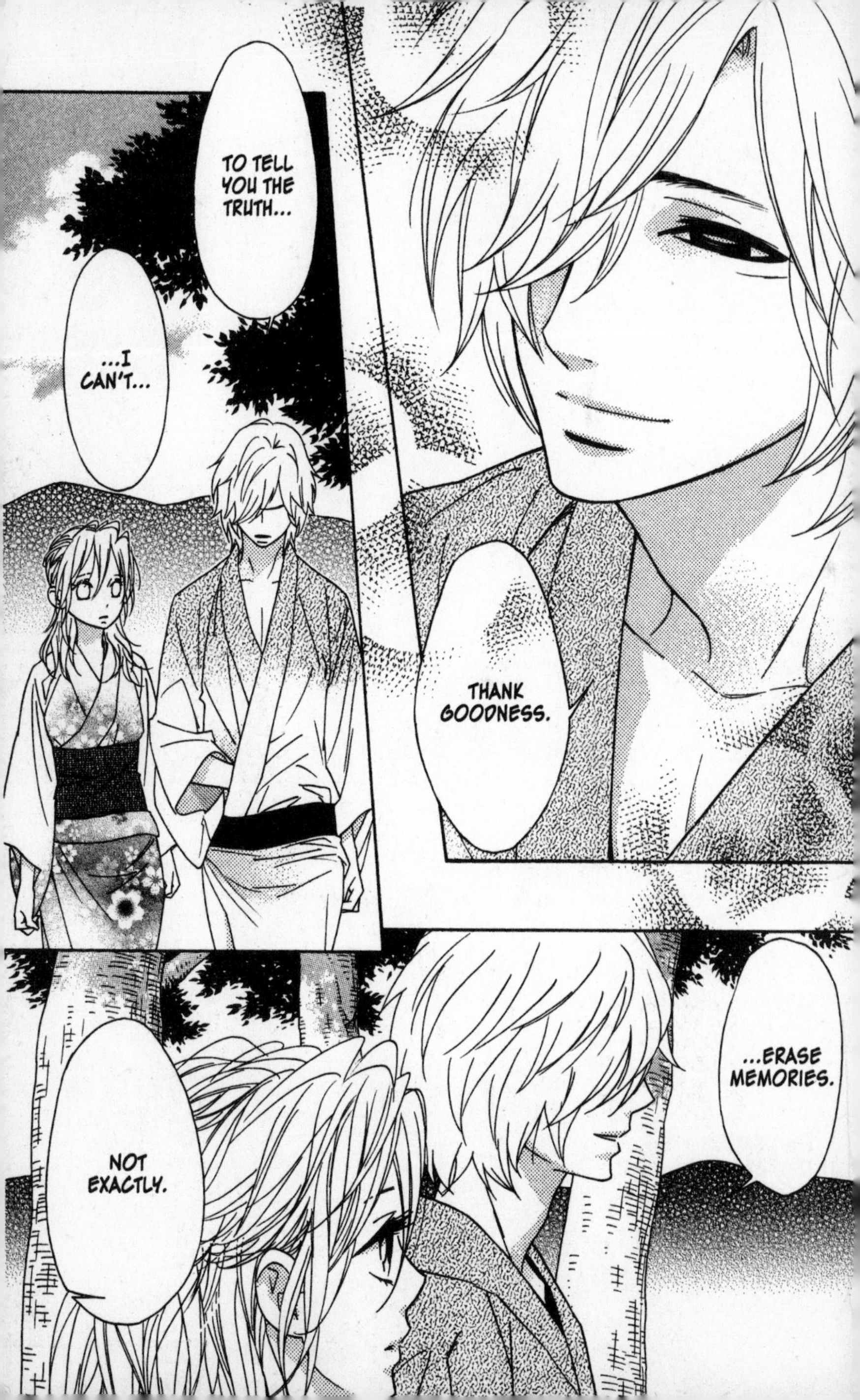
THANK GOODNESS.
TO TELL YOU THE TRUTH...
...I CAN'T...
...ERASE MEMORIES.
NOT EXACTLY.

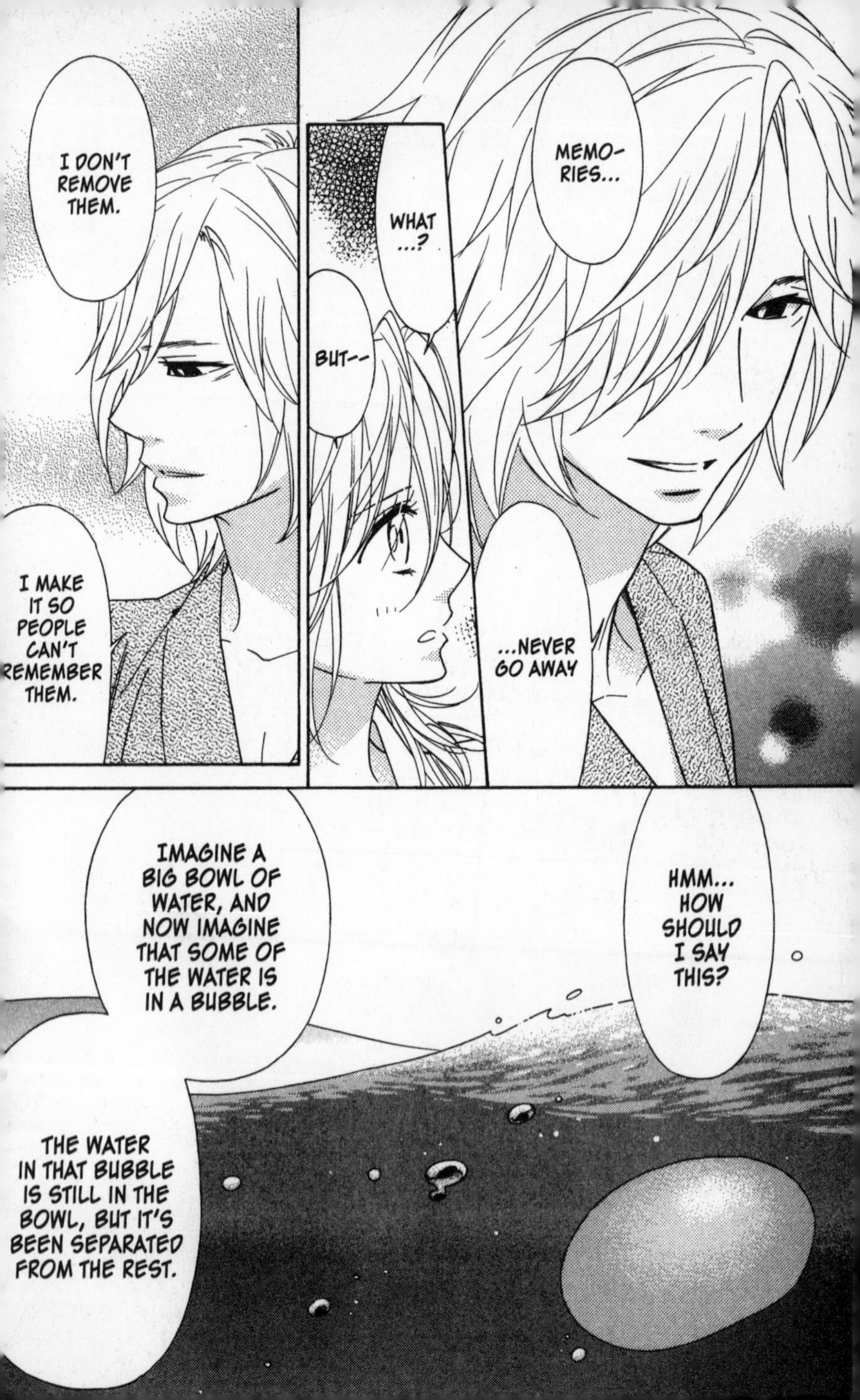
MEMO-RIES...
...NEVER GO AWAY
WHAT ...?
BUT--
I DON'T REMOVE THEM.
I MAKE IT SO PEOPLE CAN'T REMEMBER THEM.
HMM... HOW SHOULD I SAY THIS?
IMAGINE A BIG BOWL OF WATER, AND NOW IMAGINE THAT SOME OF THE WATER IS IN A BUBBLE.
THE WATER IN THAT BUBBLE IS STILL IN THE BOWL, BUT IT'S BEEN SEPARATED FROM THE REST.

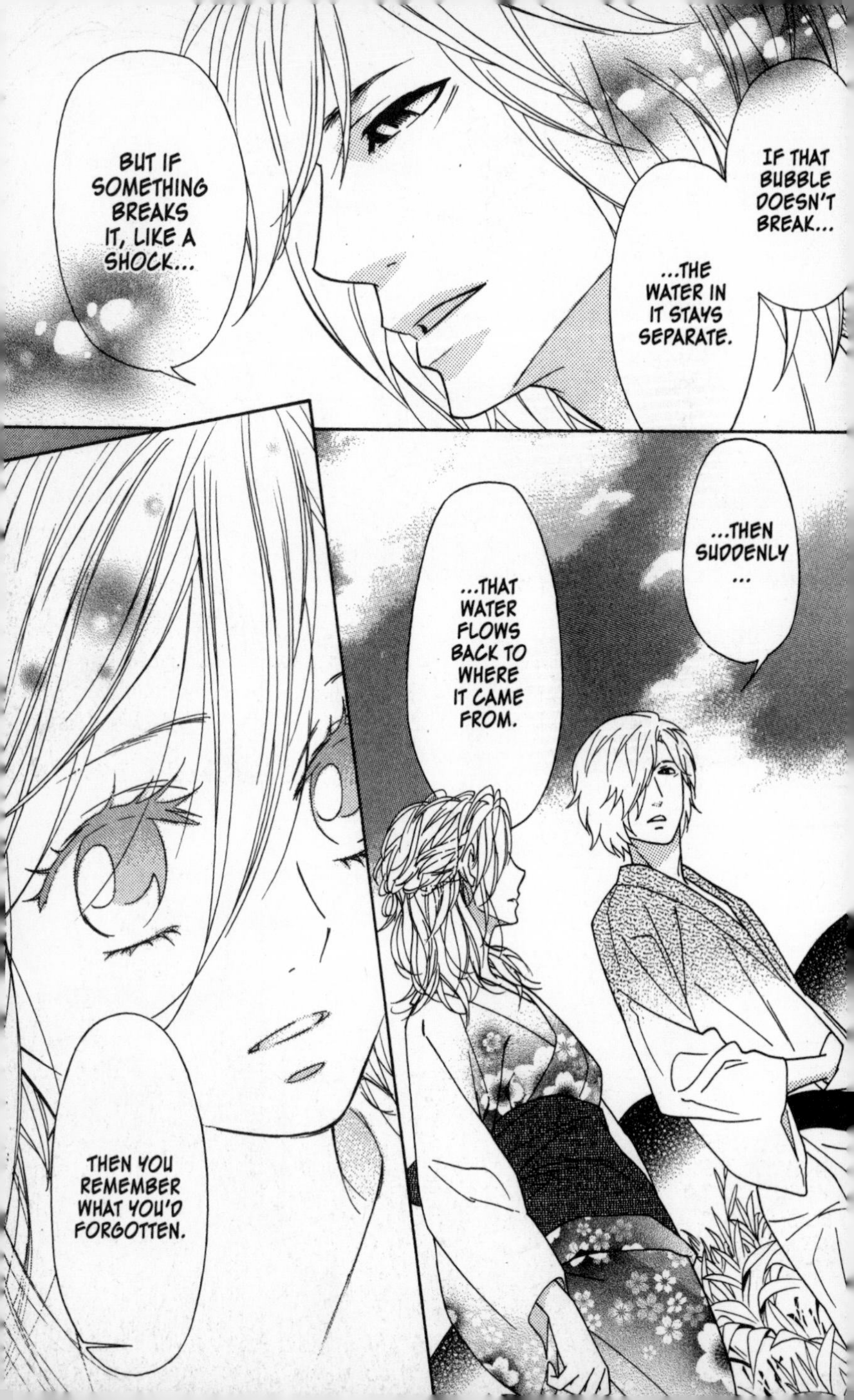
IF THAT BUBBLE DOESN'T BREAK...
...THE WATER IN IT STAYS SEPARATE.
BUT IF SOMETHING BREAKS IT, LIKE A SHOCK...
...THEN SUDDENLY...
...THAT WATER FLOWS BACK TO WHERE IT CAME FROM.
THEN YOU REMEMBER WHAT YOU'D FORGOTTEN.

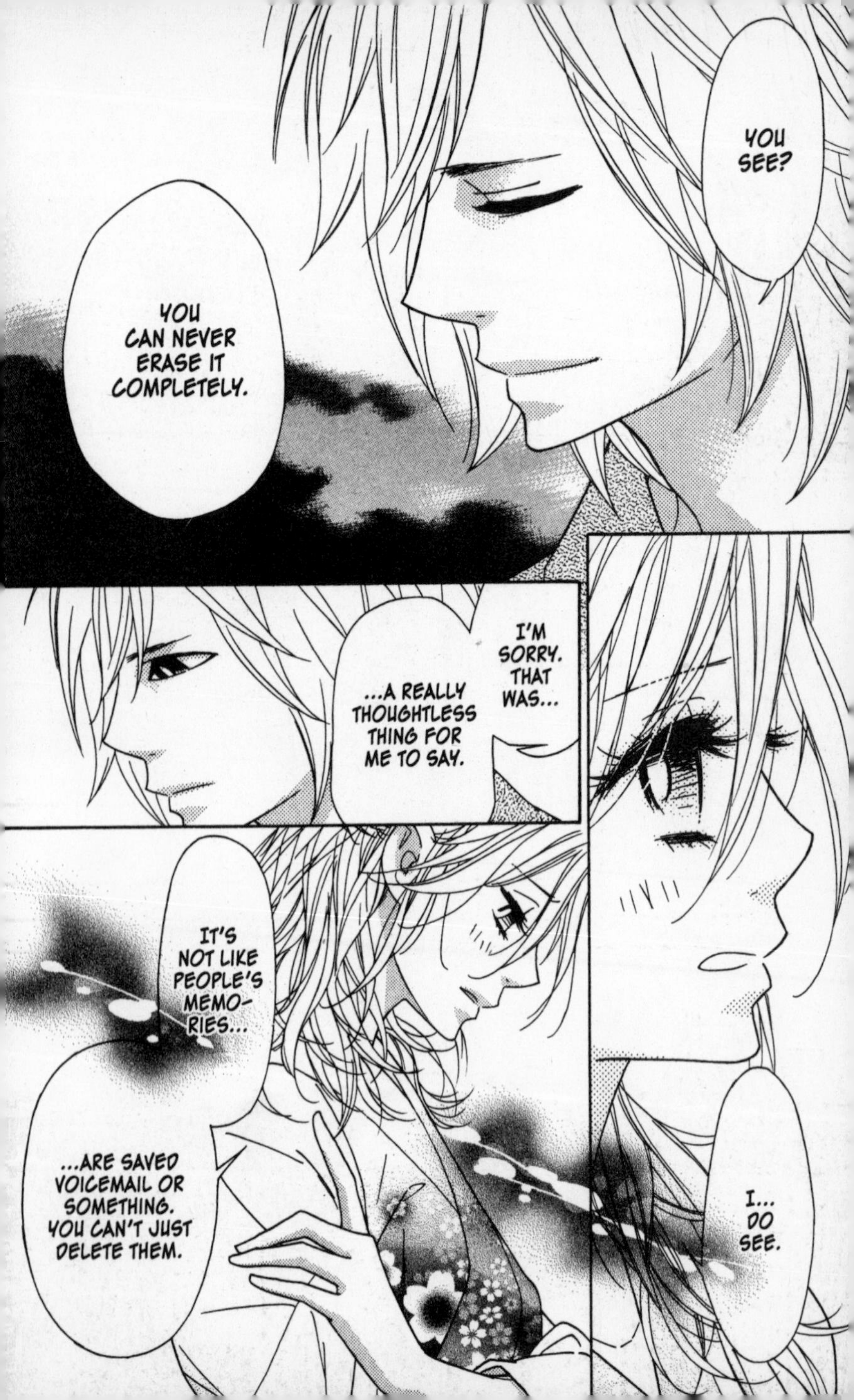
YOU SEE?
YOU CAN NEVER ERASE IT COMPLETELY.
I... DO SEE.
I'M SORRY. THAT WAS...
...A REALLY THOUGHTLESS THING FOR ME TO SAY.
IT'S NOT LIKE PEOPLE'S MEMO-RIES...
...ARE SAVED VOICEMAIL OR SOMETHING. YOU CAN'T JUST DELETE THEM.

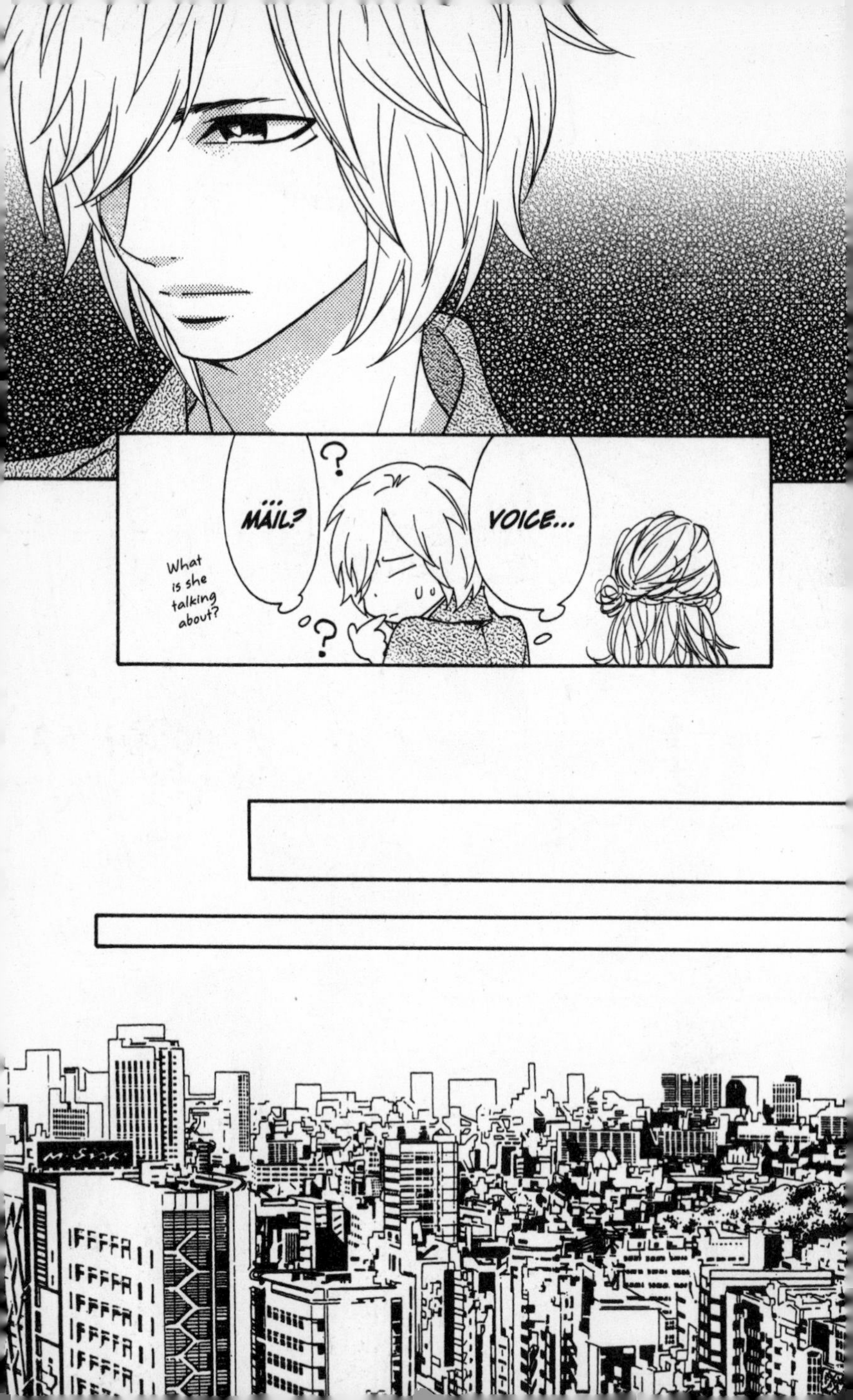
VOICE...
MÄIL?
What is she talking about?

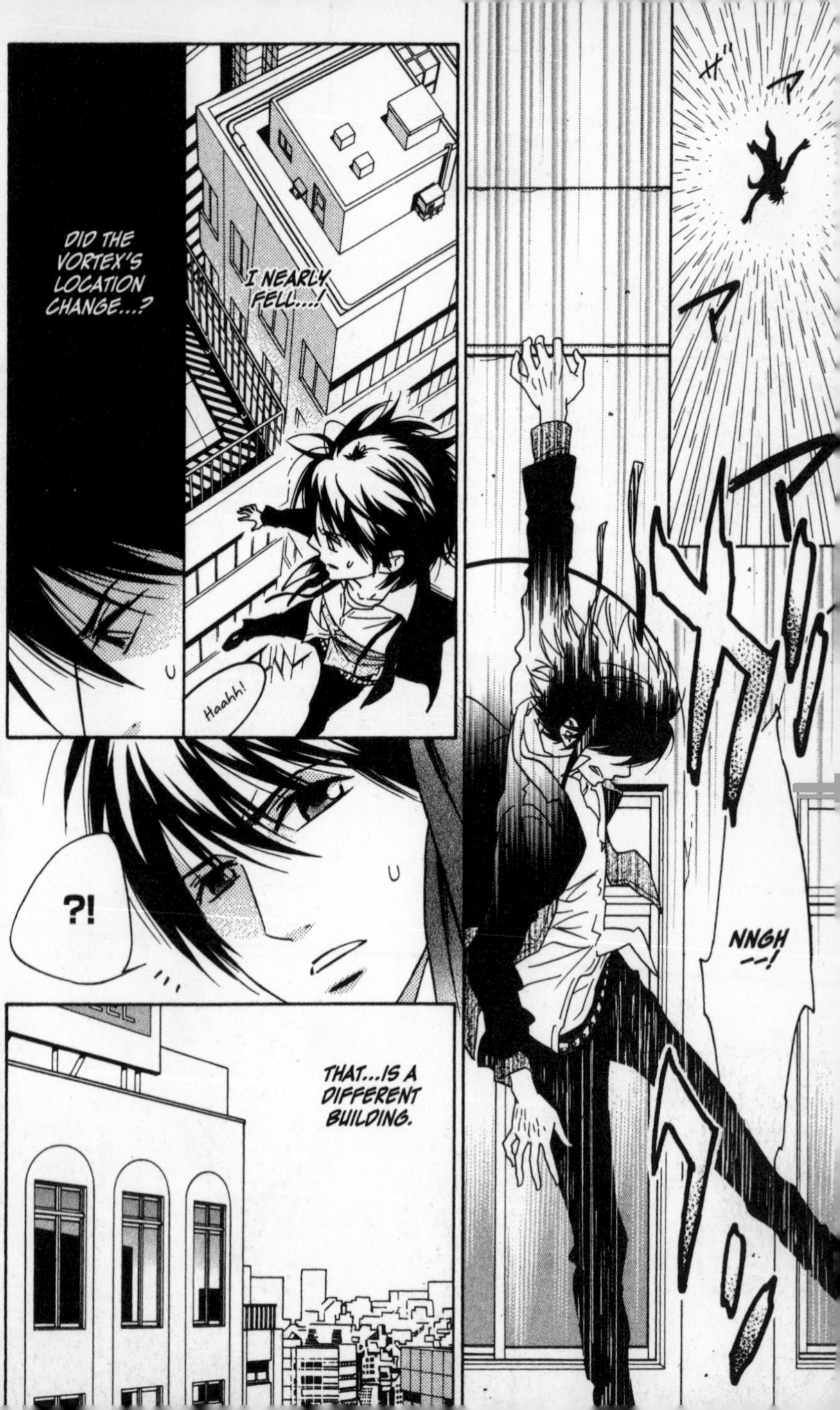
NNGH --!
I NEARLY FELL...!
Haahh!
DID THE VORTEX'S LOCATION CHANGE...?
?!
THAT...IS A DIFFERENT BUILDING.

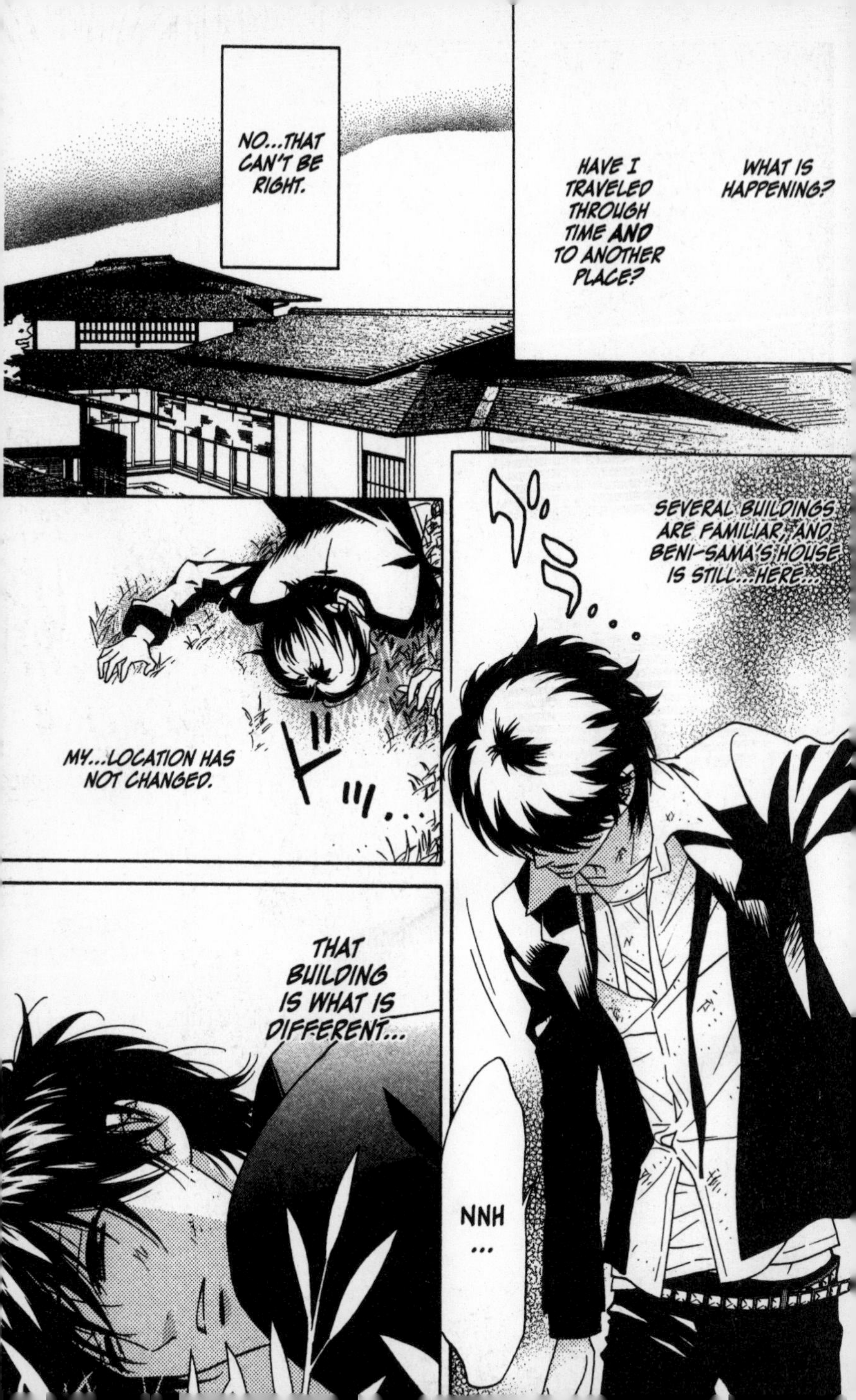
WHAT IS HAPPENING?
HAVE I TRAVELED THROUGH TIME AND TO ANOTHER PLACE?
NO...THAT CAN'T BE RIGHT.
SEVERAL BUILDINGS ARE FAMILIAR, AND BENI-SAMA'S HOUSE IS STILL...HERE...
NNH ...
MY...LOCATION HAS NOT CHANGED.
THAT BUILDING IS WHAT IS DIFFERENT...

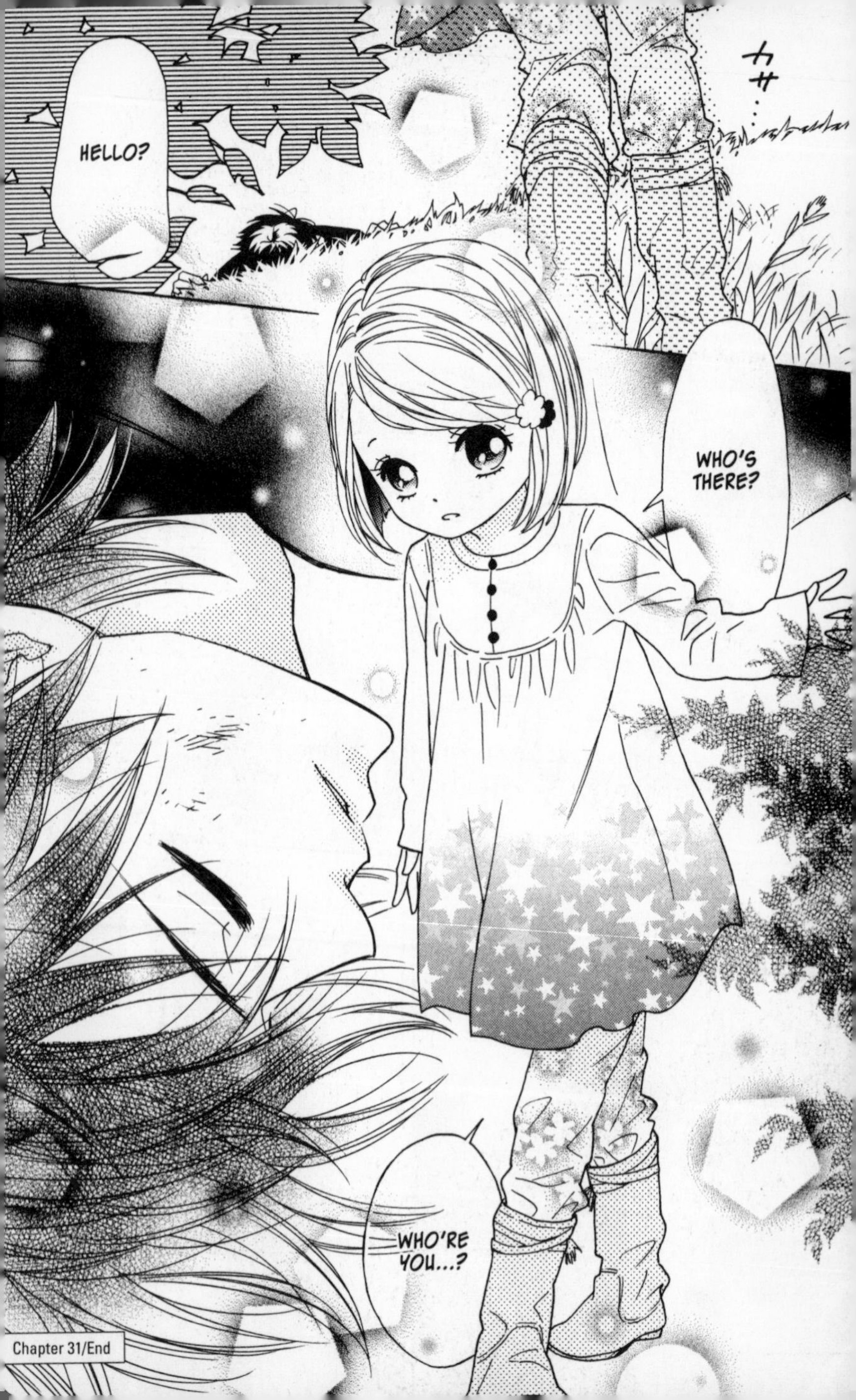
カサ…
HELLO?
WHO'S THERE?
WHO'RE YOU...?
Chapter 31/End

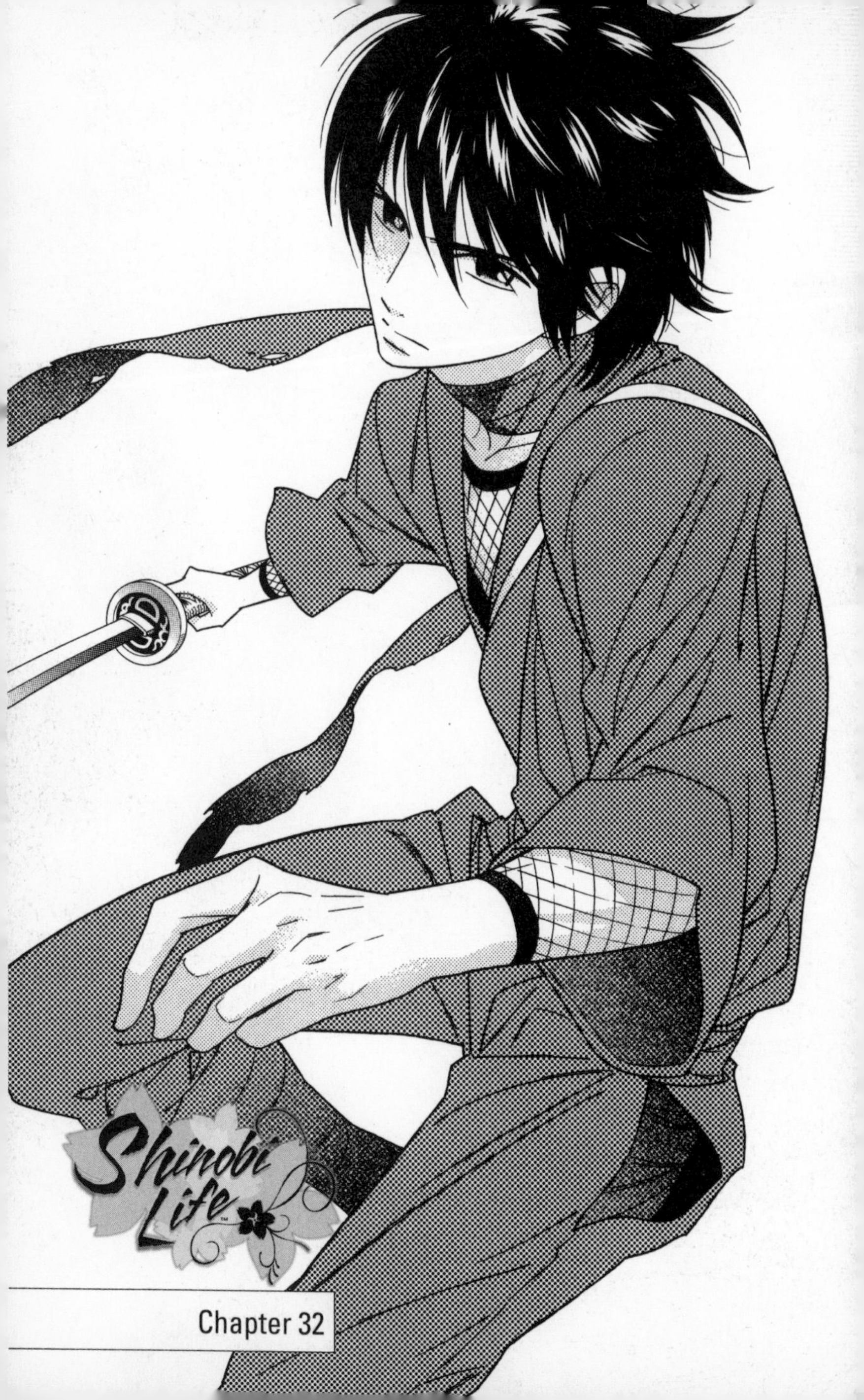
Shinobi Life™
Chapter 32

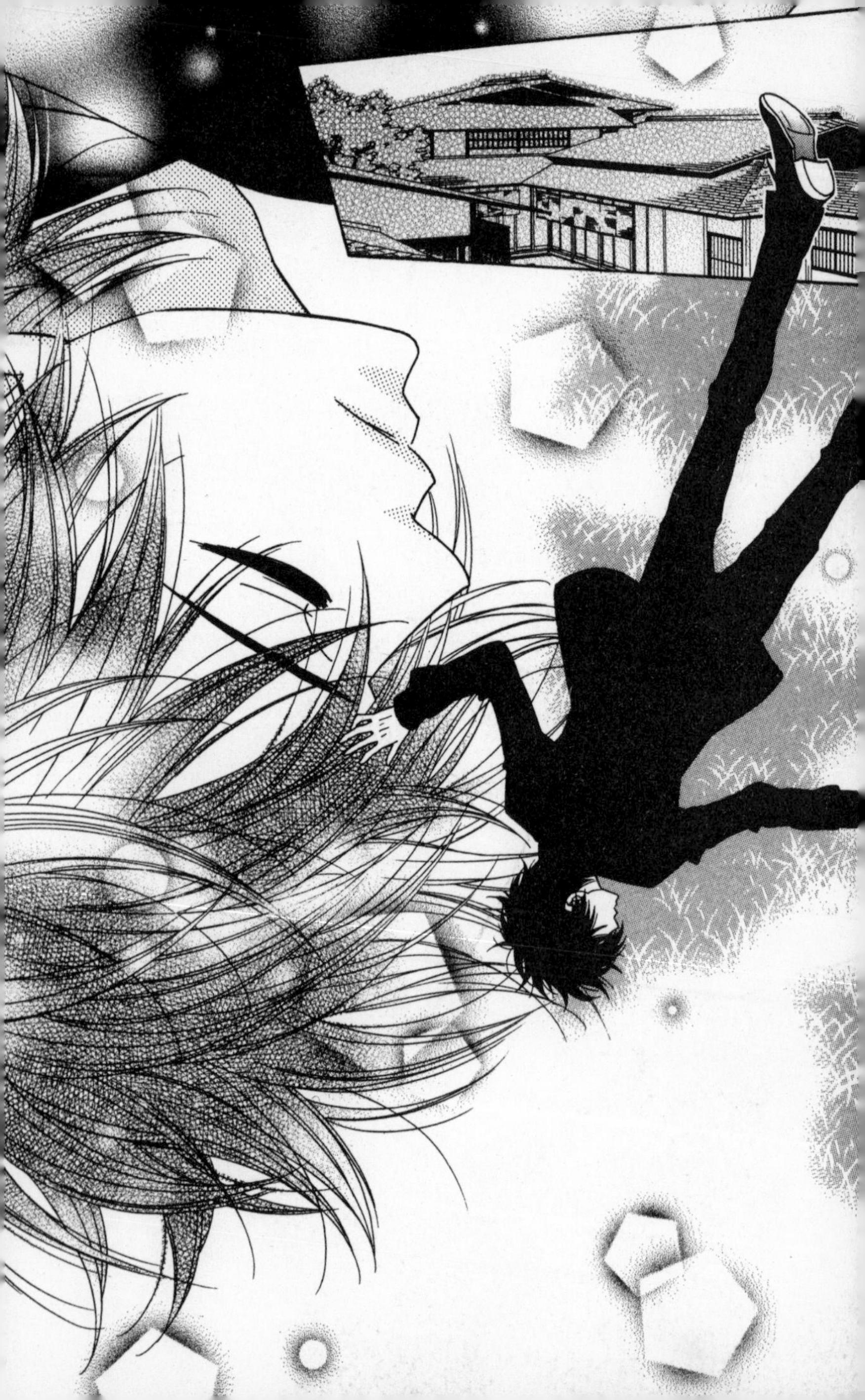

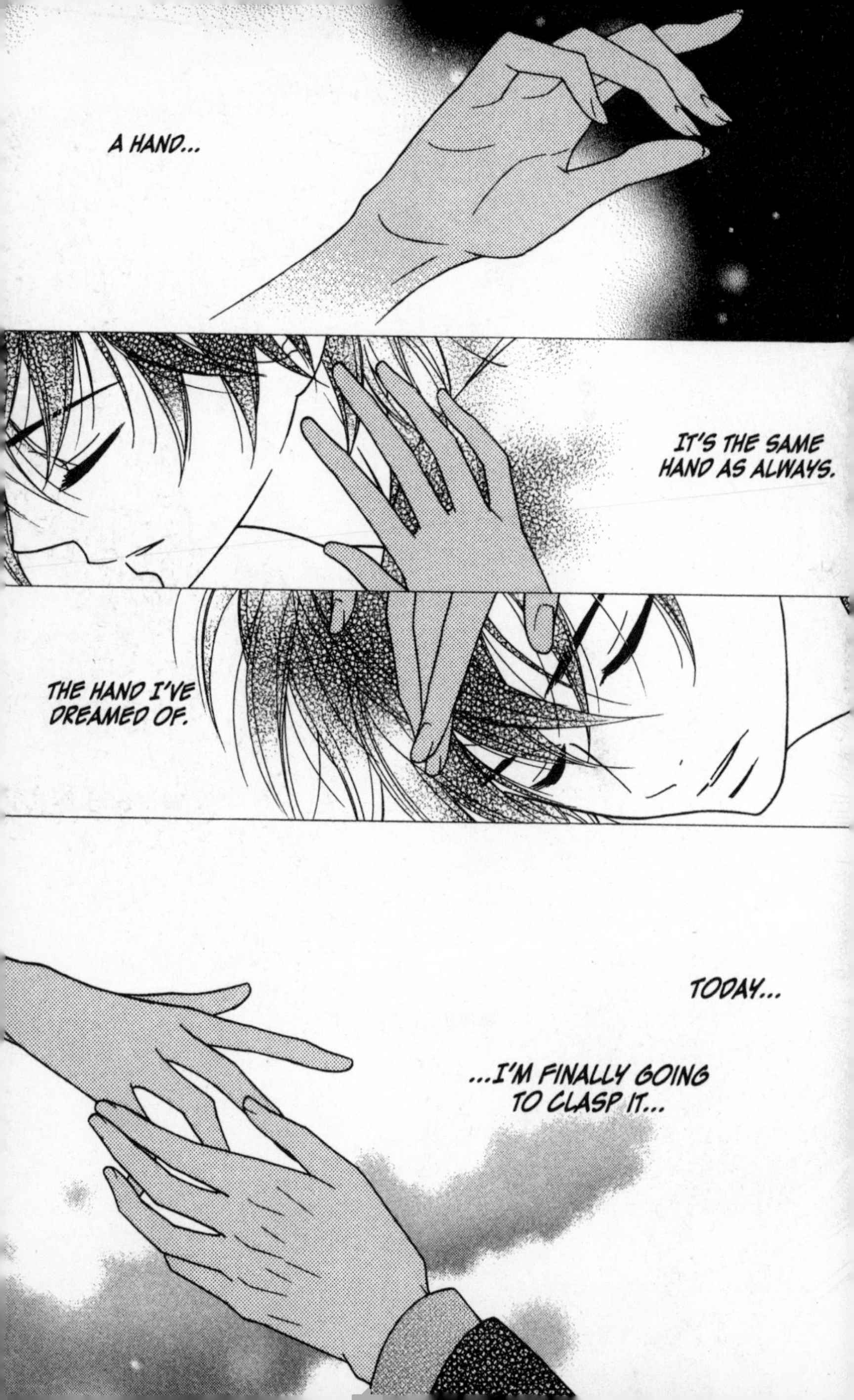
A HAND...
IT'S THE SAME HAND AS ALWAYS.
THE HAND I'VE DREAMED OF.
TODAY...
...I'M FINALLY GOING TO CLASP IT...

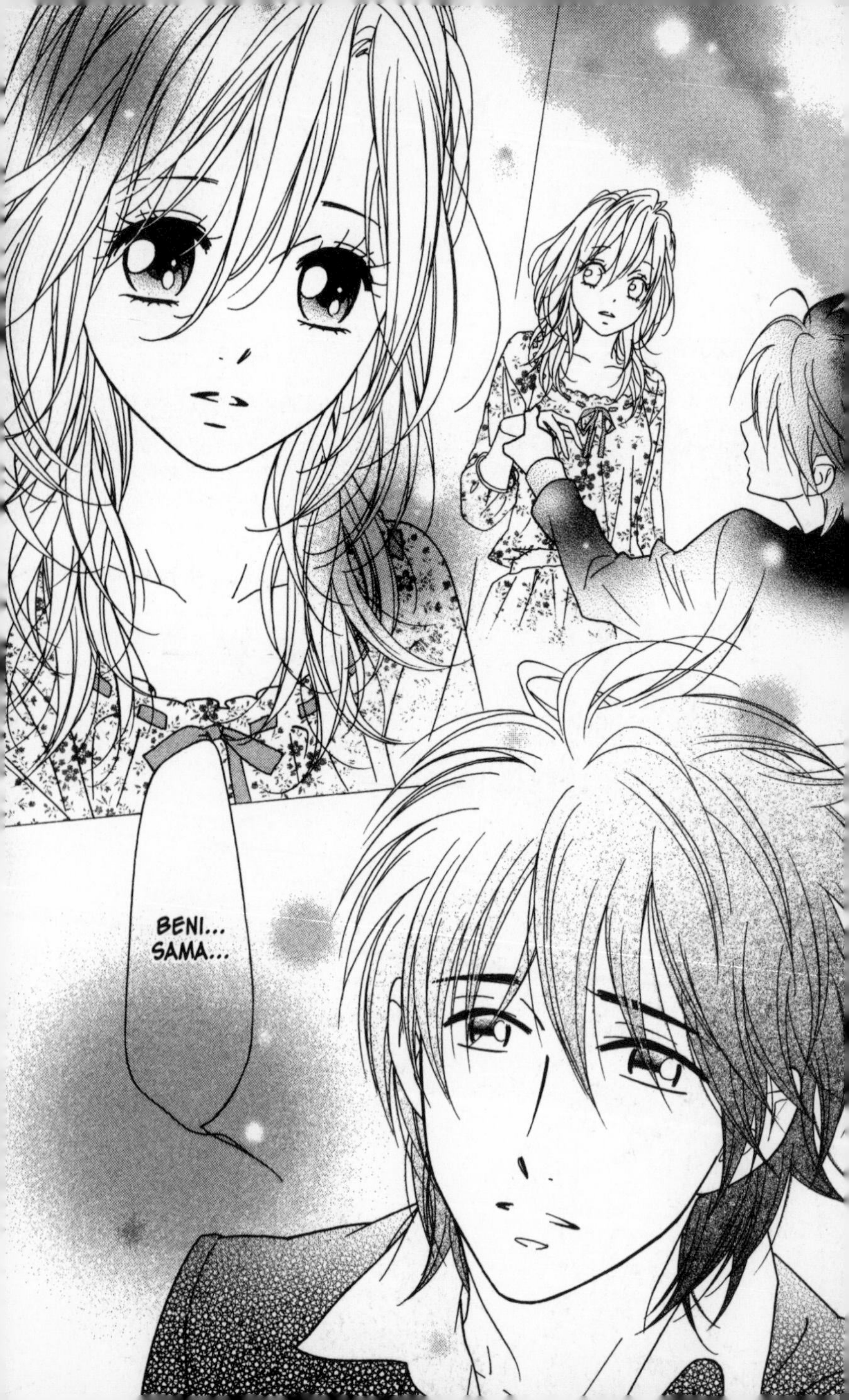
BENI... SAMA...

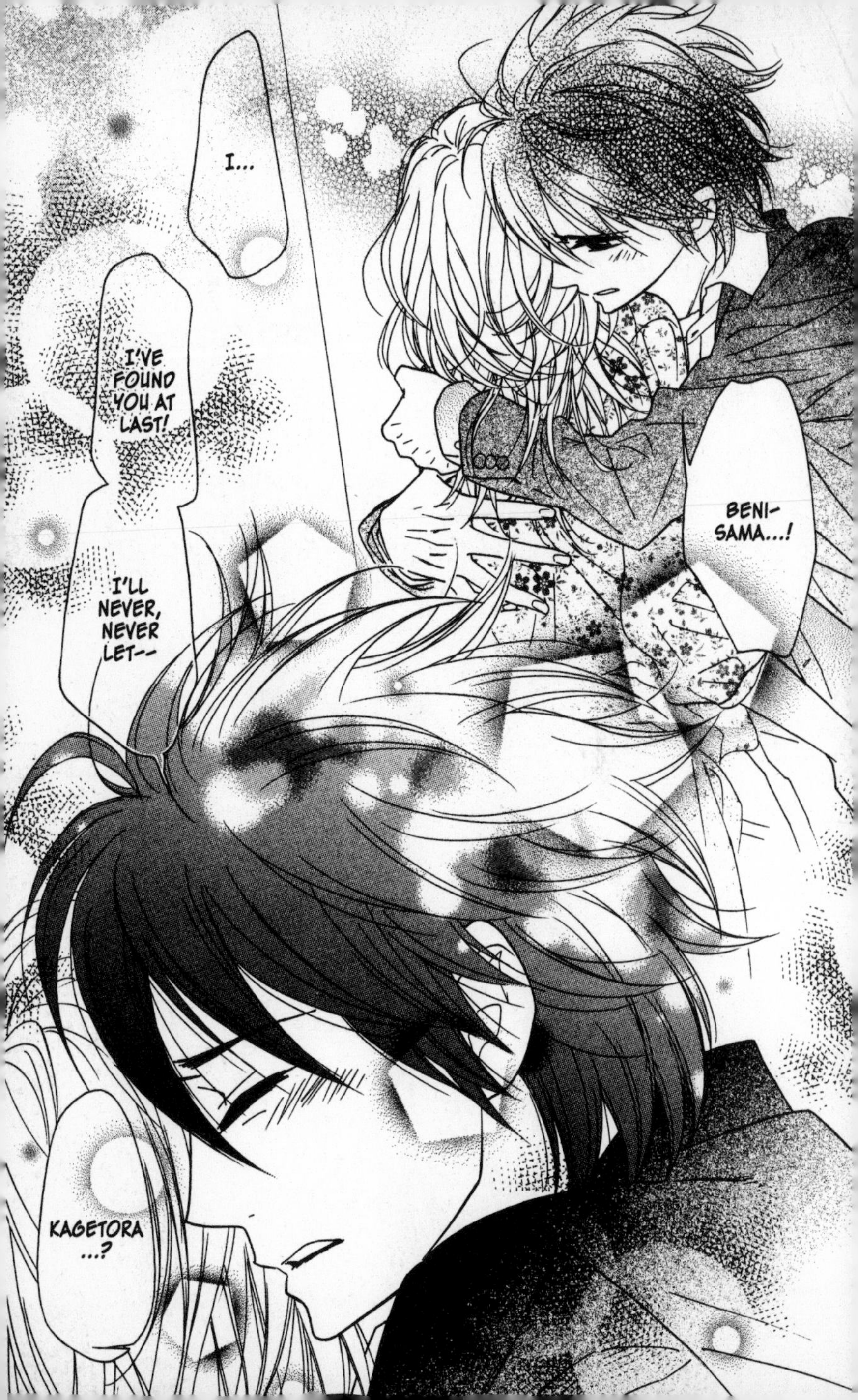
BENI-SAMA...!
I...
I'VE FOUND YOU AT LAST!
I'LL NEVER, NEVER LET--
KAGETORA ...?

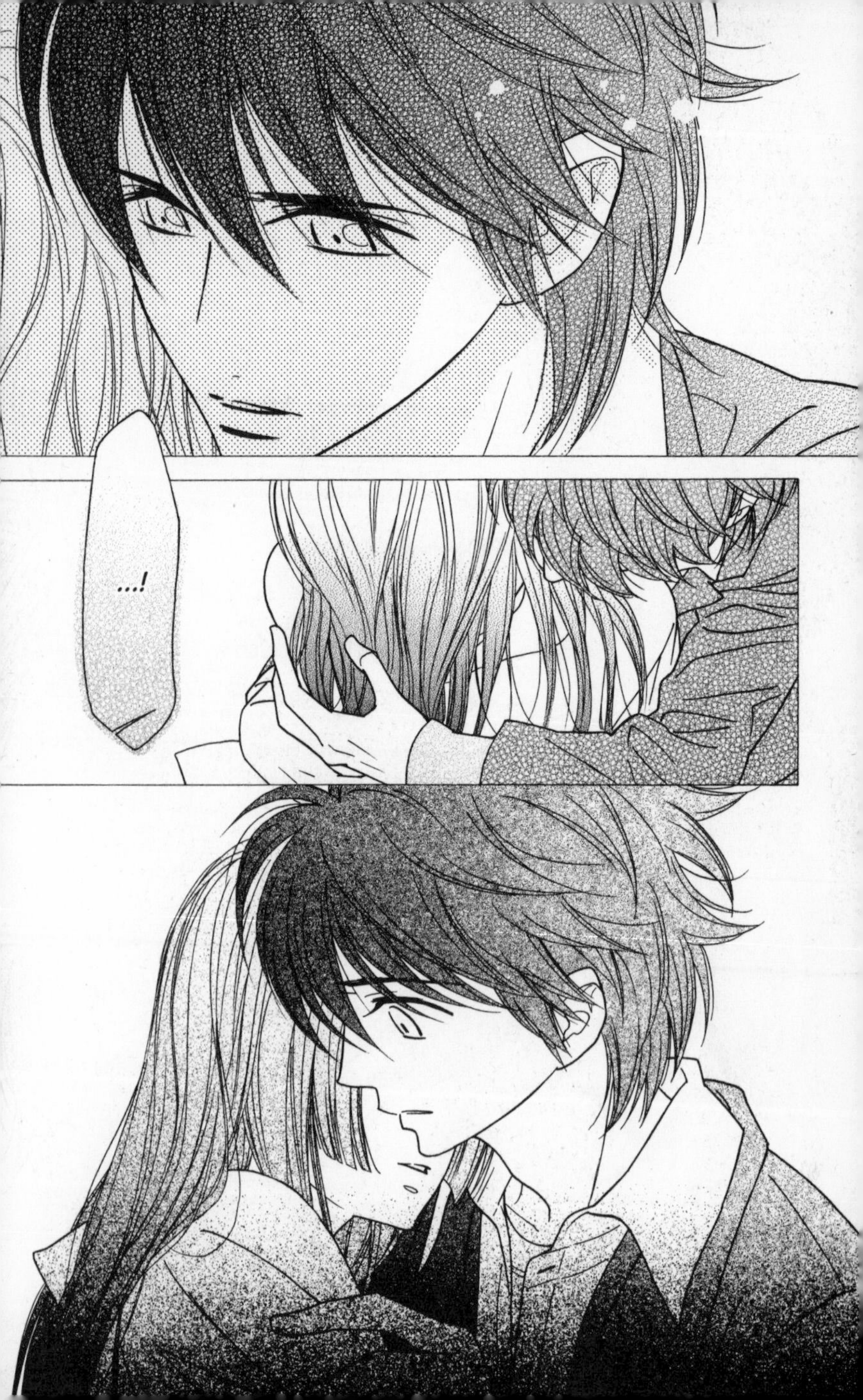
...!

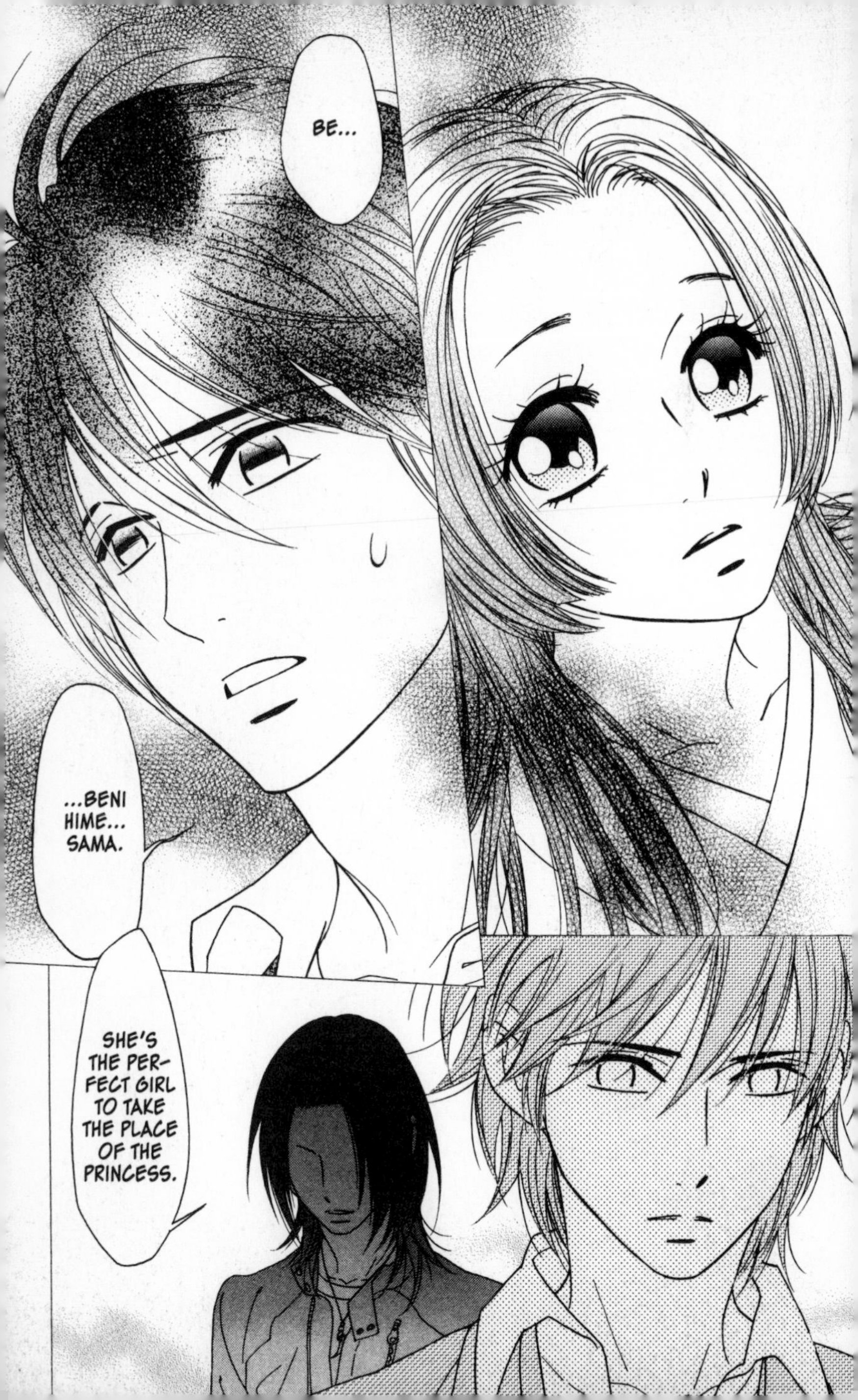
BE...
...BENI HIME... SAMA.
SHE'S THE PER-FECT GIRL TO TAKE THE PLACE OF THE PRINCESS.

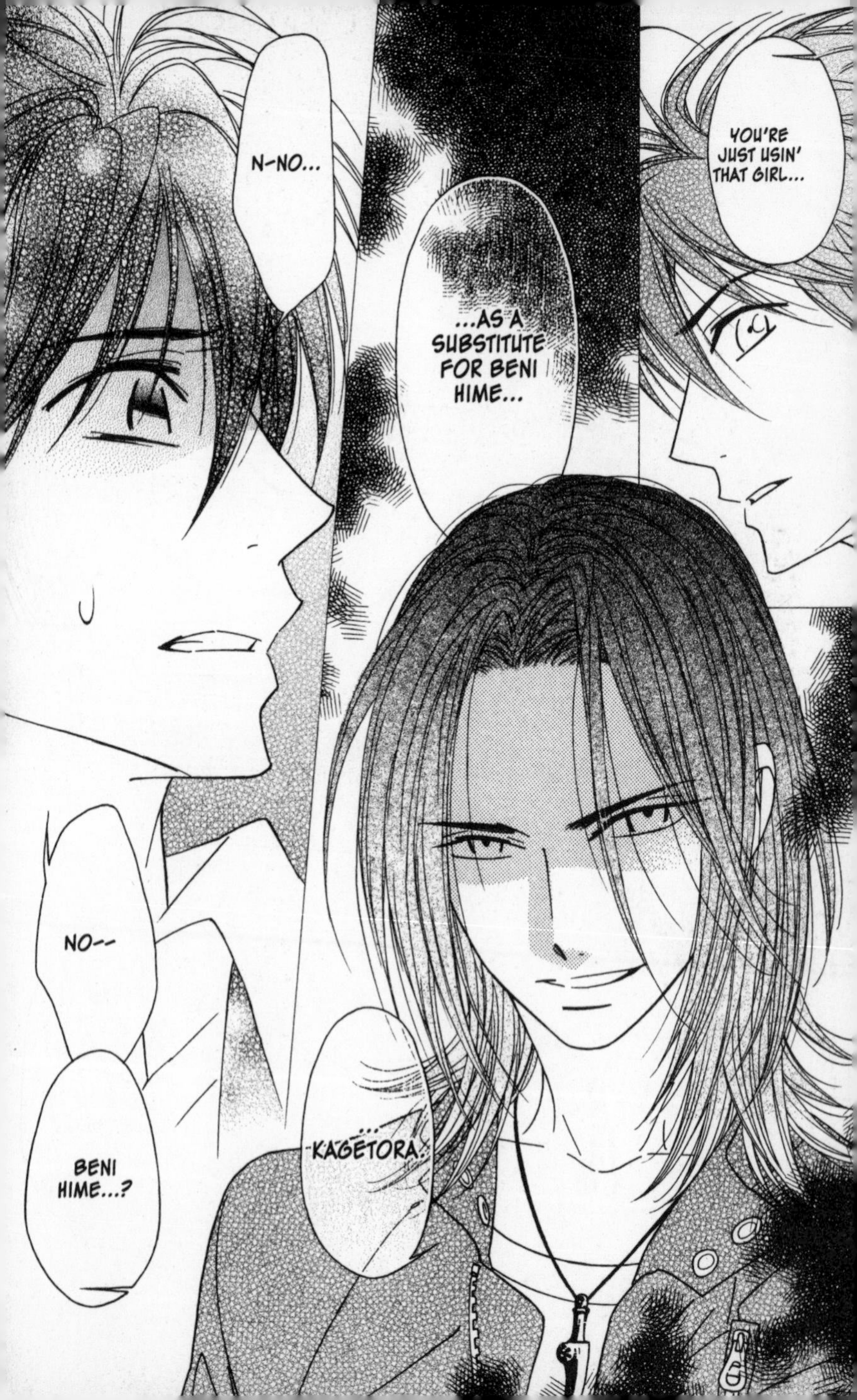
YOU'RE JUST USIN' THAT GIRL...
...AS A SUBSTITUTE FOR BENI HIME...
N-NO...
NO--
BENI HIME...?
...KAGETORA.

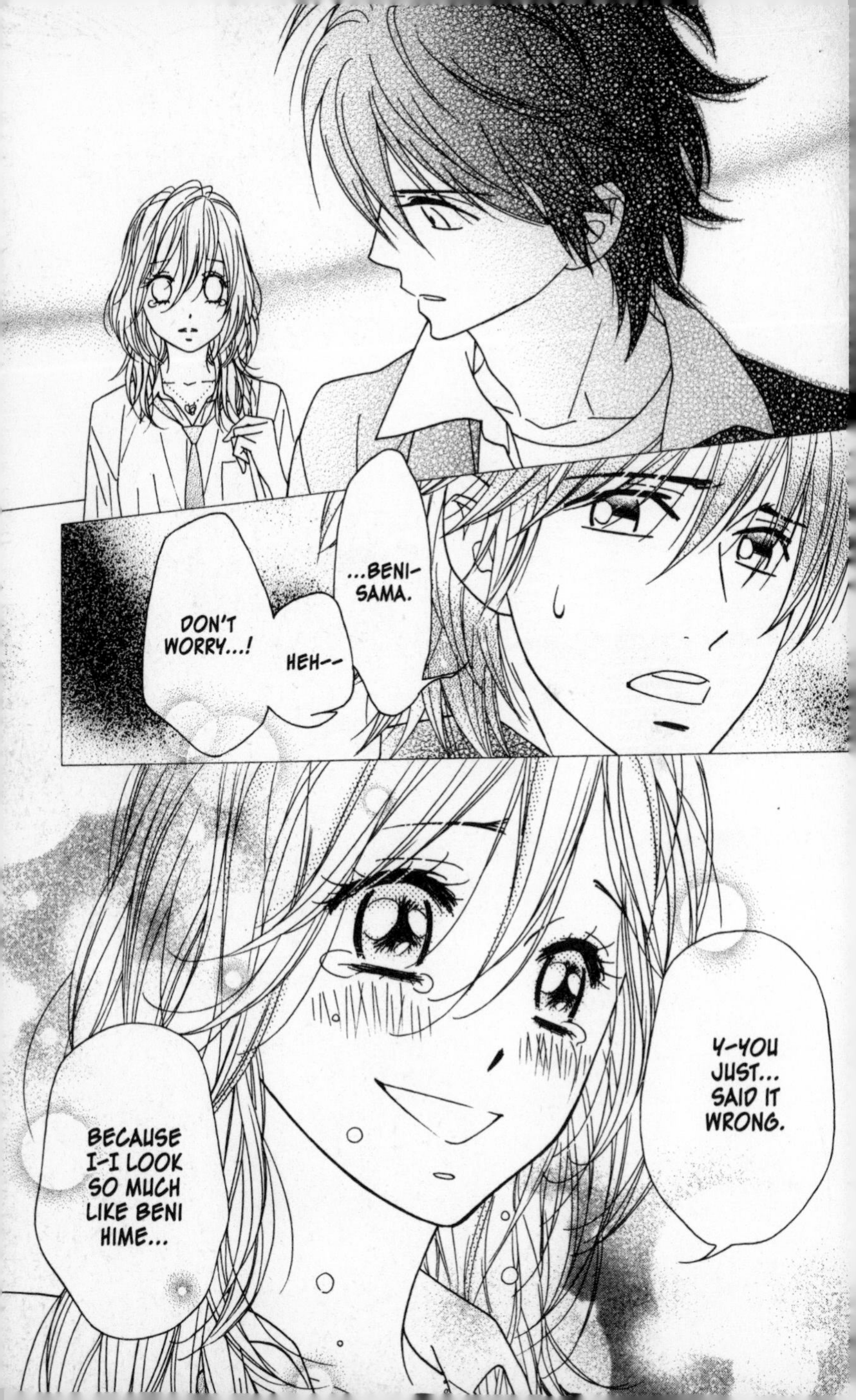
...BENI-SAMA.
HEH--
DON'T WORRY...!
Y-YOU JUST... SAID IT WRONG.
BECAUSE I-I LOOK SO MUCH LIKE BENI HIME...

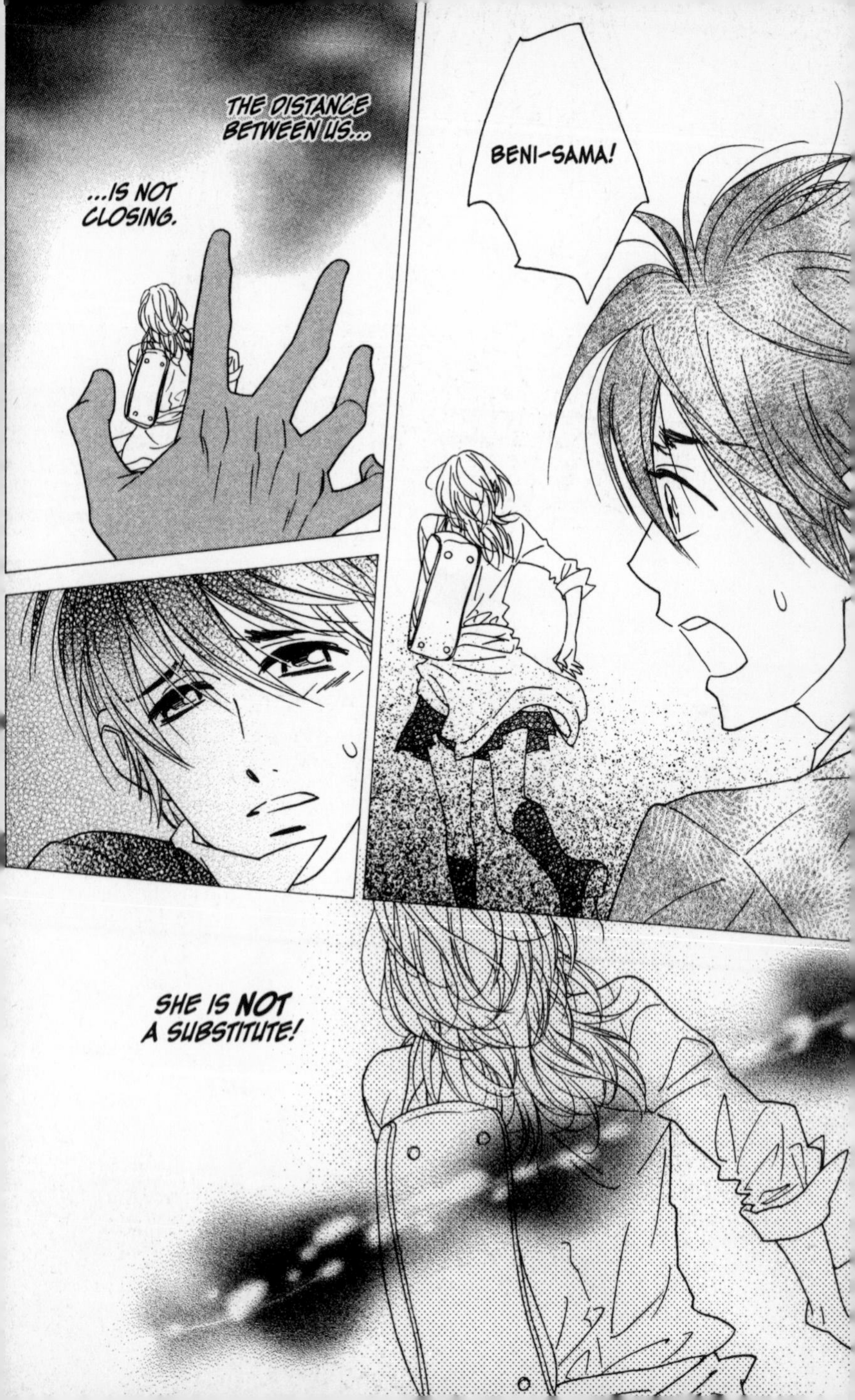
BENI-SAMA!
THE DISTANCE BETWEEN US...
...IS NOT CLOSING.
SHE IS **NOT** A SUBSTITUTE!

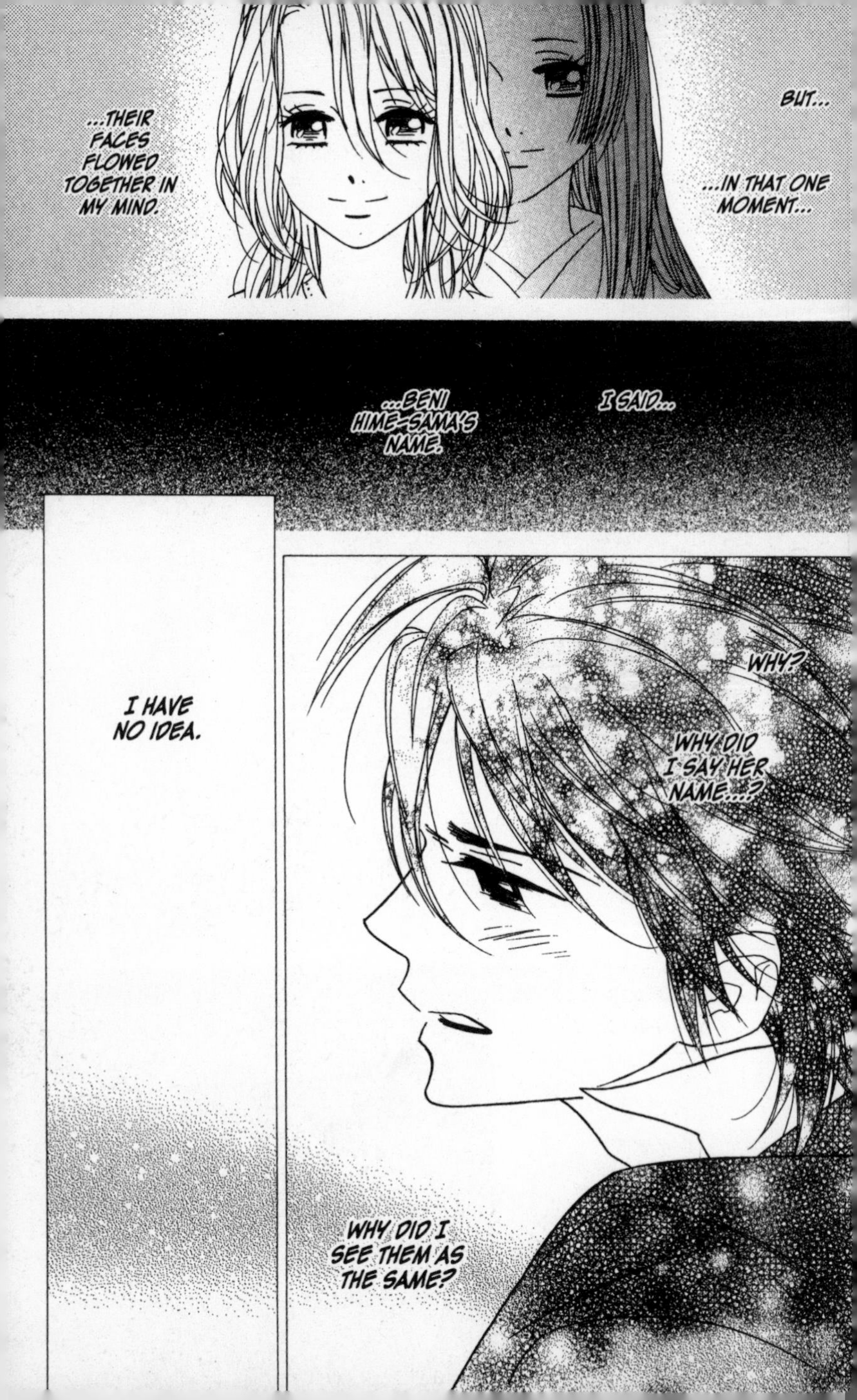
BUT...
...IN THAT ONE MOMENT...
...THEIR FACES FLOWED TOGETHER IN MY MIND.
I SAID...
...BENI HIME-SAMA'S NAME.
WHY?
WHY DID I SAY HER NAME...?
WHY DID I SEE THEM AS THE SAME?
I HAVE NO IDEA.

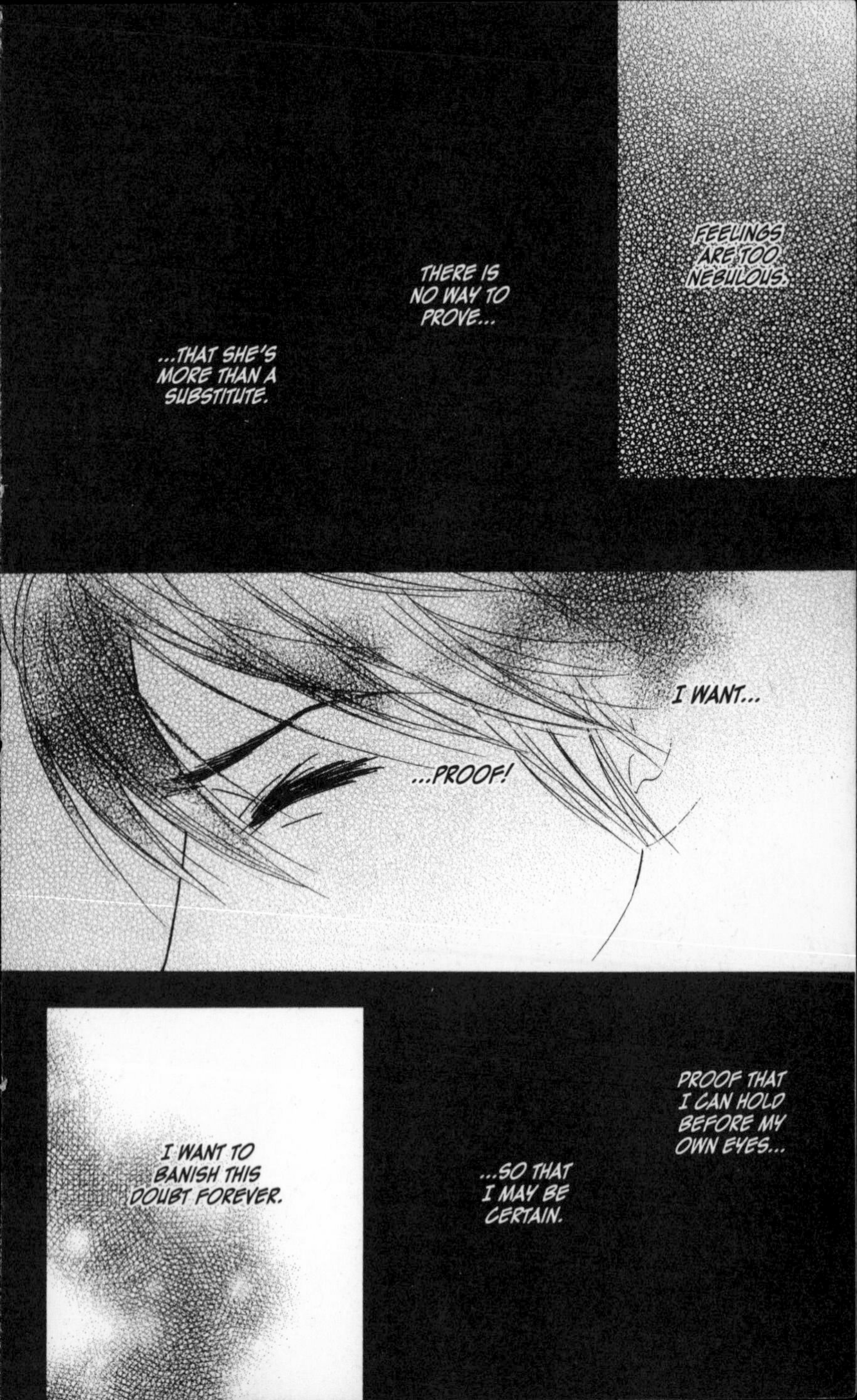
FEELINGS ARE TOO NEBULOUS.
THERE IS NO WAY TO PROVE...
...THAT SHE'S MORE THAN A SUBSTITUTE.
I WANT...
...PROOF!
PROOF THAT I CAN HOLD BEFORE MY OWN EYES...
...SO THAT I MAY BE CERTAIN.
I WANT TO BANISH THIS DOUBT FOREVER.

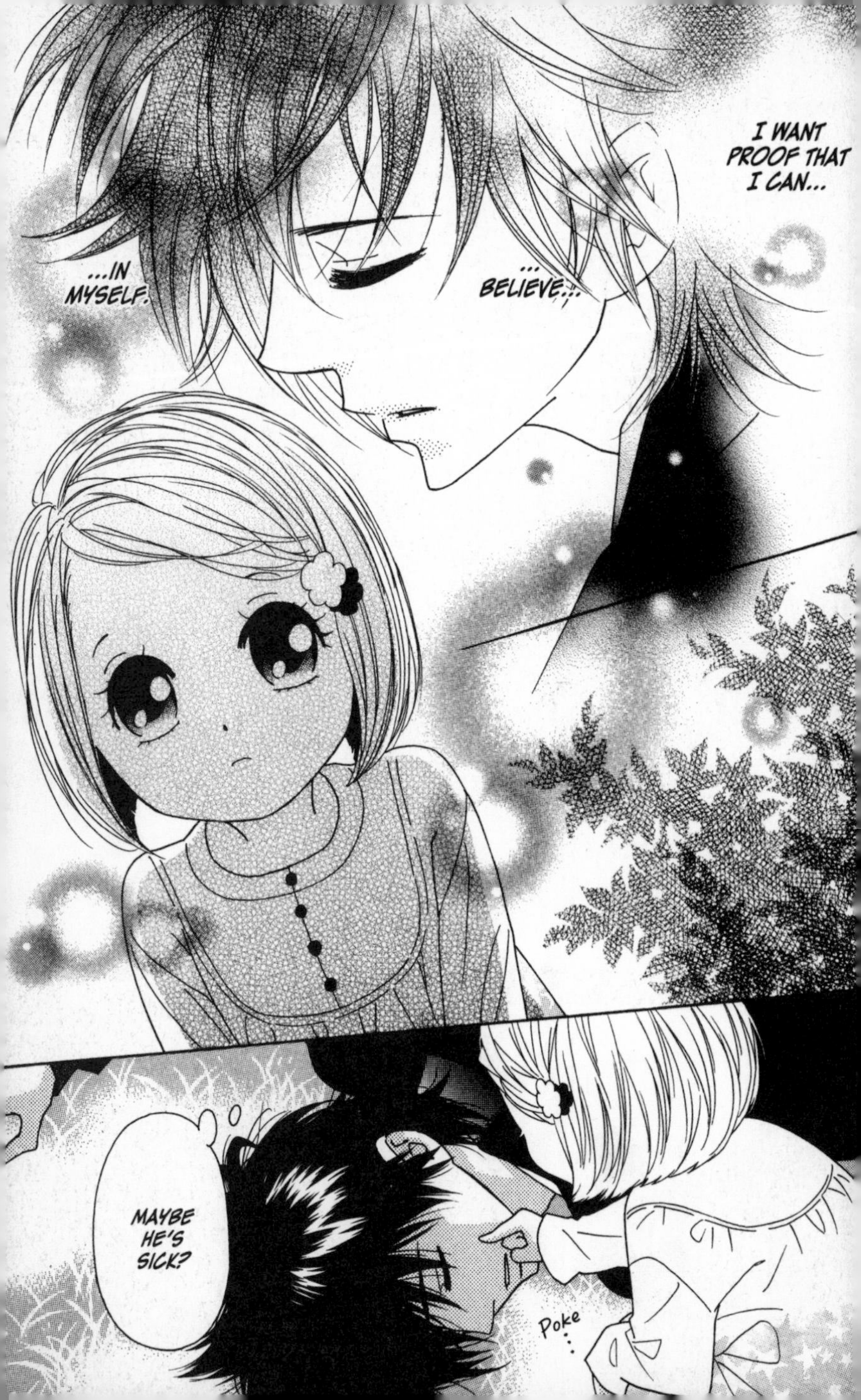
I WANT PROOF THAT I CAN...
... BELIEVE...
...IN MYSELF.
Poke...
MAYBE HE'S SICK?

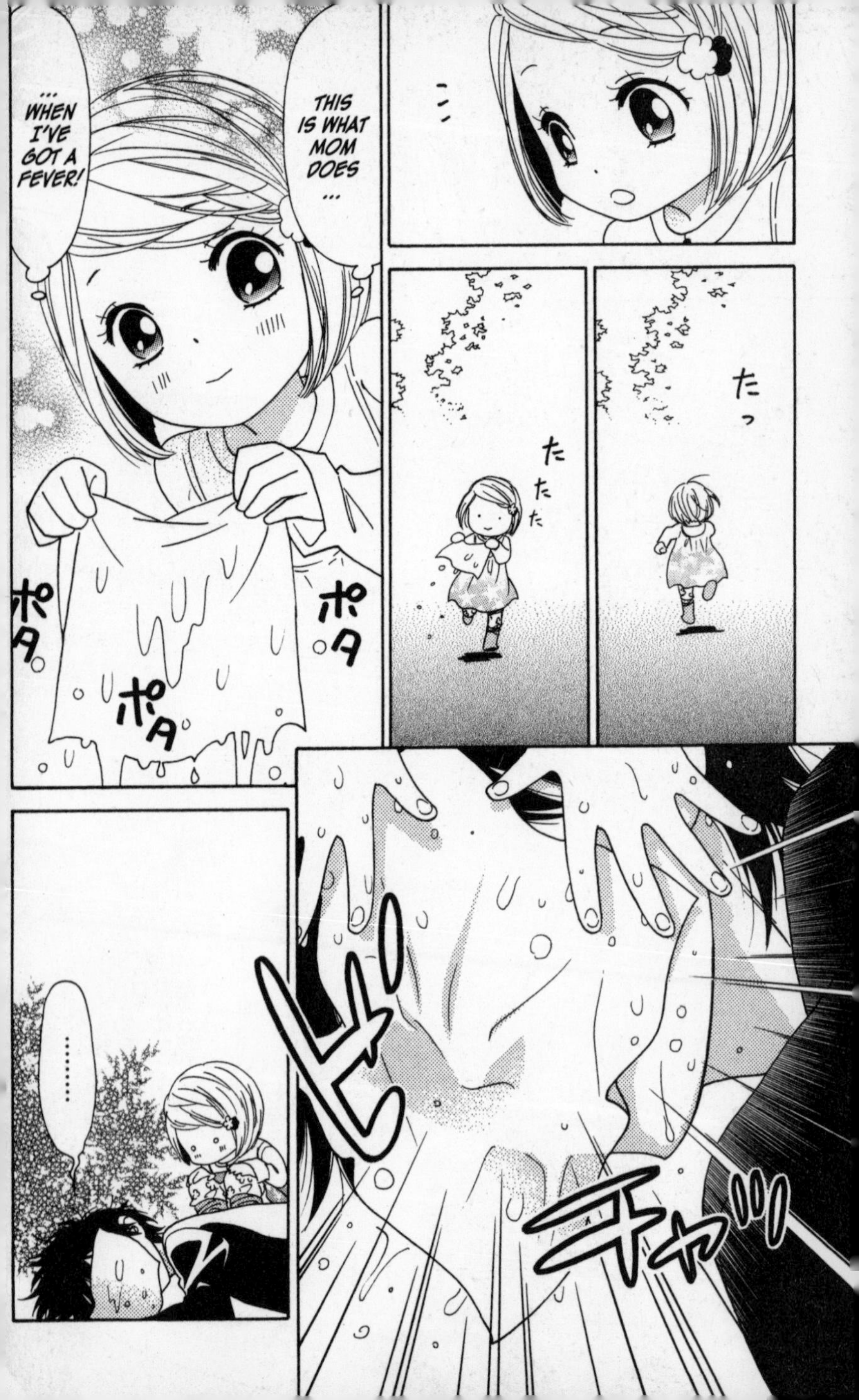
たっ
たたたた
THIS IS WHAT MOM DOES...
...WHEN I'VE GOT A FEVER!
ポタ
ポタ
ポタ
ビチャッ
....

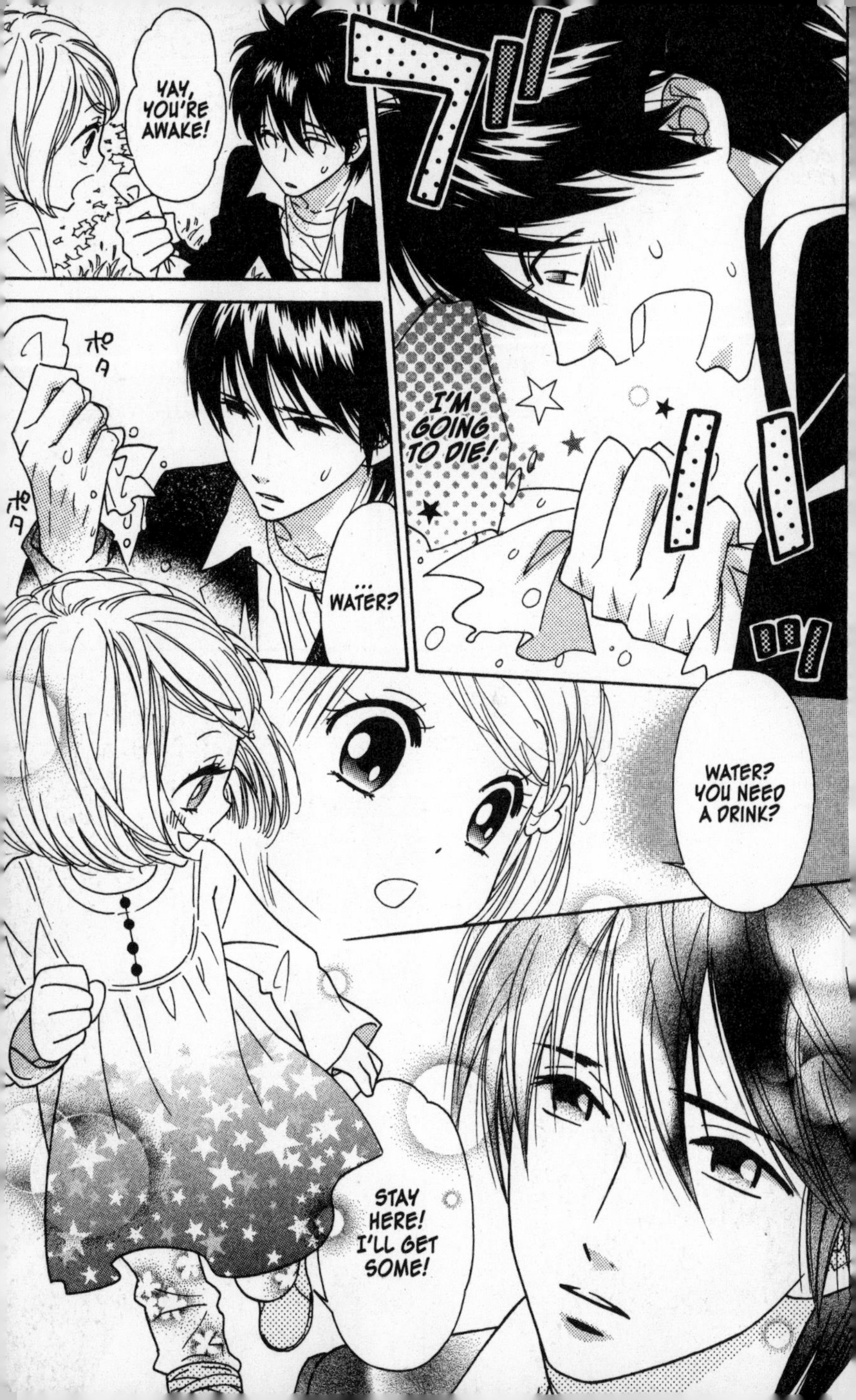
ブ
I'M GOING TO DIE!
YAY, YOU'RE AWAKE!
ポタ
ポタ
... WATER?
WATER? YOU NEED A DRINK?
STAY HERE! I'LL GET SOME!

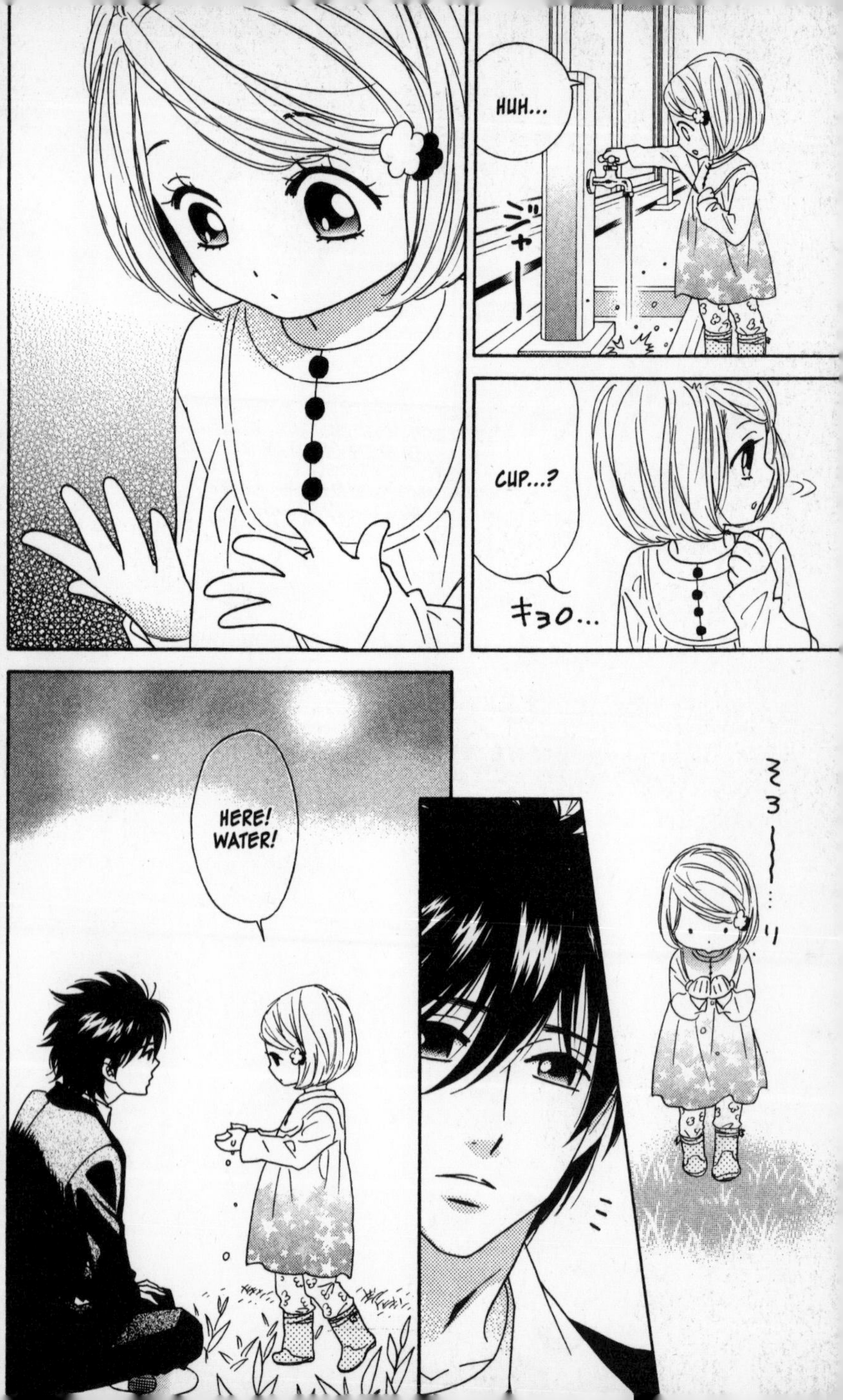
HUH...
ジャー
CUP...?
キョロ...
HERE! WATER!

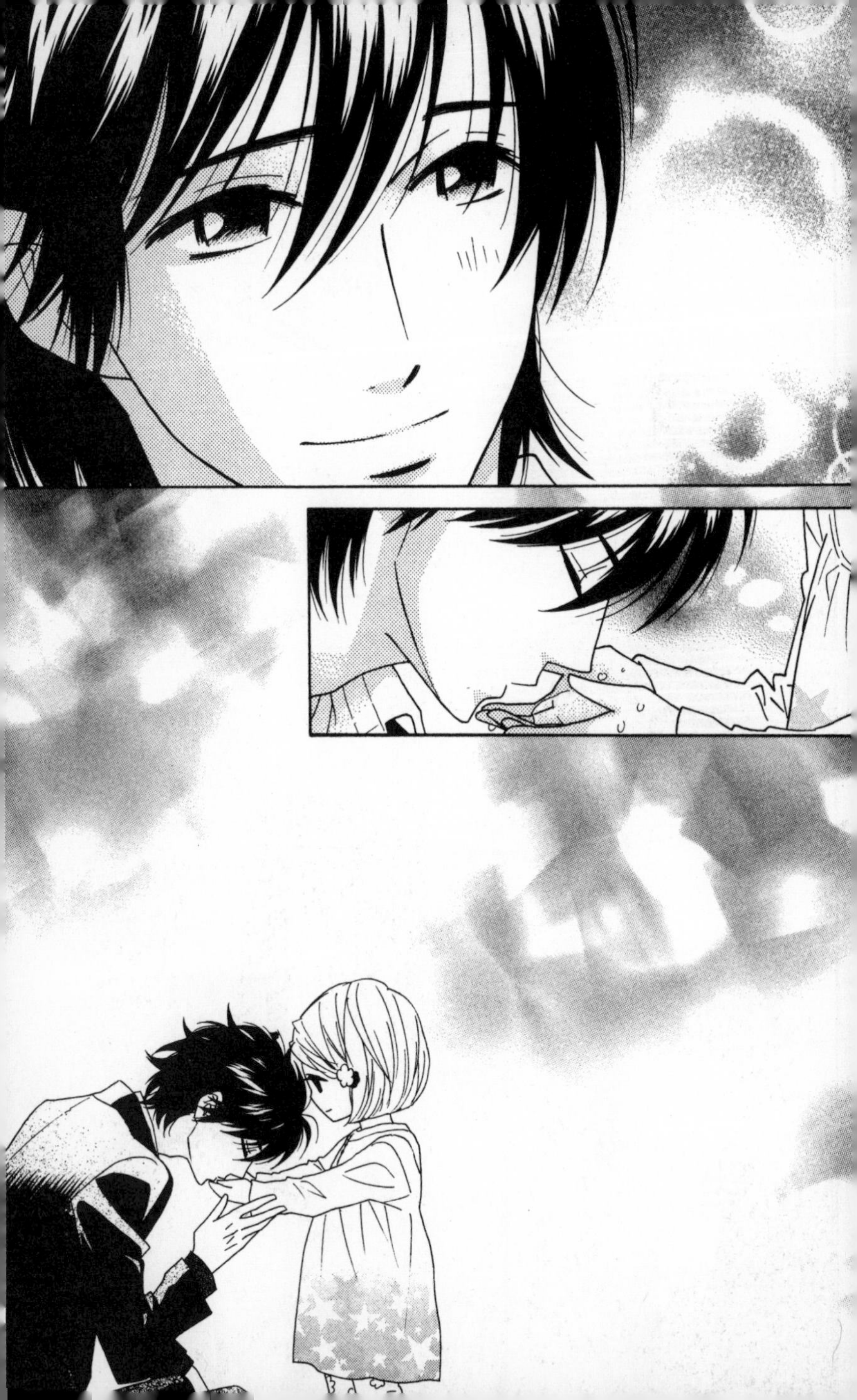

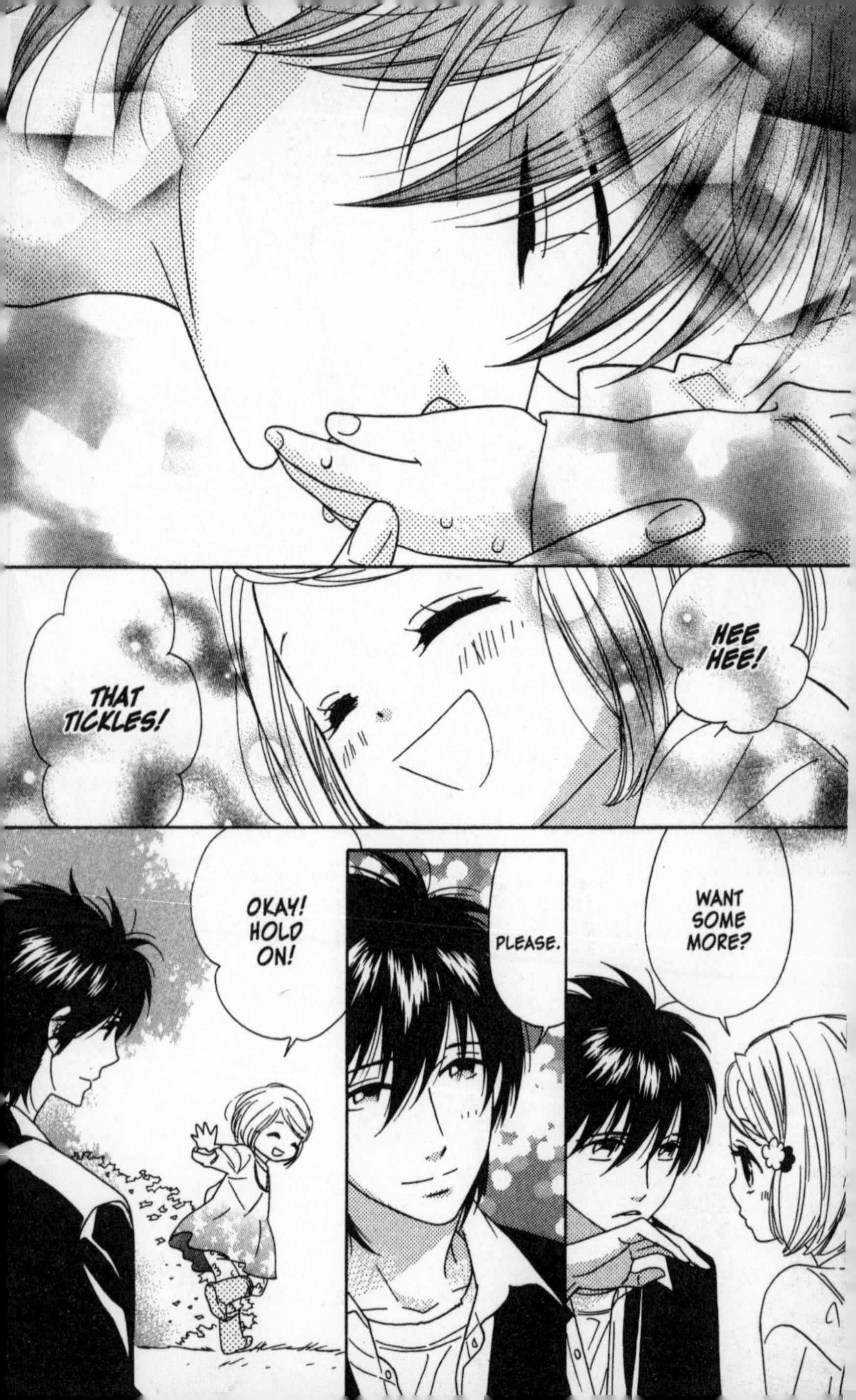
HEE HEE!
THAT TICKLES!
WANT SOME MORE?
PLEASE.
OKAY! HOLD ON!

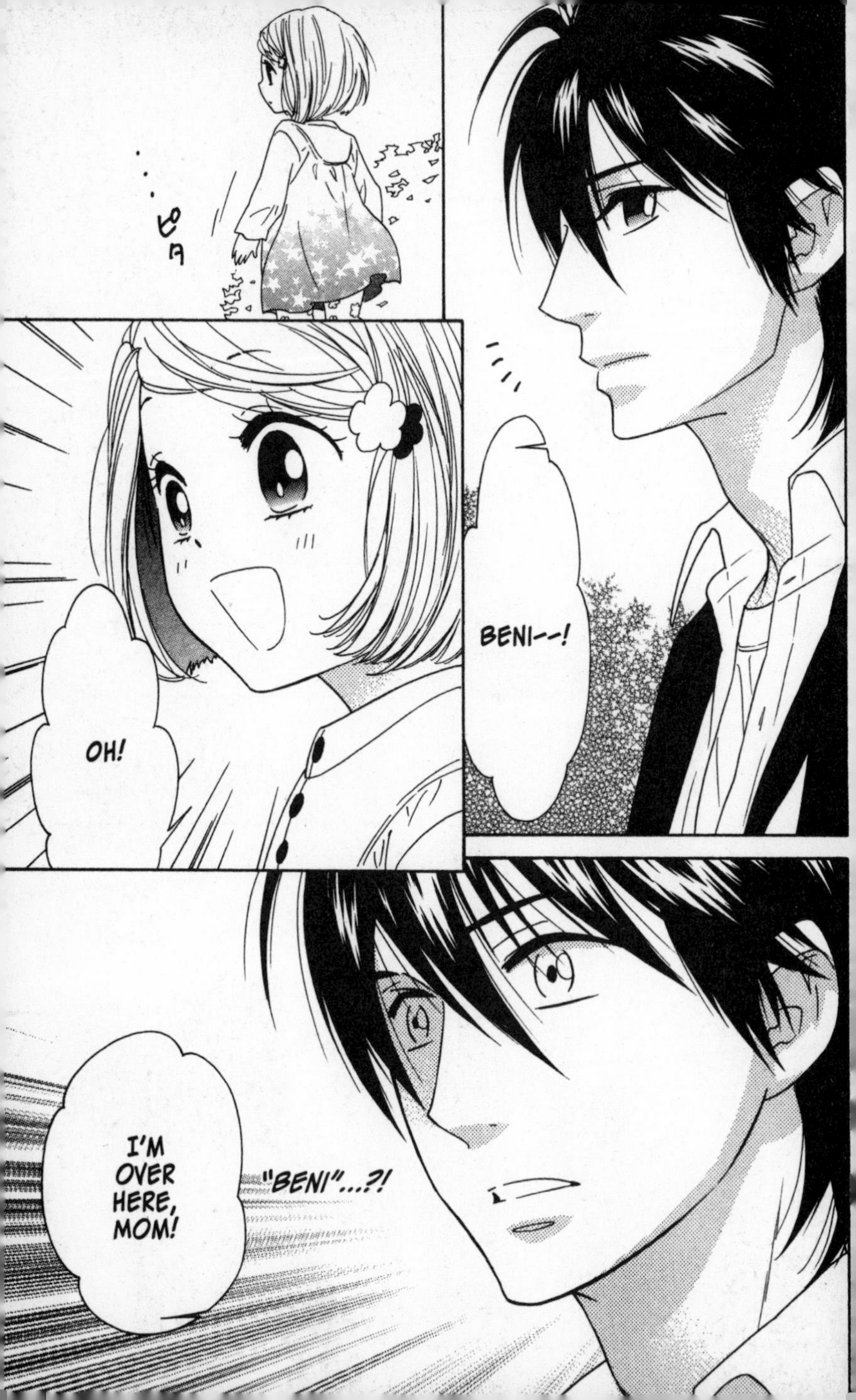
BENI--!
…ピタ
OH!
I'M OVER HERE, MOM!
"BENI"...?!

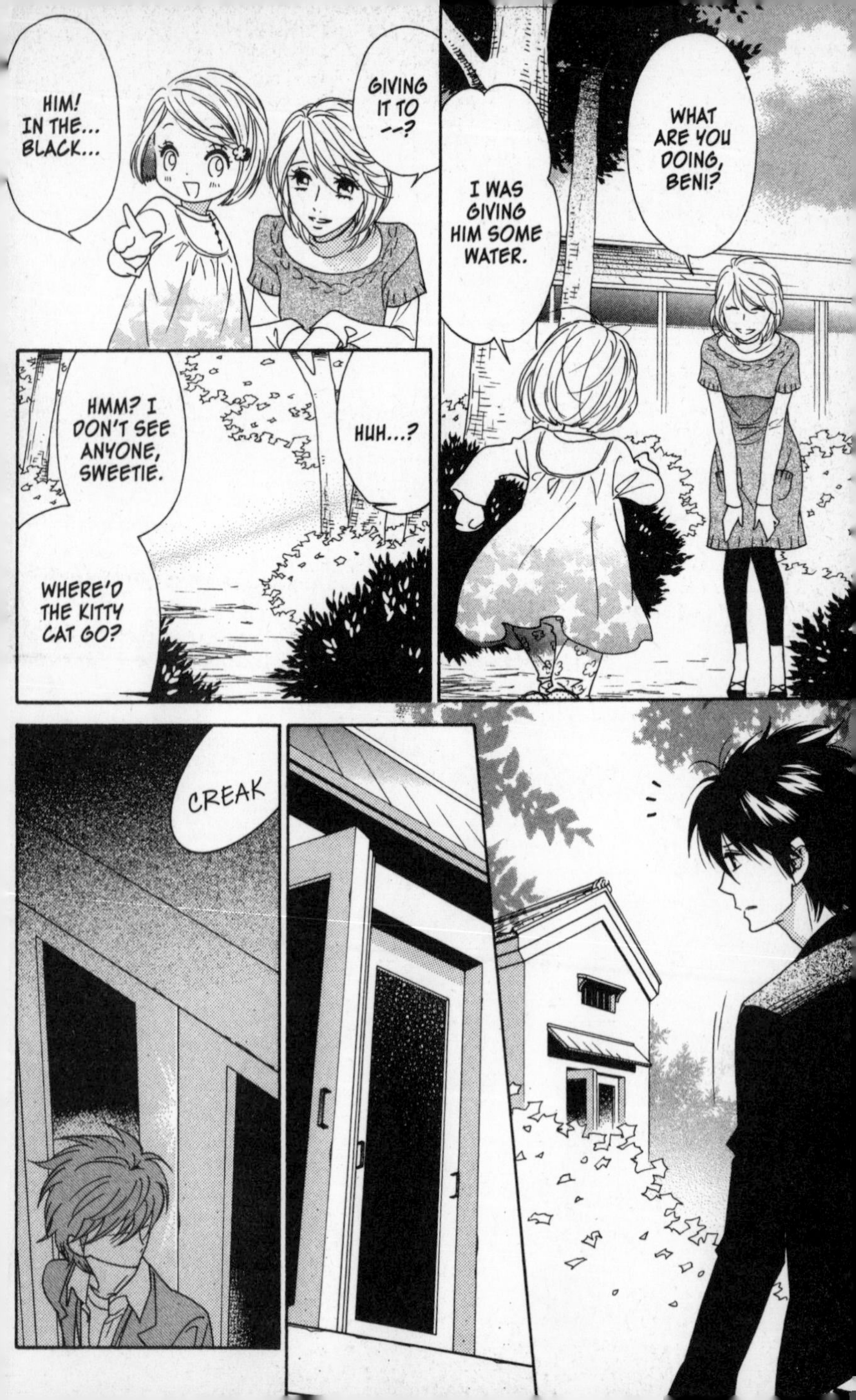
WHAT ARE YOU DOING, BENI?
I WAS GIVING HIM SOME WATER.
GIVING IT TO --?
HIM! IN THE... BLACK...
HUH...?
HMM? I DON'T SEE ANYONE, SWEETIE.
WHERE'D THE KITTY CAT GO?
CREAK

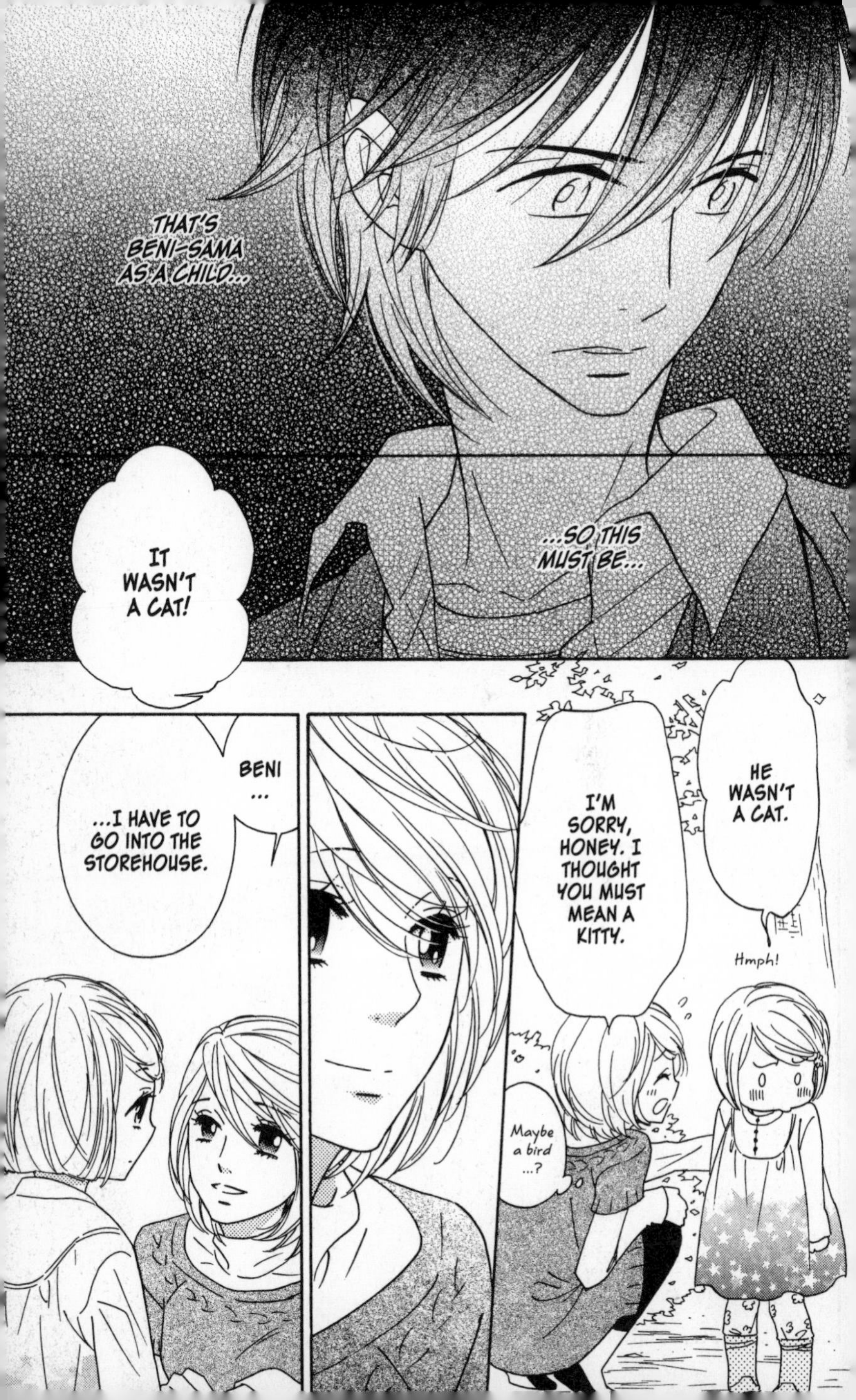

THAT'S BENI-SAMA AS A CHILD...
...SO THIS MUST BE...
IT WASN'T A CAT!
HE WASN'T A CAT.
Hmph!
I'M SORRY, HONEY. I THOUGHT YOU MUST MEAN A KITTY.
Maybe a bird ...?
BENI ...
...I HAVE TO GO INTO THE STOREHOUSE.

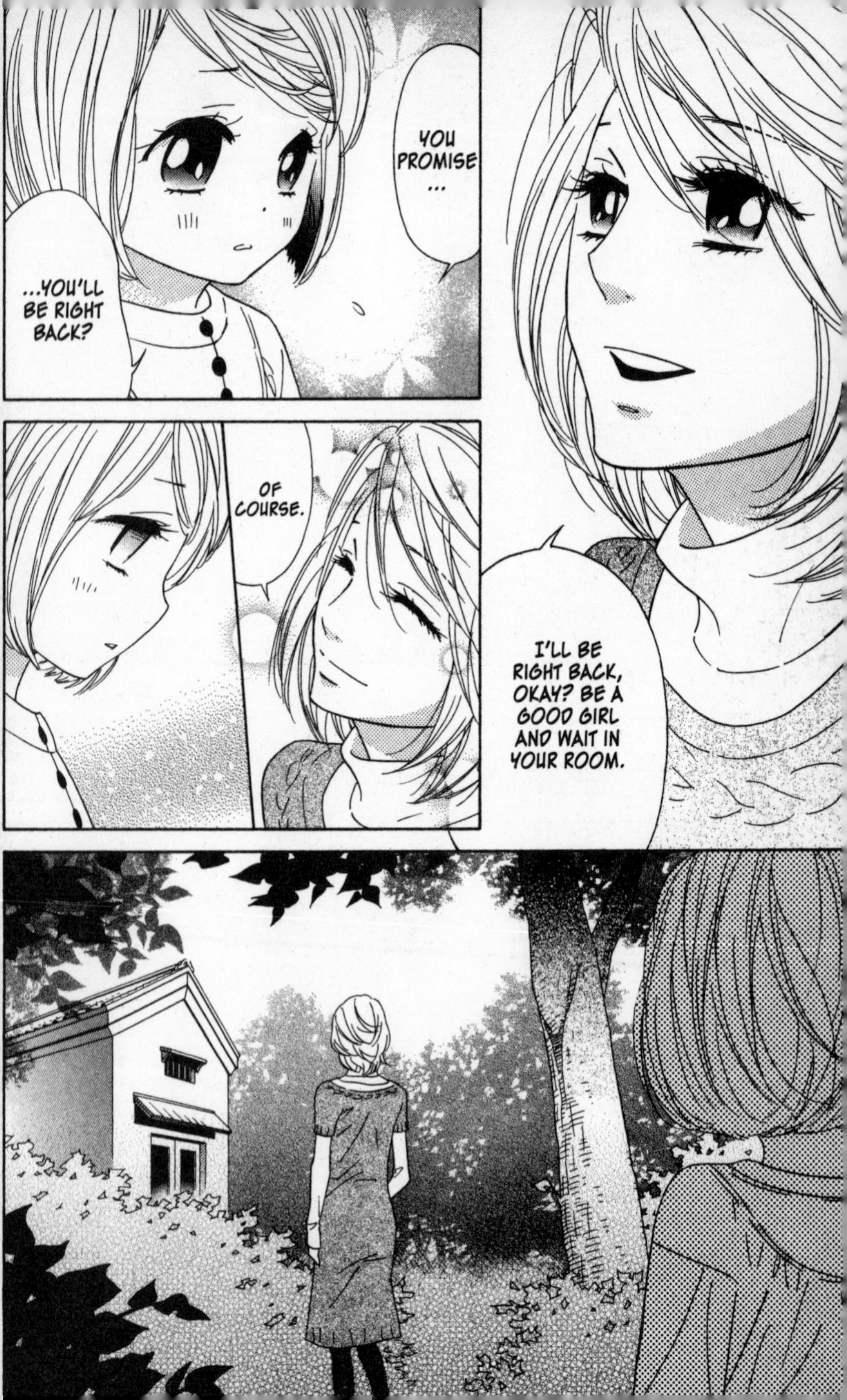
I'LL BE RIGHT BACK, OKAY? BE A GOOD GIRL AND WAIT IN YOUR ROOM.
YOU PROMISE ...
...YOU'LL BE RIGHT BACK?
OF COURSE.

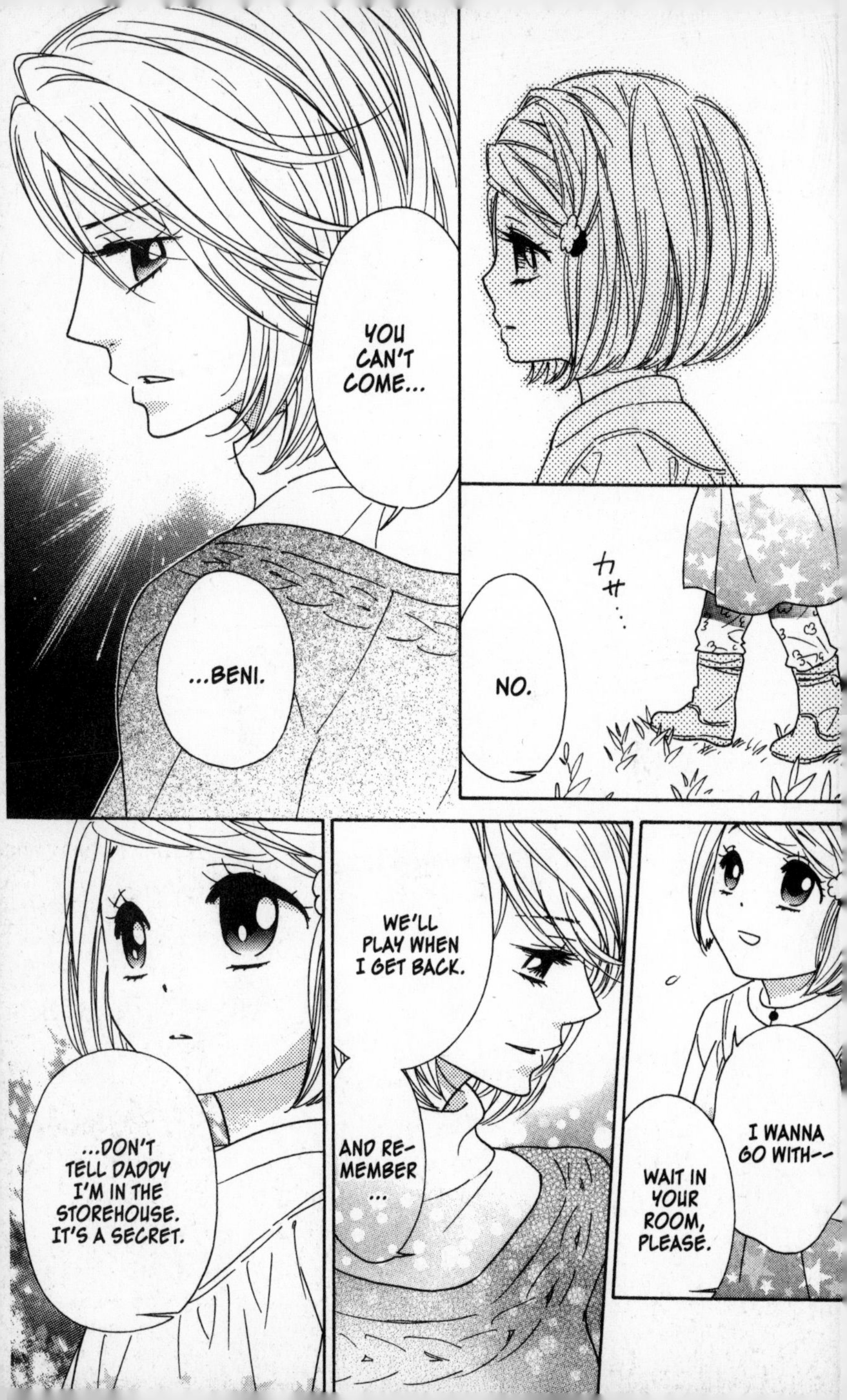
カサ…
NO.
YOU CAN'T COME...
...BENI.
I WANNA GO WITH--
WAIT IN YOUR ROOM, PLEASE.
WE'LL PLAY WHEN I GET BACK.
AND RE-MEMBER ...
...DON'T TELL DADDY I'M IN THE STOREHOUSE. IT'S A SECRET.

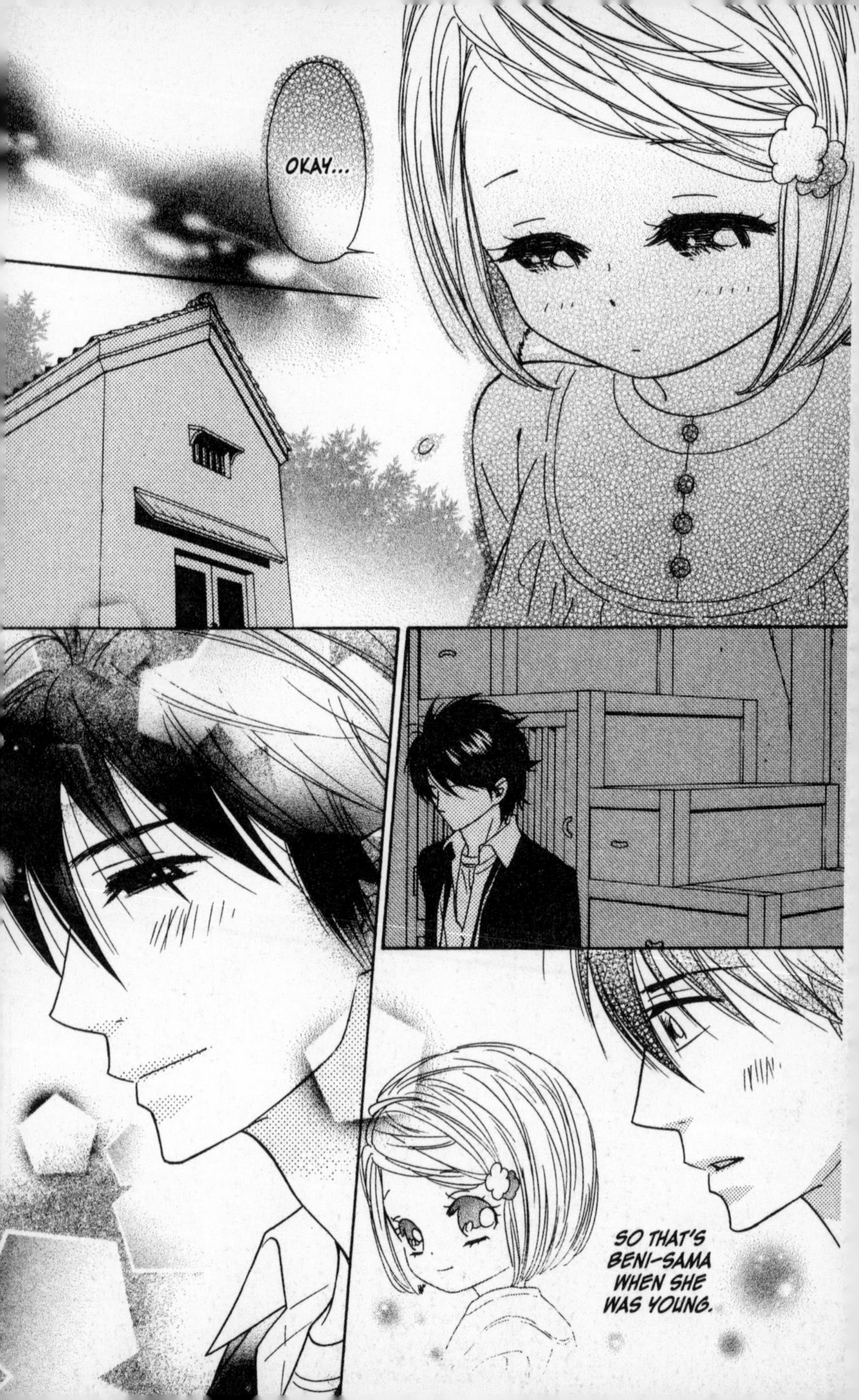
OKAY...
SO THAT'S BENI-SAMA WHEN SHE WAS YOUNG.

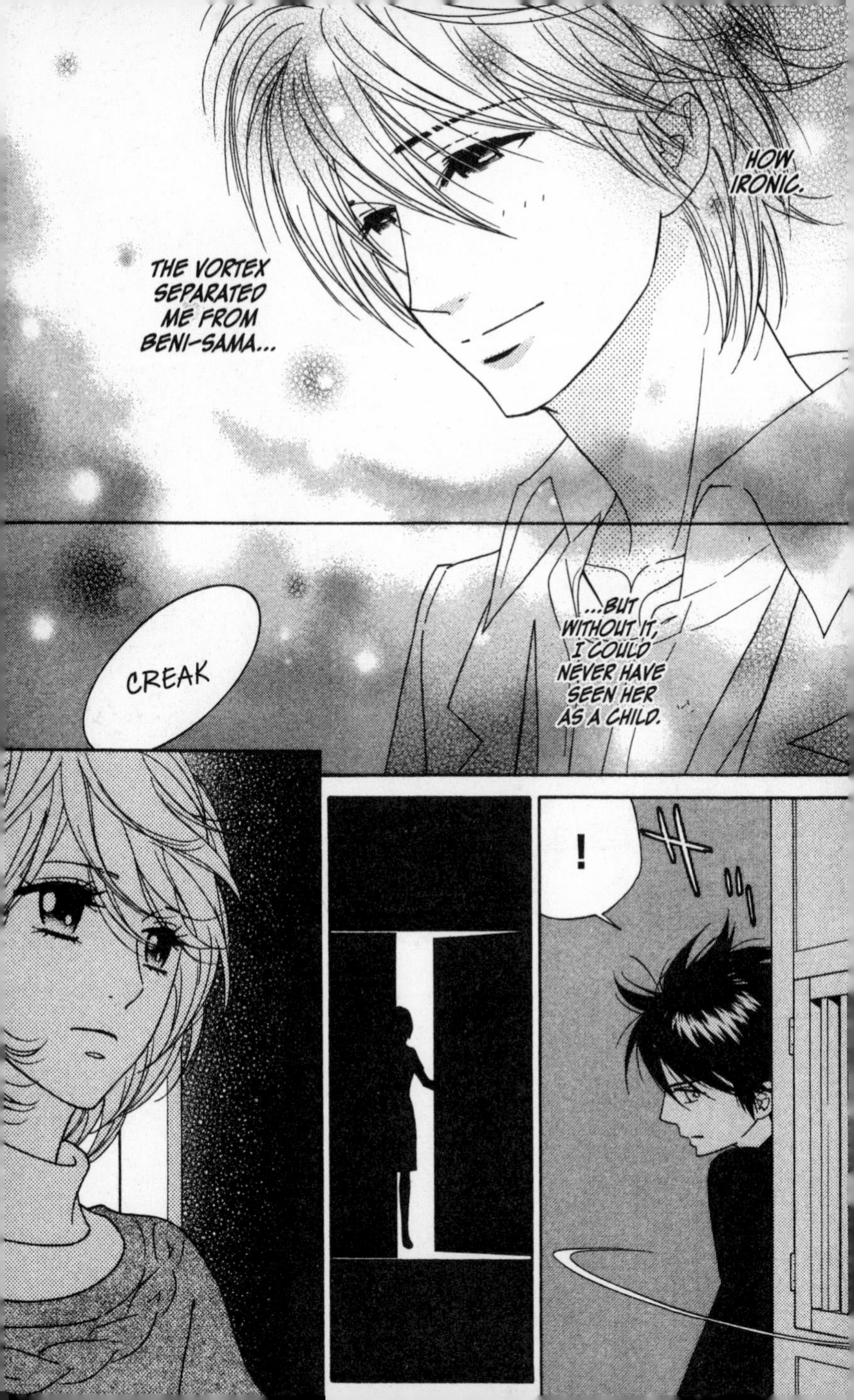
HOW IRONIC.
THE VORTEX SEPARATED ME FROM BENI-SAMA...
...BUT WITHOUT IT, I COULD NEVER HAVE SEEN HER AS A CHILD.
CREAK
!

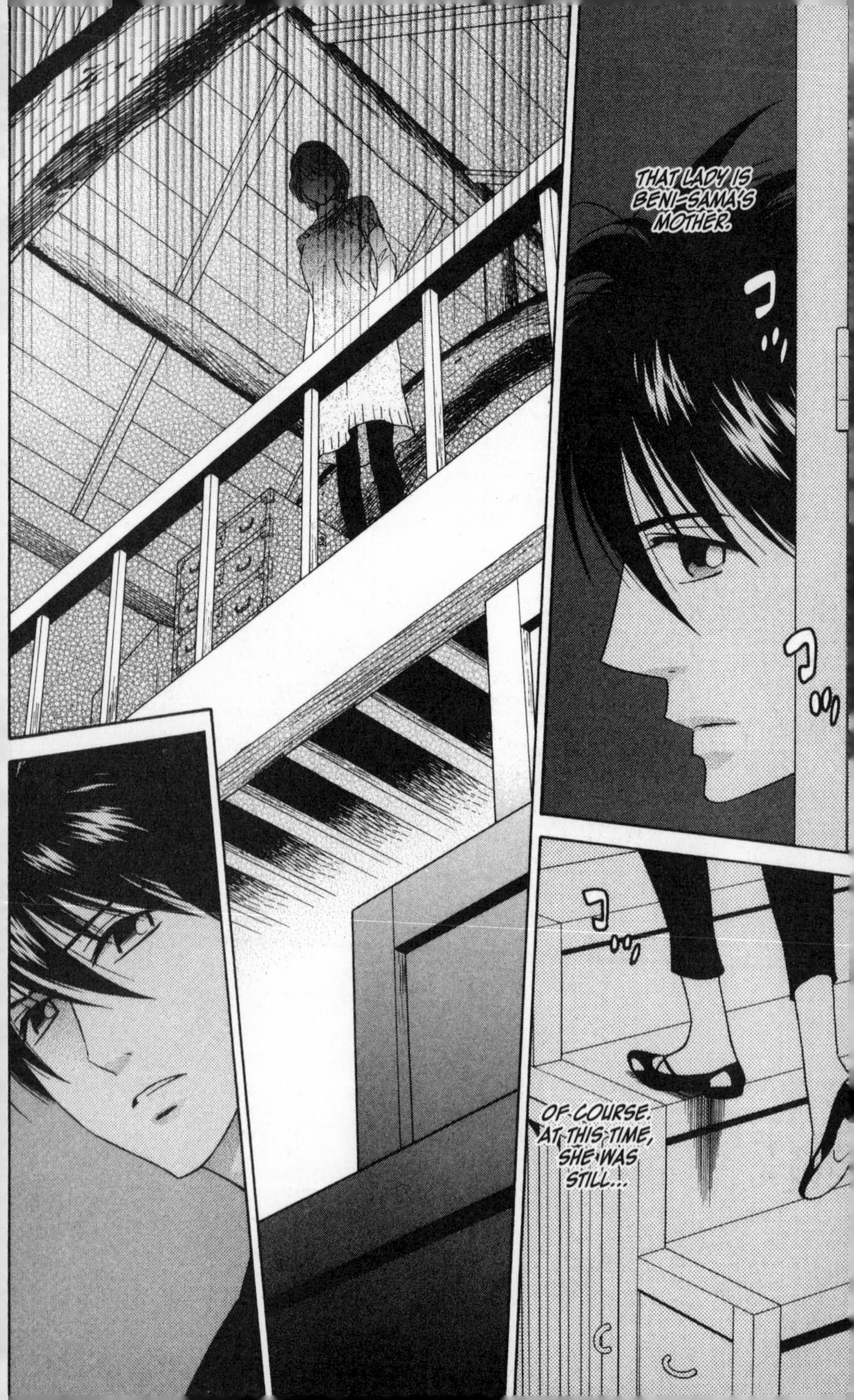
THAT LADY IS BENI-SAMA'S MOTHER.
OF COURSE. AT THIS TIME, SHE WAS STILL...

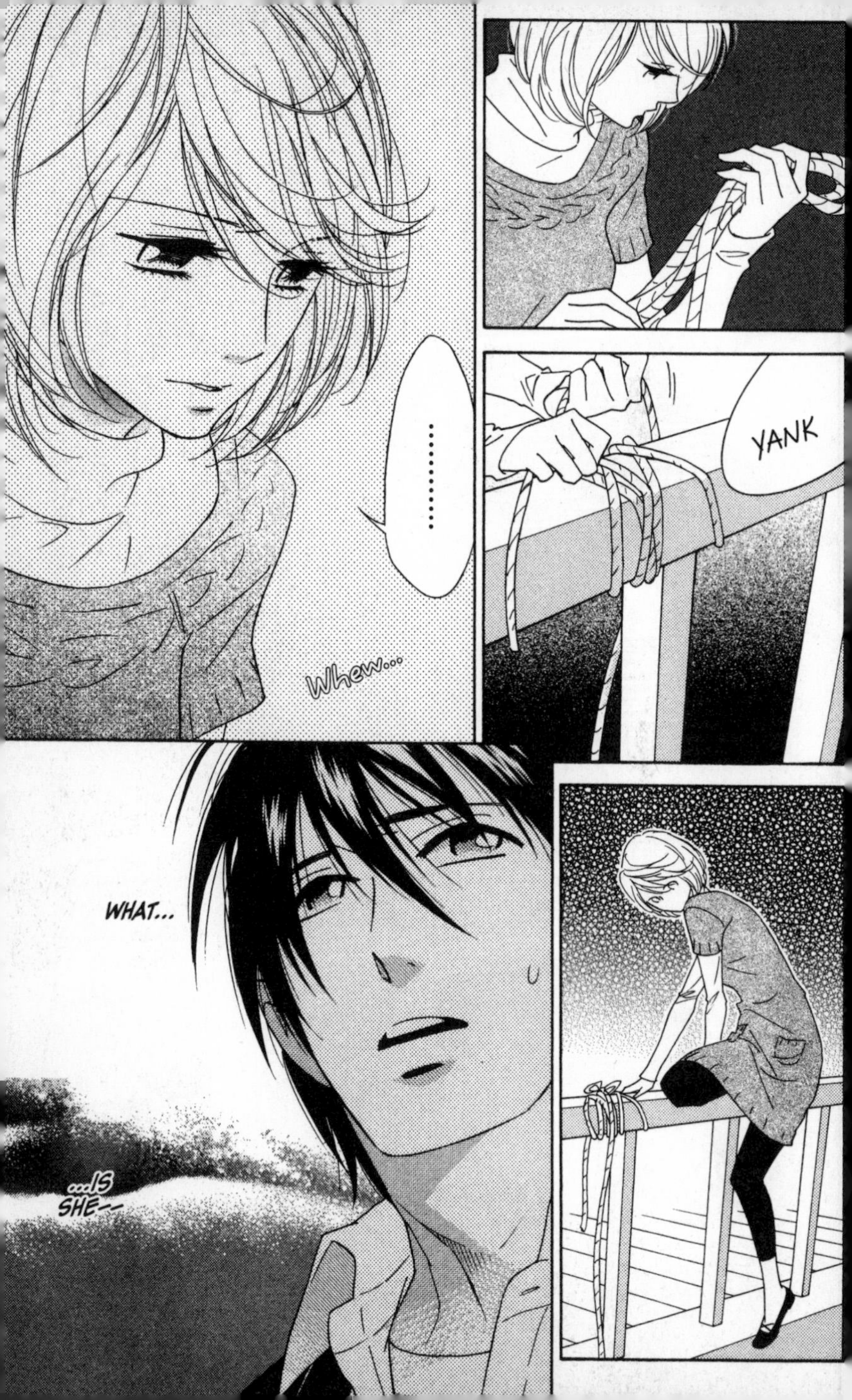
YANK
....
Whew...
WHAT...
...IS SHE--

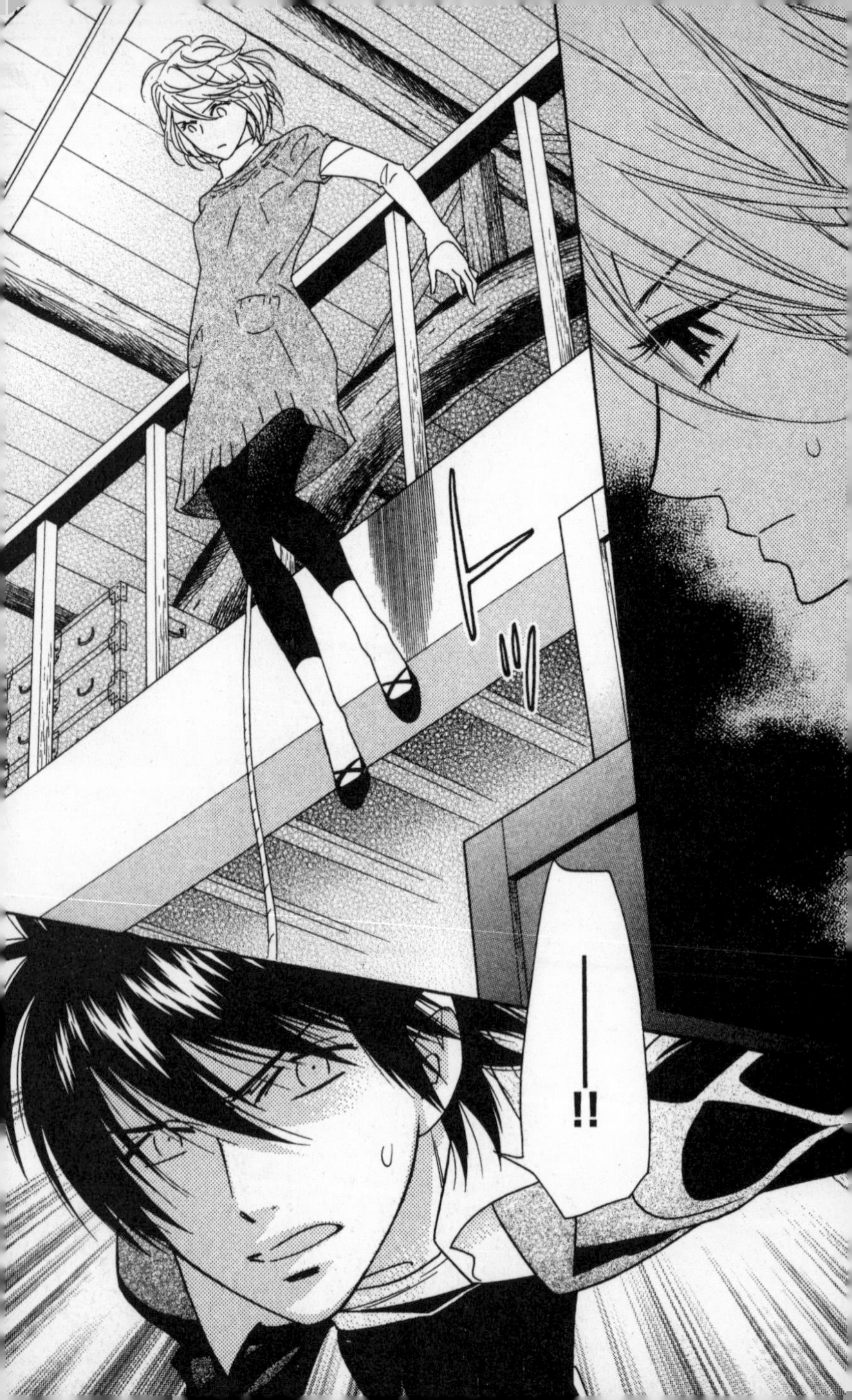
ド
――!!

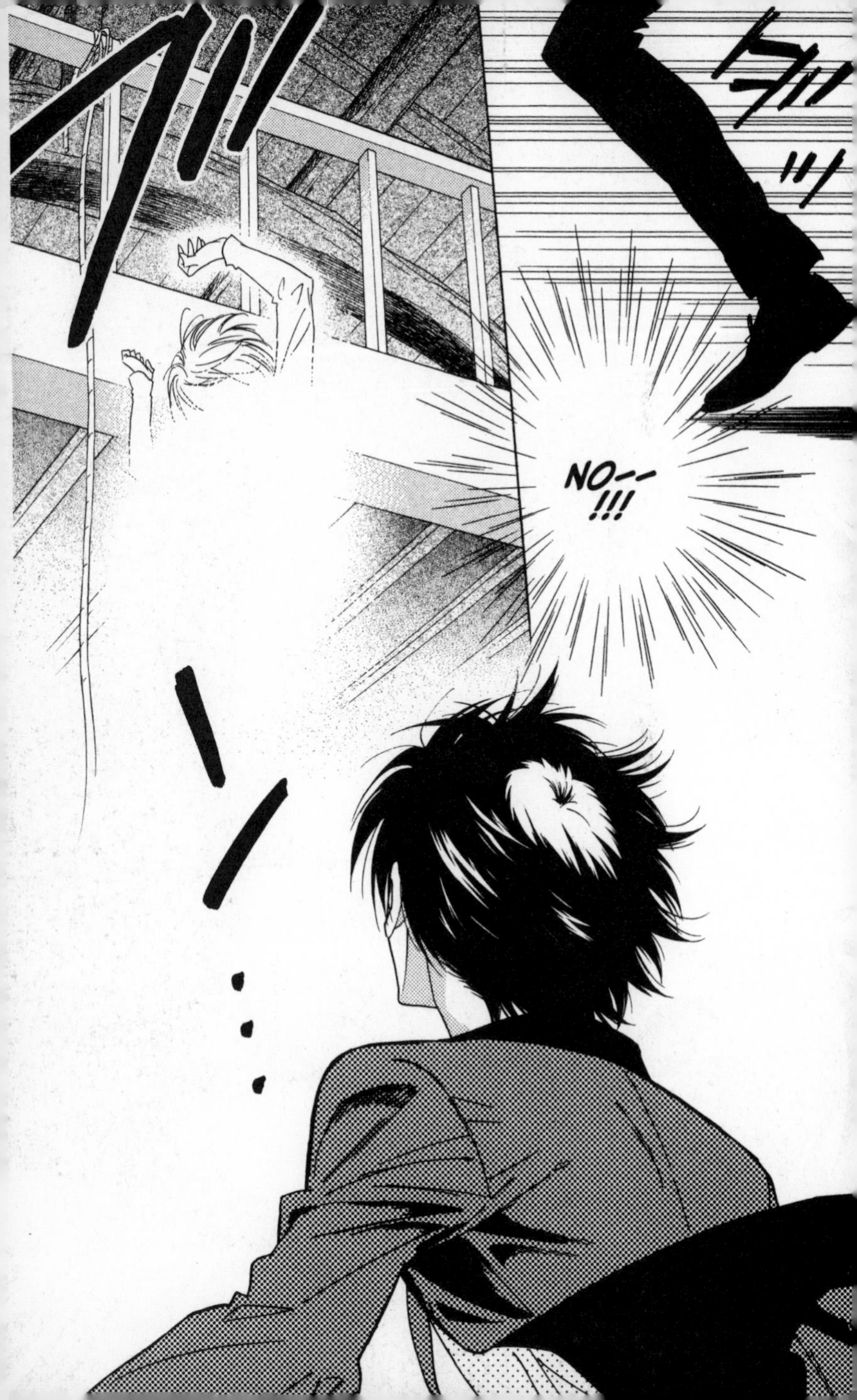
NO-- !!!

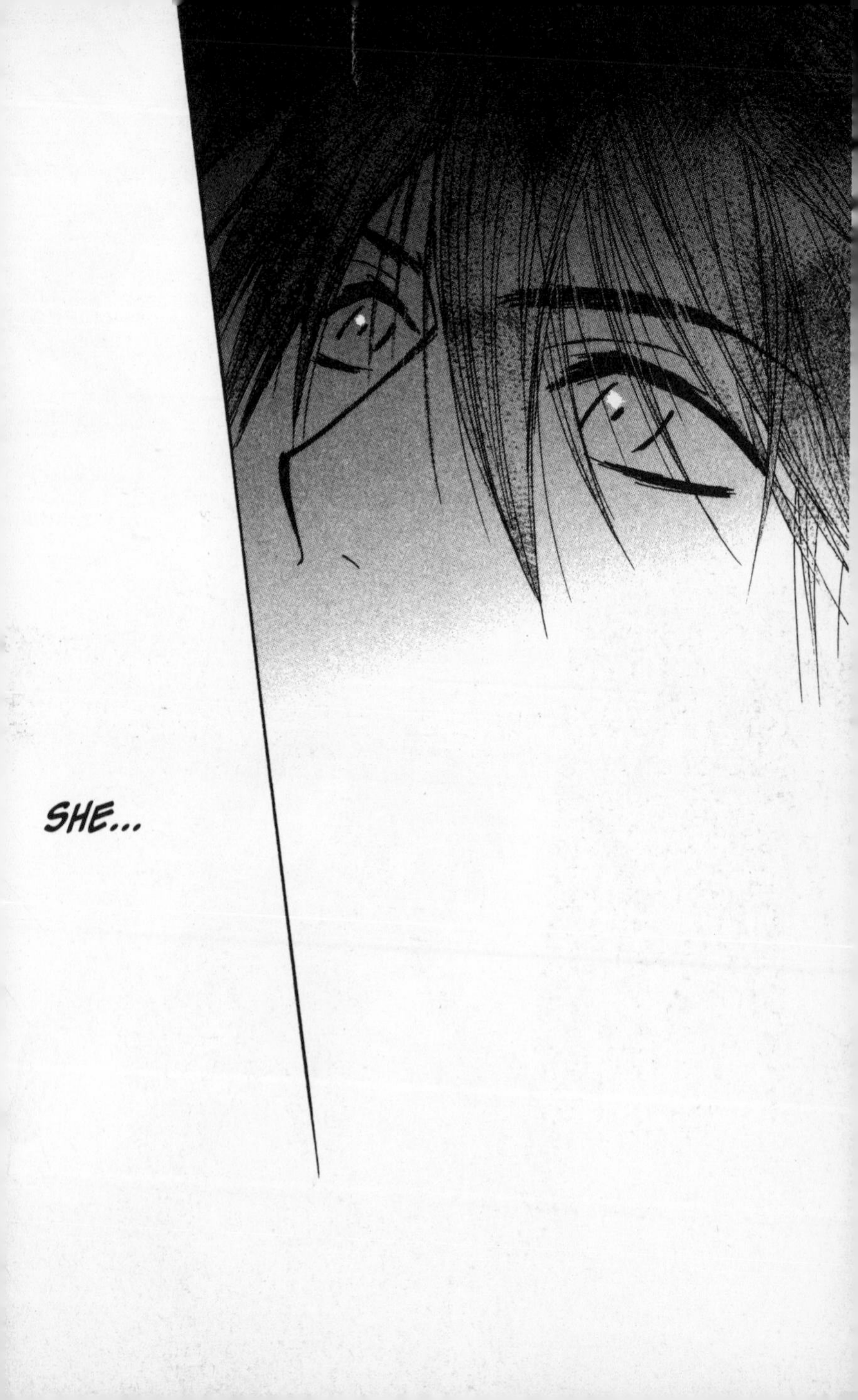
SHE...

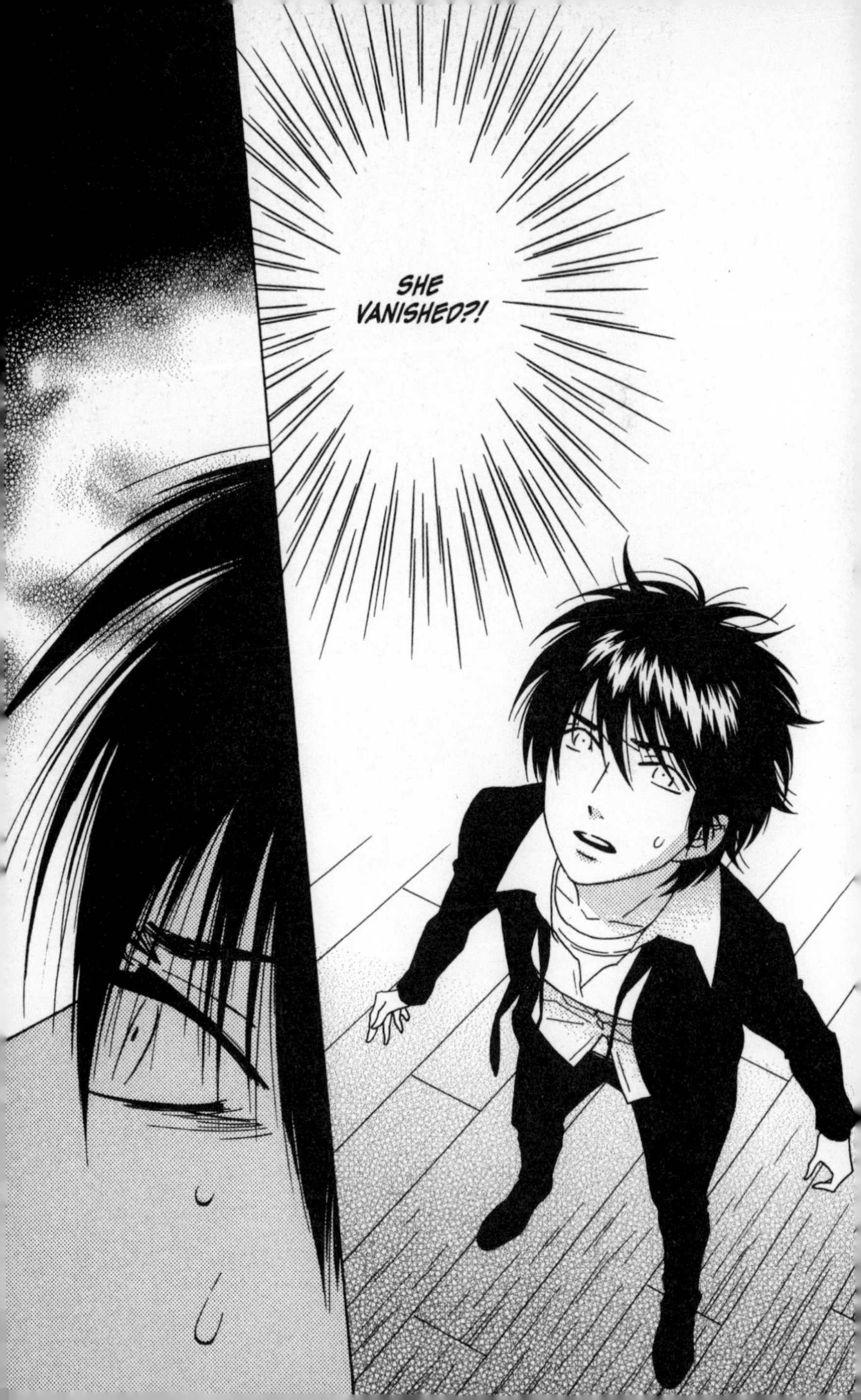
SHE VANISHED?!

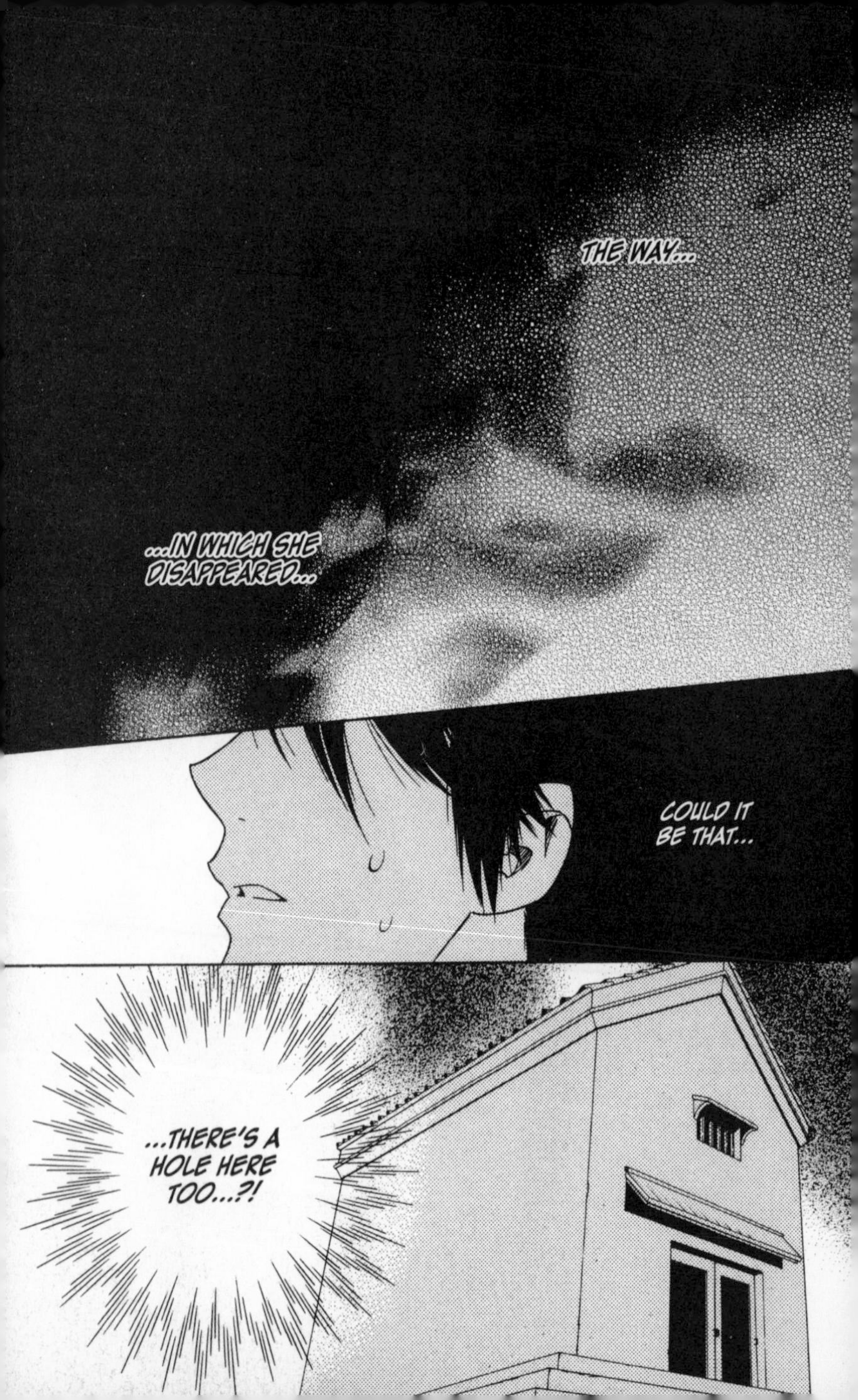
THE WAY...
...IN WHICH SHE DISAPPEARED...
COULD IT BE THAT...
...THERE'S A HOLE HERE TOO...?!

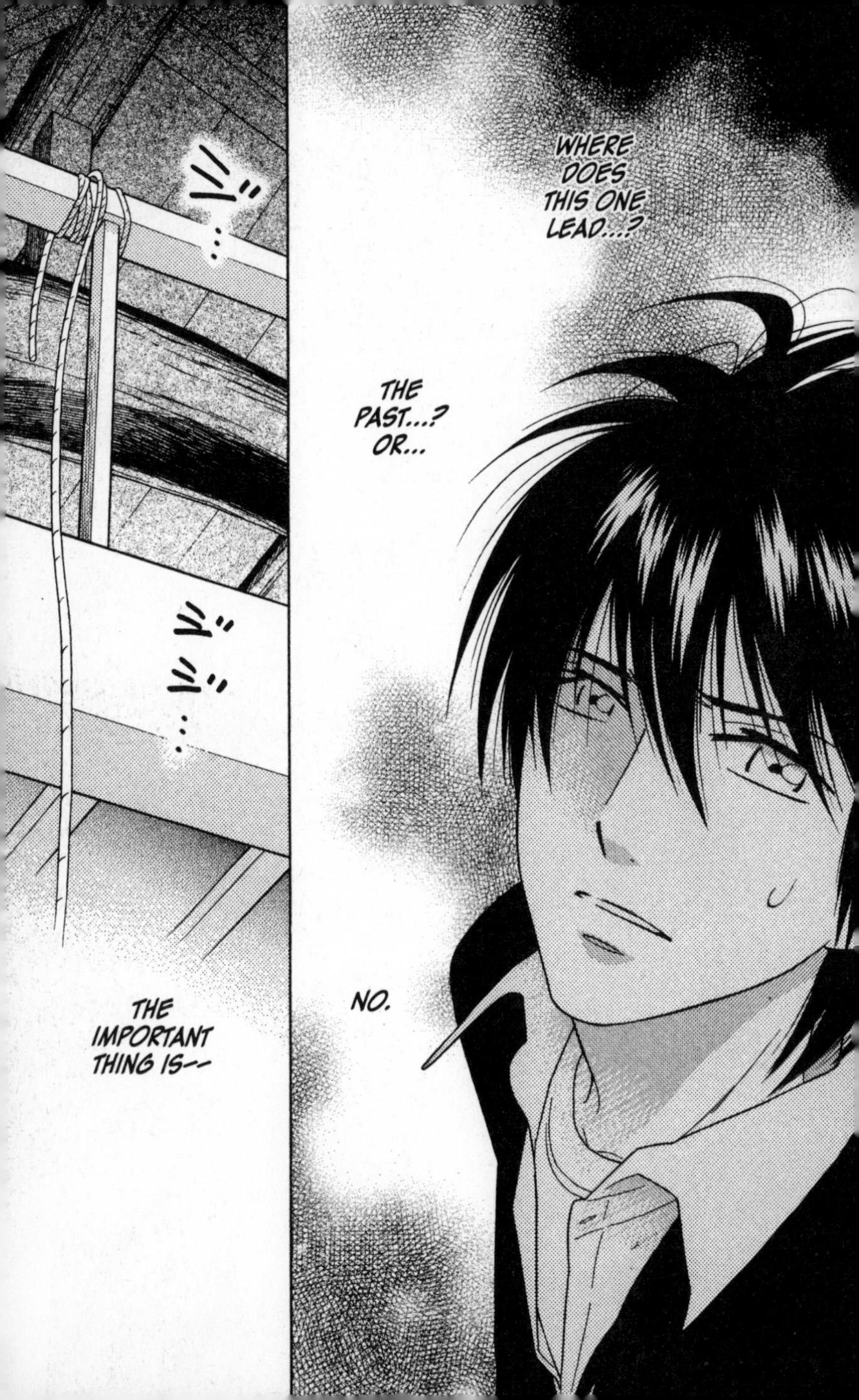
WHERE DOES THIS ONE LEAD...?
THE PAST...? OR...
NO.
ジ…
ジジ…
THE IMPORTANT THING IS--

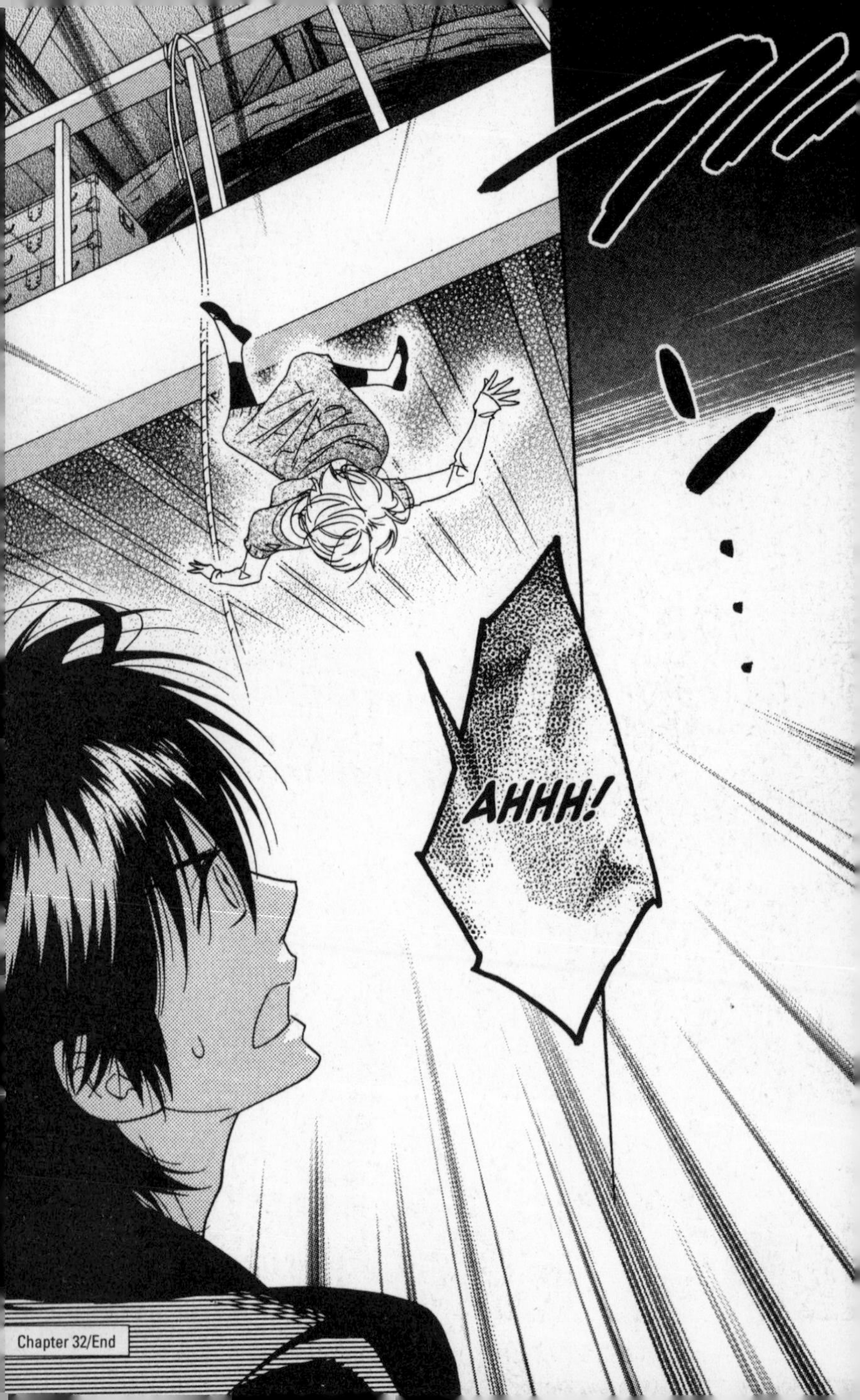
AHHH!
Chapter 32/End

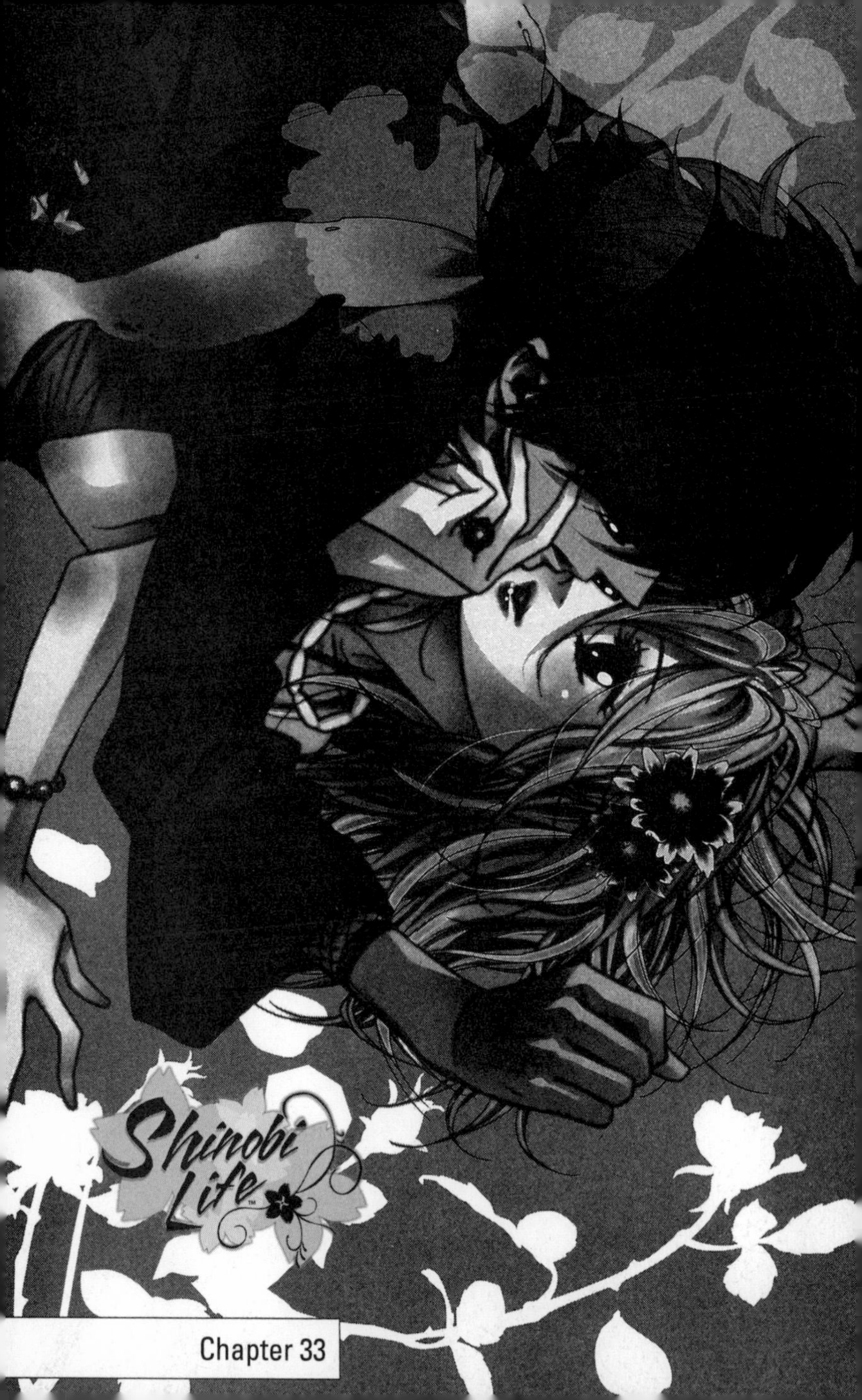
Shinobi Life
Chapter 33

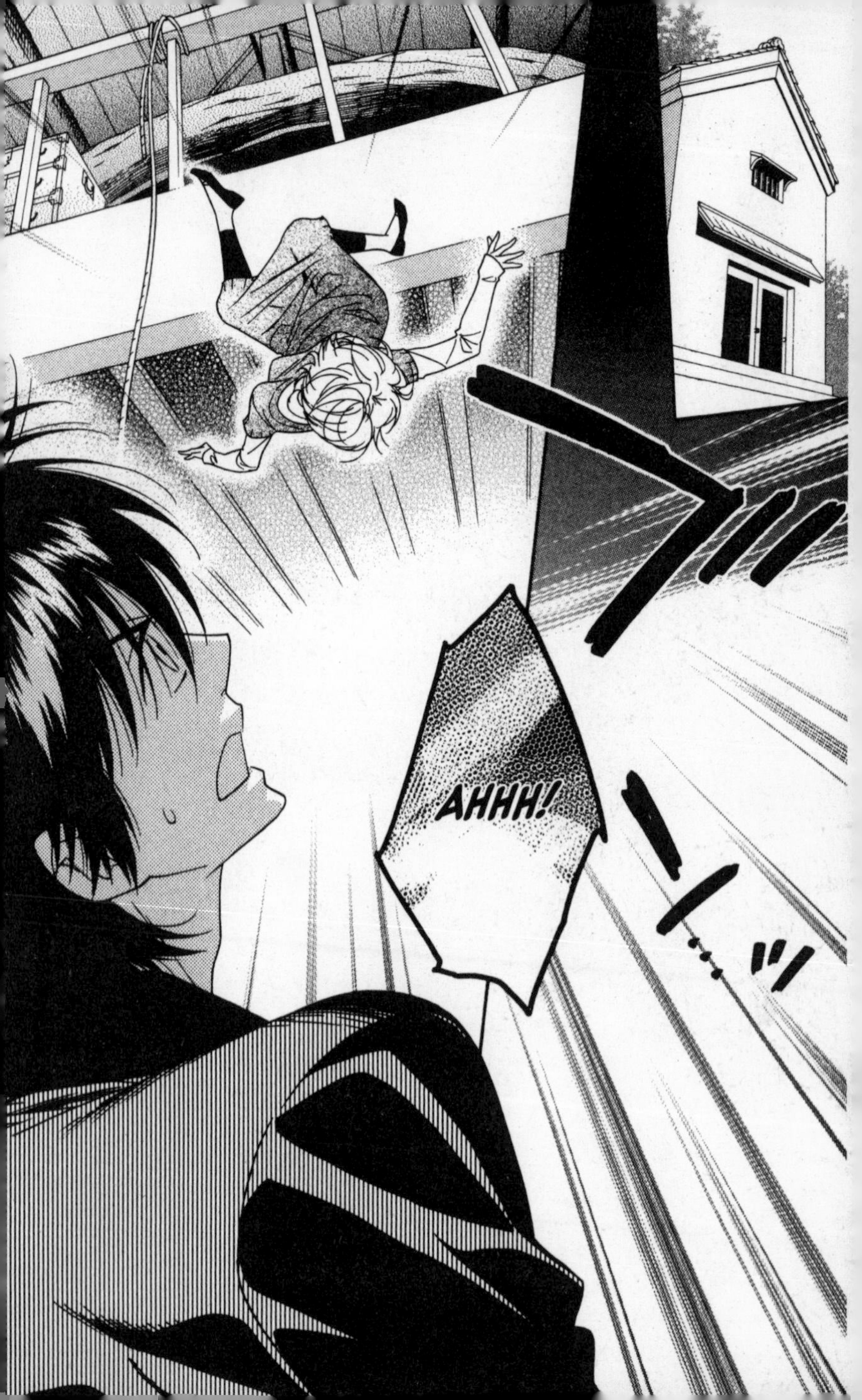
AHHH!

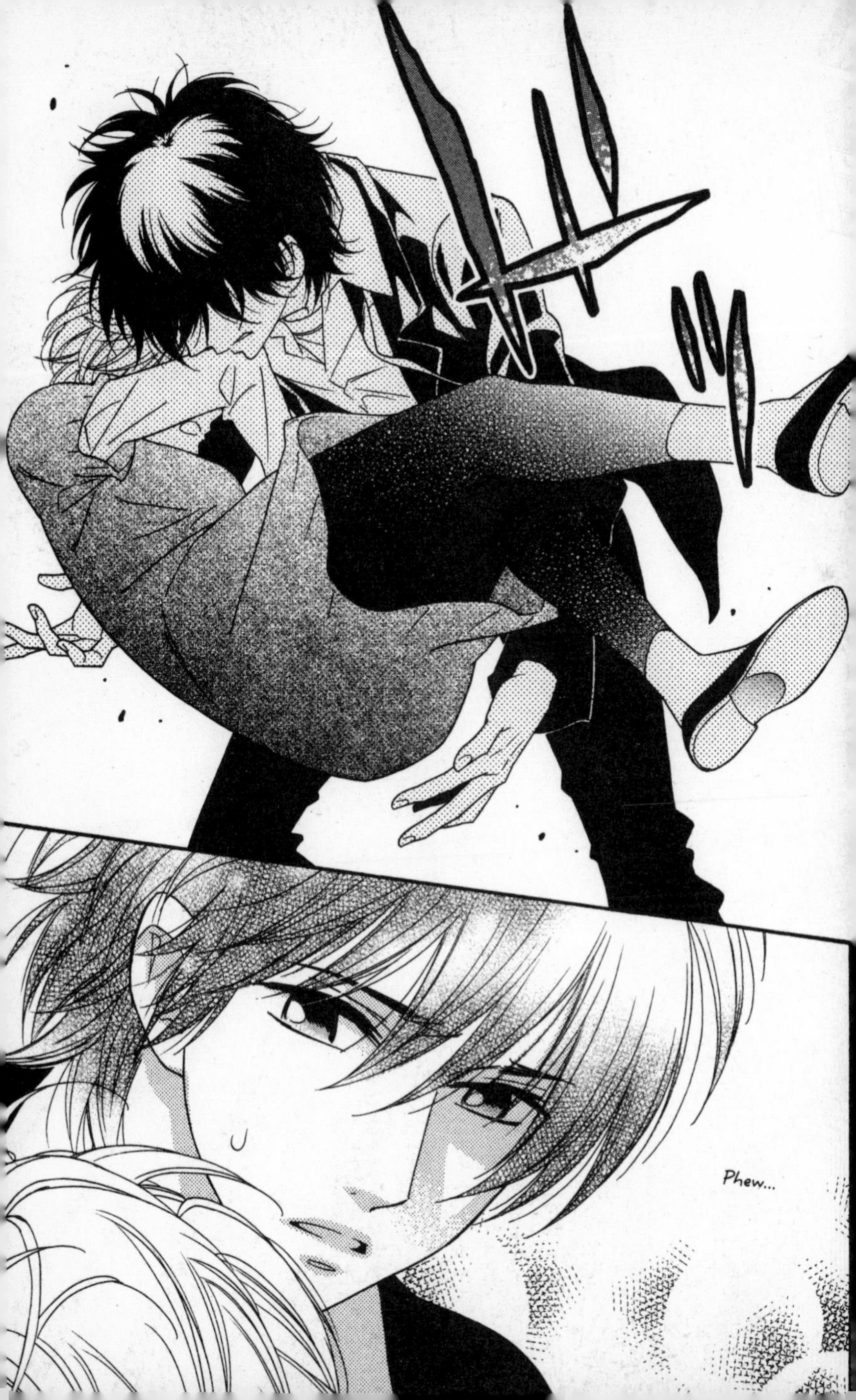
Phew...

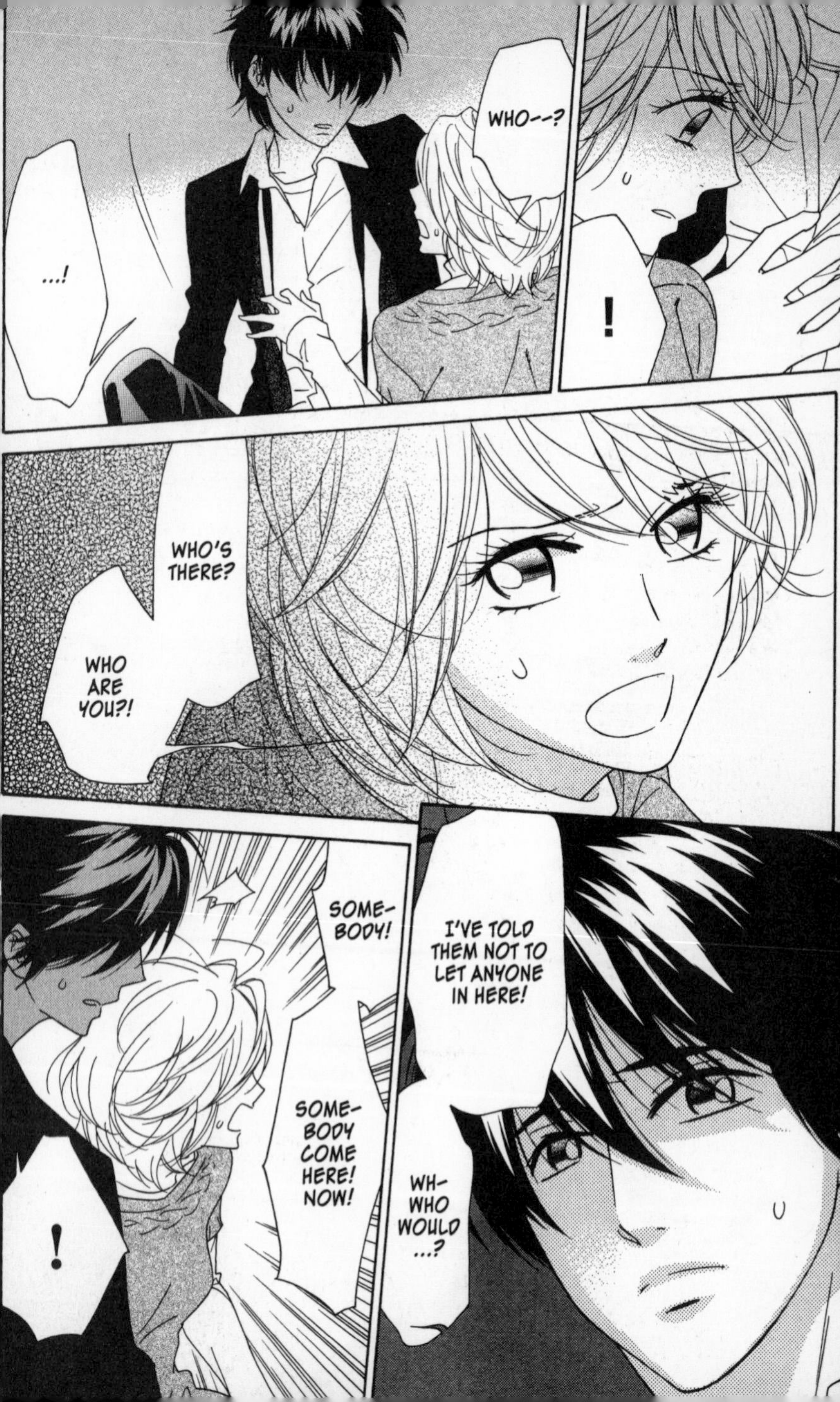
!
WHO--?
...!
WHO'S THERE?
WHO ARE YOU?!
I'VE TOLD THEM NOT TO LET ANYONE IN HERE!
WH-WHO WOULD ...?
SOME-BODY!
SOME-BODY COME HERE! NOW!
!

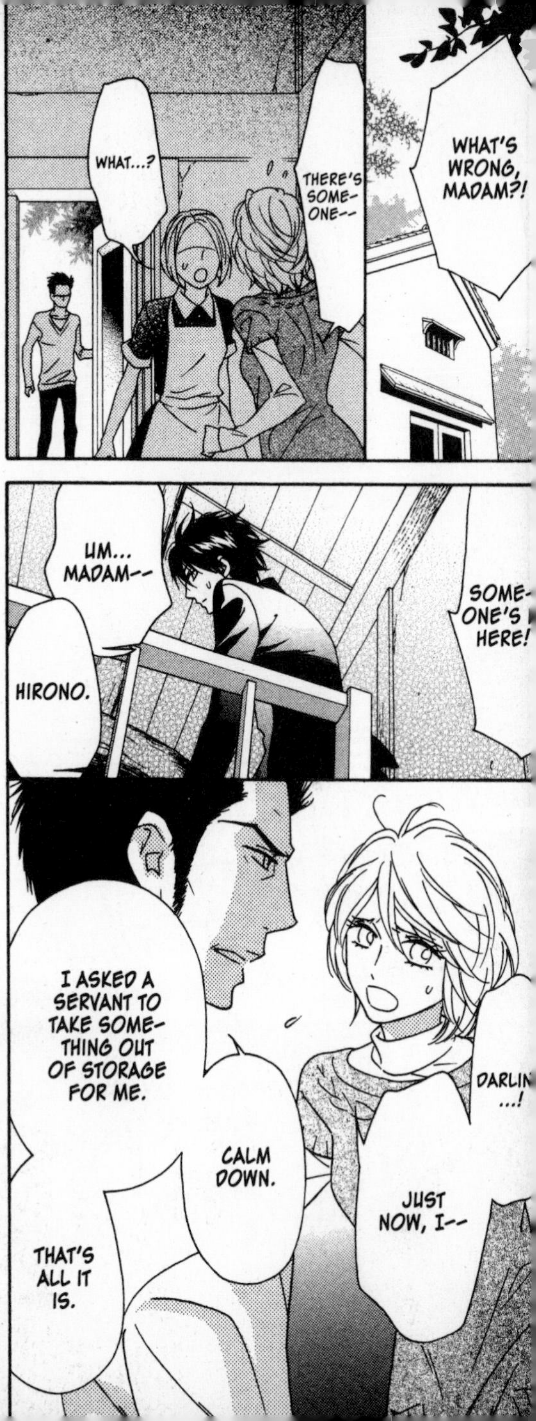
WHAT'S WRONG, MADAM?!
THERE'S SOME-ONE--
WHAT...?
SOME-ONE'S HERE!
UM... MADAM--
HIRONO.
DARLIN ...!
JUST NOW, I--
CALM DOWN.
I ASKED A SERVANT TO TAKE SOME-THING OUT OF STORAGE FOR ME.
THAT'S ALL IT IS.

Hi there! This is Conami. I haven't written anything in this space for a while now...

Thank you so much for reading this manga! You're my sunshine for reading all seven volumes!

Something very special happened completely out of the blue! Get this--they've made a drama CD for Shinobi Life! I've written a report about the recording, and it's at the back of this volume, so please read through it. ♡

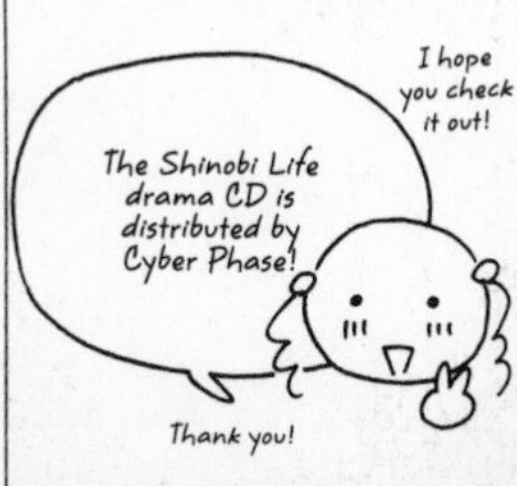
I hope you check it out!
The Shinobi Life drama CD is distributed by Cyber Phase!
Thank you!

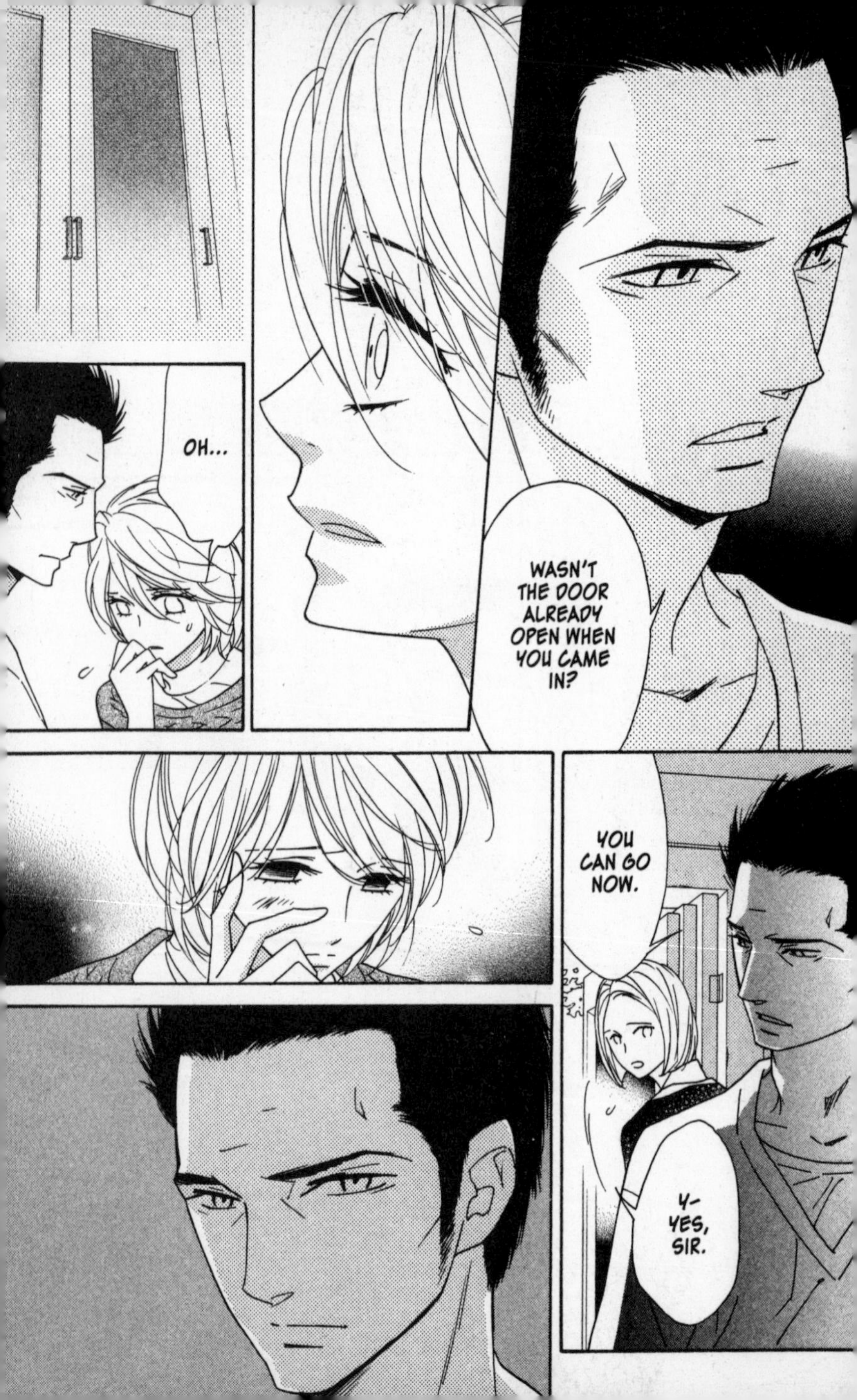
WASN'T THE DOOR ALREADY OPEN WHEN YOU CAME IN?
OH...
YOU CAN GO NOW.
Y-YES, SIR.

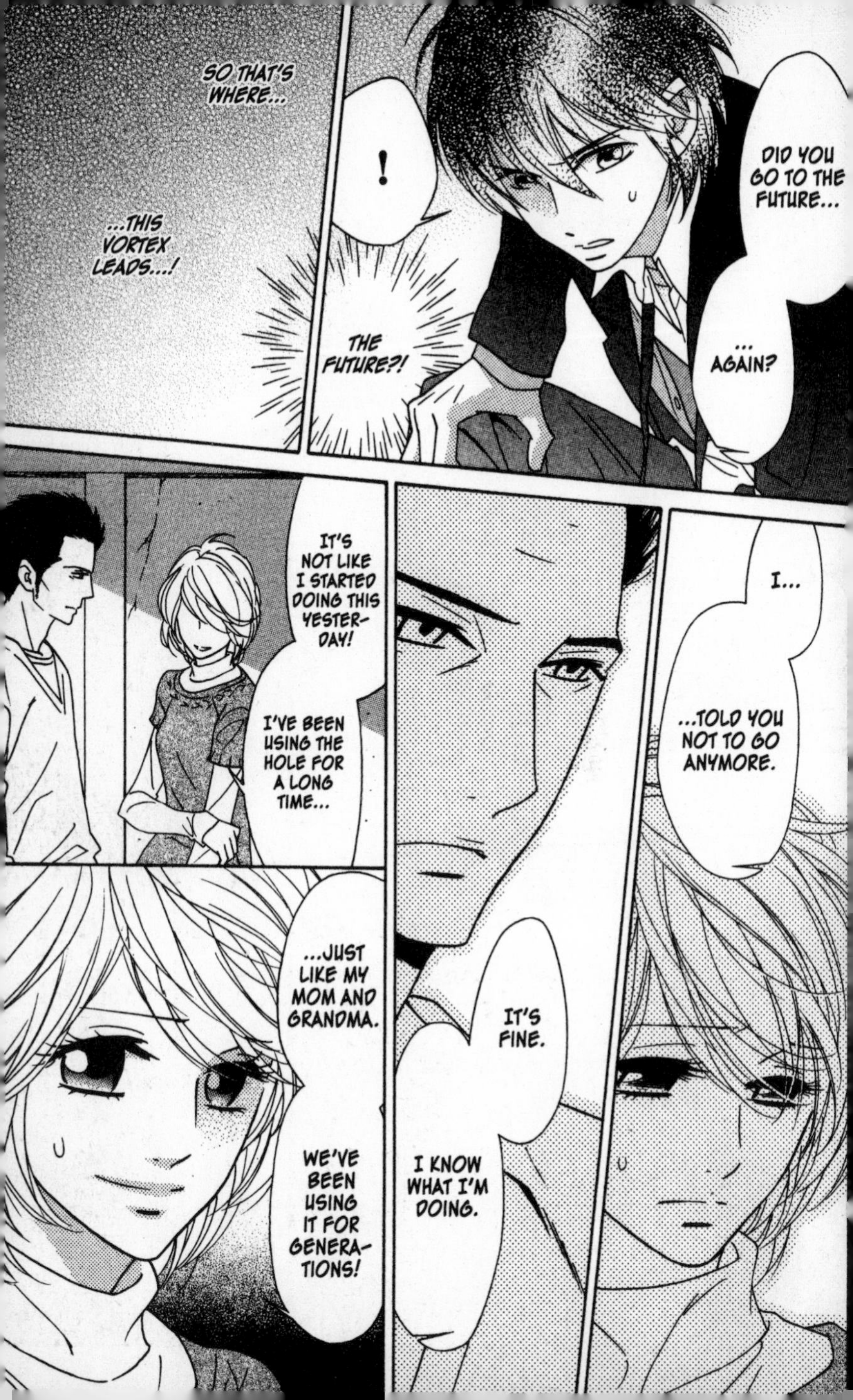
DID YOU GO TO THE FUTURE...
... AGAIN?
!
THE FUTURE?!
SO THAT'S WHERE...
...THIS VORTEX LEADS...!
I...
...TOLD YOU NOT TO GO ANYMORE.
IT'S FINE.
I KNOW WHAT I'M DOING.
IT'S NOT LIKE I STARTED DOING THIS YESTER-DAY!
I'VE BEEN USING THE HOLE FOR A LONG TIME...
...JUST LIKE MY MOM AND GRANDMA.
WE'VE BEEN USING IT FOR GENERA-TIONS!

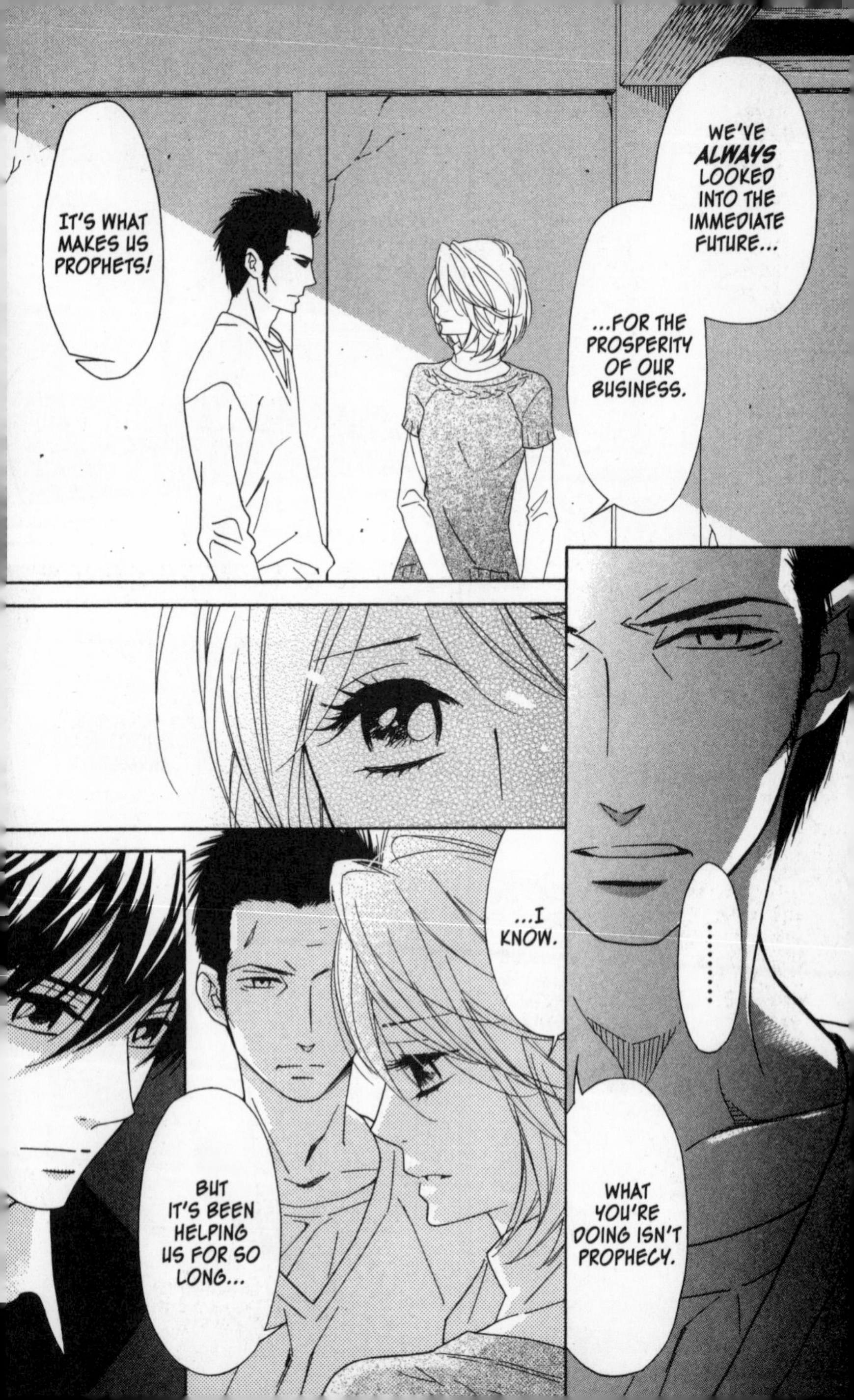
WE'VE ***ALWAYS*** LOOKED INTO THE IMMEDIATE FUTURE...
...FOR THE PROSPERITY OF OUR BUSINESS.
IT'S WHAT MAKES US PROPHETS!
......
WHAT YOU'RE DOING ISN'T PROPHECY.
...I KNOW.
BUT IT'S BEEN HELPING US FOR SO LONG...

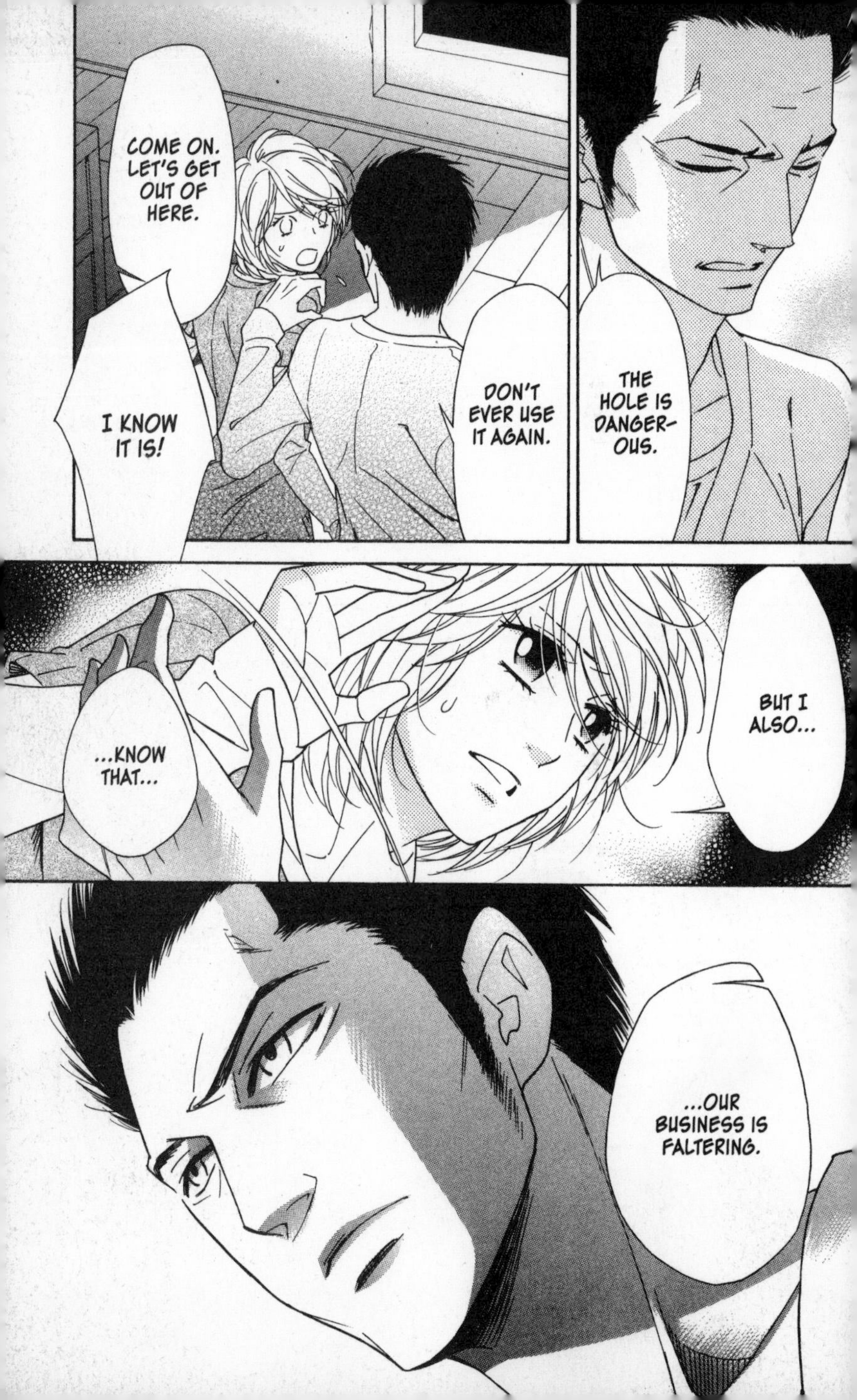
THE HOLE IS DANGER-OUS.
DON'T EVER USE IT AGAIN.
COME ON. LET'S GET OUT OF HERE.
I KNOW IT IS!
BUT I ALSO...
...KNOW THAT...
...OUR BUSINESS IS FALTERING.

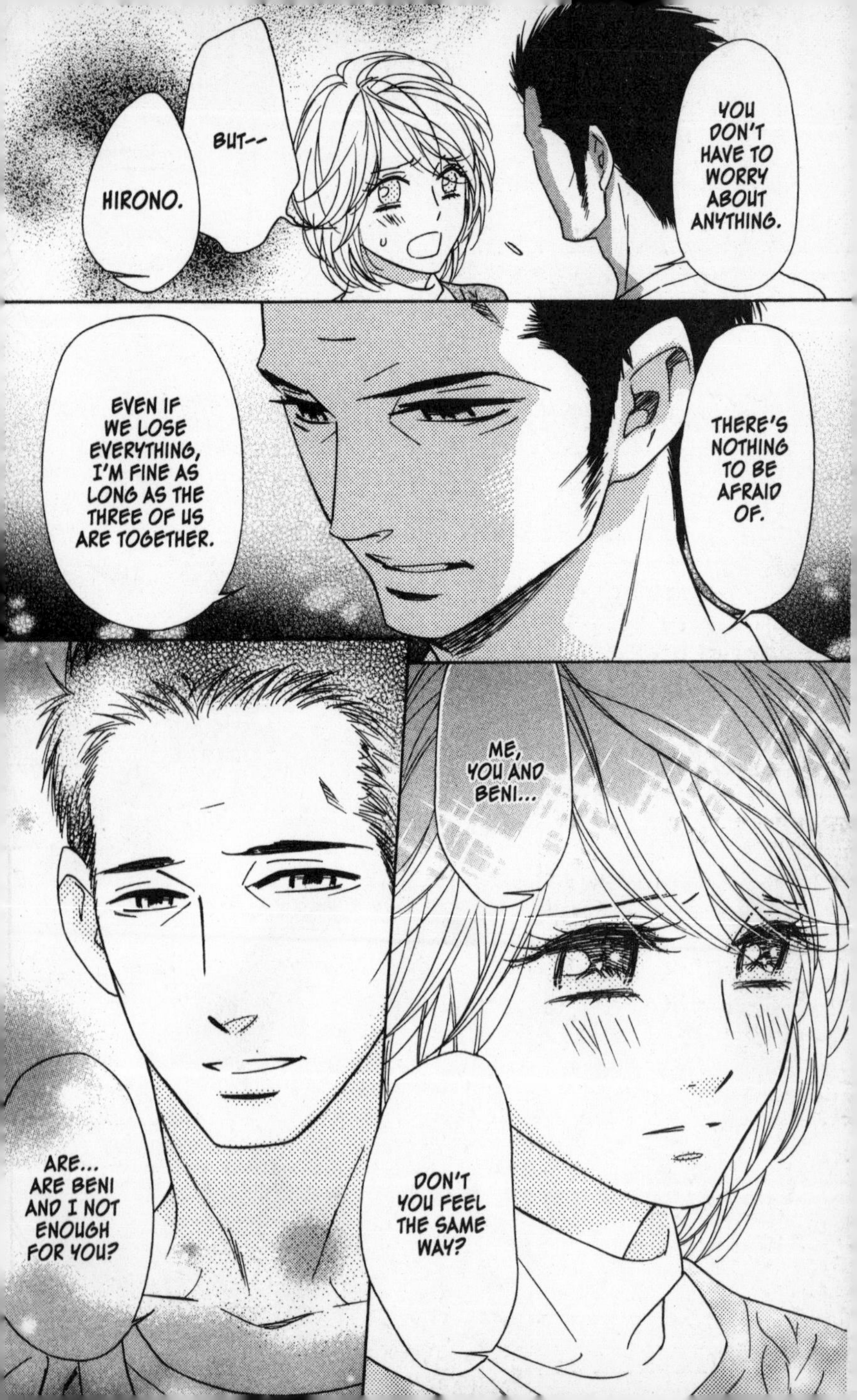
YOU DON'T HAVE TO WORRY ABOUT ANYTHING.
BUT--
HIRONO.
THERE'S NOTHING TO BE AFRAID OF.
EVEN IF WE LOSE EVERYTHING, I'M FINE AS LONG AS THE THREE OF US ARE TOGETHER.
ME, YOU AND BENI...
DON'T YOU FEEL THE SAME WAY?
ARE... ARE BENI AND I NOT ENOUGH FOR YOU?

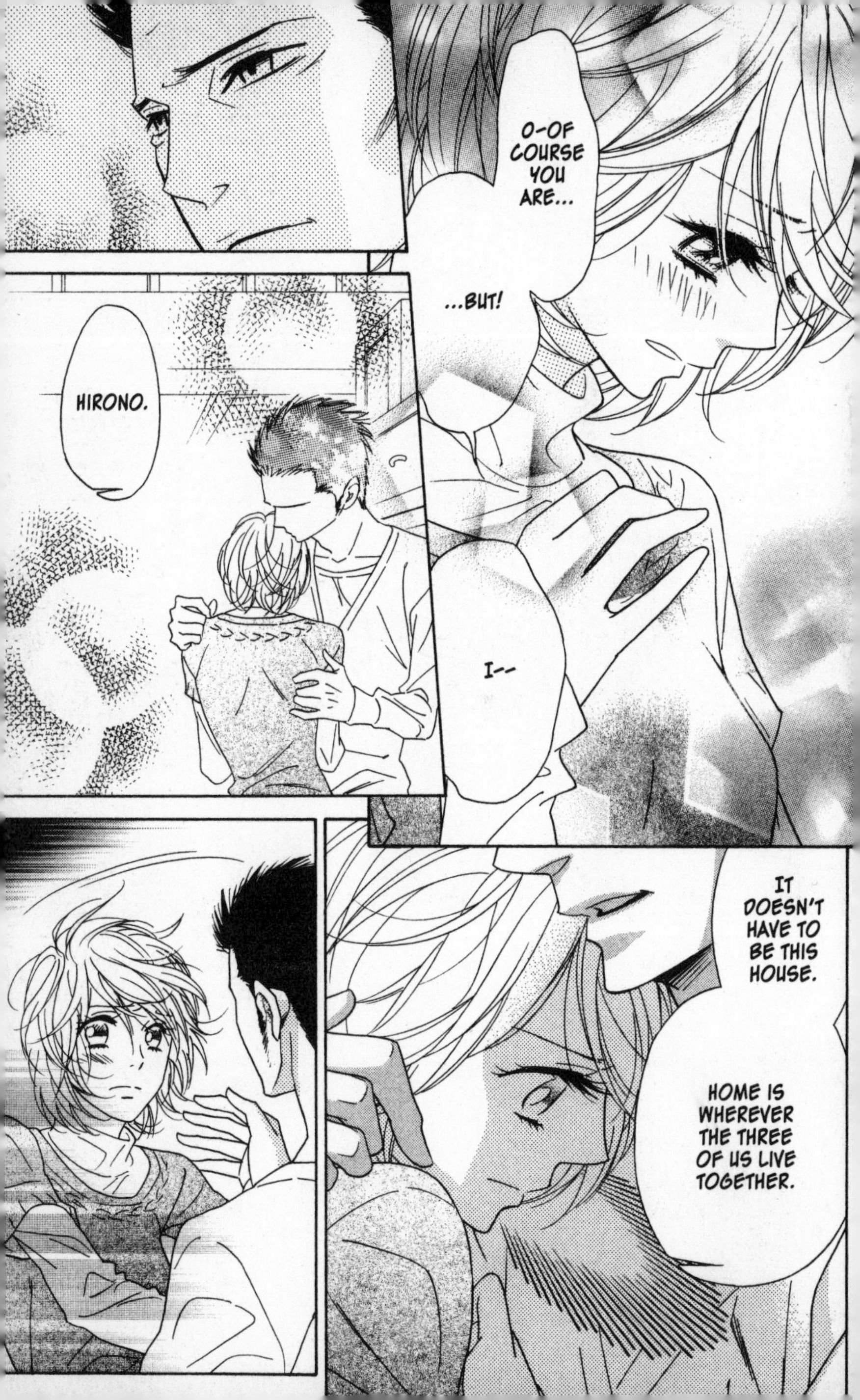
O-OF COURSE YOU ARE...
...BUT!
I--
HIRONO.
IT DOESN'T HAVE TO BE THIS HOUSE.
HOME IS WHEREVER THE THREE OF US LIVE TOGETHER.

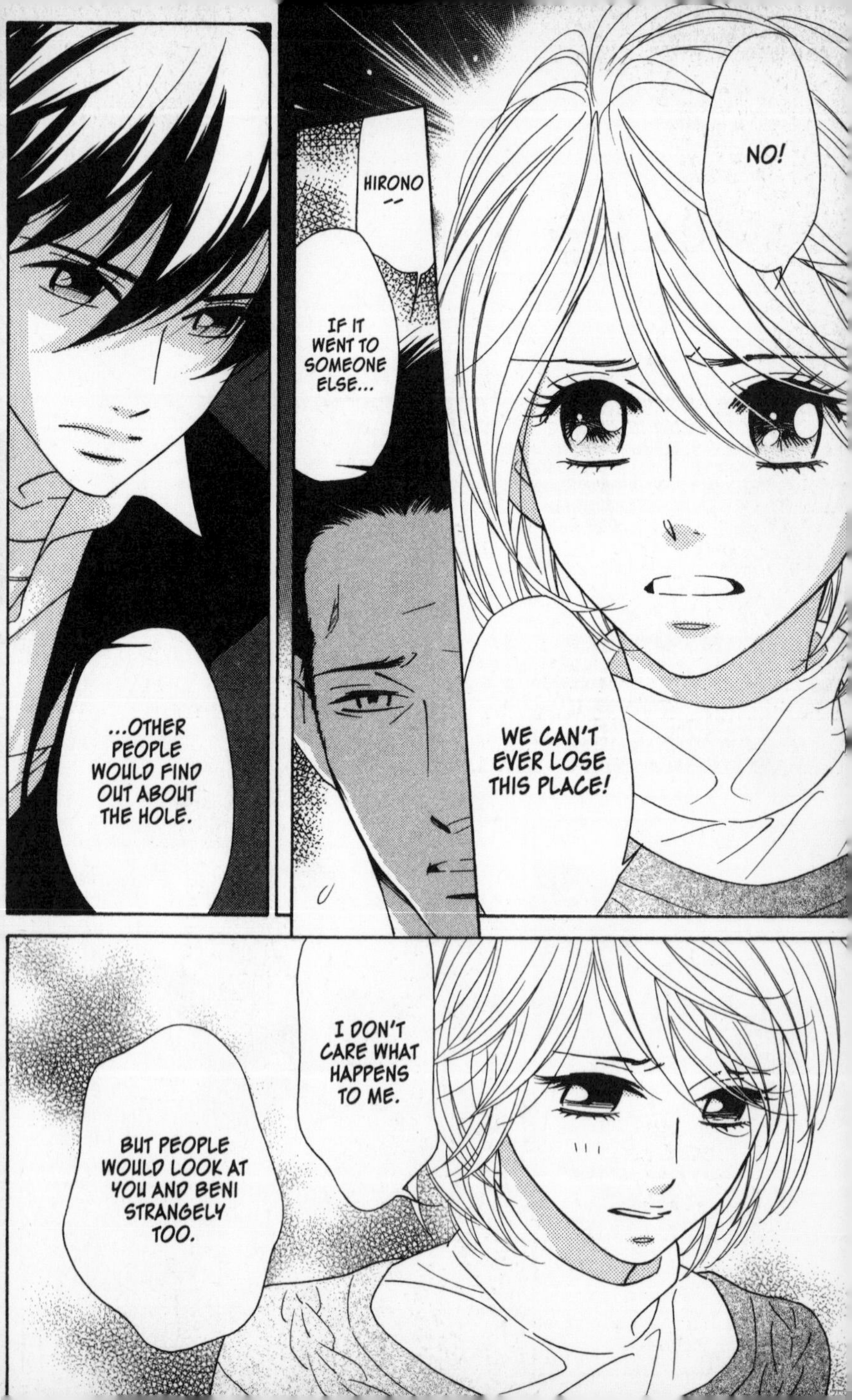
NO!
WE CAN'T EVER LOSE THIS PLACE!
HIRONO --
IF IT WENT TO SOMEONE ELSE...
...OTHER PEOPLE WOULD FIND OUT ABOUT THE HOLE.
I DON'T CARE WHAT HAPPENS TO ME.
BUT PEOPLE WOULD LOOK AT YOU AND BENI STRANGELY TOO.

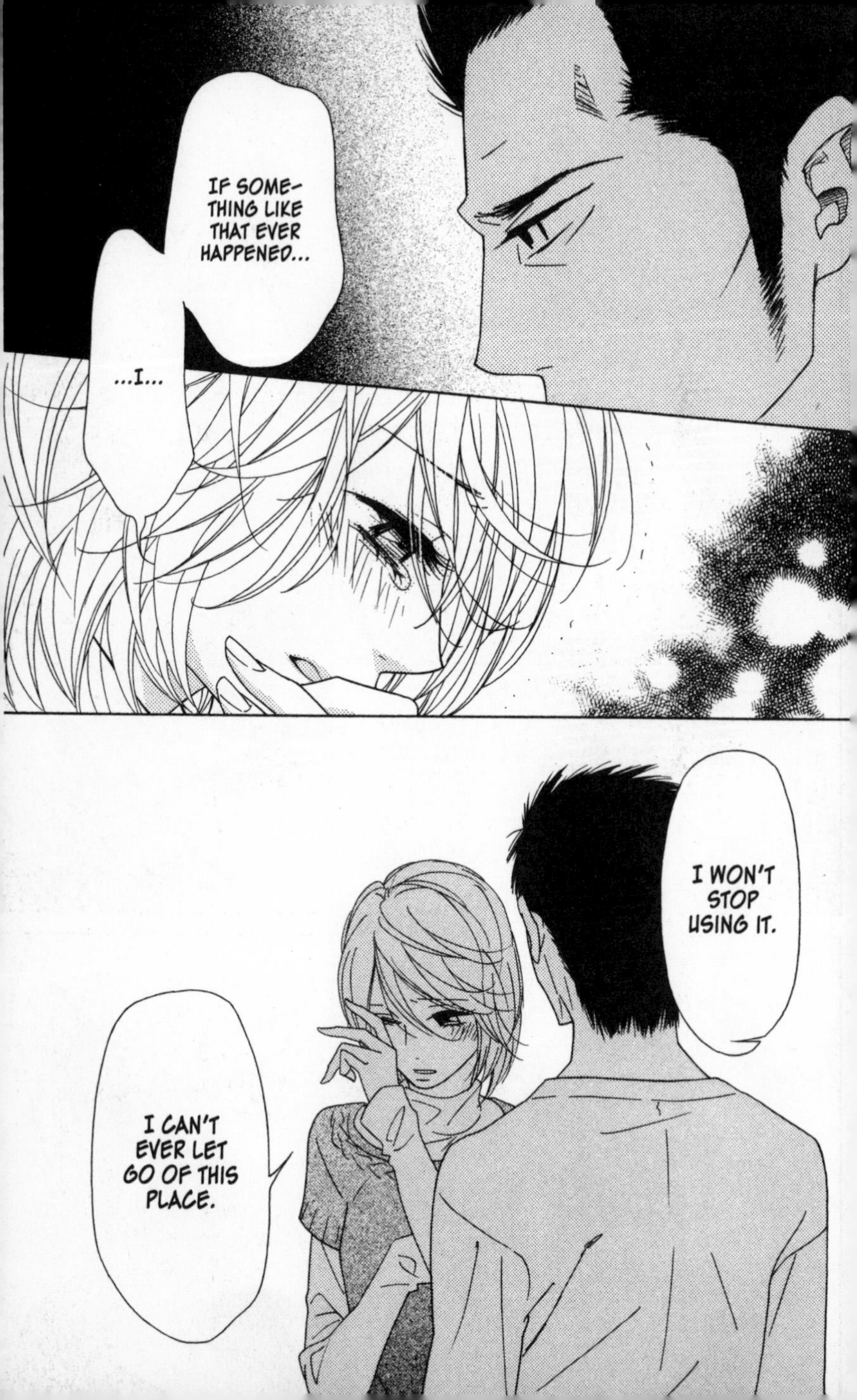
IF SOME-THING LIKE THAT EVER HAPPENED...
...I...
I WON'T STOP USING IT.
I CAN'T EVER LET GO OF THIS PLACE.

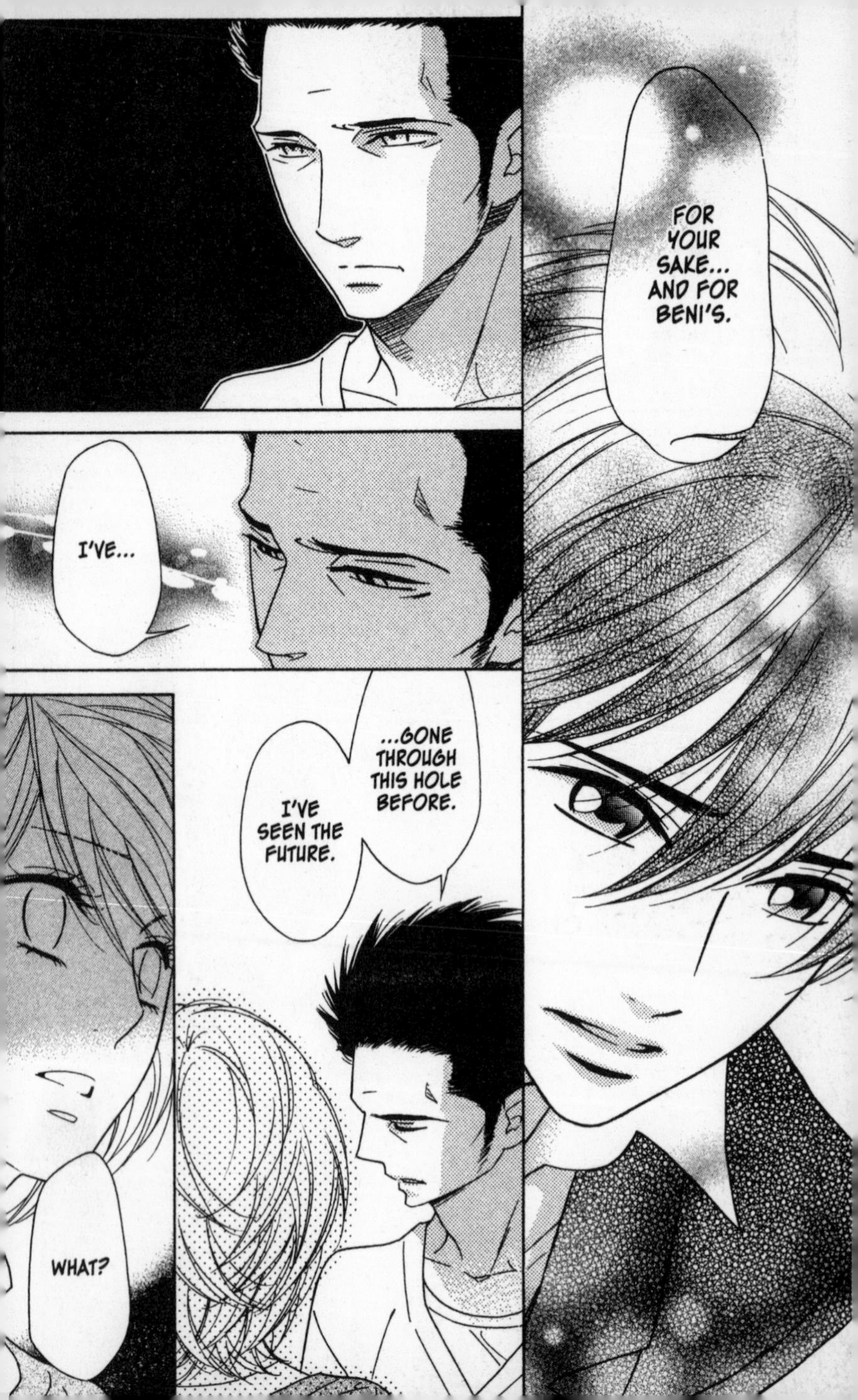
FOR YOUR SAKE... AND FOR BENI'S.
I'VE...
...GONE THROUGH THIS HOLE BEFORE.
I'VE SEEN THE FUTURE.
WHAT?

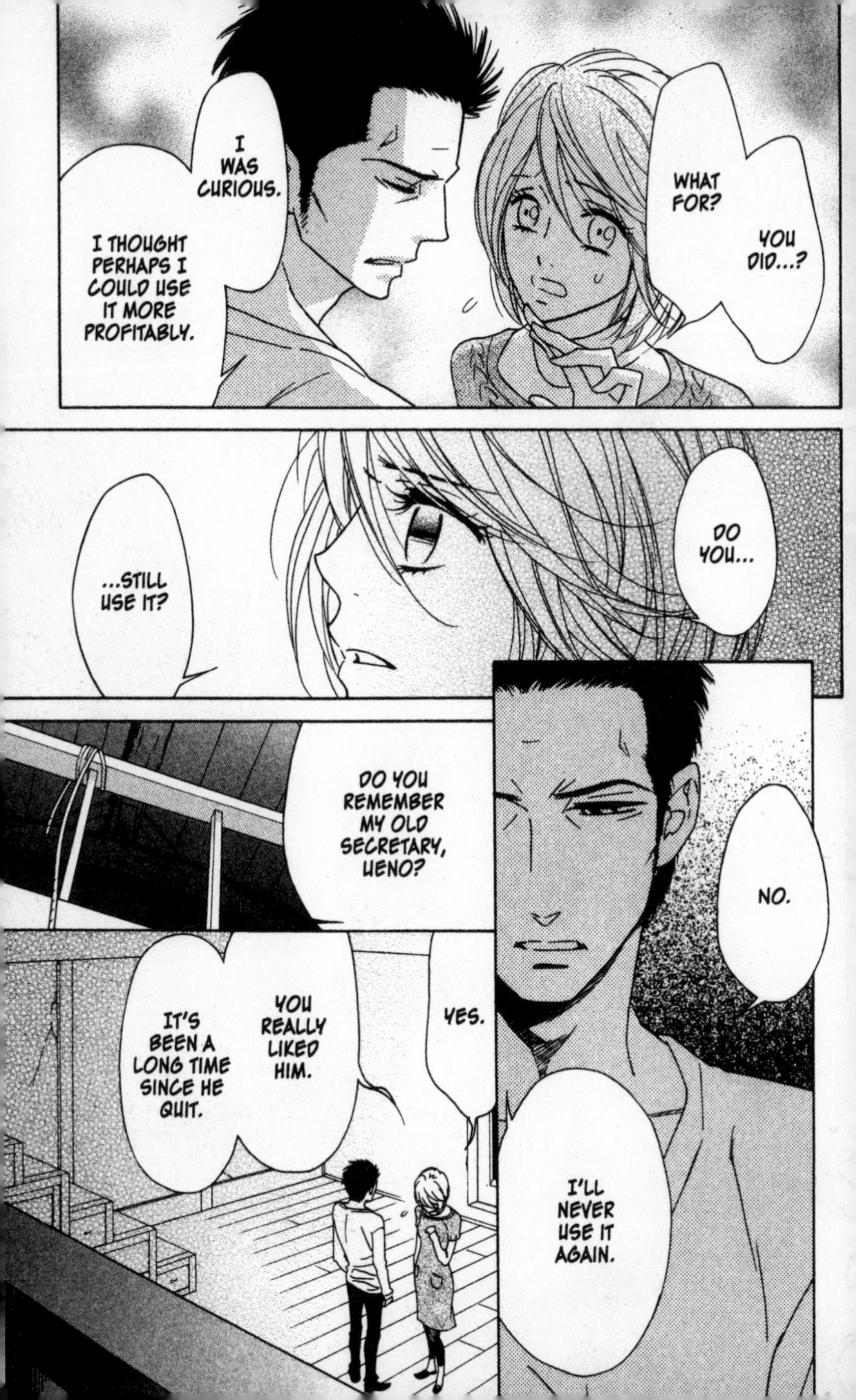
WHAT FOR?
YOU DID...?
I WAS CURIOUS.
I THOUGHT PERHAPS I COULD USE IT MORE PROFITABLY.
DO YOU...
...STILL USE IT?
NO.
I'LL NEVER USE IT AGAIN.
DO YOU REMEMBER MY OLD SECRETARY, UENO?
YES.
YOU REALLY LIKED HIM.
IT'S BEEN A LONG TIME SINCE HE QUIT.

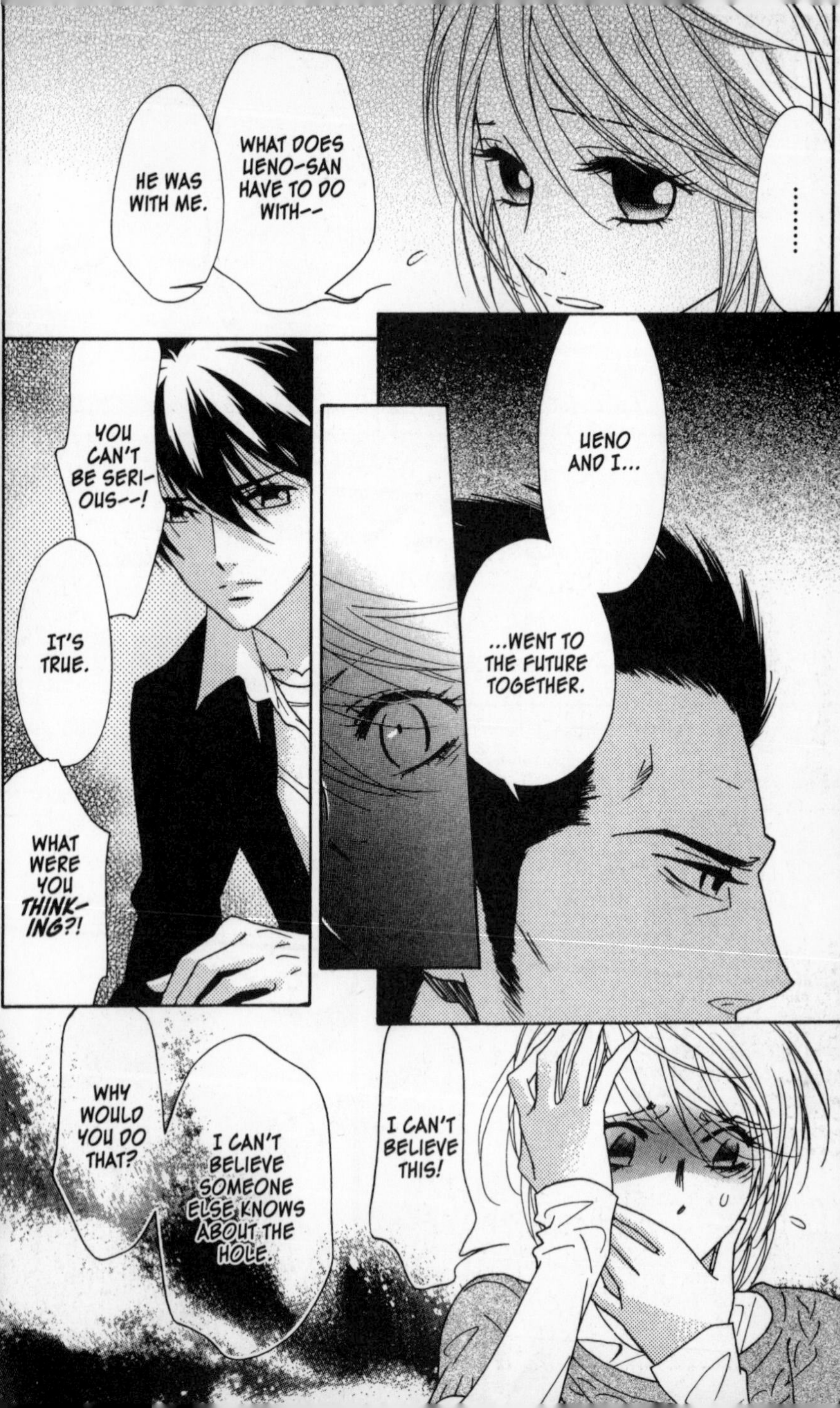
......
WHAT DOES UENO-SAN HAVE TO DO WITH--
HE WAS WITH ME.
UENO AND I...
...WENT TO THE FUTURE TOGETHER.
YOU CAN'T BE SERI-OUS--!
IT'S TRUE.
WHAT WERE YOU *THINKING*?!
I CAN'T BELIEVE THIS!
I CAN'T BELIEVE SOMEONE ELSE KNOWS ABOUT THE HOLE.
WHY WOULD YOU DO THAT?

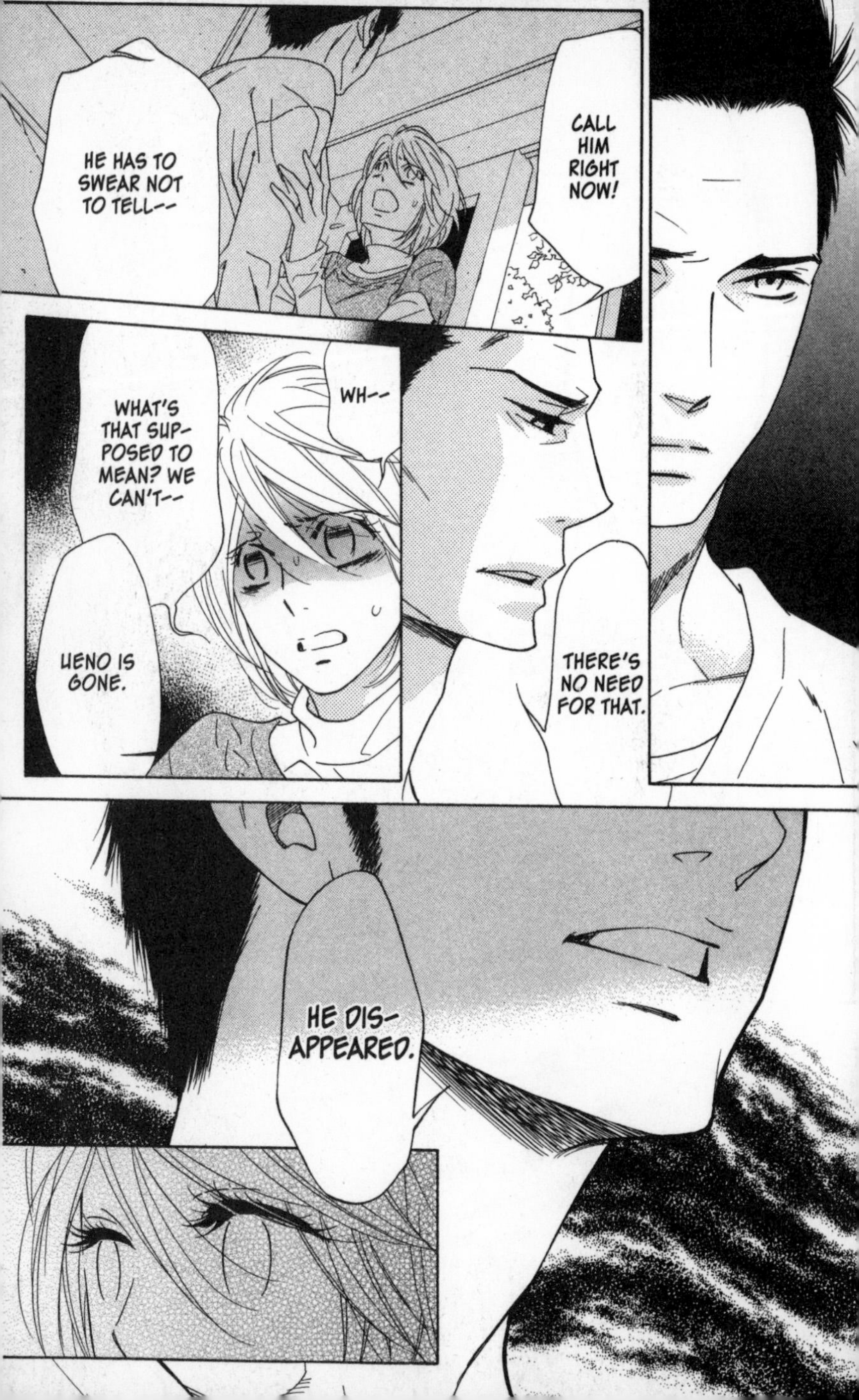
CALL HIM RIGHT NOW!
HE HAS TO SWEAR NOT TO TELL--
THERE'S NO NEED FOR THAT.
WH--
WHAT'S THAT SUP-POSED TO MEAN? WE CAN'T--
UENO IS GONE.
HE DIS-APPEARED.

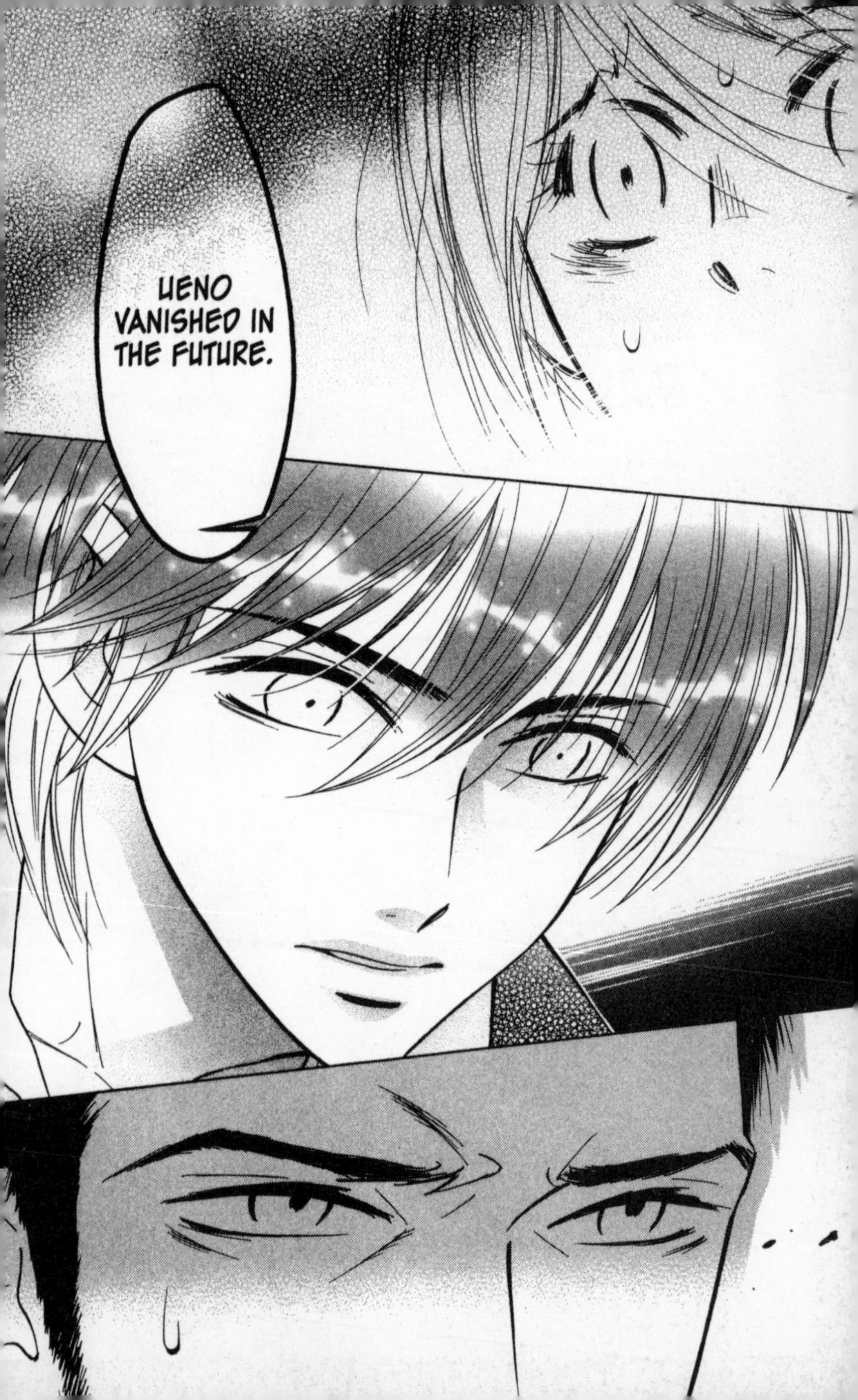
UENO VANISHED IN THE FUTURE.

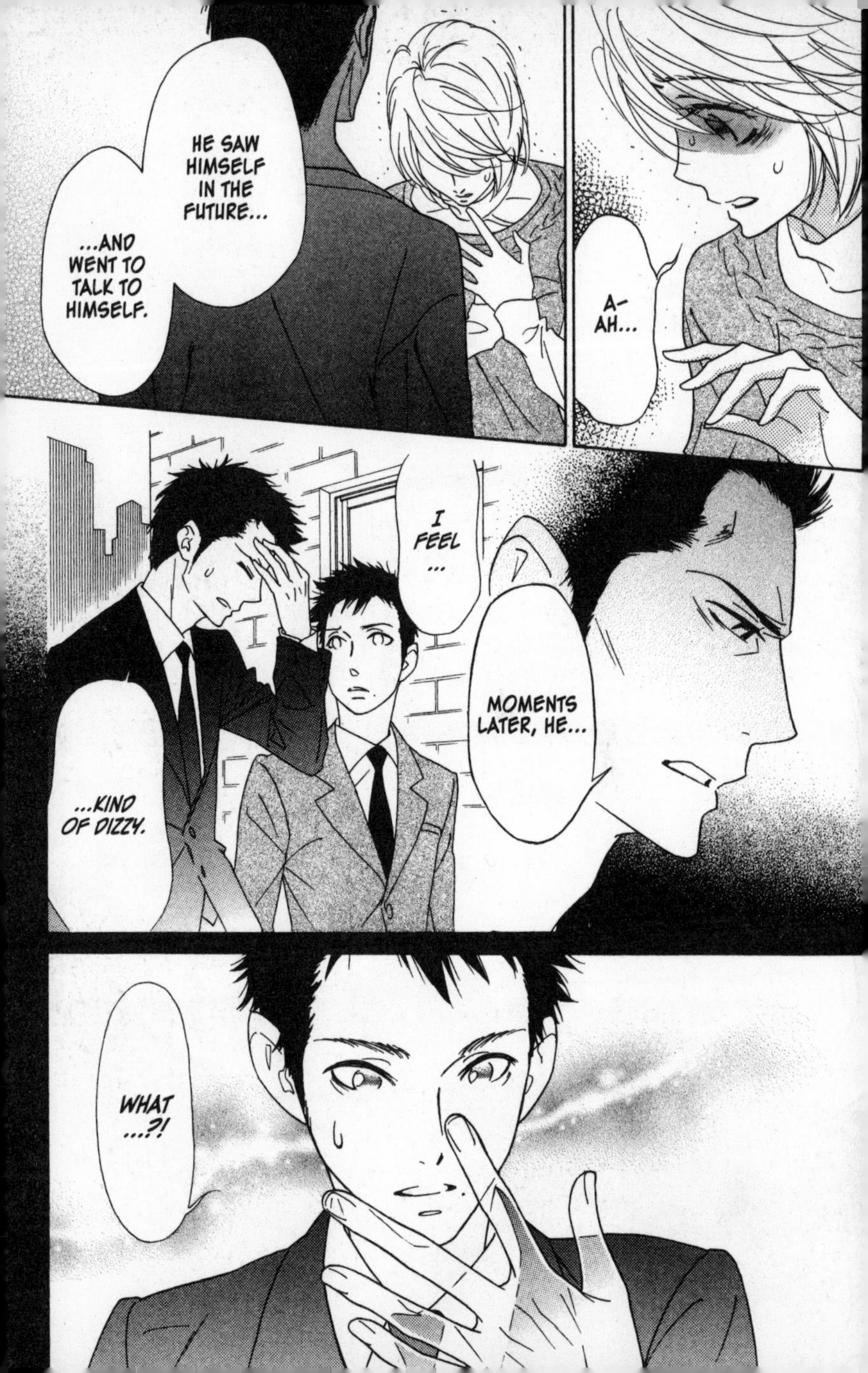
A-AH...
HE SAW HIMSELF IN THE FUTURE...
...AND WENT TO TALK TO HIMSELF.
MOMENTS LATER, HE...
I FEEL ...
...KIND OF DIZZY.
WHAT ...?!

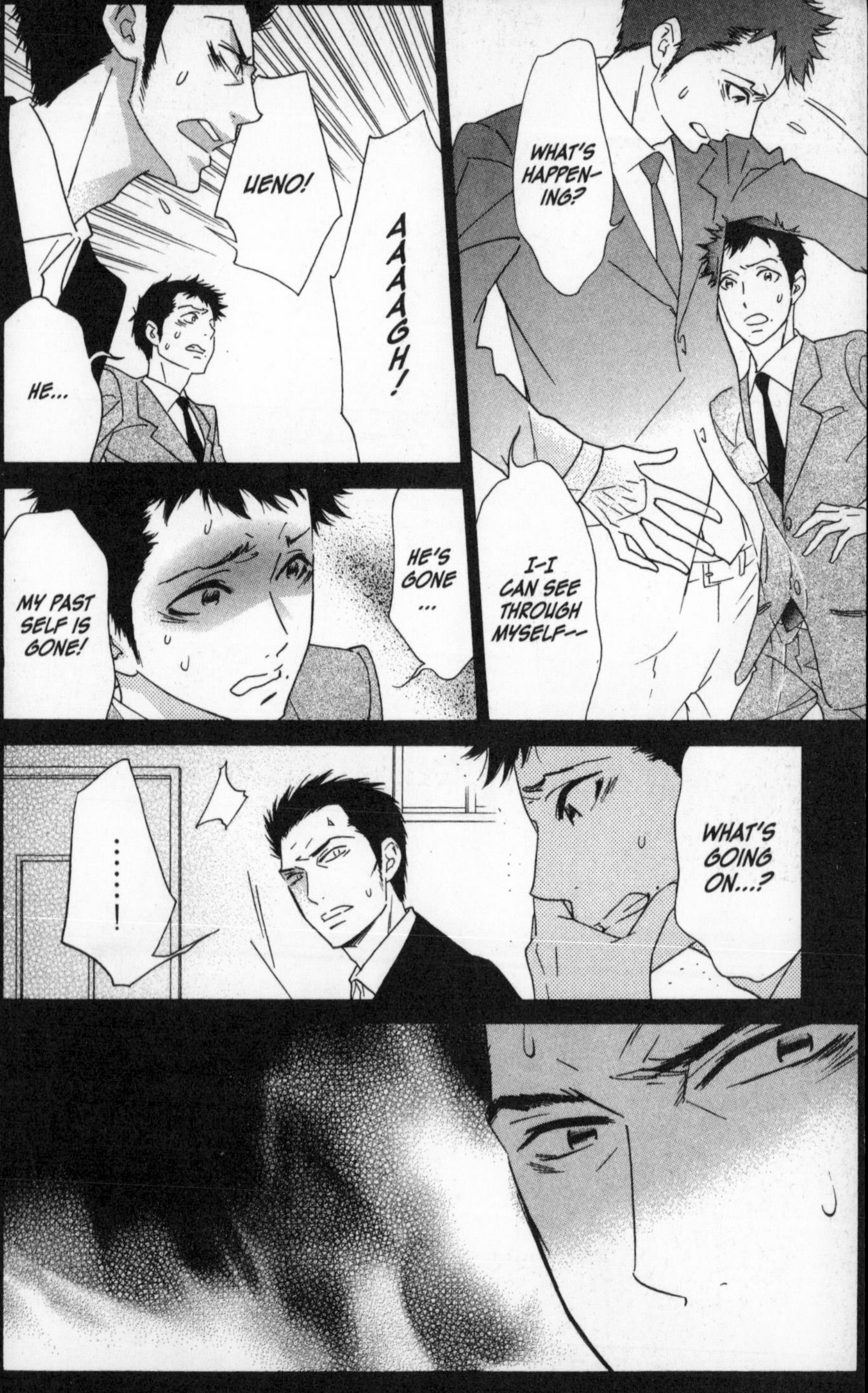
WHAT'S HAPPENING?
I-I CAN SEE THROUGH MYSELF--
AAAAGH!
UENO!
HE...
HE'S GONE ...
MY PAST SELF IS GONE!
WHAT'S GOING ON...?
......!

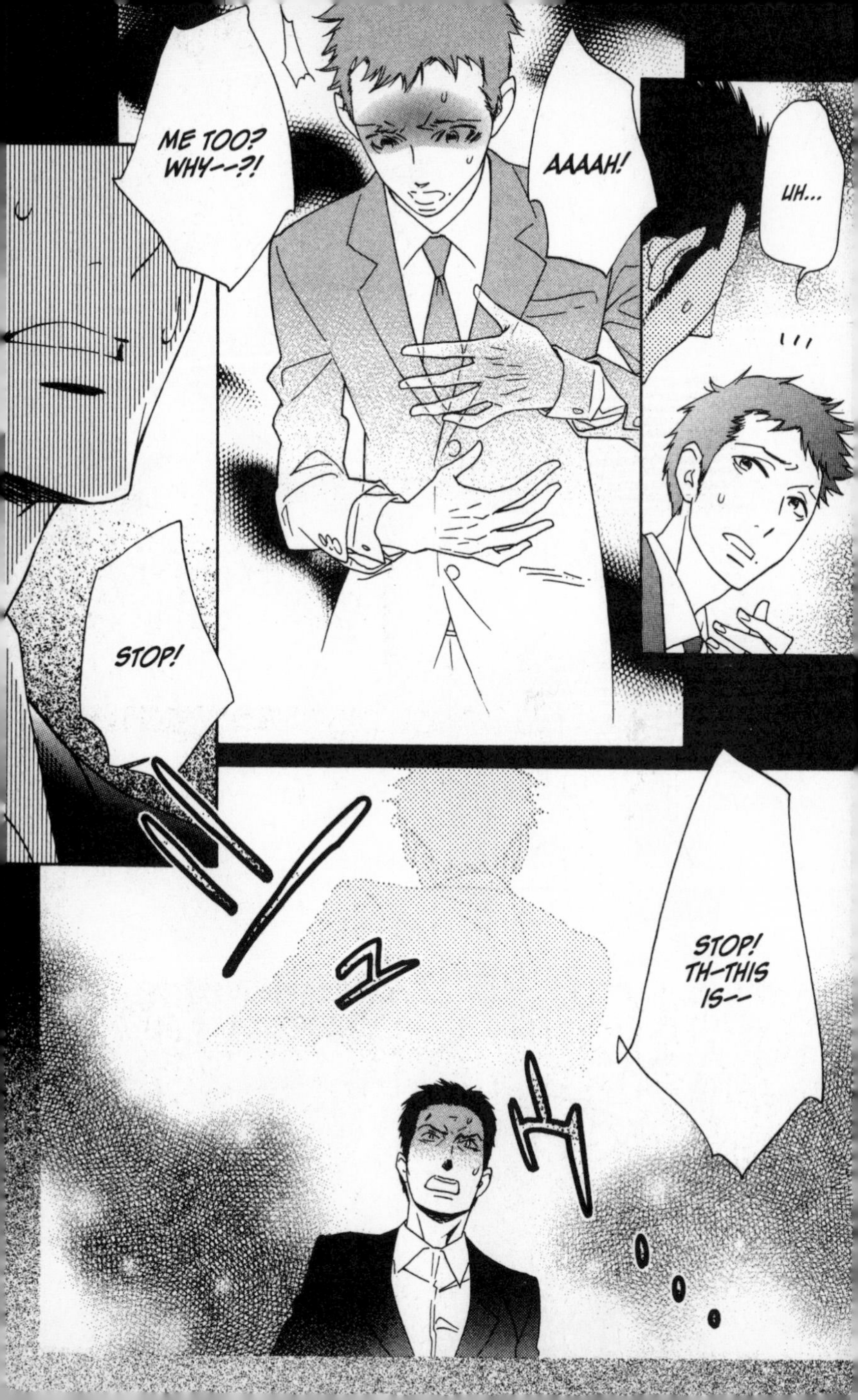
UH...
AAAAH!
ME TOO? WHY--?!
STOP!
STOP! TH-THIS IS--

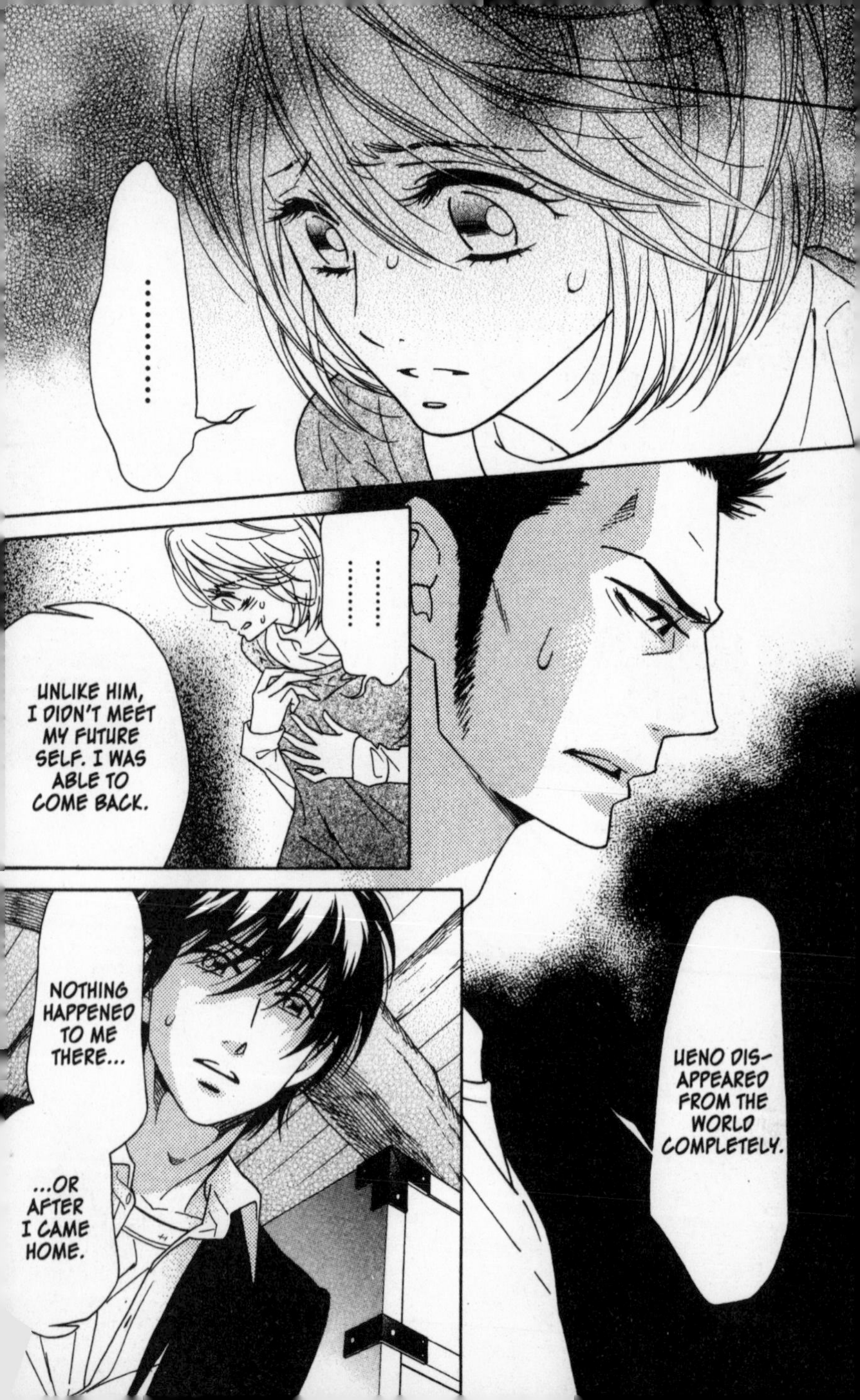
......
UENO DISAPPEARED FROM THE WORLD COMPLETELY.
......
UNLIKE HIM, I DIDN'T MEET MY FUTURE SELF. I WAS ABLE TO COME BACK.
NOTHING HAPPENED TO ME THERE...
...OR AFTER I CAME HOME.

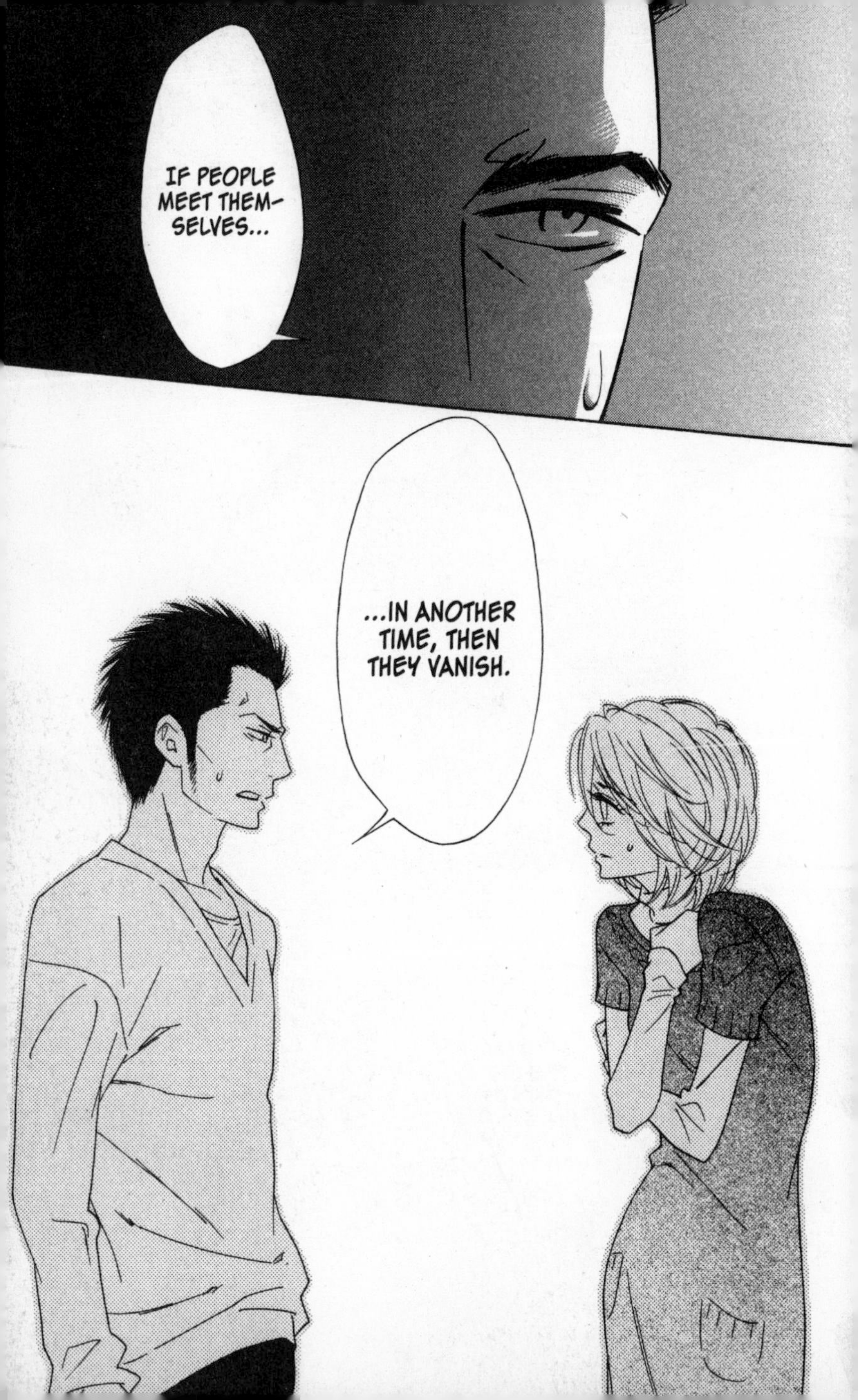
IF PEOPLE MEET THEM-SELVES...
...IN ANOTHER TIME, THEN THEY VANISH.

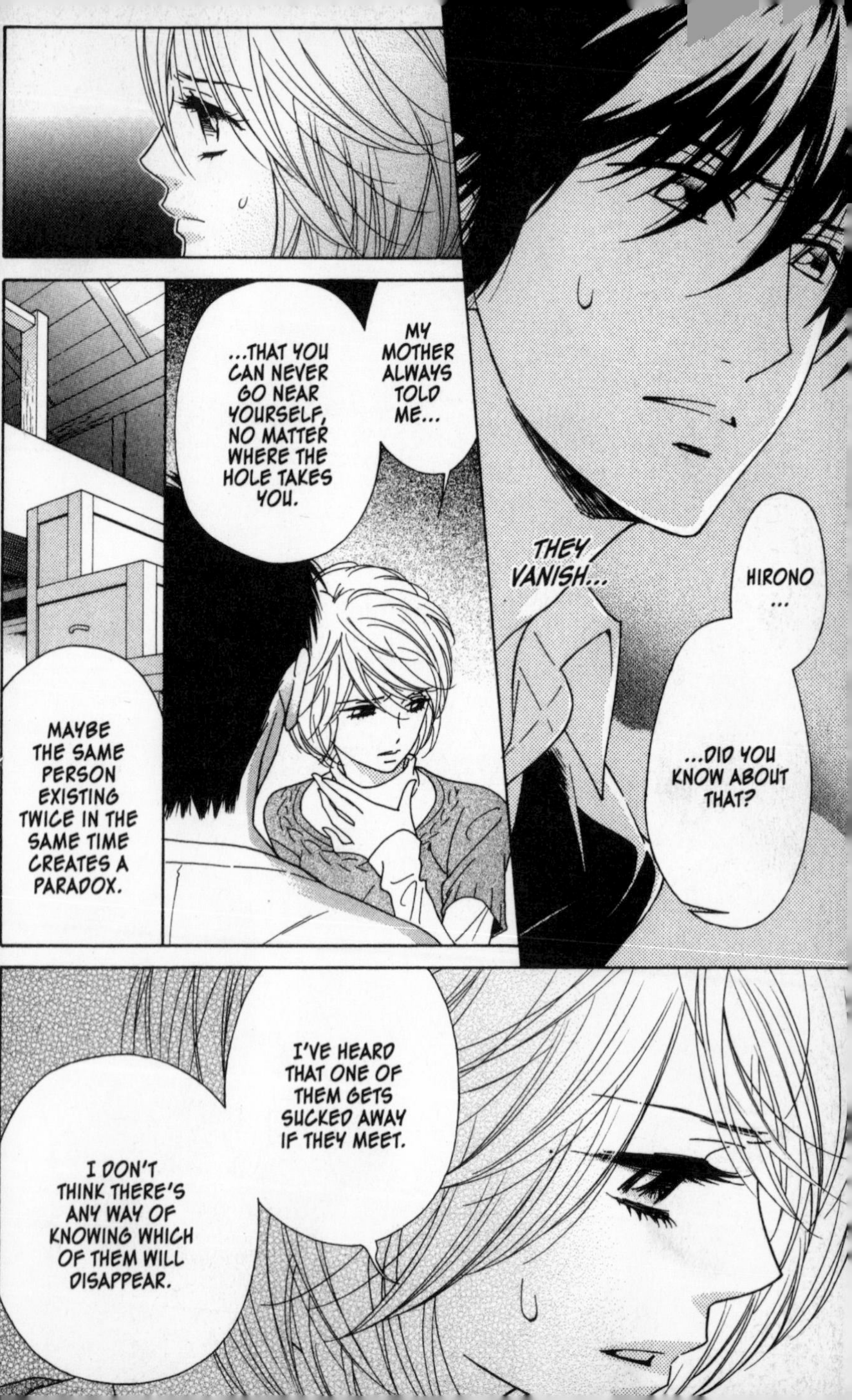
HIRONO ...
...DID YOU KNOW ABOUT THAT?
THEY VANISH...
MY MOTHER ALWAYS TOLD ME...
...THAT YOU CAN NEVER GO NEAR YOURSELF, NO MATTER WHERE THE HOLE TAKES YOU.
MAYBE THE SAME PERSON EXISTING TWICE IN THE SAME TIME CREATES A PARADOX.
I'VE HEARD THAT ONE OF THEM GETS SUCKED AWAY IF THEY MEET.
I DON'T THINK THERE'S ANY WAY OF KNOWING WHICH OF THEM WILL DISAPPEAR.

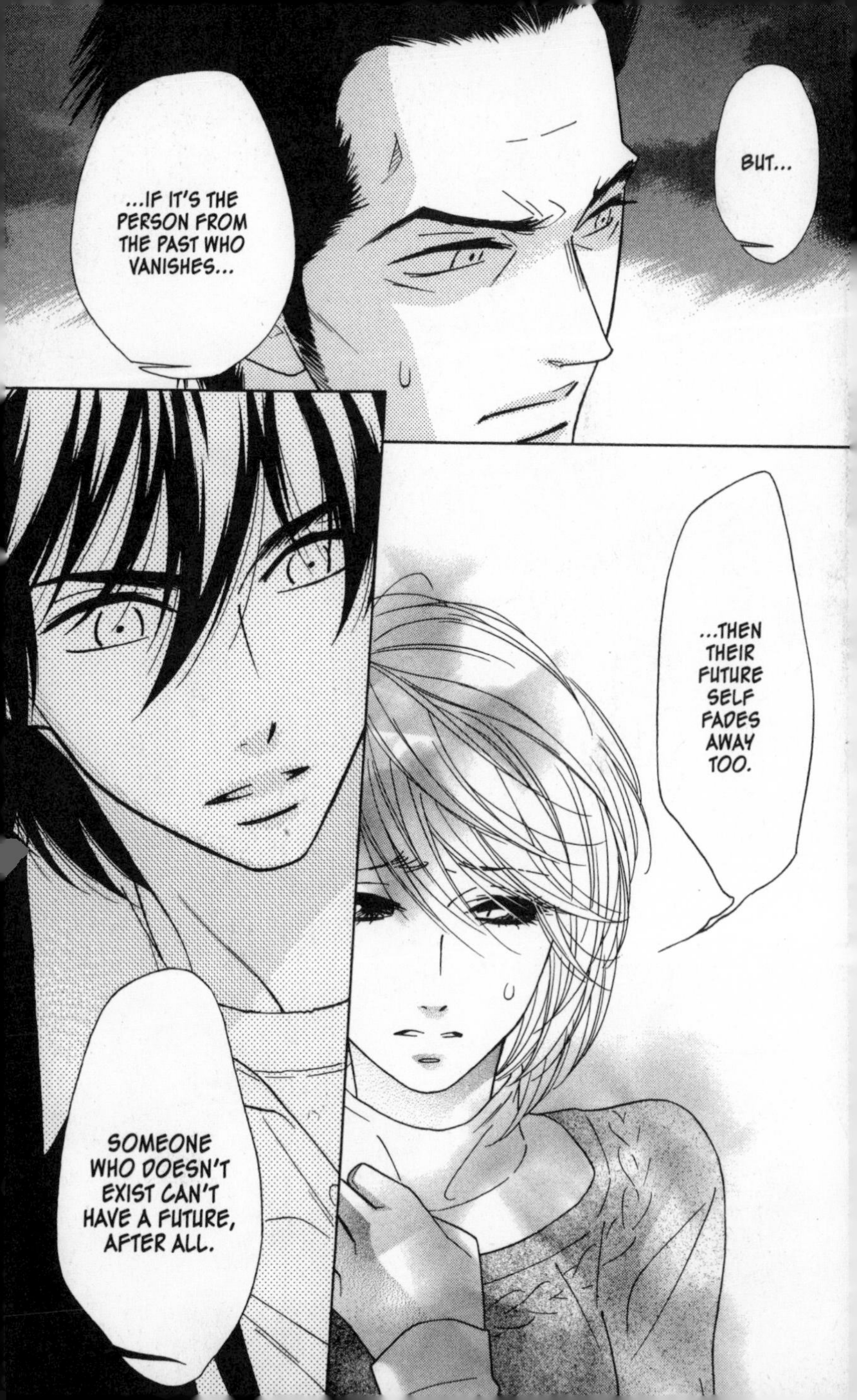
BUT...
...IF IT'S THE PERSON FROM THE PAST WHO VANISHES...
...THEN THEIR FUTURE SELF FADES AWAY TOO.
SOMEONE WHO DOESN'T EXIST CAN'T HAVE A FUTURE, AFTER ALL.

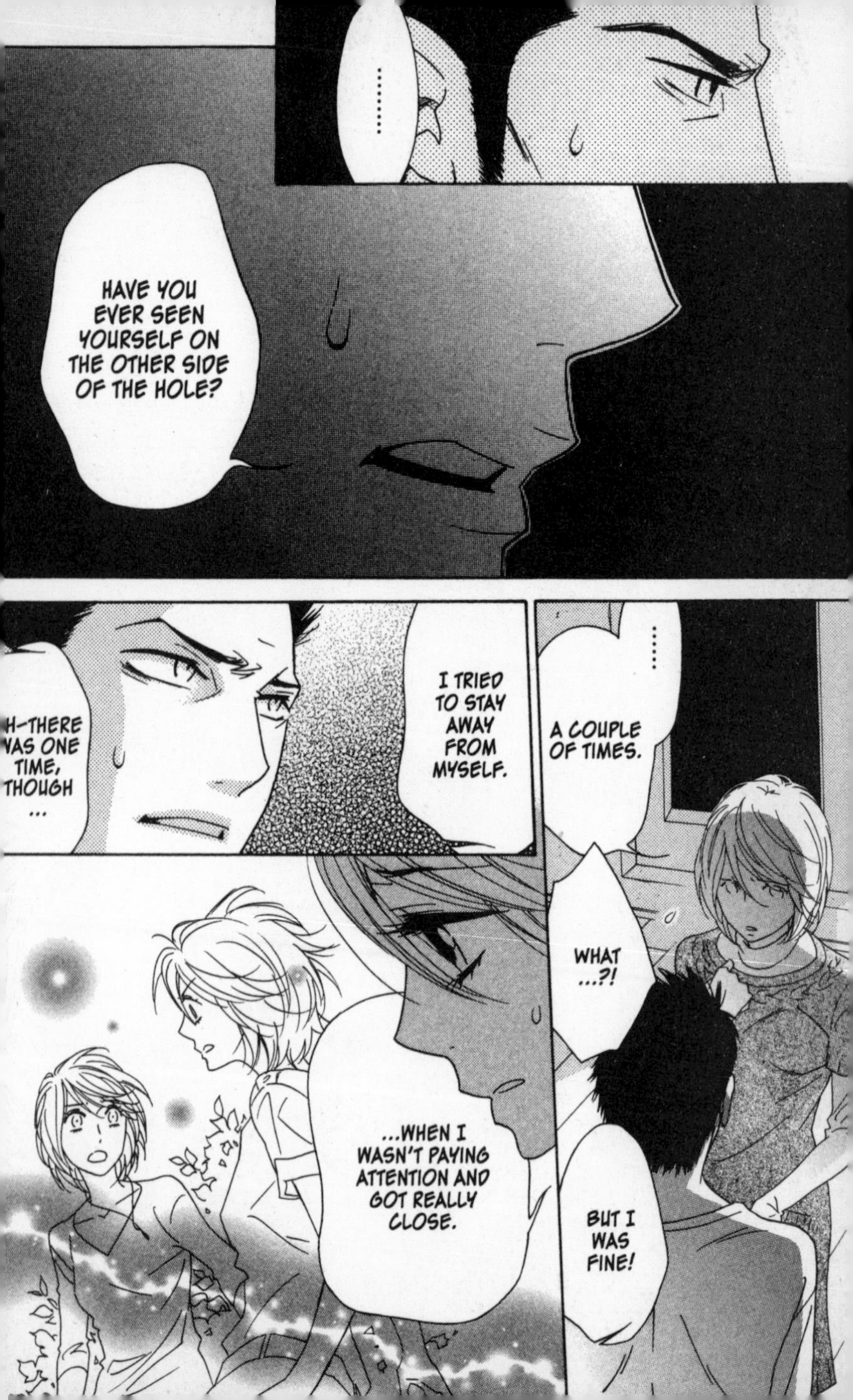
......
HAVE YOU EVER SEEN YOURSELF ON THE OTHER SIDE OF THE HOLE?
......
A COUPLE OF TIMES.
WHAT ...?!
BUT I WAS FINE!
I TRIED TO STAY AWAY FROM MYSELF.
H-THERE WAS ONE TIME, THOUGH ...
...WHEN I WASN'T PAYING ATTENTION AND GOT REALLY CLOSE.

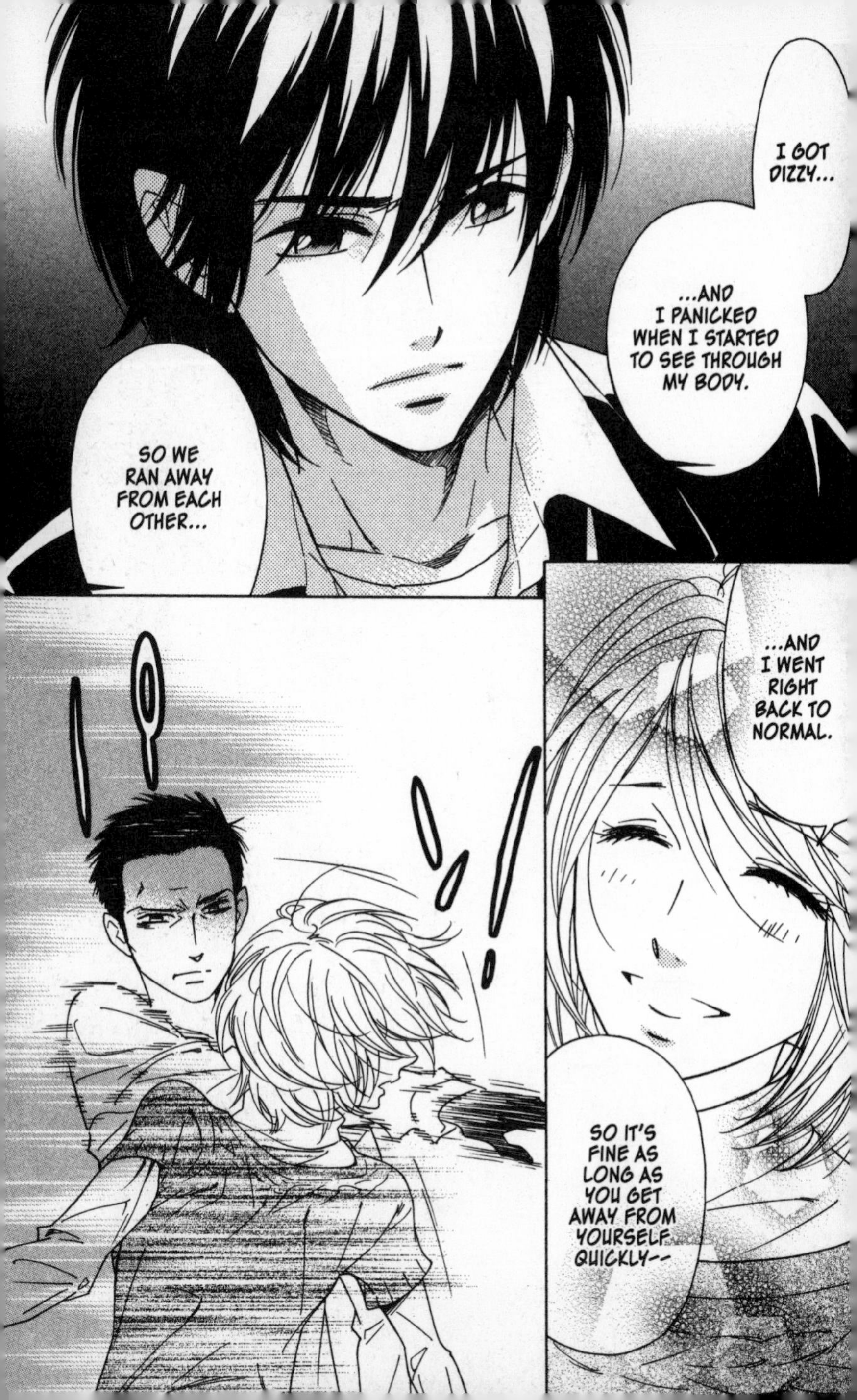
I GOT DIZZY...
...AND I PANICKED WHEN I STARTED TO SEE THROUGH MY BODY.
SO WE RAN AWAY FROM EACH OTHER...
...AND I WENT RIGHT BACK TO NORMAL.
SO IT'S FINE AS LONG AS YOU GET AWAY FROM YOURSELF QUICKLY--
!!

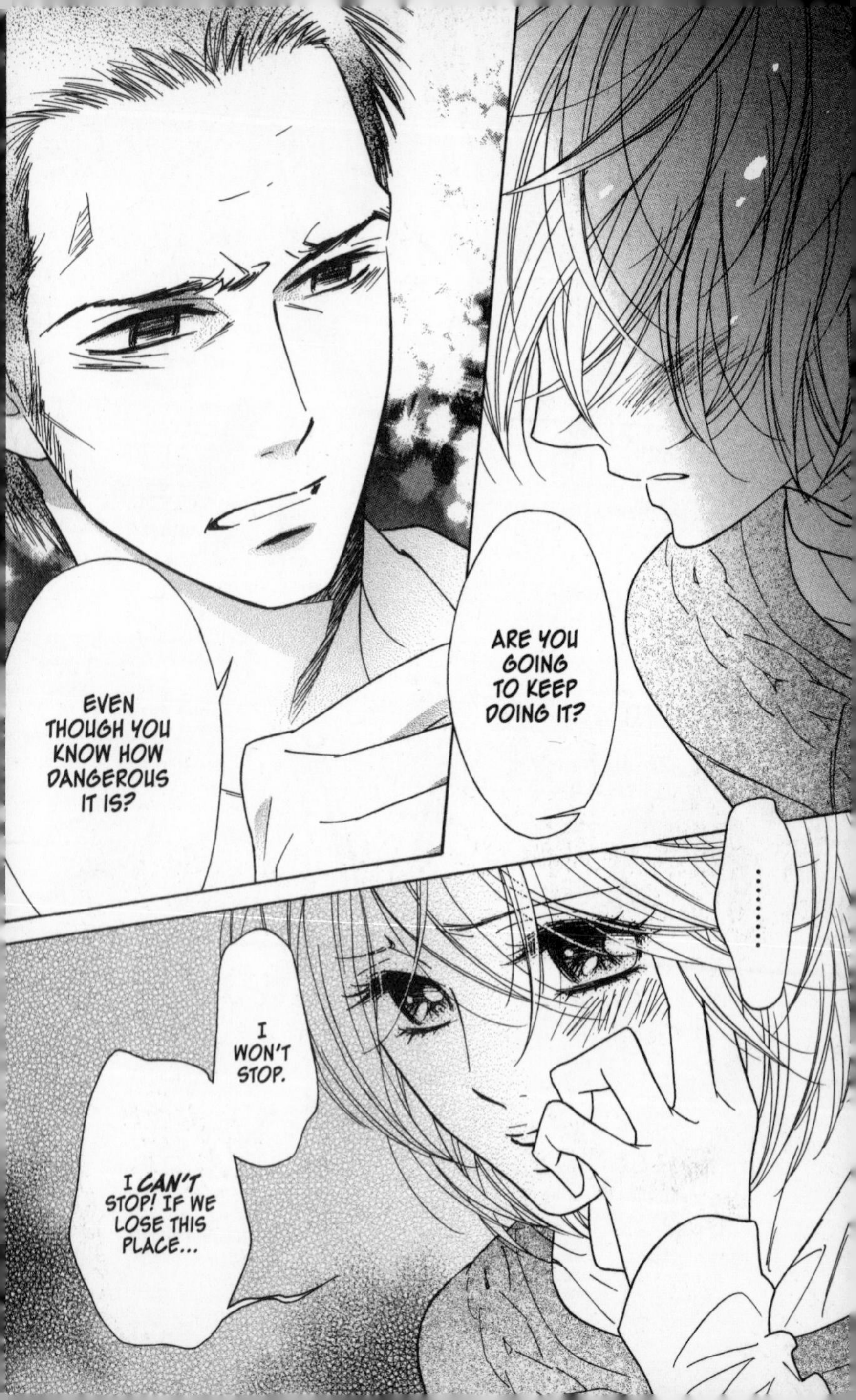
ARE YOU GOING TO KEEP DOING IT?
EVEN THOUGH YOU KNOW HOW DANGEROUS IT IS?
......
I WON'T STOP.
I *CAN'T* STOP! IF WE LOSE THIS PLACE...

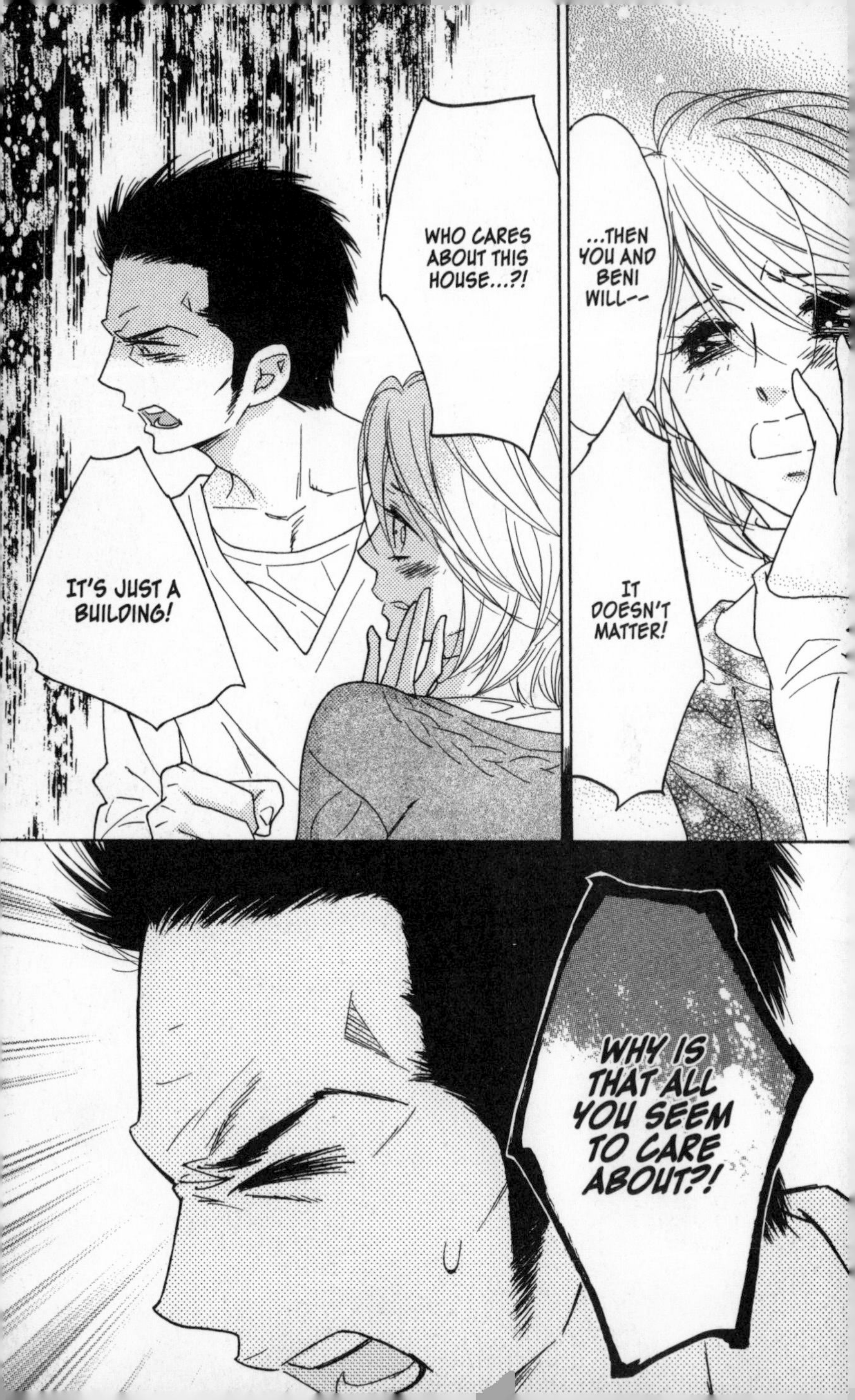
...THEN YOU AND BENI WILL--
IT DOESN'T MATTER!
WHO CARES ABOUT THIS HOUSE...?!
IT'S JUST A BUILDING!
WHY IS THAT ALL YOU SEEM TO CARE ABOUT?!

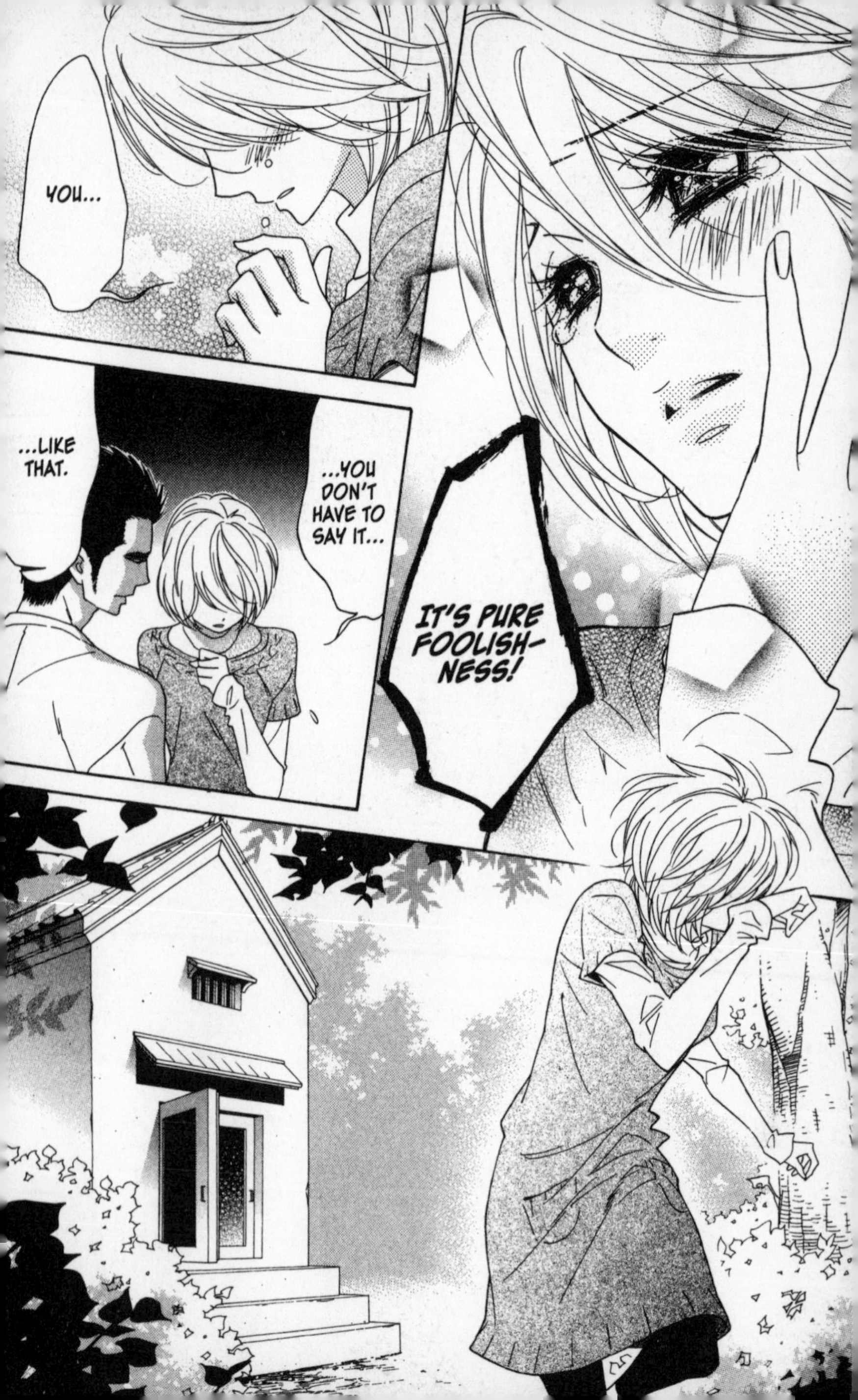
IT'S PURE FOOLISHNESS!
YOU...
...YOU DON'T HAVE TO SAY IT...
...LIKE THAT.

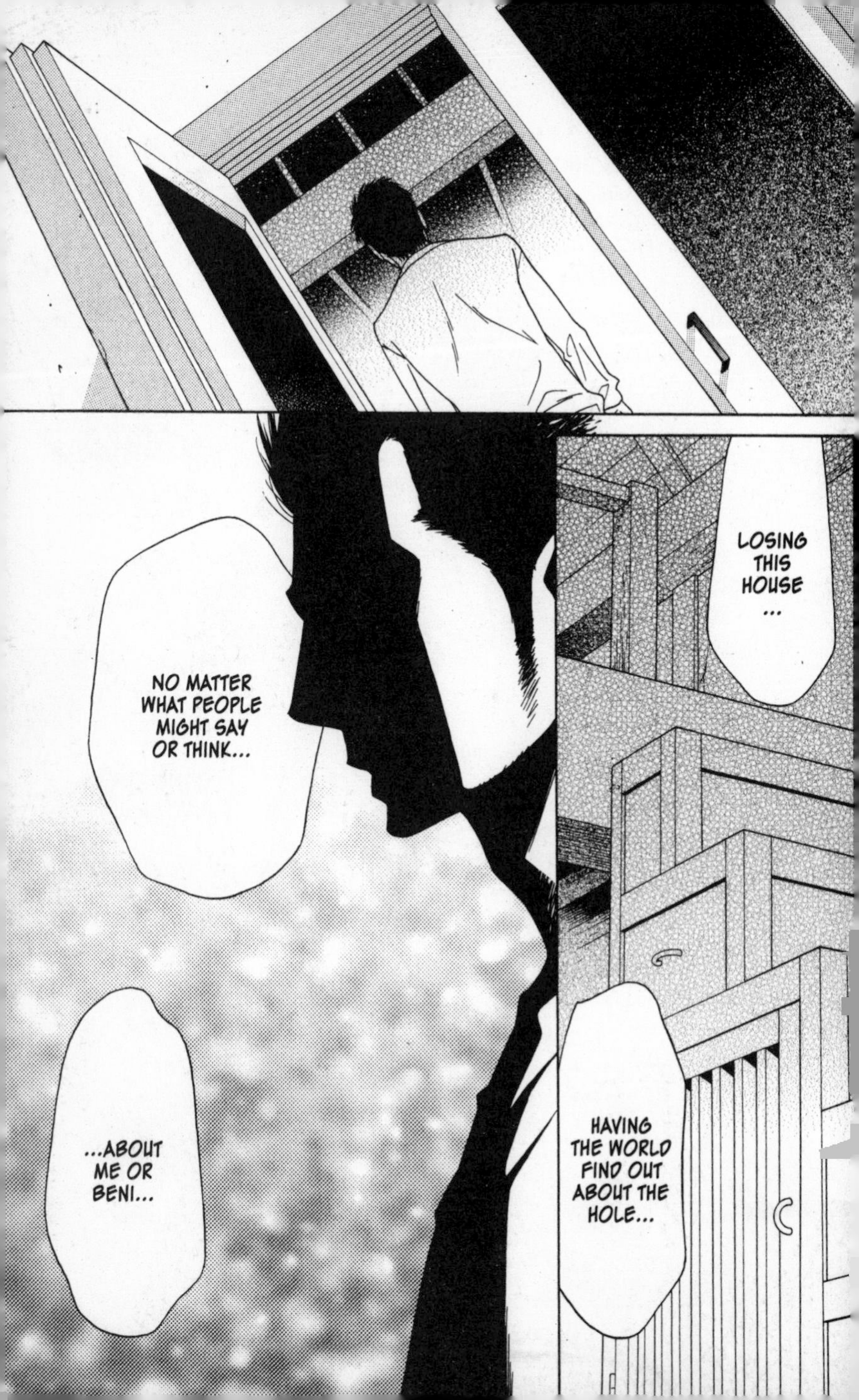
LOSING THIS HOUSE ...
HAVING THE WORLD FIND OUT ABOUT THE HOLE...
NO MATTER WHAT PEOPLE MIGHT SAY OR THINK...
...ABOUT ME OR BENI...

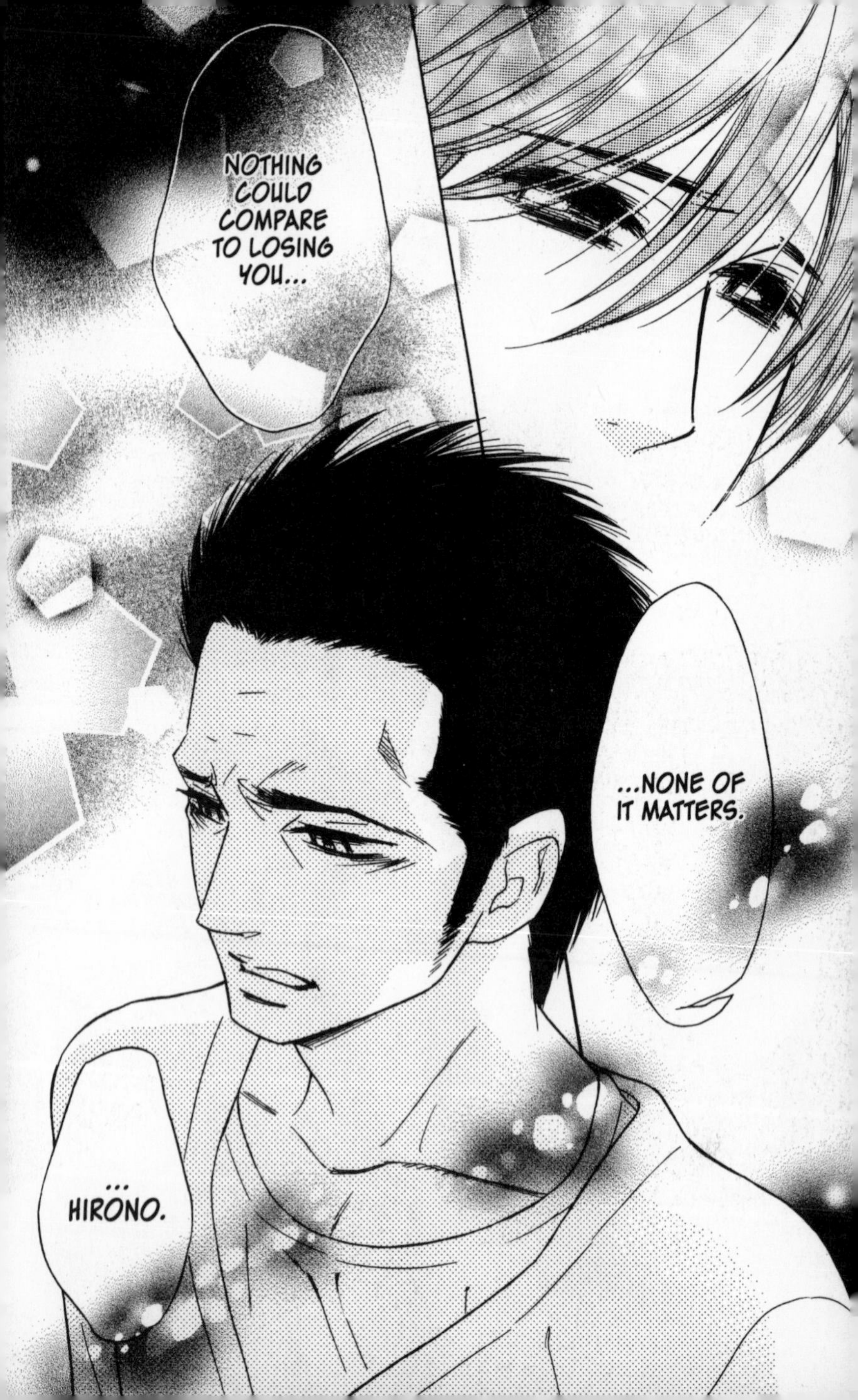
NOTHING COULD COMPARE TO LOSING YOU...
...NONE OF IT MATTERS.
...HIRONO.

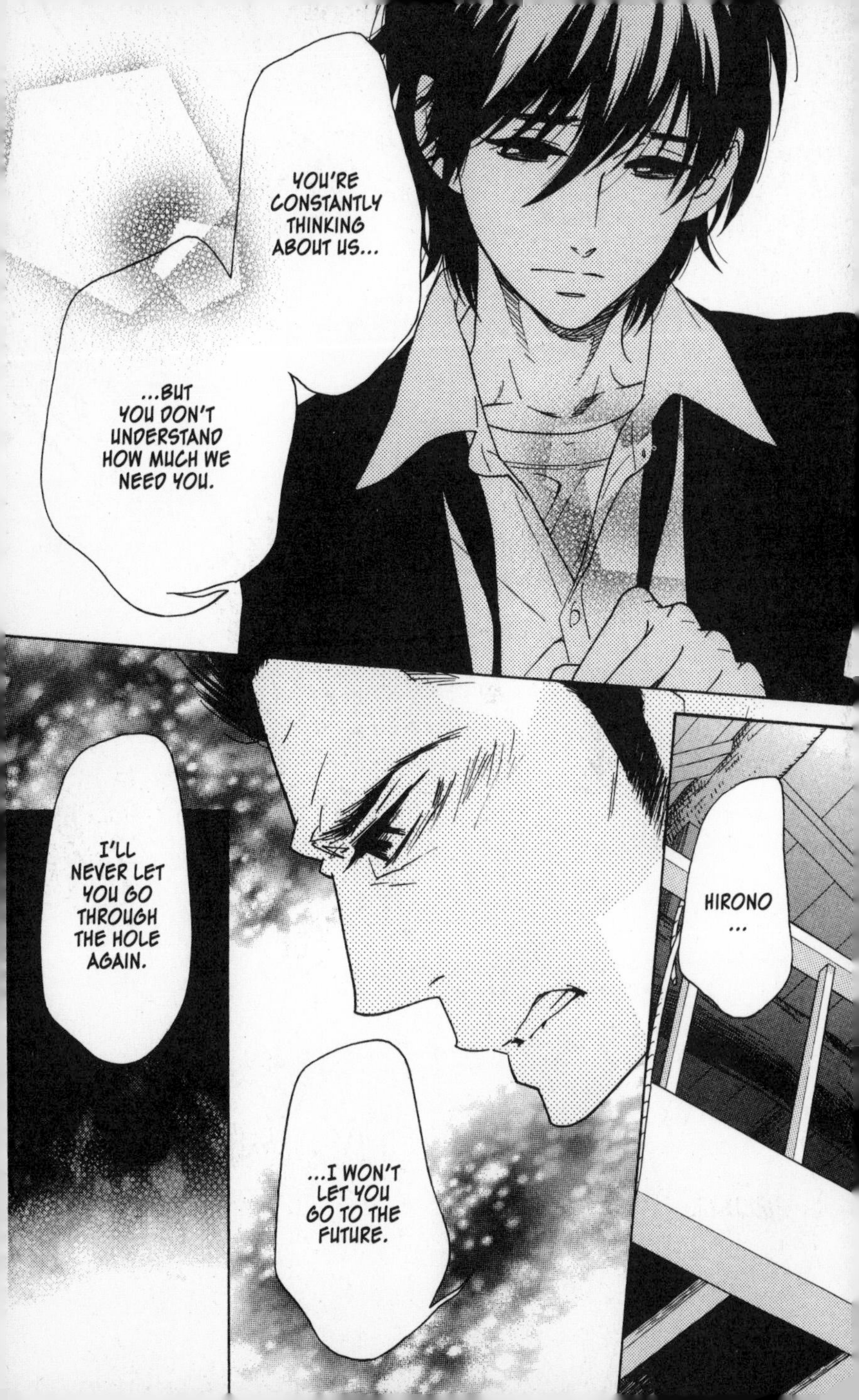
YOU'RE CONSTANTLY THINKING ABOUT US...
...BUT YOU DON'T UNDERSTAND HOW MUCH WE NEED YOU.
HIRONO ...
I'LL NEVER LET YOU GO THROUGH THE HOLE AGAIN.
...I WON'T LET YOU GO TO THE FUTURE.

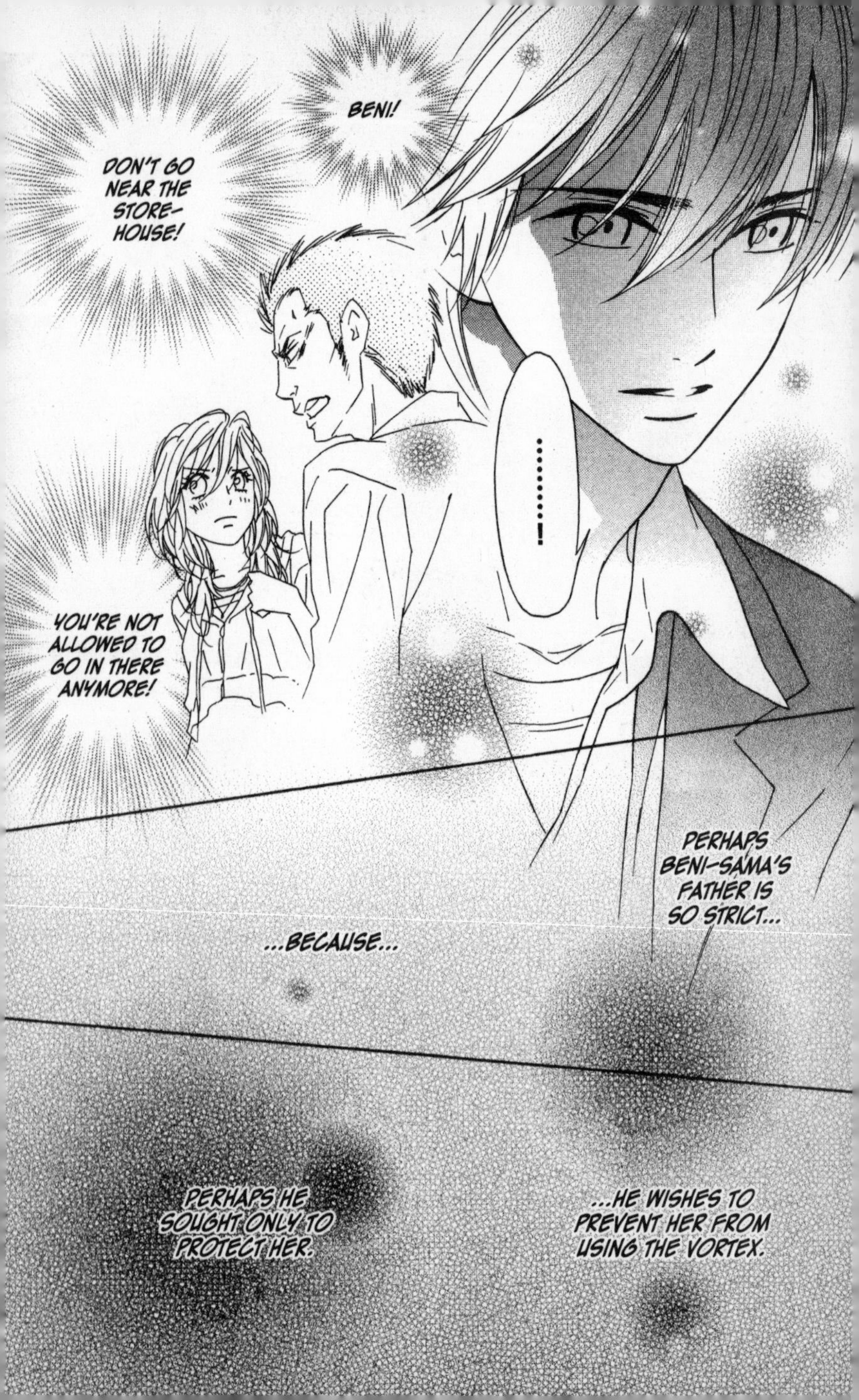
BENI!
DON'T GO NEAR THE STORE-HOUSE!
......!
YOU'RE NOT ALLOWED TO GO IN THERE ANYMORE!
PERHAPS BENI-SAMA'S FATHER IS SO STRICT...
...BECAUSE...
...HE WISHES TO PREVENT HER FROM USING THE VORTEX.
PERHAPS HE SOUGHT ONLY TO PROTECT HER.

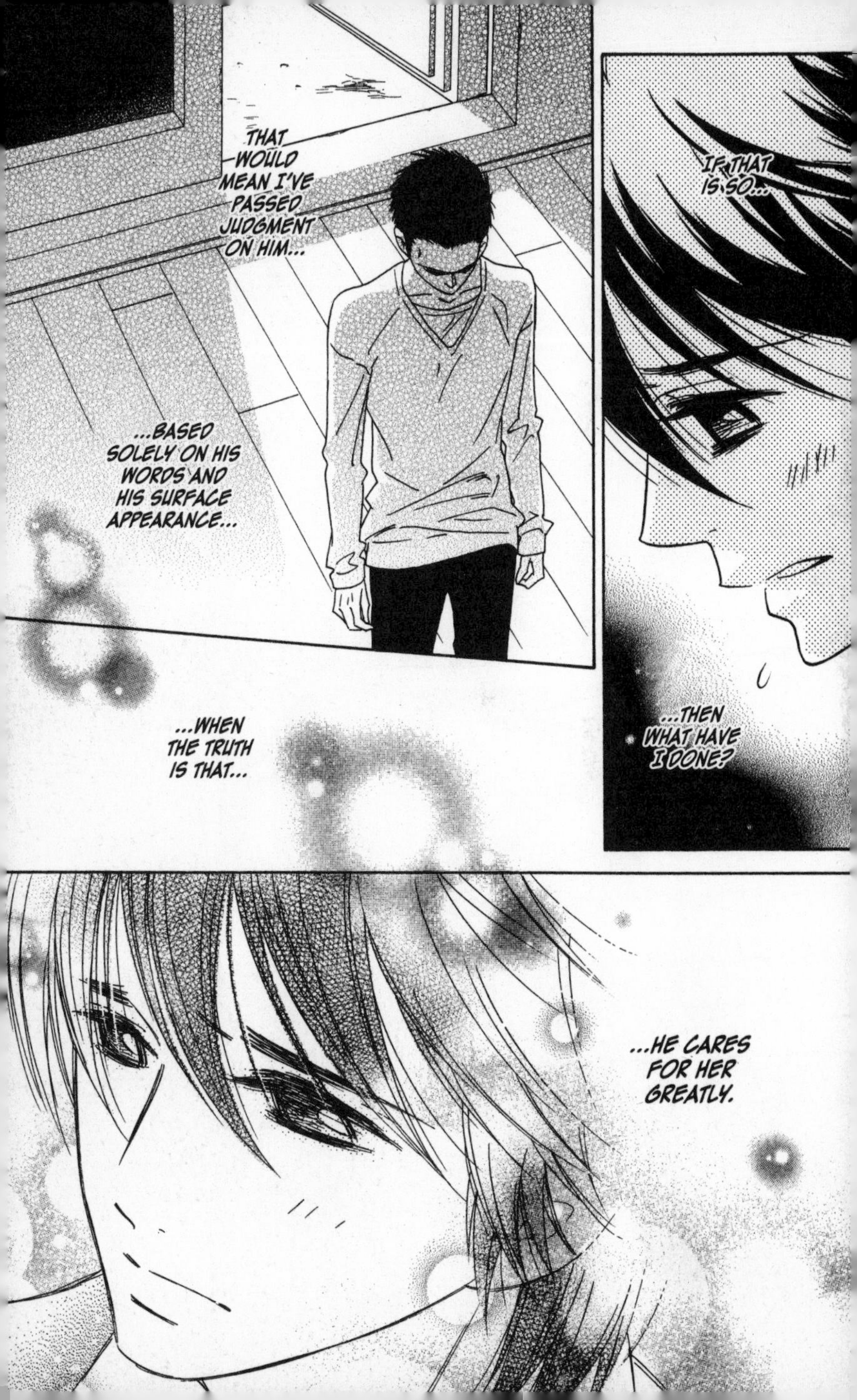
IF THAT IS SO...
...THEN WHAT HAVE I DONE?
THAT WOULD MEAN I'VE PASSED JUDGMENT ON HIM...
...BASED SOLELY ON HIS WORDS AND HIS SURFACE APPEARANCE...
...WHEN THE TRUTH IS THAT...
...HE CARES FOR HER GREATLY.

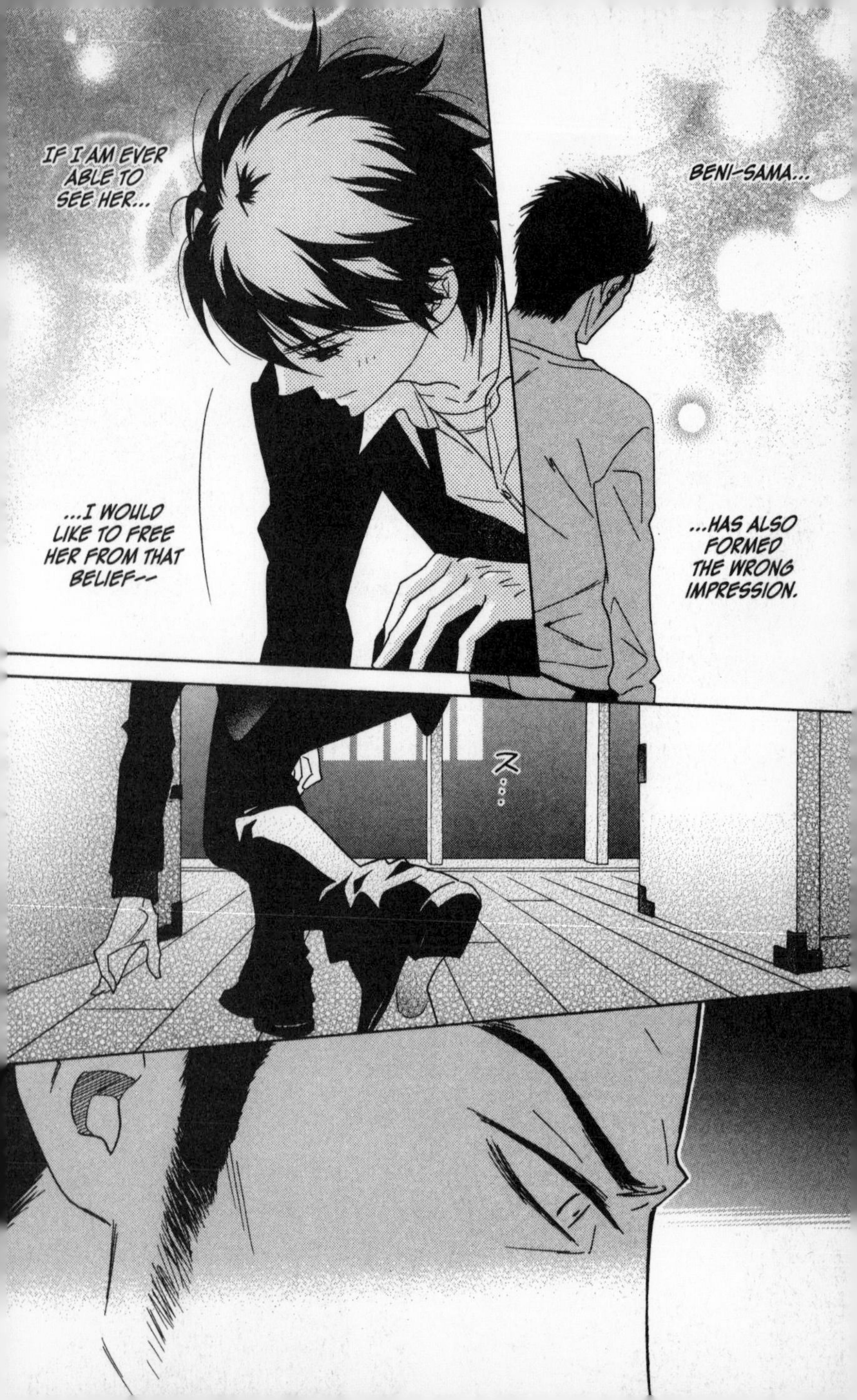
BENI-SAMA...
...HAS ALSO FORMED THE WRONG IMPRESSION.
IF I AM EVER ABLE TO SEE HER...
...I WOULD LIKE TO FREE HER FROM THAT BELIEF--
ス...

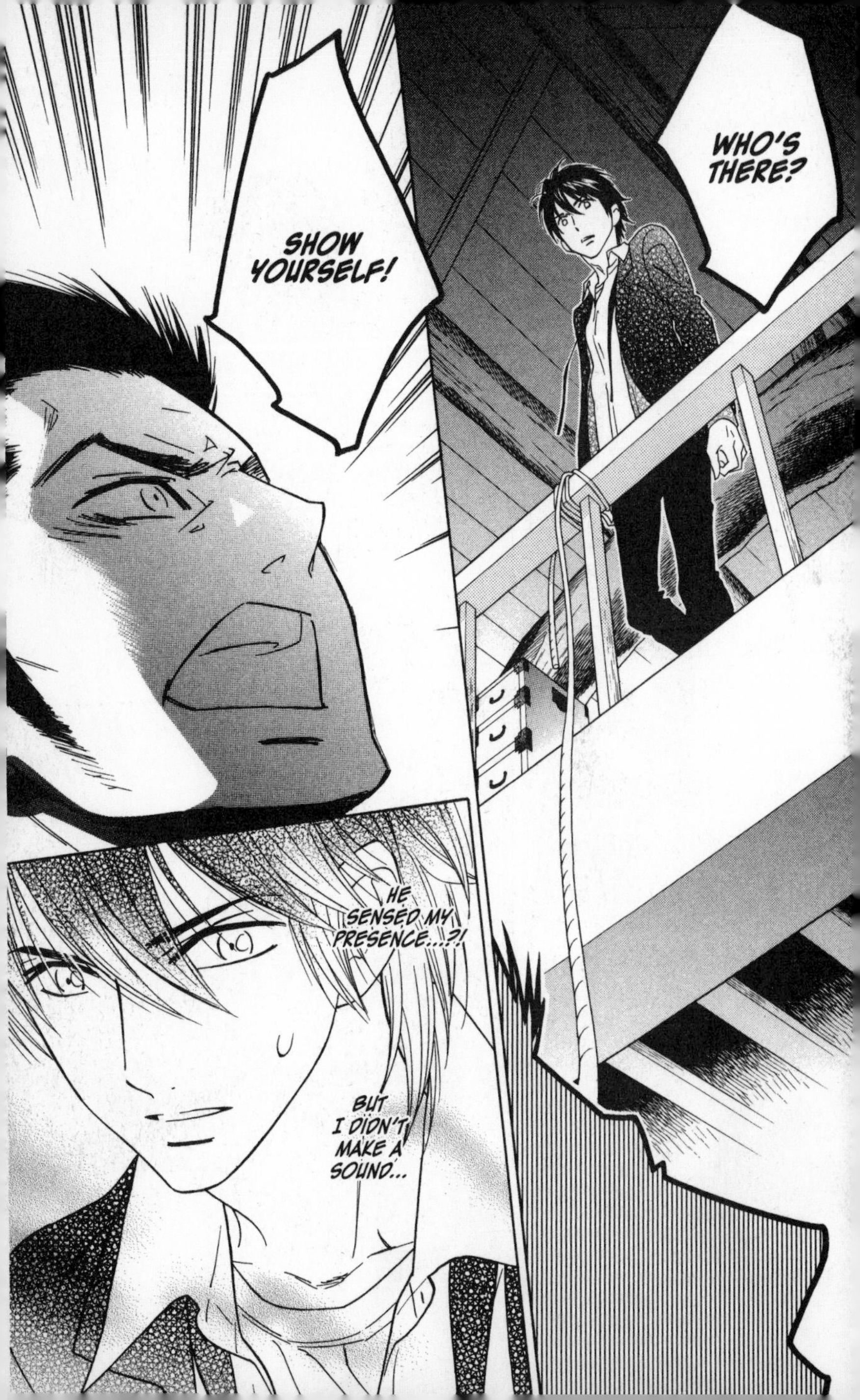
WHO'S THERE?
SHOW YOURSELF!
HE SENSED MY PRESENCE...?!
BUT I DIDN'T MAKE A SOUND...

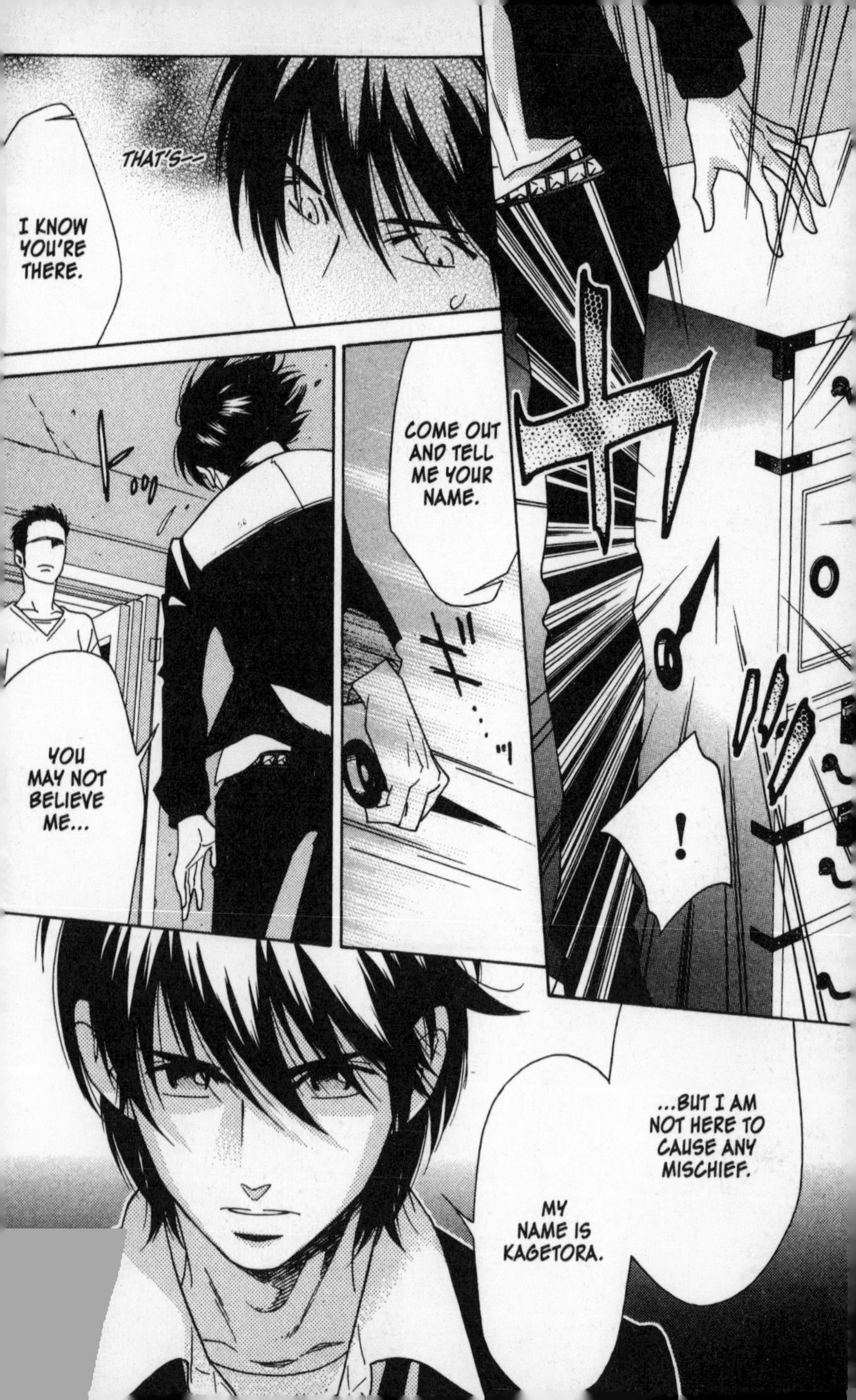
!
THAT'S--
I KNOW YOU'RE THERE.
COME OUT AND TELL ME YOUR NAME.
YOU MAY NOT BELIEVE ME...
...BUT I AM NOT HERE TO CAUSE ANY MISCHIEF.
MY NAME IS KAGETORA.

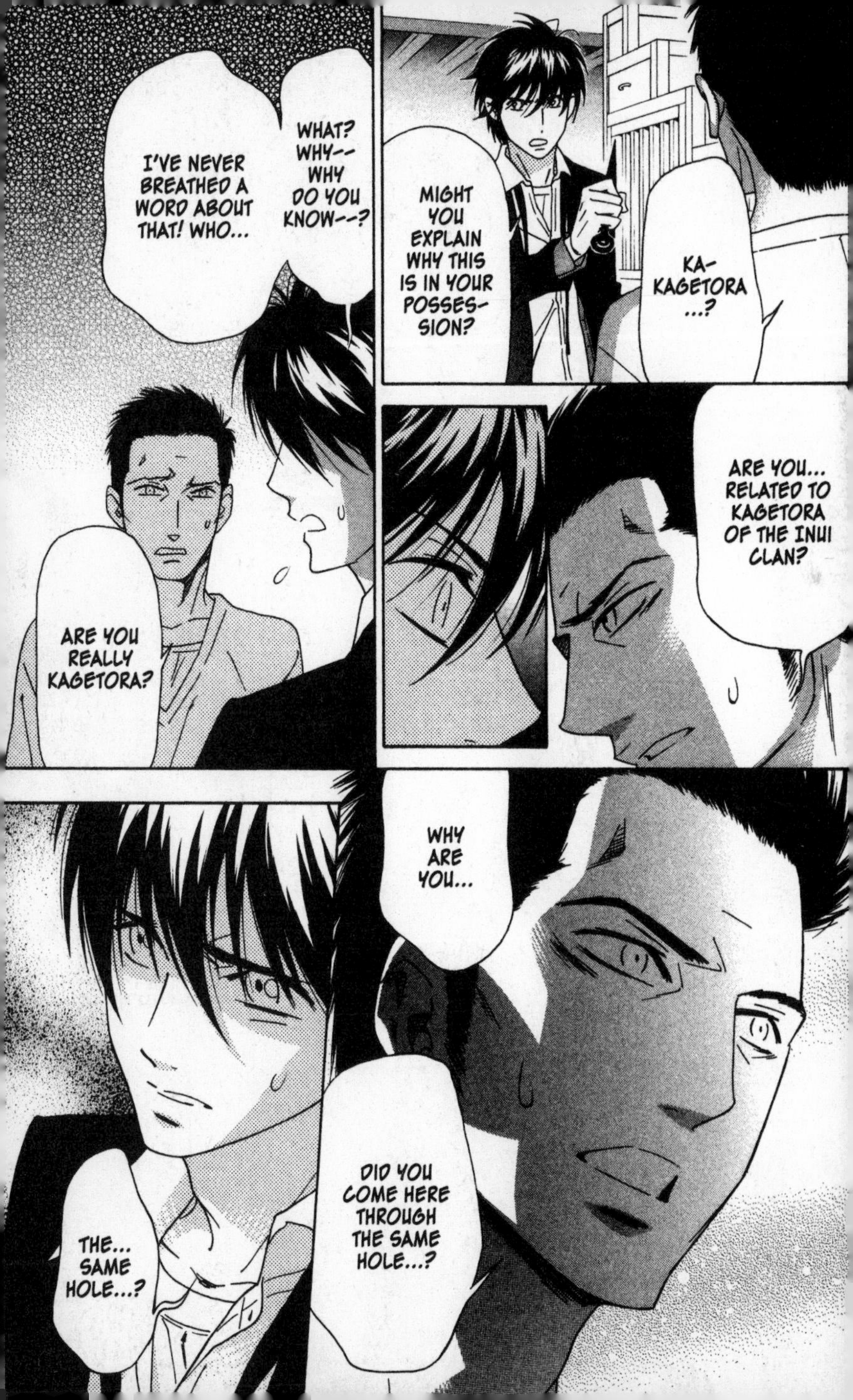
KA-KAGETORA...?
MIGHT YOU EXPLAIN WHY THIS IS IN YOUR POSSESSION?
ARE YOU... RELATED TO KAGETORA OF THE INUI CLAN?
WHAT? WHY--WHY DO YOU KNOW--?
I'VE NEVER BREATHED A WORD ABOUT THAT! WHO...
ARE YOU REALLY KAGETORA?
WHY ARE YOU...
DID YOU COME HERE THROUGH THE SAME HOLE...?
THE... SAME HOLE...?

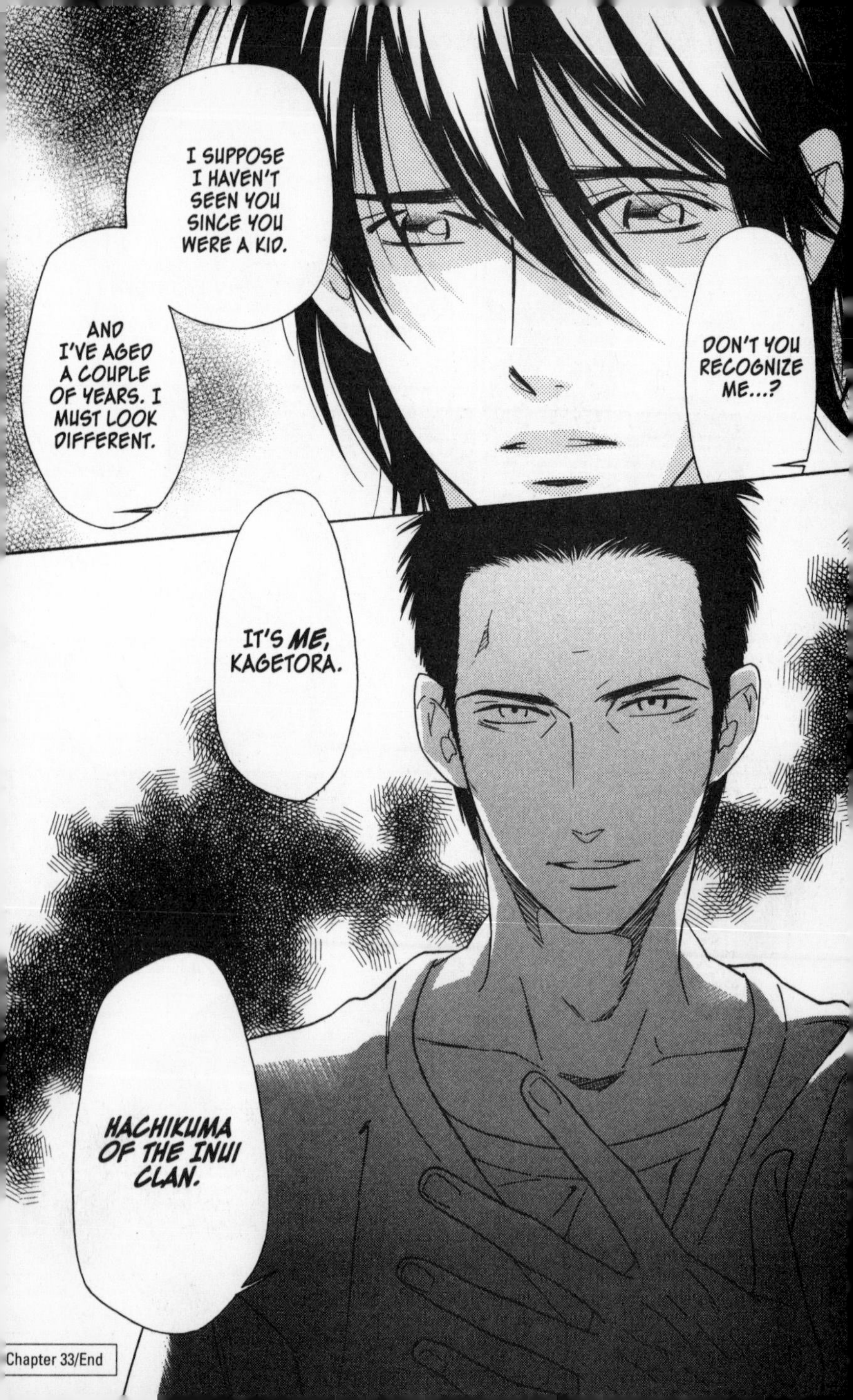
DON'T YOU RECOGNIZE ME...?
I SUPPOSE I HAVEN'T SEEN YOU SINCE YOU WERE A KID.
AND I'VE AGED A COUPLE OF YEARS. I MUST LOOK DIFFERENT.
IT'S *ME*, KAGETORA.
HACHIKUMA OF THE INUI CLAN.

Chapter 33/End

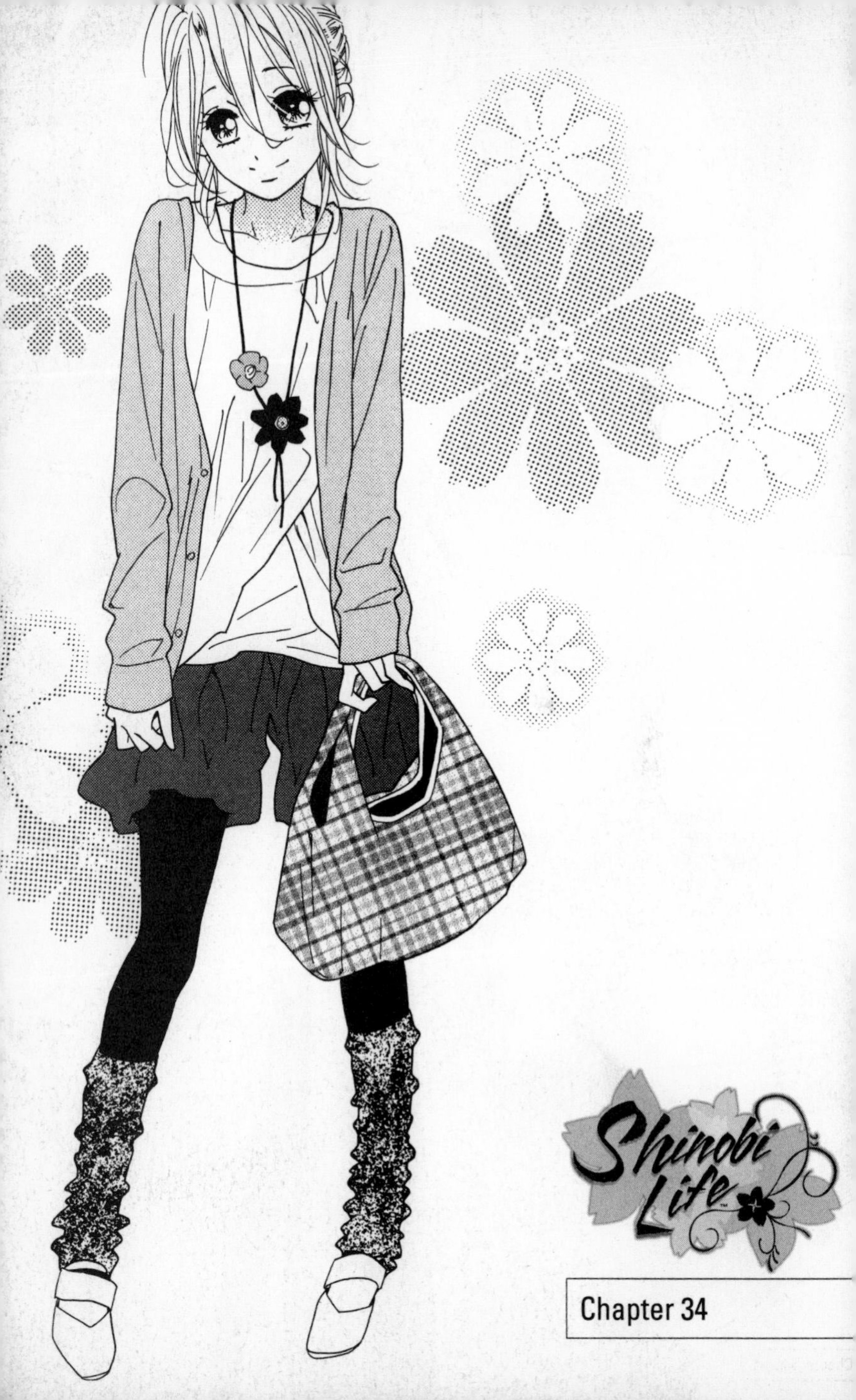

Shinobi Life

Chapter 34

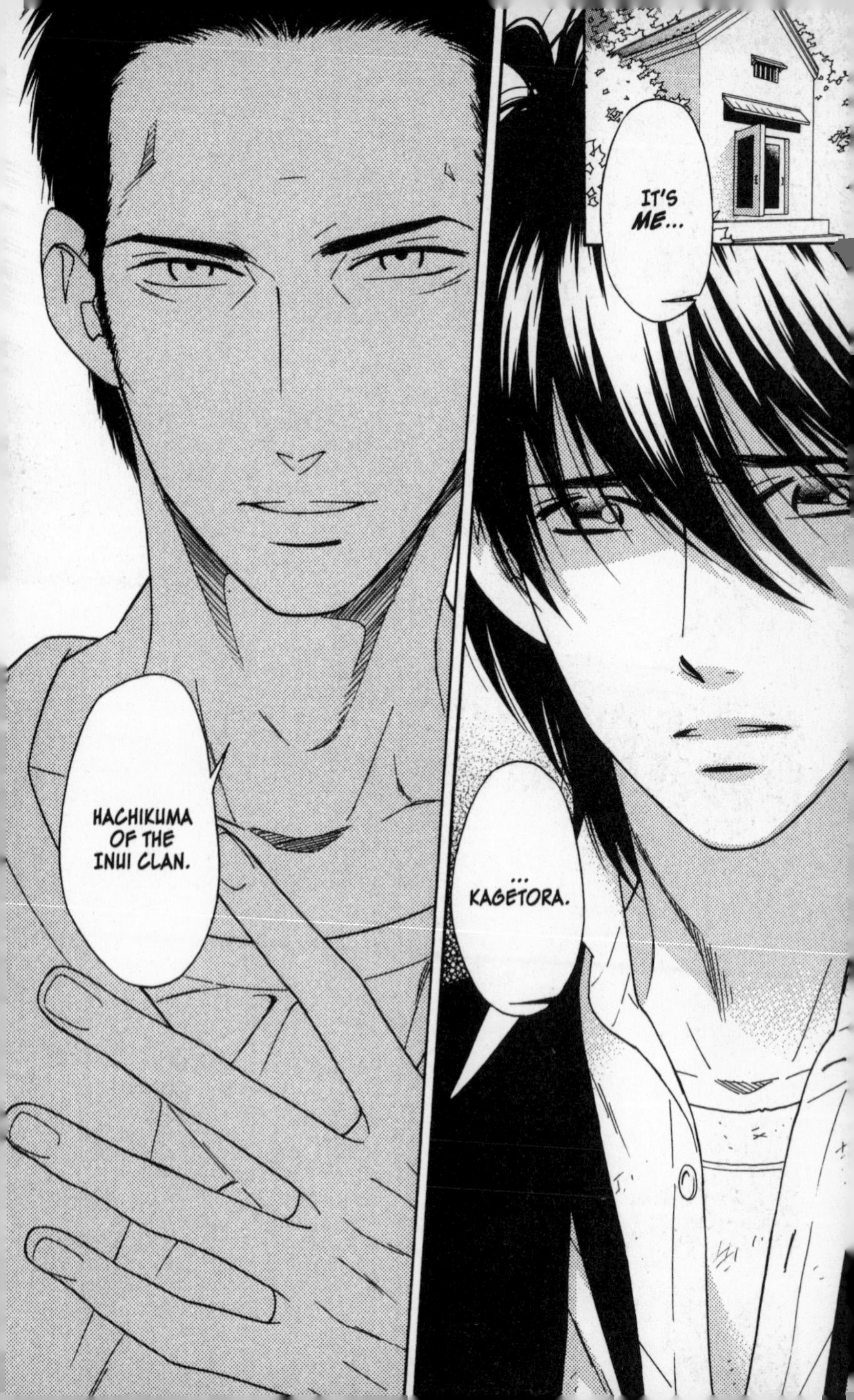
IT'S ME...
... KAGETORA.
HACHIKUMA OF THE INUI CLAN.

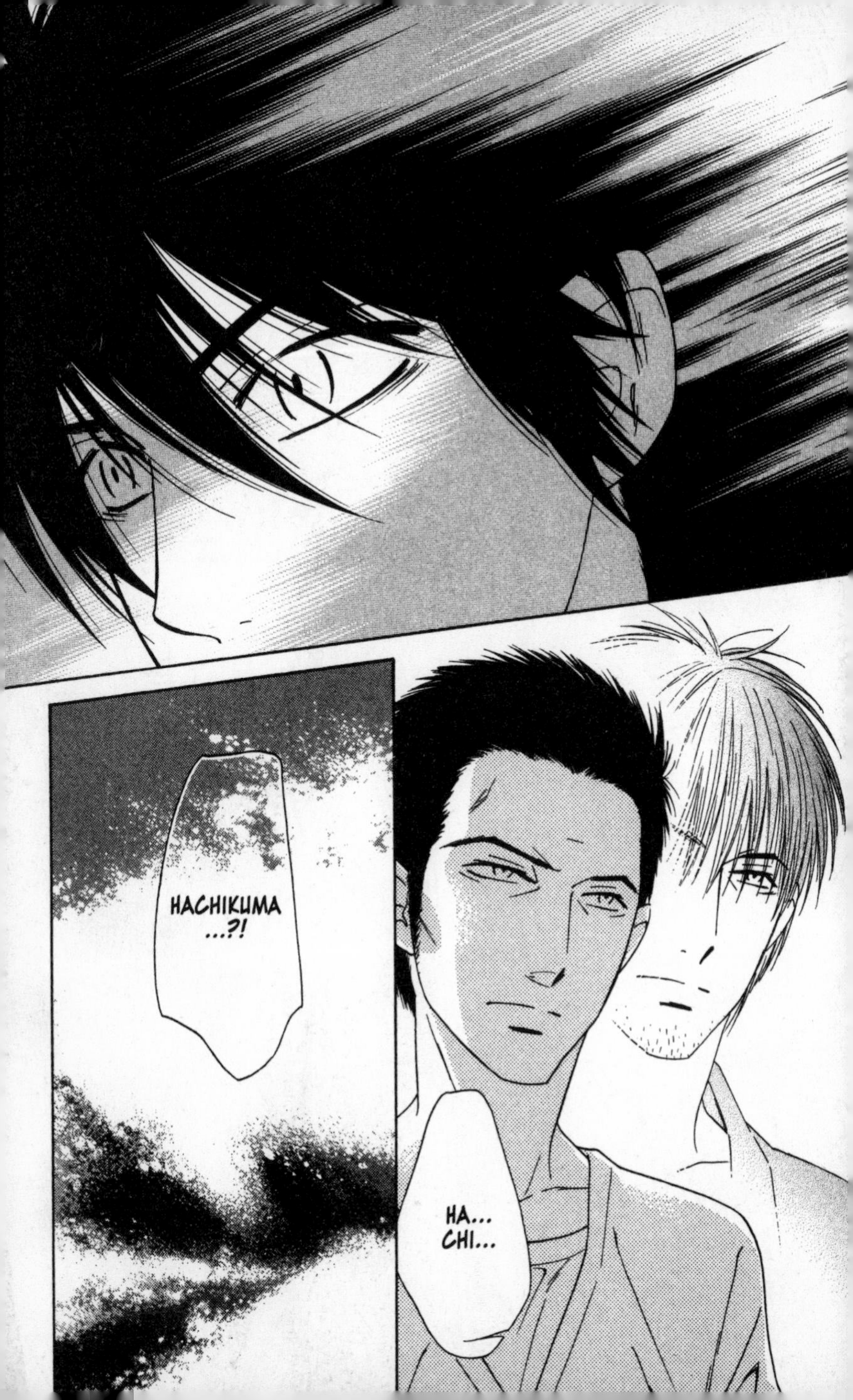
HA... CHI...
HACHIKUMA ...?!

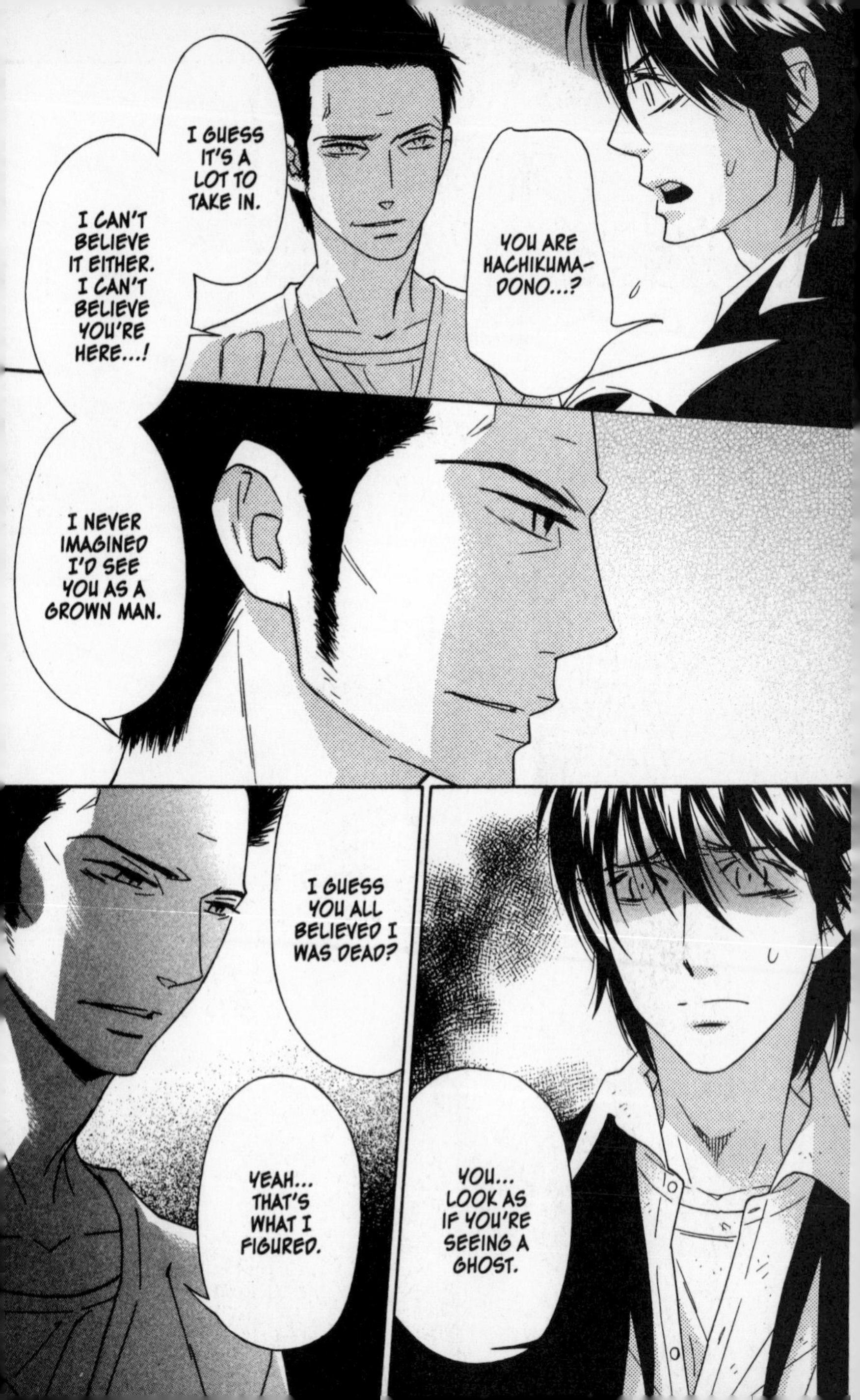
YOU ARE HACHIKUMA-DONO...?
I GUESS IT'S A LOT TO TAKE IN.
I CAN'T BELIEVE IT EITHER. I CAN'T BELIEVE YOU'RE HERE...!
I NEVER IMAGINED I'D SEE YOU AS A GROWN MAN.
YOU... LOOK AS IF YOU'RE SEEING A GHOST.
I GUESS YOU ALL BELIEVED I WAS DEAD?
YEAH... THAT'S WHAT I FIGURED.

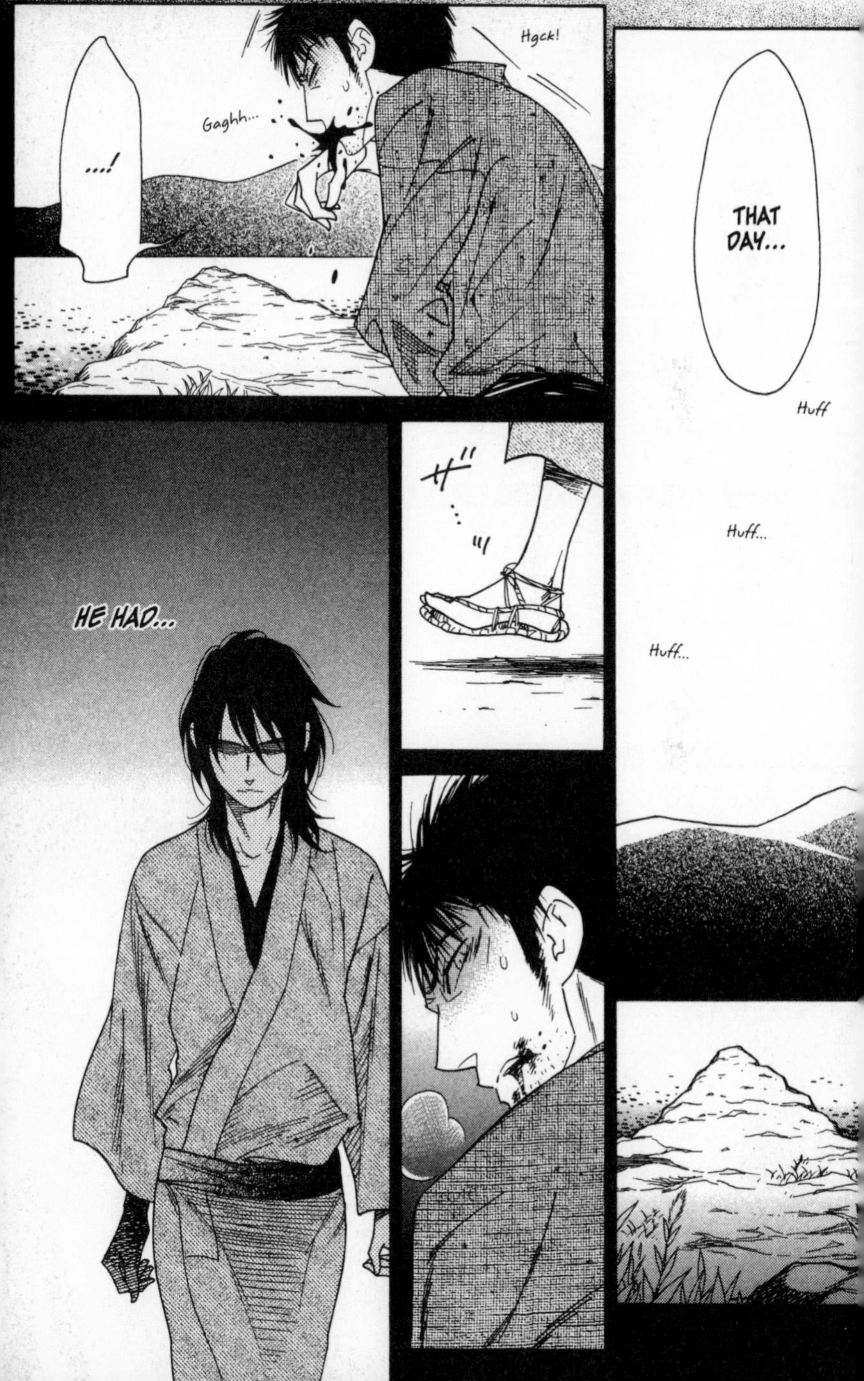
THAT DAY...
Huff
Huff...
Huff...
Hgck!
Gaghh...
...!
ザ…ッ
HE HAD...

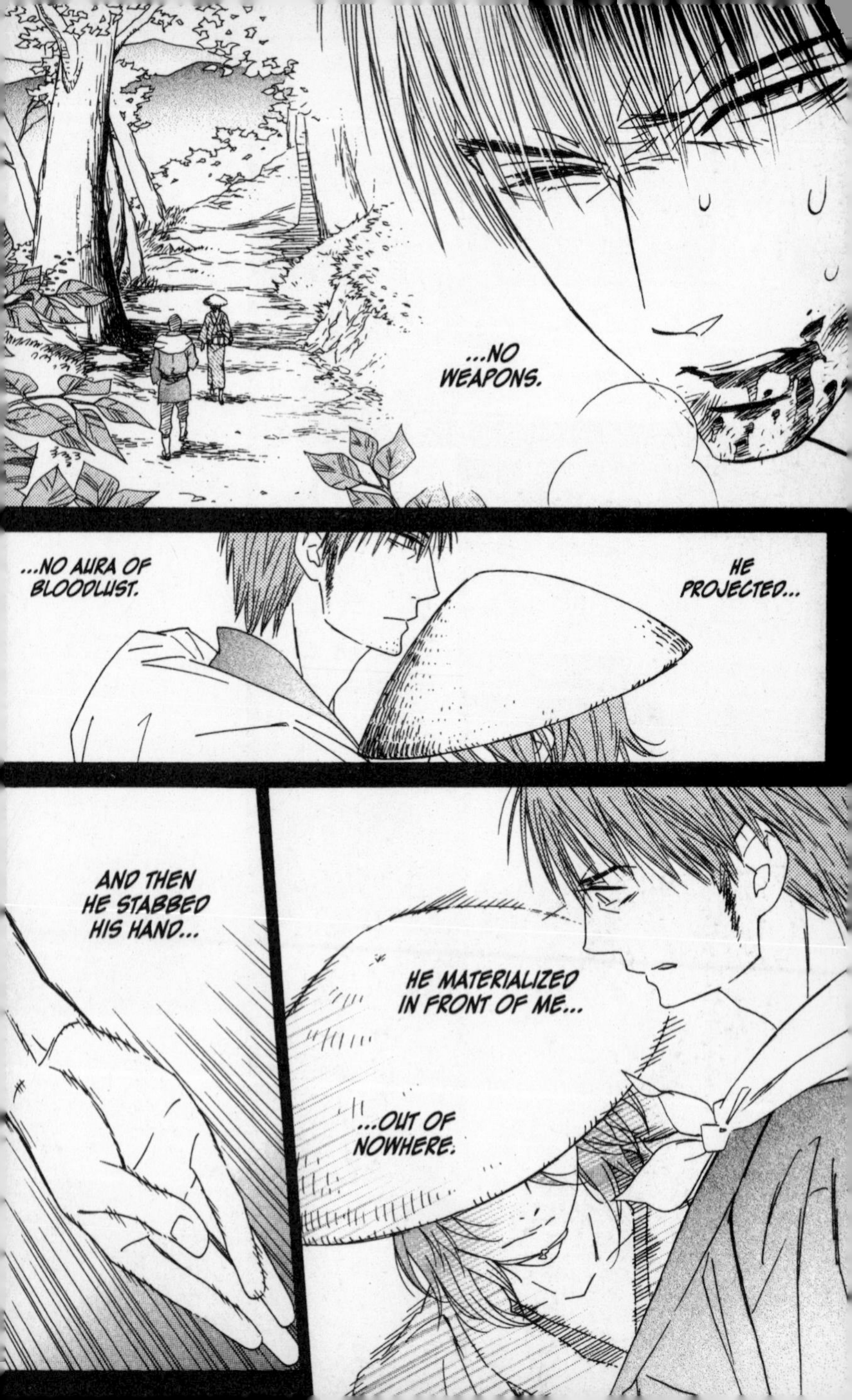
...NO WEAPONS.
HE PROJECTED...
...NO AURA OF BLOODLUST.
HE MATERIALIZED IN FRONT OF ME...
...OUT OF NOWHERE.
AND THEN HE STABBED HIS HAND...

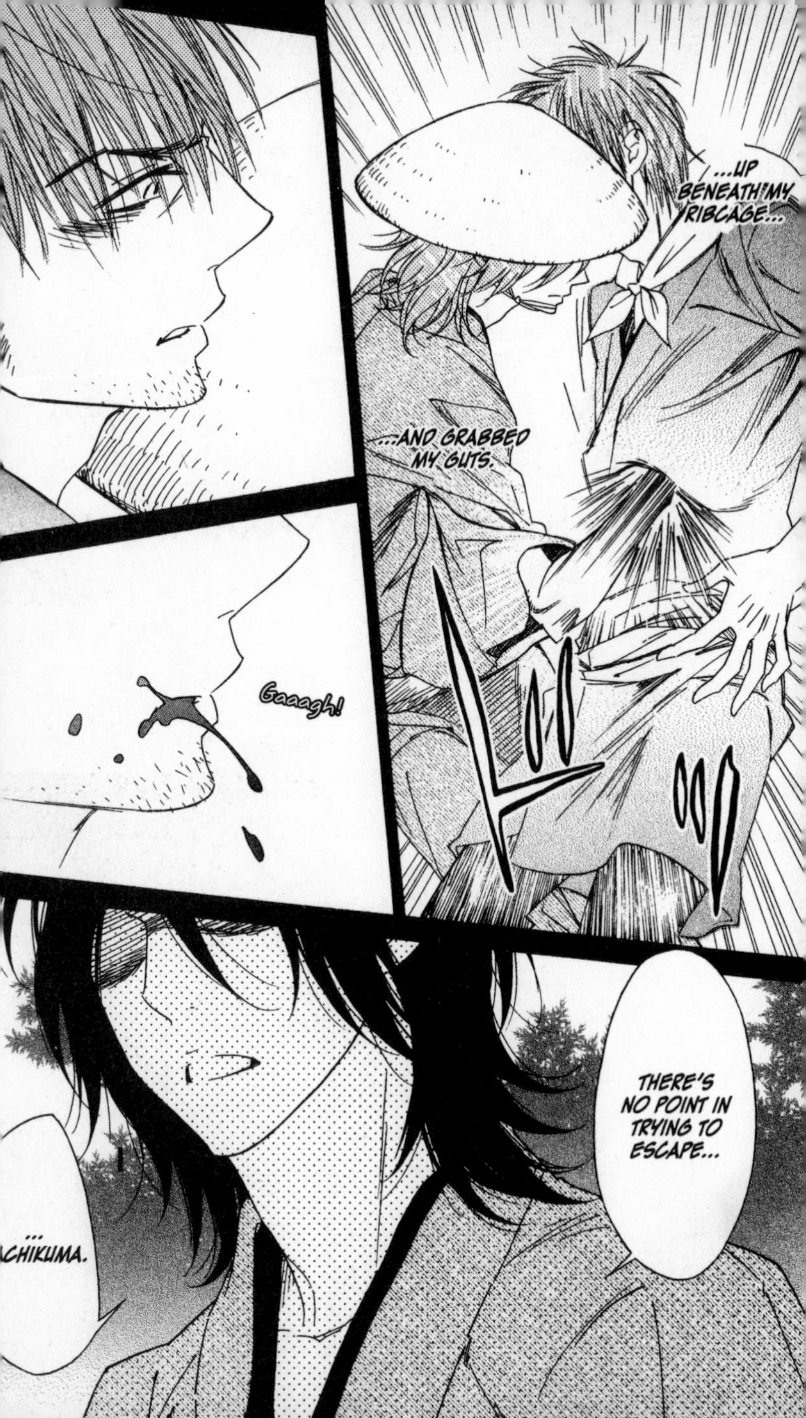
...UP BENEATH MY RIBCAGE...
...AND GRABBED MY GUTS.
Gaaagh!
THERE'S NO POINT IN TRYING TO ESCAPE...
...CHIKUMA.

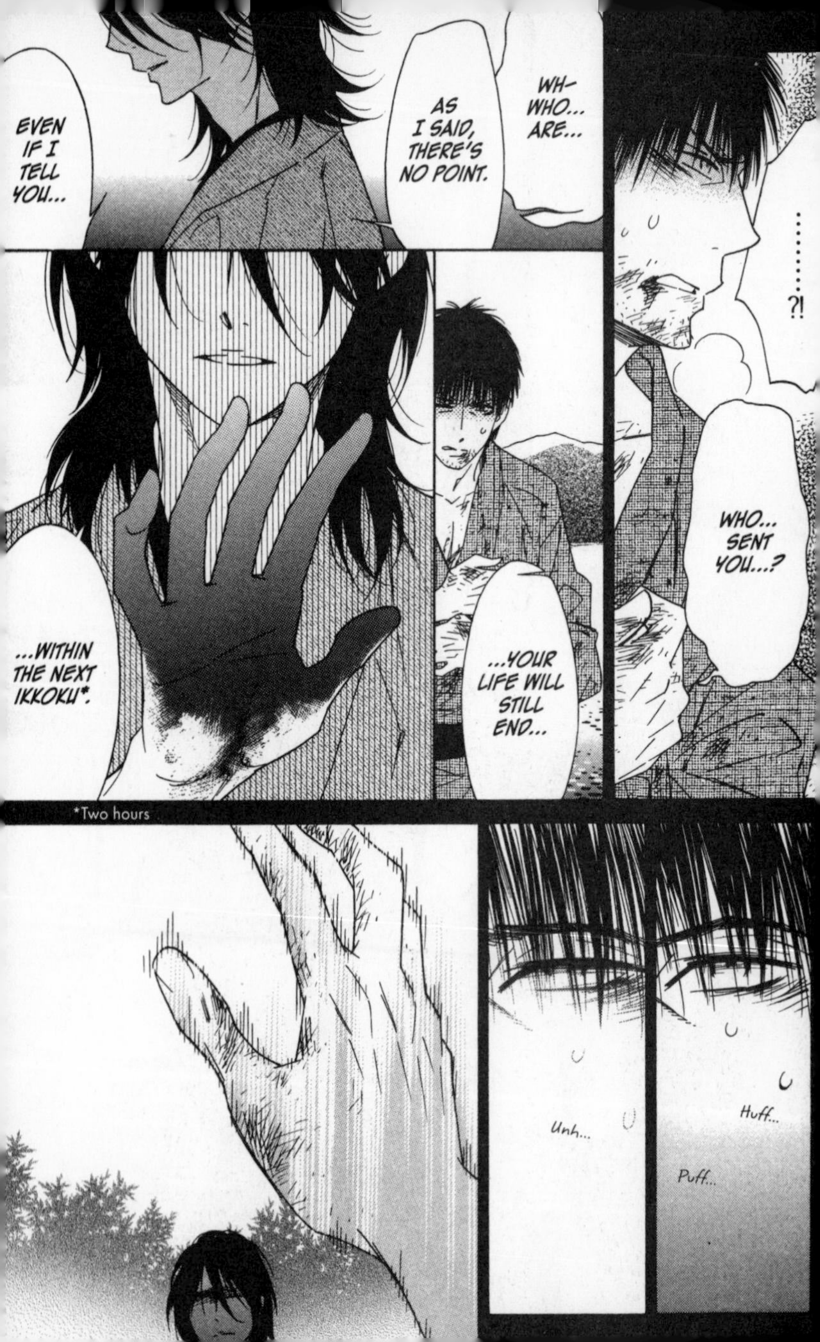
......?!
WHO... SENT YOU...?
WH- WHO... ARE...
AS I SAID, THERE'S NO POINT.
EVEN IF I TELL YOU...
...YOUR LIFE WILL STILL END...
...WITHIN THE NEXT IKKOKU*.
Huff...
Puff...
Unh...

*Two hours

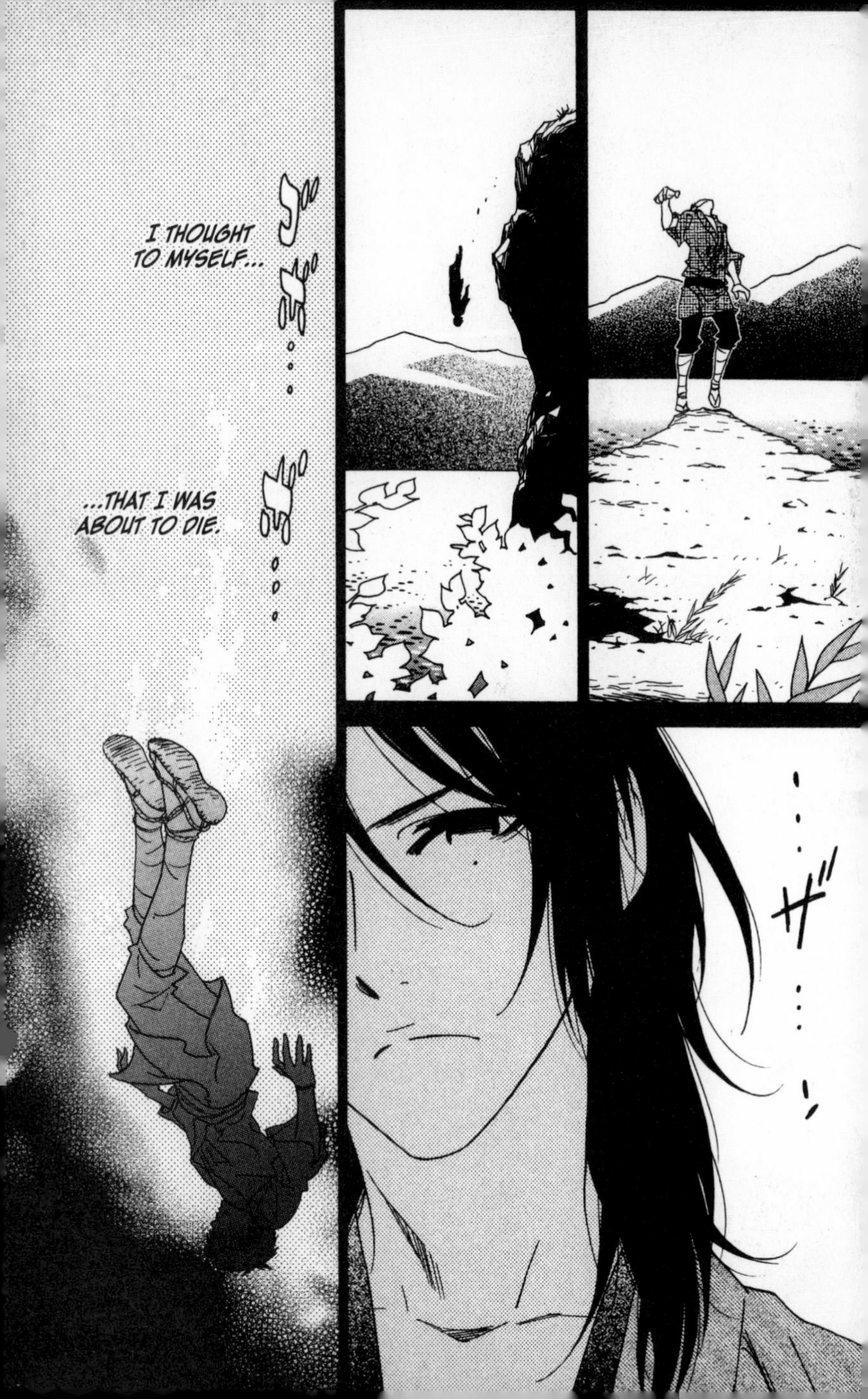
I THOUGHT TO MYSELF...
...THAT I WAS ABOUT TO DIE.

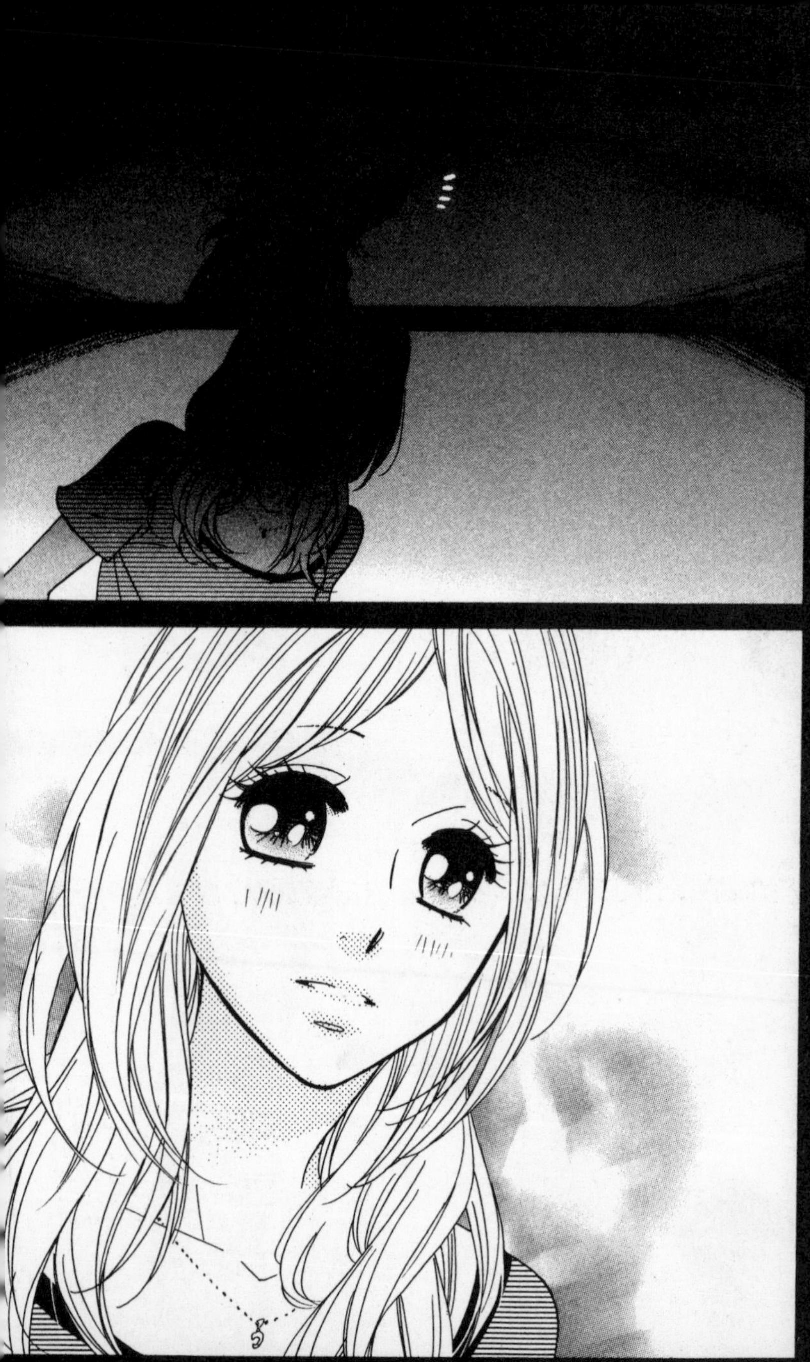

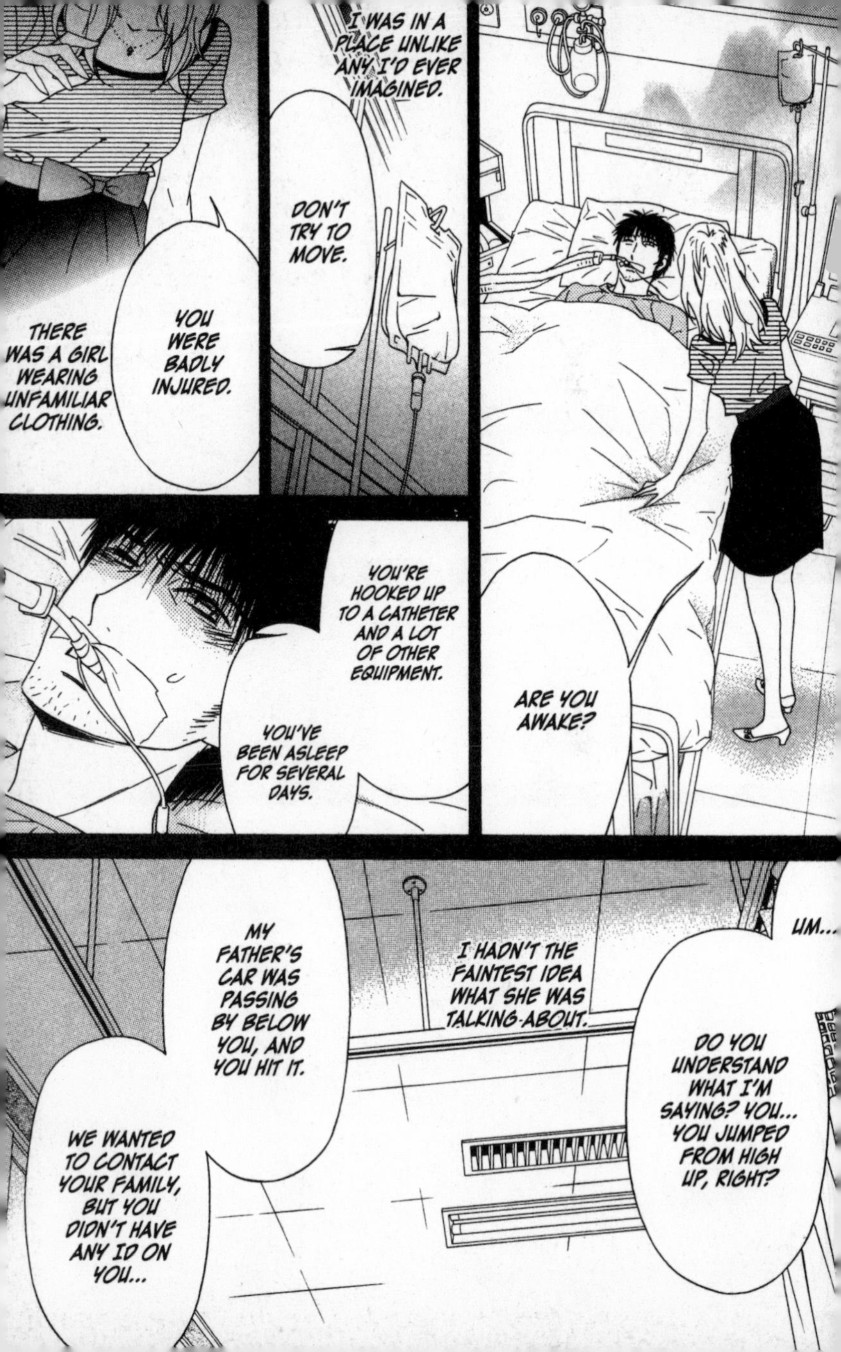
ARE YOU AWAKE?
I WAS IN A PLACE UNLIKE ANY I'D EVER IMAGINED.
DON'T TRY TO MOVE.
YOU WERE BADLY INJURED.
THERE WAS A GIRL WEARING UNFAMILIAR CLOTHING.
YOU'RE HOOKED UP TO A CATHETER AND A LOT OF OTHER EQUIPMENT.
YOU'VE BEEN ASLEEP FOR SEVERAL DAYS.
UM...
DO YOU UNDERSTAND WHAT I'M SAYING? YOU... YOU JUMPED FROM HIGH UP, RIGHT?
I HADN'T THE FAINTEST IDEA WHAT SHE WAS TALKING ABOUT.
MY FATHER'S CAR WAS PASSING BY BELOW YOU, AND YOU HIT IT.
WE WANTED TO CONTACT YOUR FAMILY, BUT YOU DIDN'T HAVE ANY ID ON YOU...

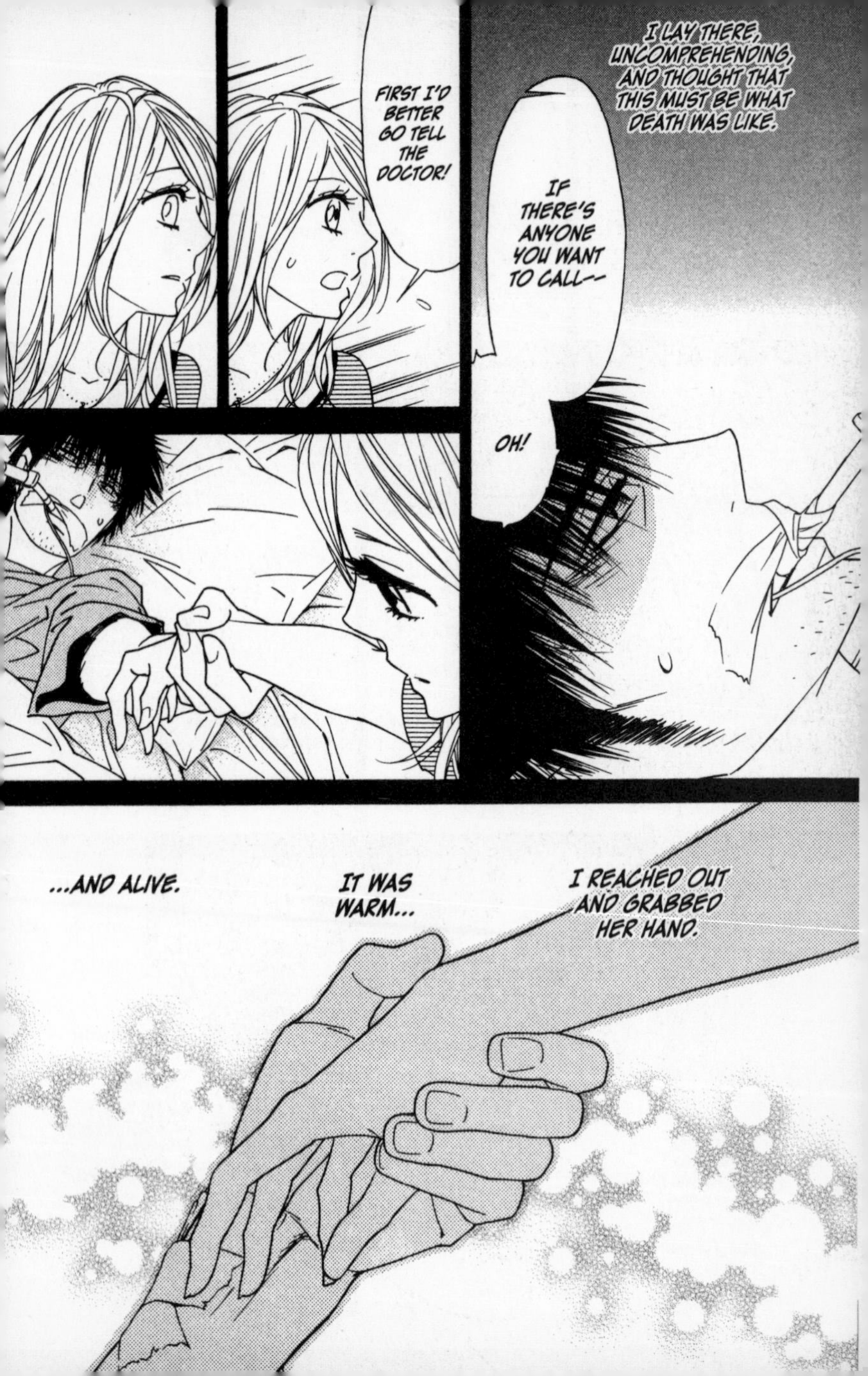
I LAY THERE, UNCOMPREHENDING, AND THOUGHT THAT THIS MUST BE WHAT DEATH WAS LIKE.
IF THERE'S ANYONE YOU WANT TO CALL--
OH!
FIRST I'D BETTER GO TELL THE DOCTOR!
I REACHED OUT AND GRABBED HER HAND.
IT WAS WARM...
...AND ALIVE.

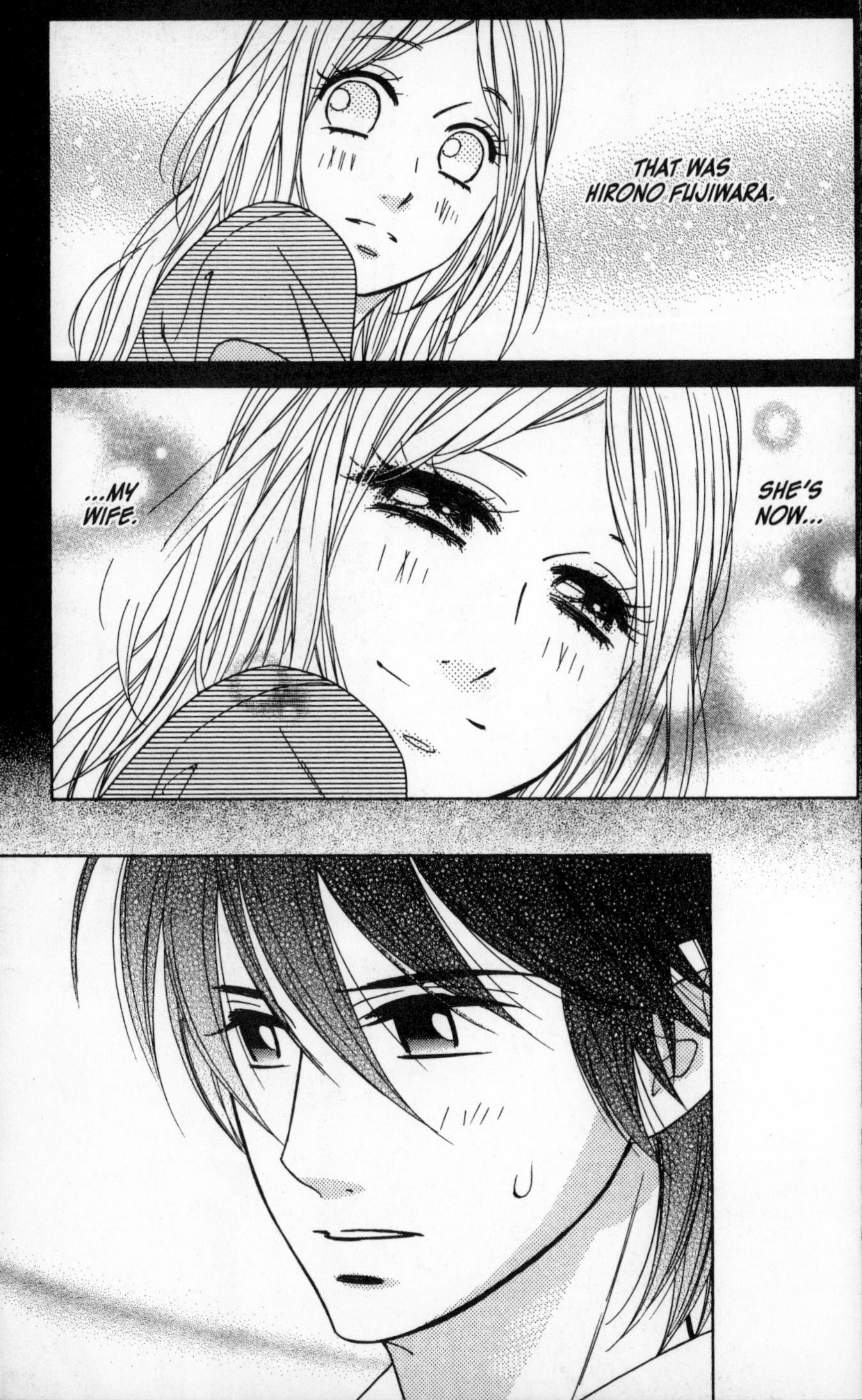
THAT WAS HIRONO FUJIWARA.
SHE'S NOW...
...MY WIFE.

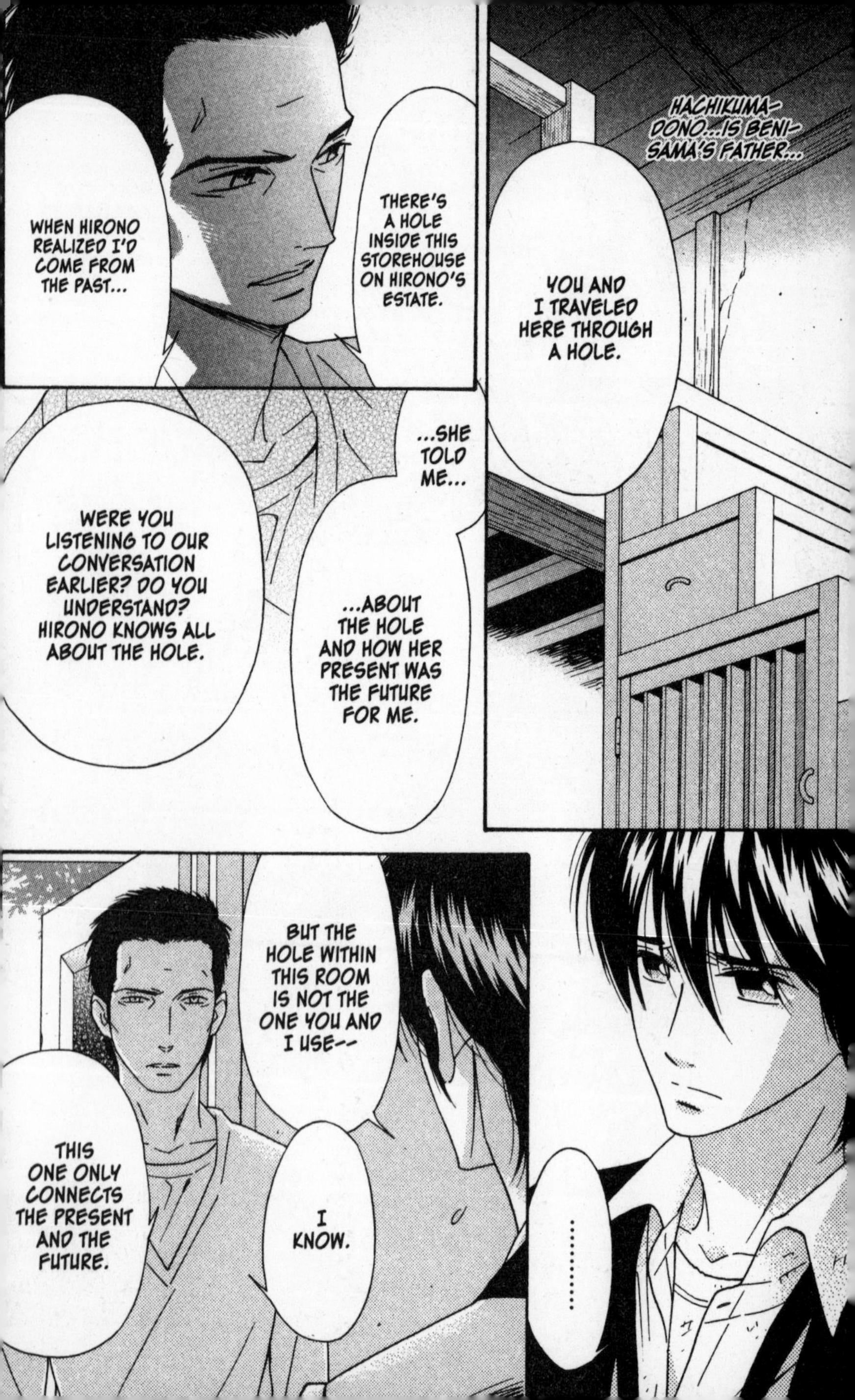
HACHIKUMA-DONO...IS BENI-SAMA'S FATHER...
YOU AND I TRAVELED HERE THROUGH A HOLE.
THERE'S A HOLE INSIDE THIS STOREHOUSE ON HIRONO'S ESTATE.
WHEN HIRONO REALIZED I'D COME FROM THE PAST...
...SHE TOLD ME...
...ABOUT THE HOLE AND HOW HER PRESENT WAS THE FUTURE FOR ME.
WERE YOU LISTENING TO OUR CONVERSATION EARLIER? DO YOU UNDERSTAND? HIRONO KNOWS ALL ABOUT THE HOLE.
......
BUT THE HOLE WITHIN THIS ROOM IS NOT THE ONE YOU AND I USE--
I KNOW.
THIS ONE ONLY CONNECTS THE PRESENT AND THE FUTURE.

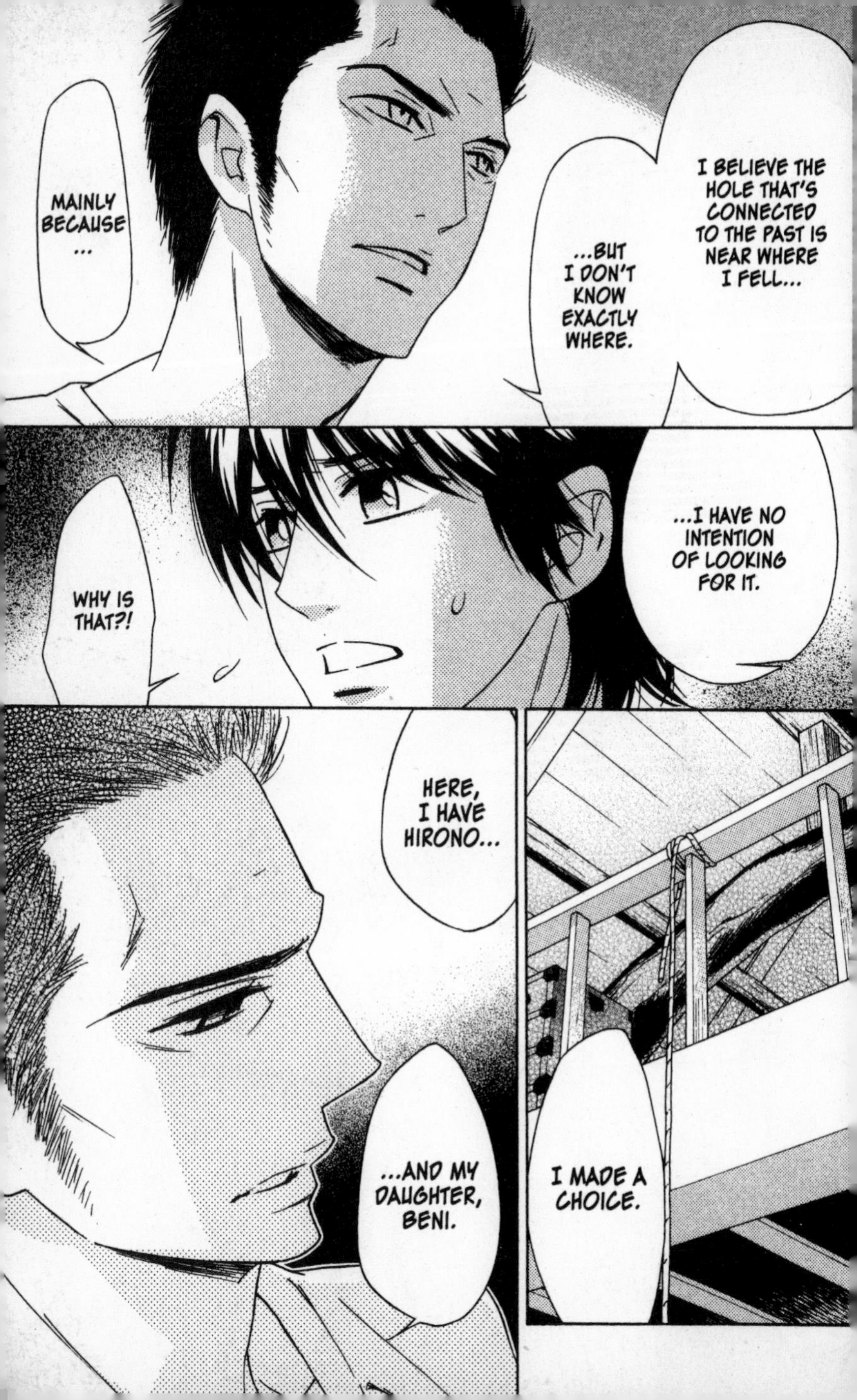
I BELIEVE THE HOLE THAT'S CONNECTED TO THE PAST IS NEAR WHERE I FELL...
...BUT I DON'T KNOW EXACTLY WHERE.
MAINLY BECAUSE ...
...I HAVE NO INTENTION OF LOOKING FOR IT.
WHY IS THAT?!
I MADE A CHOICE.
HERE, I HAVE HIRONO...
...AND MY DAUGHTER, BENI.

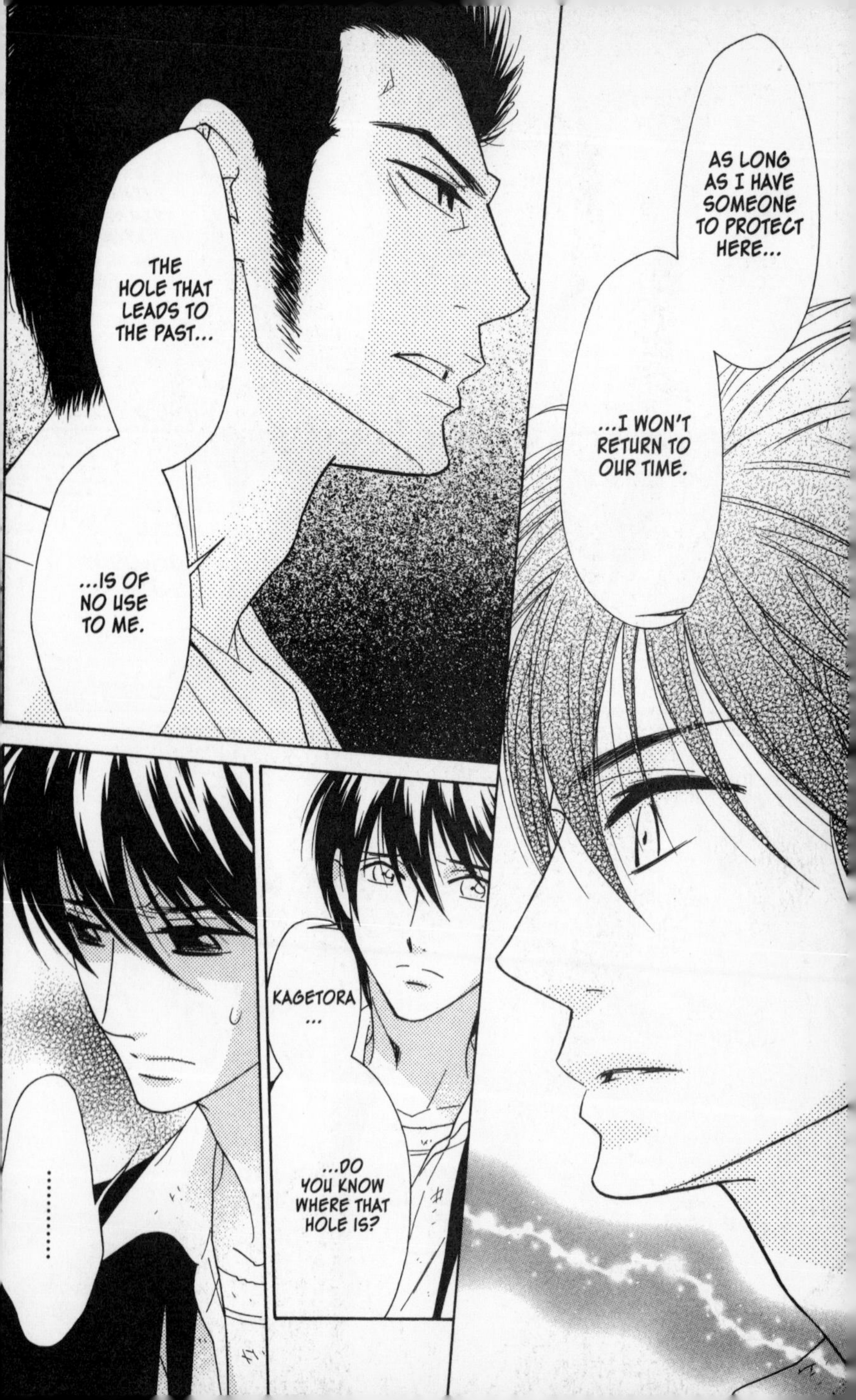
AS LONG AS I HAVE SOMEONE TO PROTECT HERE...
...I WON'T RETURN TO OUR TIME.
THE HOLE THAT LEADS TO THE PAST...
...IS OF NO USE TO ME.
KAGETORA...
...DO YOU KNOW WHERE THAT HOLE IS?
....

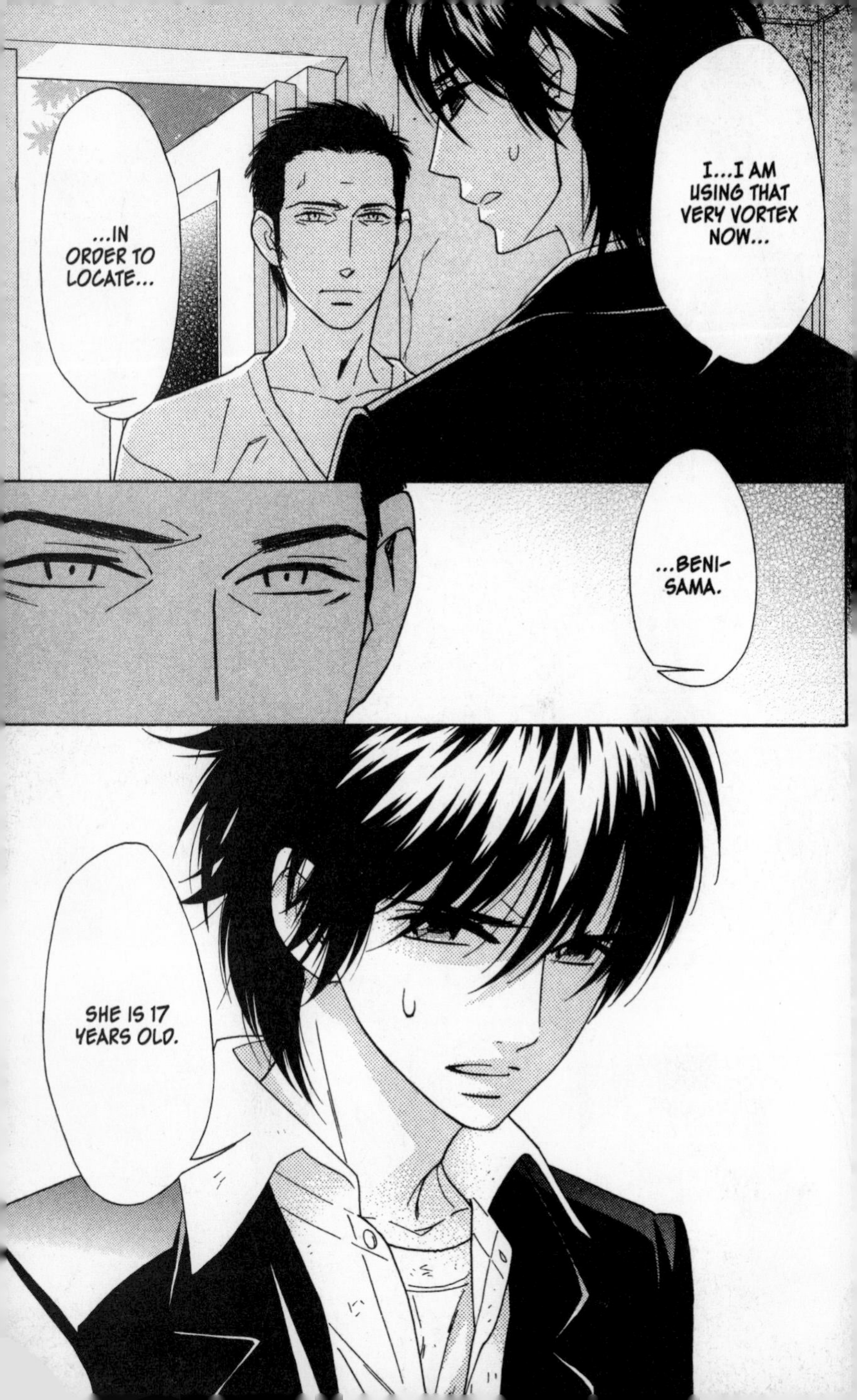
I...I AM USING THAT VERY VORTEX NOW...
...IN ORDER TO LOCATE...
...BENI-SAMA.
SHE IS 17 YEARS OLD.

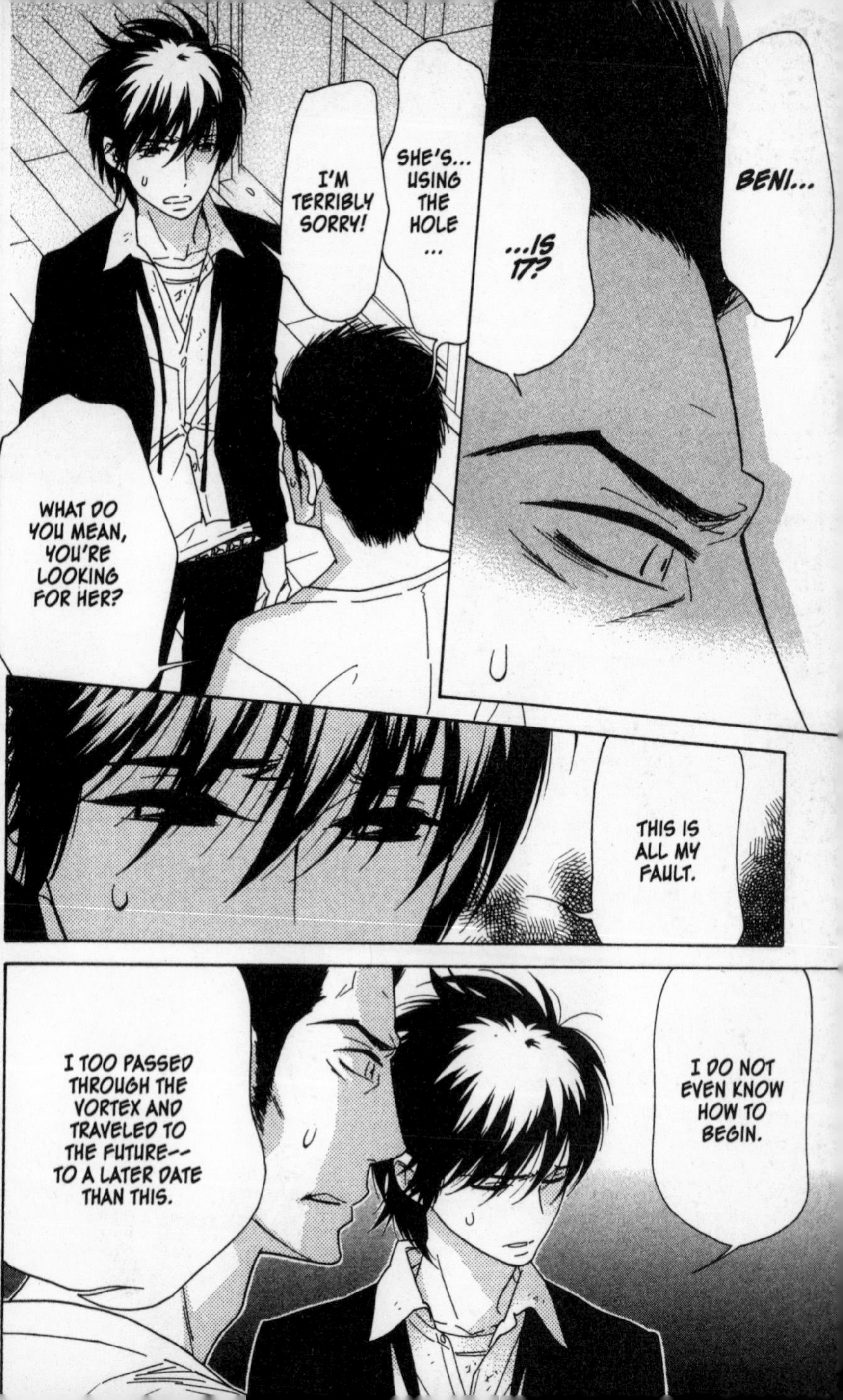
BENI...
...IS 17?
SHE'S... USING THE HOLE ...
I'M TERRIBLY SORRY!
WHAT DO YOU MEAN, YOU'RE LOOKING FOR HER?
THIS IS ALL MY FAULT.
I DO NOT EVEN KNOW HOW TO BEGIN.
I TOO PASSED THROUGH THE VORTEX AND TRAVELED TO THE FUTURE-- TO A LATER DATE THAN THIS.

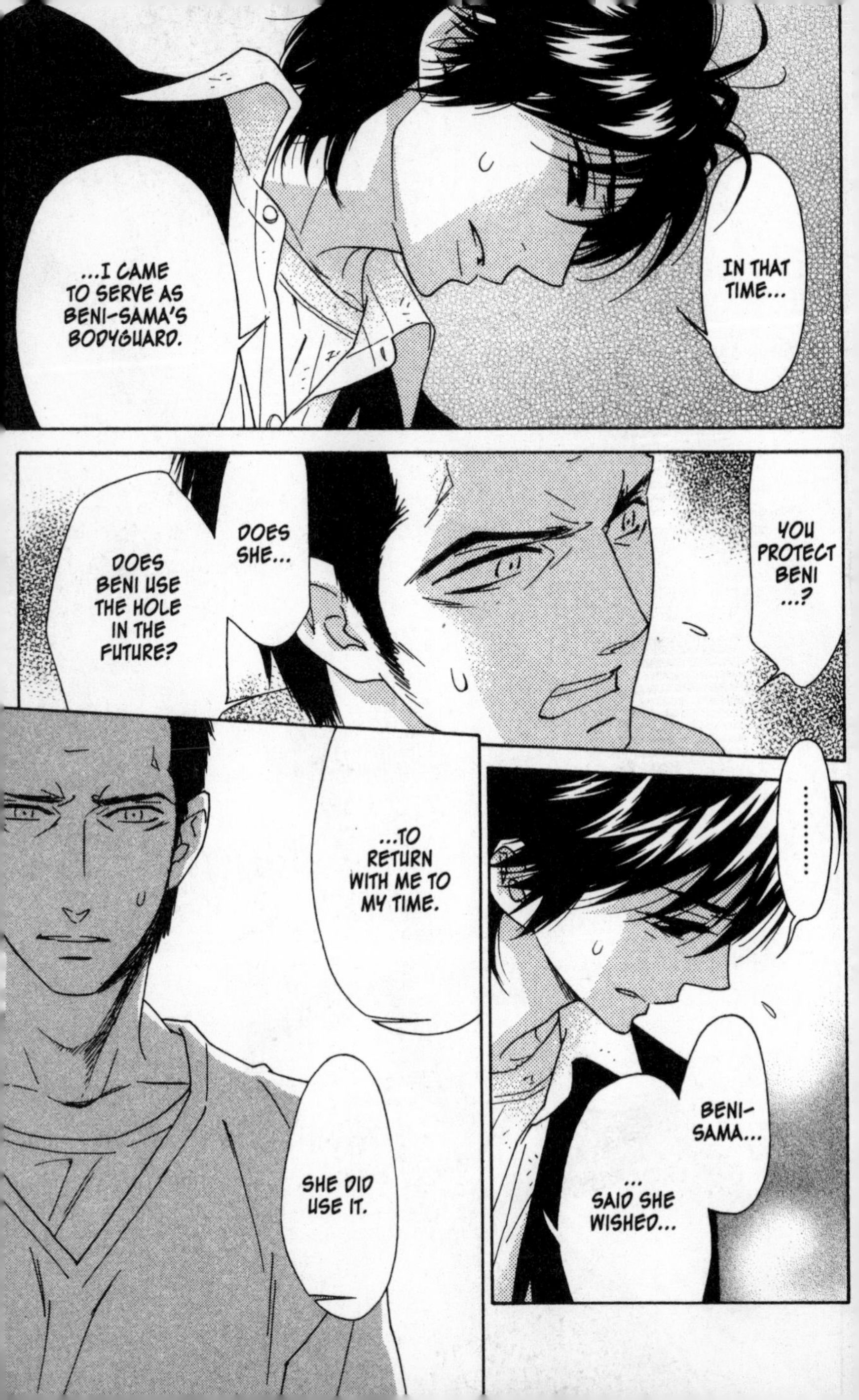
IN THAT TIME...
...I CAME TO SERVE AS BENI-SAMA'S BODYGUARD.
YOU PROTECT BENI ...?
DOES SHE...
DOES BENI USE THE HOLE IN THE FUTURE?
....
BENI-SAMA...
...SAID SHE WISHED...
...TO RETURN WITH ME TO MY TIME.
SHE DID USE IT.

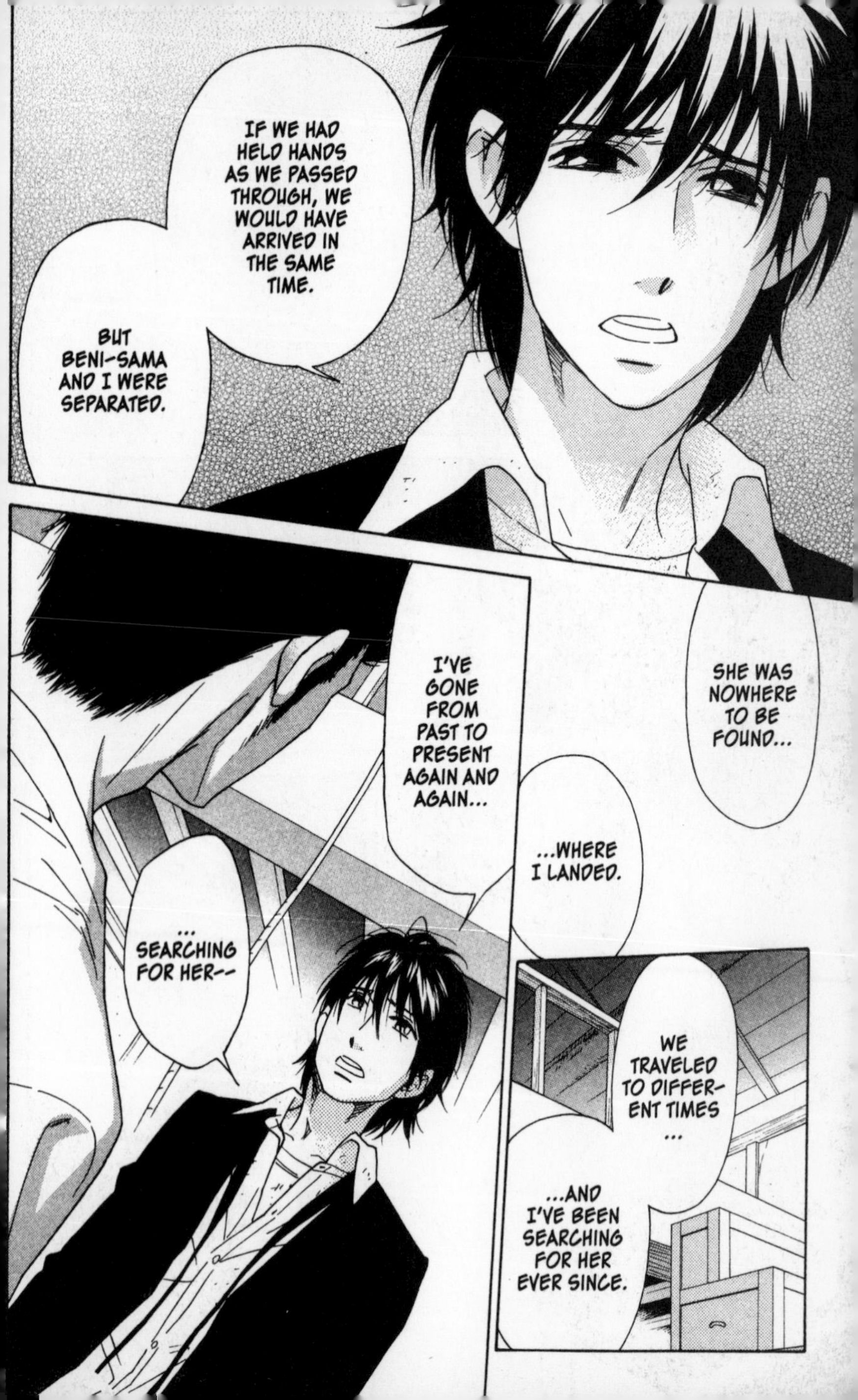
IF WE HAD HELD HANDS AS WE PASSED THROUGH, WE WOULD HAVE ARRIVED IN THE SAME TIME.
BUT BENI-SAMA AND I WERE SEPARATED.
SHE WAS NOWHERE TO BE FOUND...
...WHERE I LANDED.
WE TRAVELED TO DIFFER-ENT TIMES ...
...AND I'VE BEEN SEARCHING FOR HER EVER SINCE.
I'VE GONE FROM PAST TO PRESENT AGAIN AND AGAIN...
... SEARCHING FOR HER--

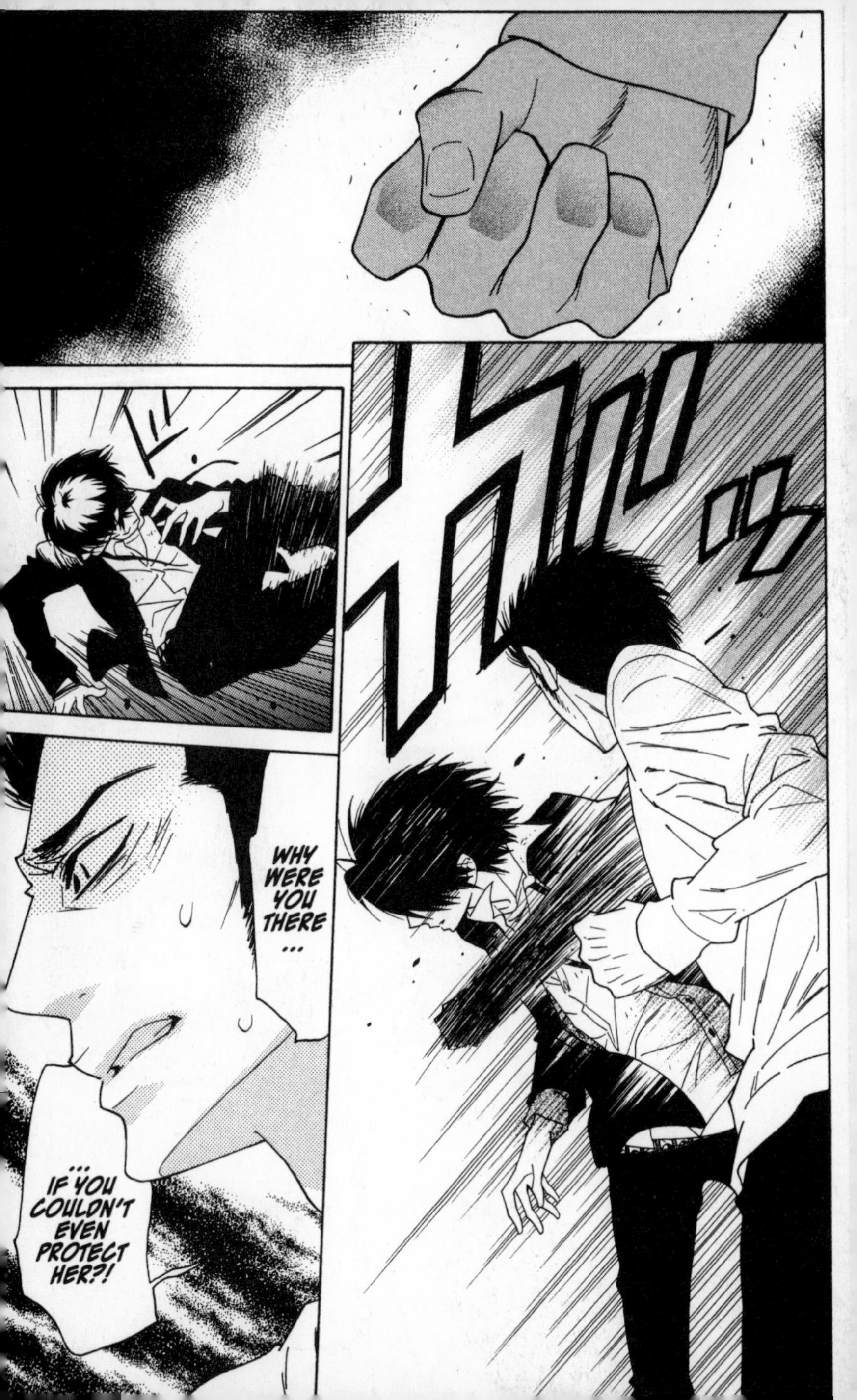
WHY WERE YOU THERE ...
... IF YOU COULDN'T EVEN PROTECT HER?!

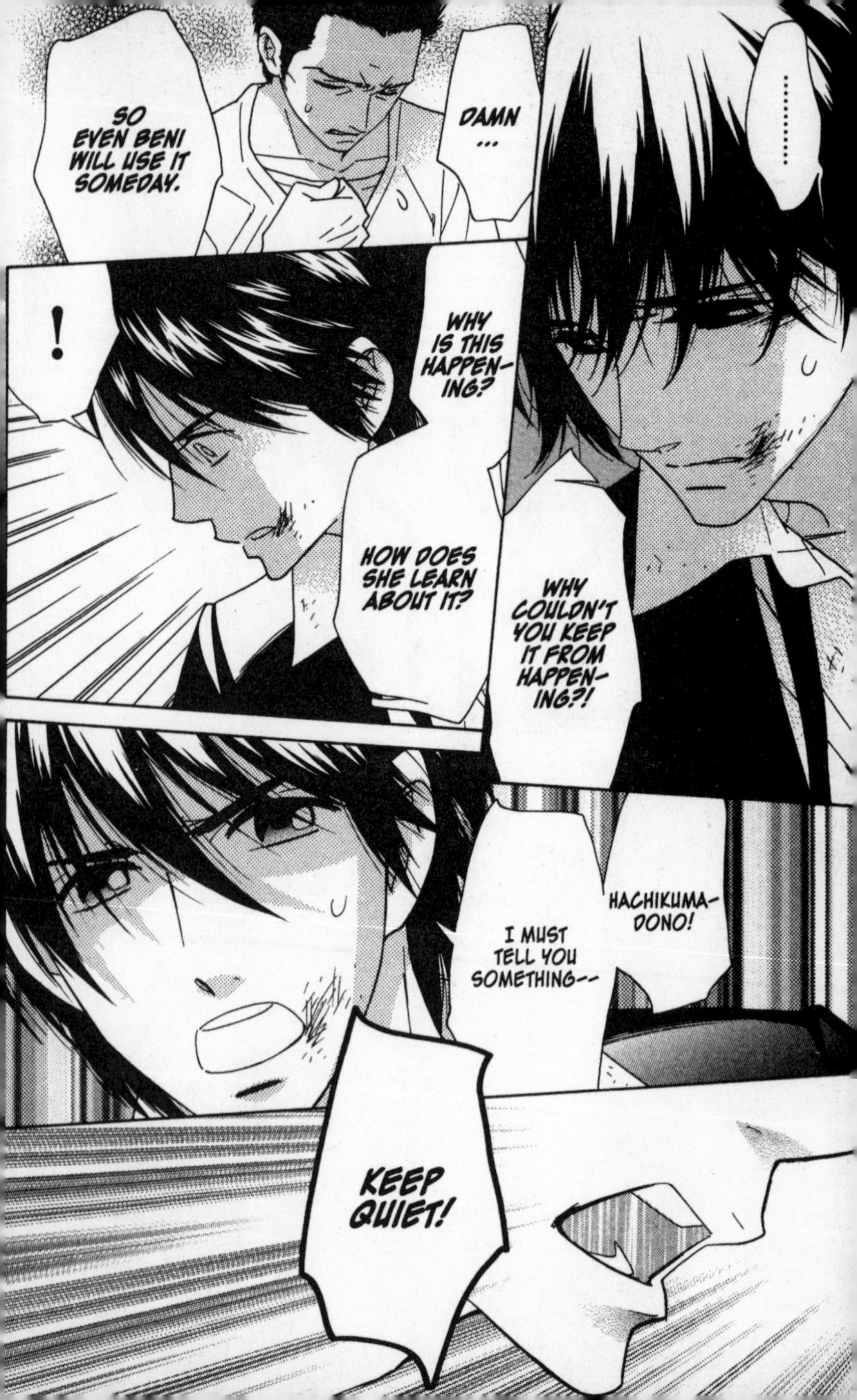

......
WHY COULDN'T YOU KEEP IT FROM HAPPENING?!
DAMN...
SO EVEN BENI WILL USE IT SOMEDAY.
WHY IS THIS HAPPENING?
HOW DOES SHE LEARN ABOUT IT?
!
HACHIKUMA-DONO!
I MUST TELL YOU SOMETHING--
KEEP QUIET!

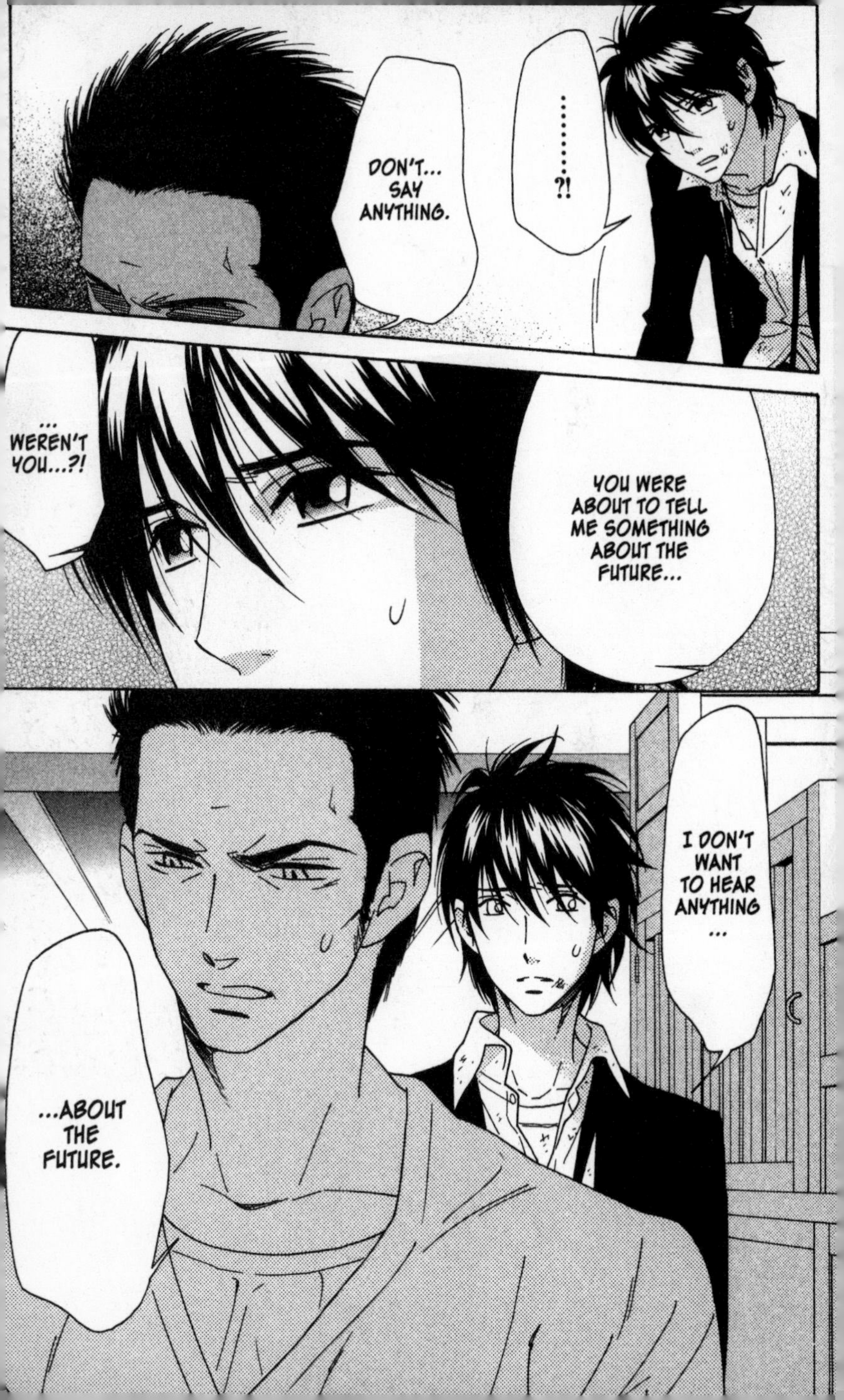

......
?!
DON'T... SAY ANYTHING.
YOU WERE ABOUT TO TELL ME SOMETHING ABOUT THE FUTURE...
... WEREN'T YOU...?!
I DON'T WANT TO HEAR ANYTHING ...
...ABOUT THE FUTURE.

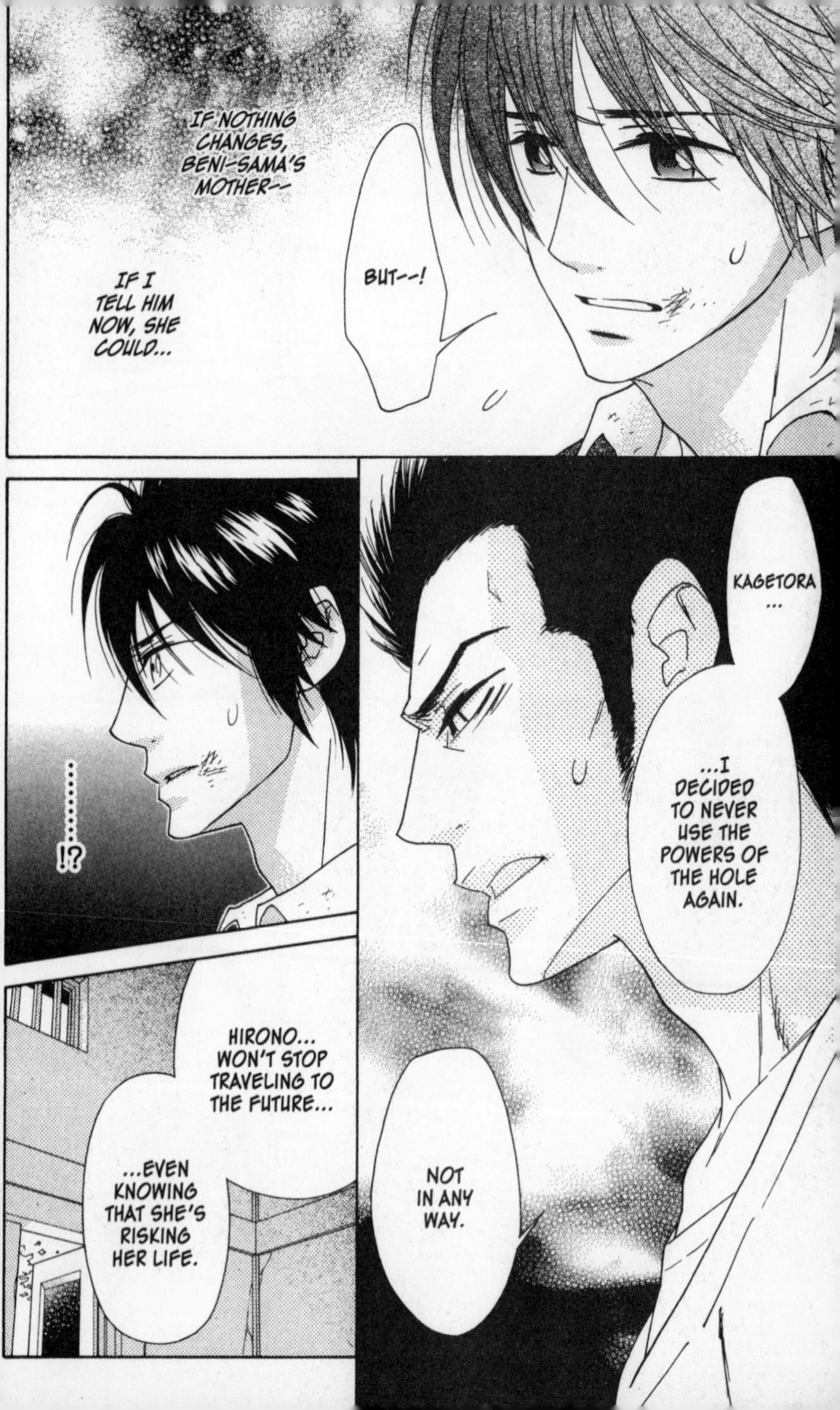
IF NOTHING CHANGES, BENI-SAMA'S MOTHER--
IF I TELL HIM NOW, SHE COULD...
BUT--!
KAGETORA ...
...I DECIDED TO NEVER USE THE POWERS OF THE HOLE AGAIN.
NOT IN ANY WAY.
......!?
HIRONO... WON'T STOP TRAVELING TO THE FUTURE...
...EVEN KNOWING THAT SHE'S RISKING HER LIFE.

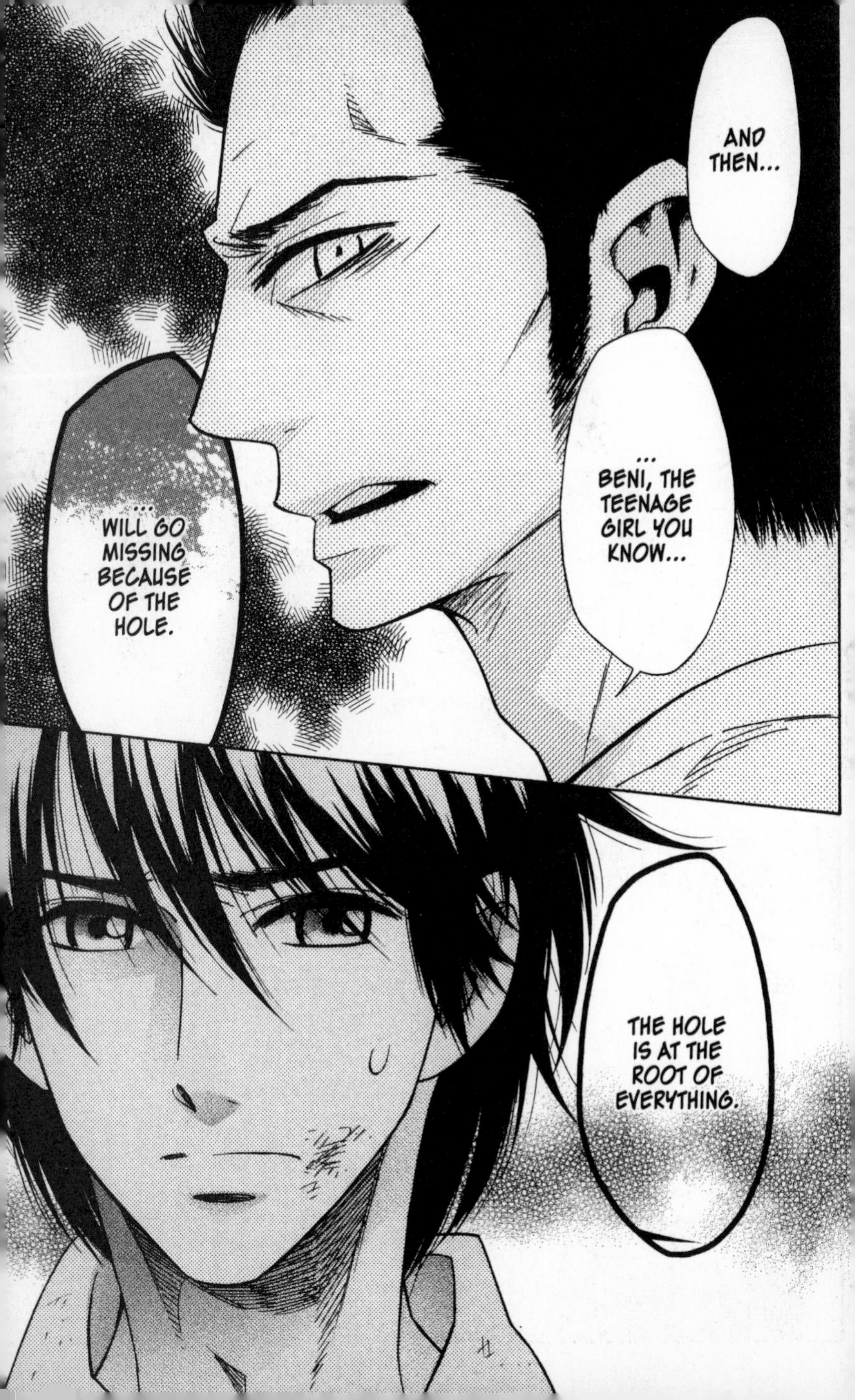
AND THEN...
... BENI, THE TEENAGE GIRL YOU KNOW...
... WILL GO MISSING BECAUSE OF THE HOLE.
THE HOLE IS AT THE ROOT OF EVERYTHING.

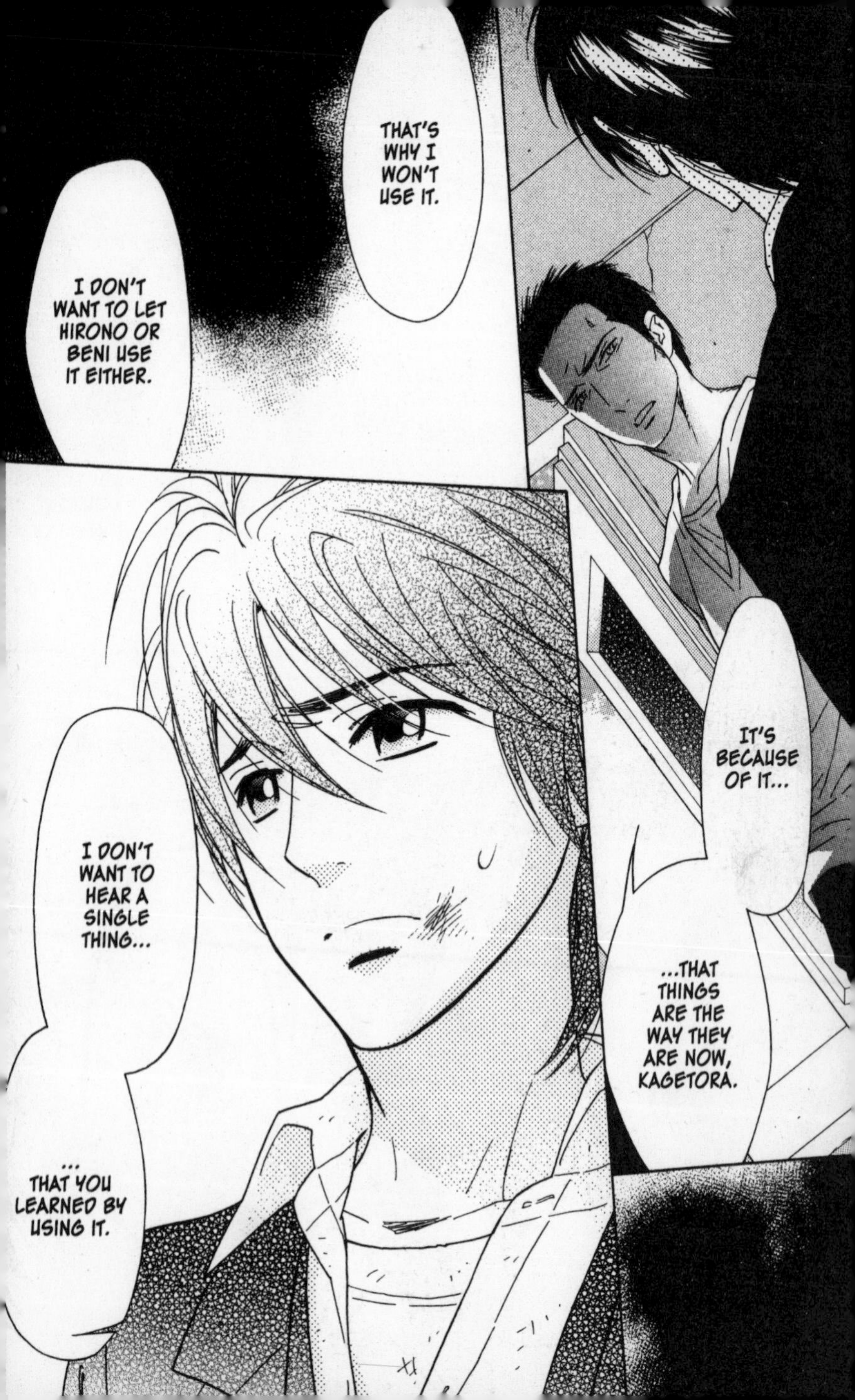
IT'S BECAUSE OF IT...
...THAT THINGS ARE THE WAY THEY ARE NOW, KAGETORA.
THAT'S WHY I WON'T USE IT.
I DON'T WANT TO LET HIRONO OR BENI USE IT EITHER.
I DON'T WANT TO HEAR A SINGLE THING...
...THAT YOU LEARNED BY USING IT.

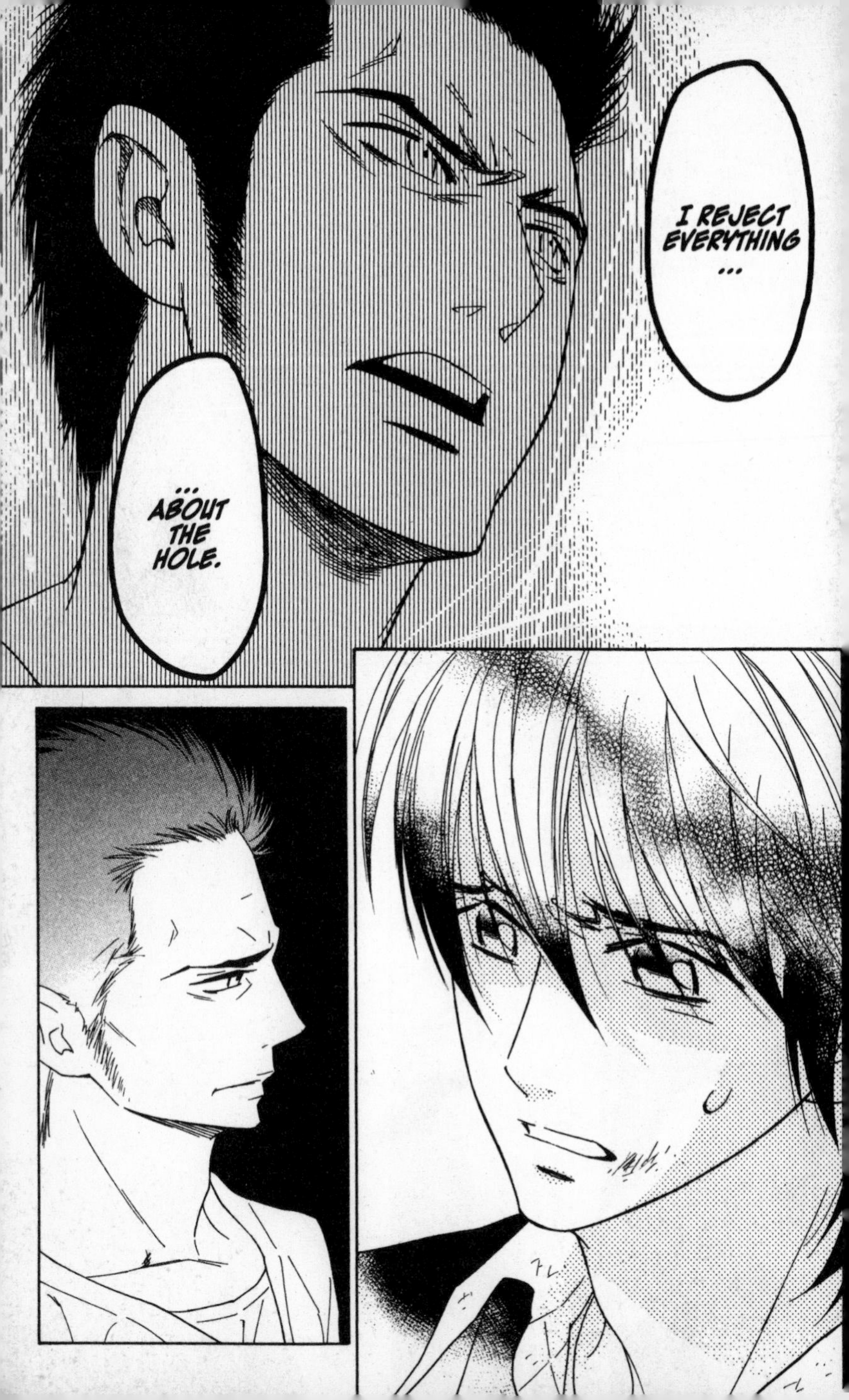
I REJECT EVERYTHING ...
... ABOUT THE HOLE.

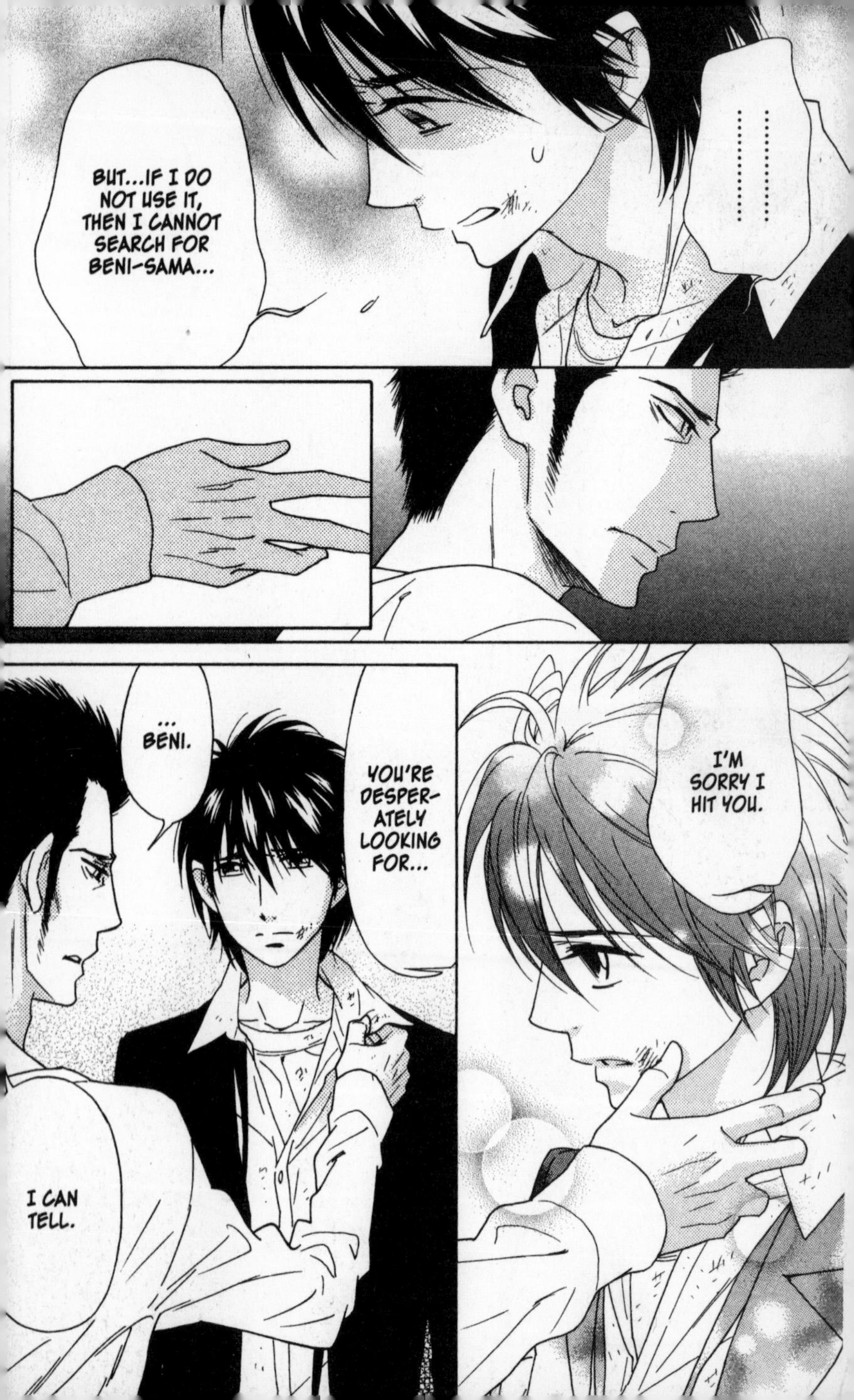
......
BUT...IF I DO NOT USE IT, THEN I CANNOT SEARCH FOR BENI-SAMA...
I'M SORRY I HIT YOU.
YOU'RE DESPER-ATELY LOOKING FOR...
...BENI.
I CAN TELL.

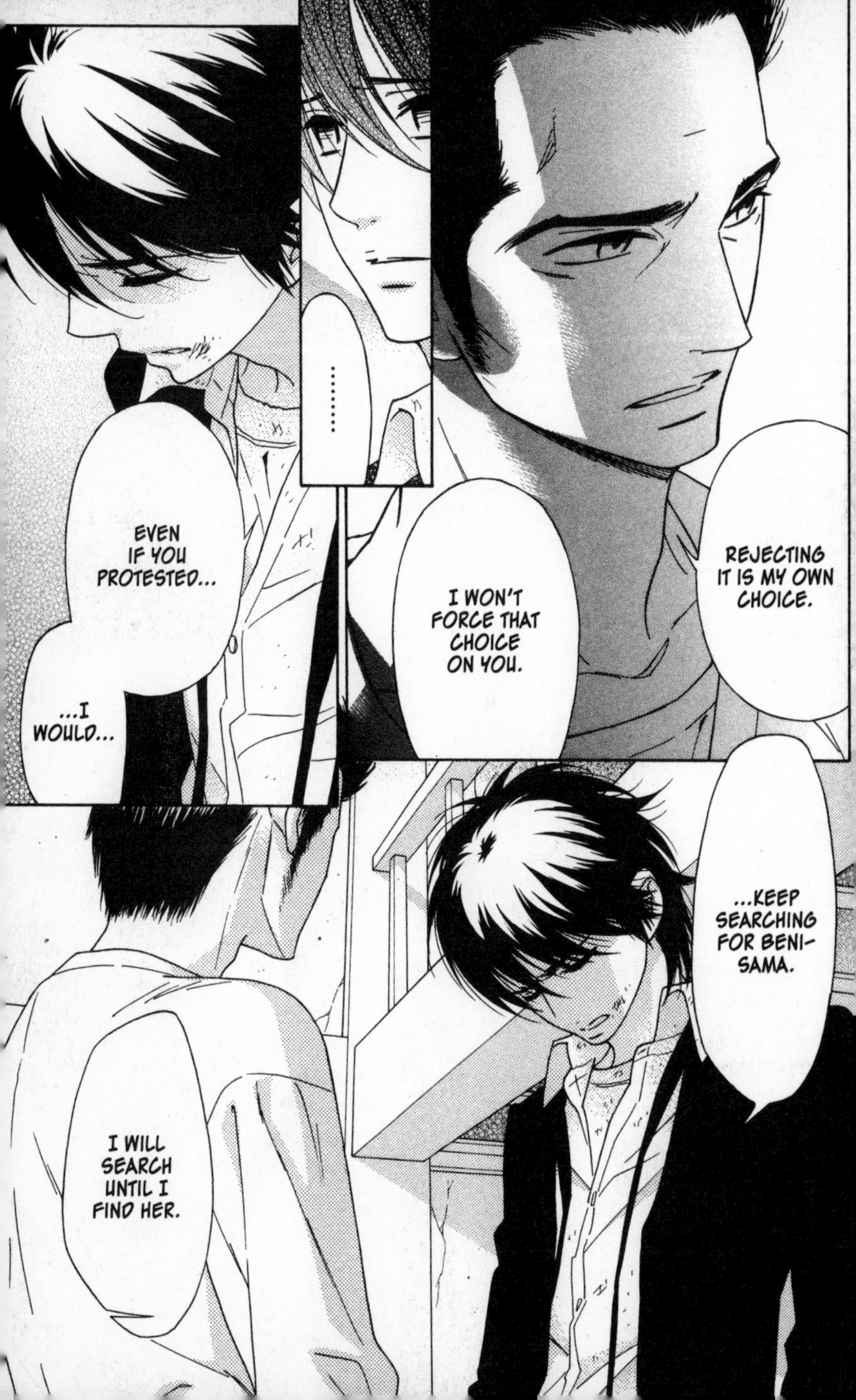
REJECTING IT IS MY OWN CHOICE.
I WON'T FORCE THAT CHOICE ON YOU.
......
EVEN IF YOU PROTESTED...
...I WOULD...
...KEEP SEARCHING FOR BENI-SAMA.
I WILL SEARCH UNTIL I FIND HER.

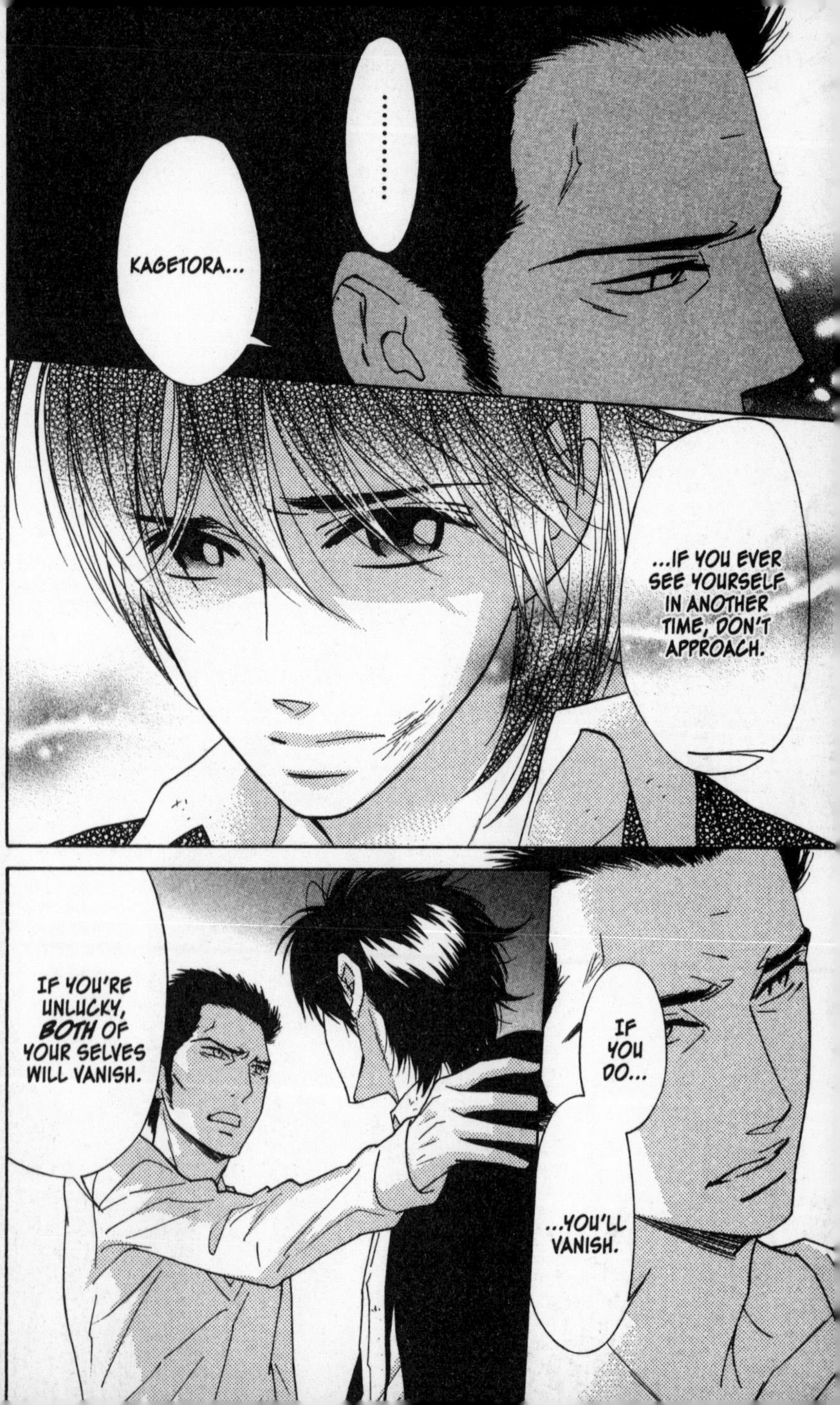

......
KAGETORA...
...IF YOU EVER SEE YOURSELF IN ANOTHER TIME, DON'T APPROACH.
IF YOU DO...
...YOU'LL VANISH.
IF YOU'RE UNLUCKY, ***BOTH*** OF YOUR SELVES WILL VANISH.

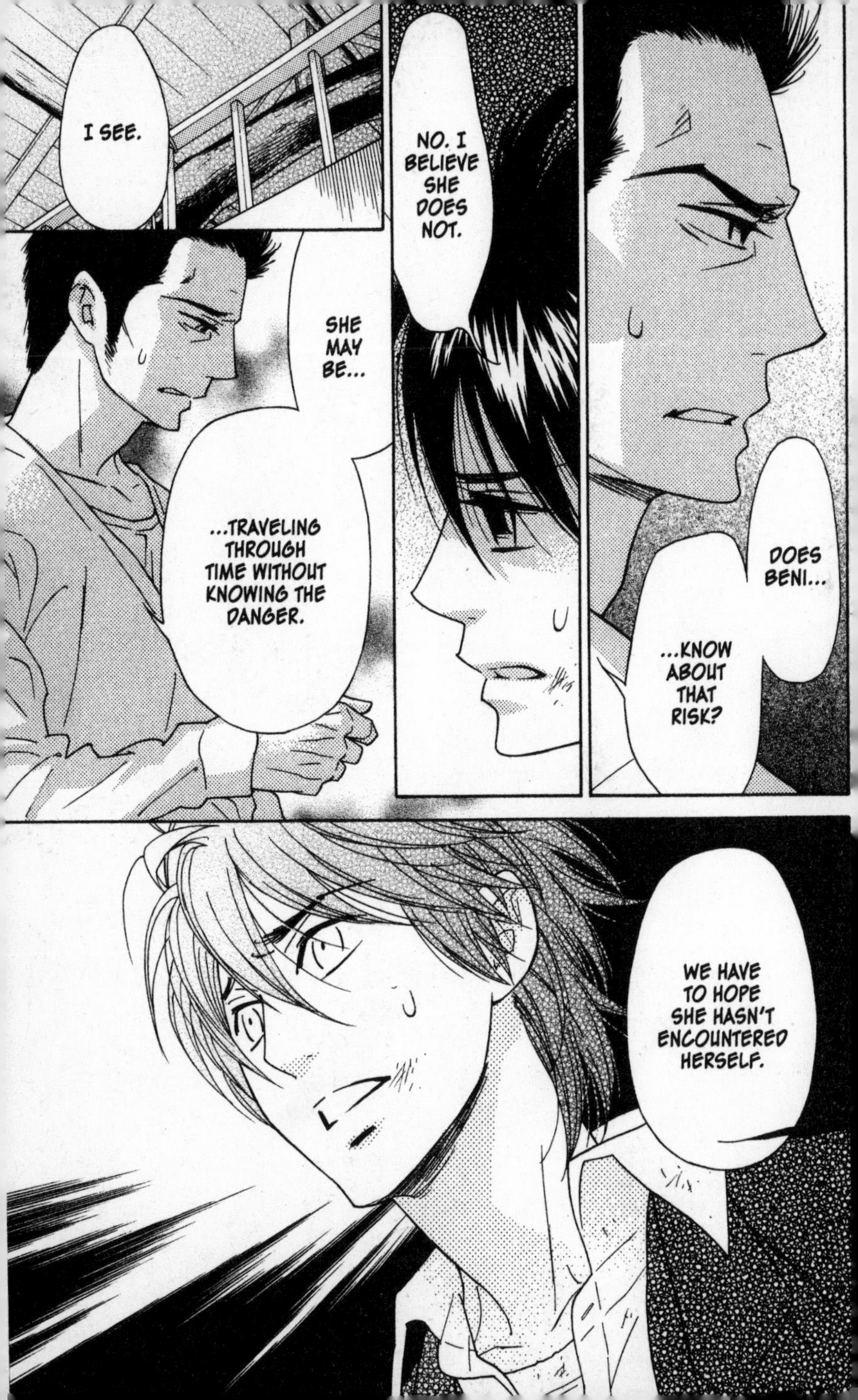
DOES BENI...
...KNOW ABOUT THAT RISK?
NO. I BELIEVE SHE DOES NOT.
I SEE.
SHE MAY BE...
...TRAVELING THROUGH TIME WITHOUT KNOWING THE DANGER.
WE HAVE TO HOPE SHE HASN'T ENCOUNTERED HERSELF.

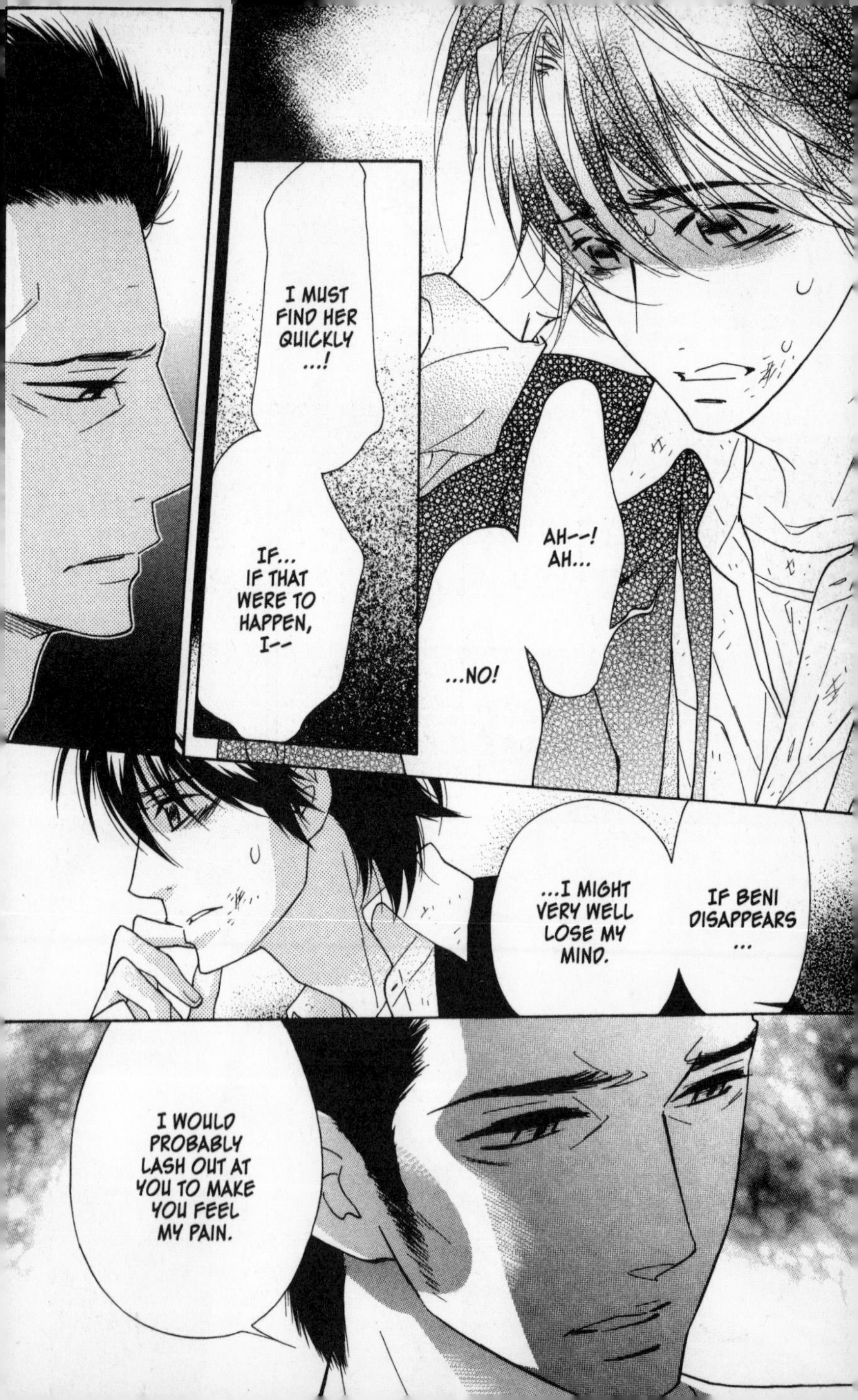
AH--! AH...
...NO!
I MUST FIND HER QUICKLY ...!
IF... IF THAT WERE TO HAPPEN, I--
IF BENI DISAPPEARS ...
...I MIGHT VERY WELL LOSE MY MIND.
I WOULD PROBABLY LASH OUT AT YOU TO MAKE YOU FEEL MY PAIN.

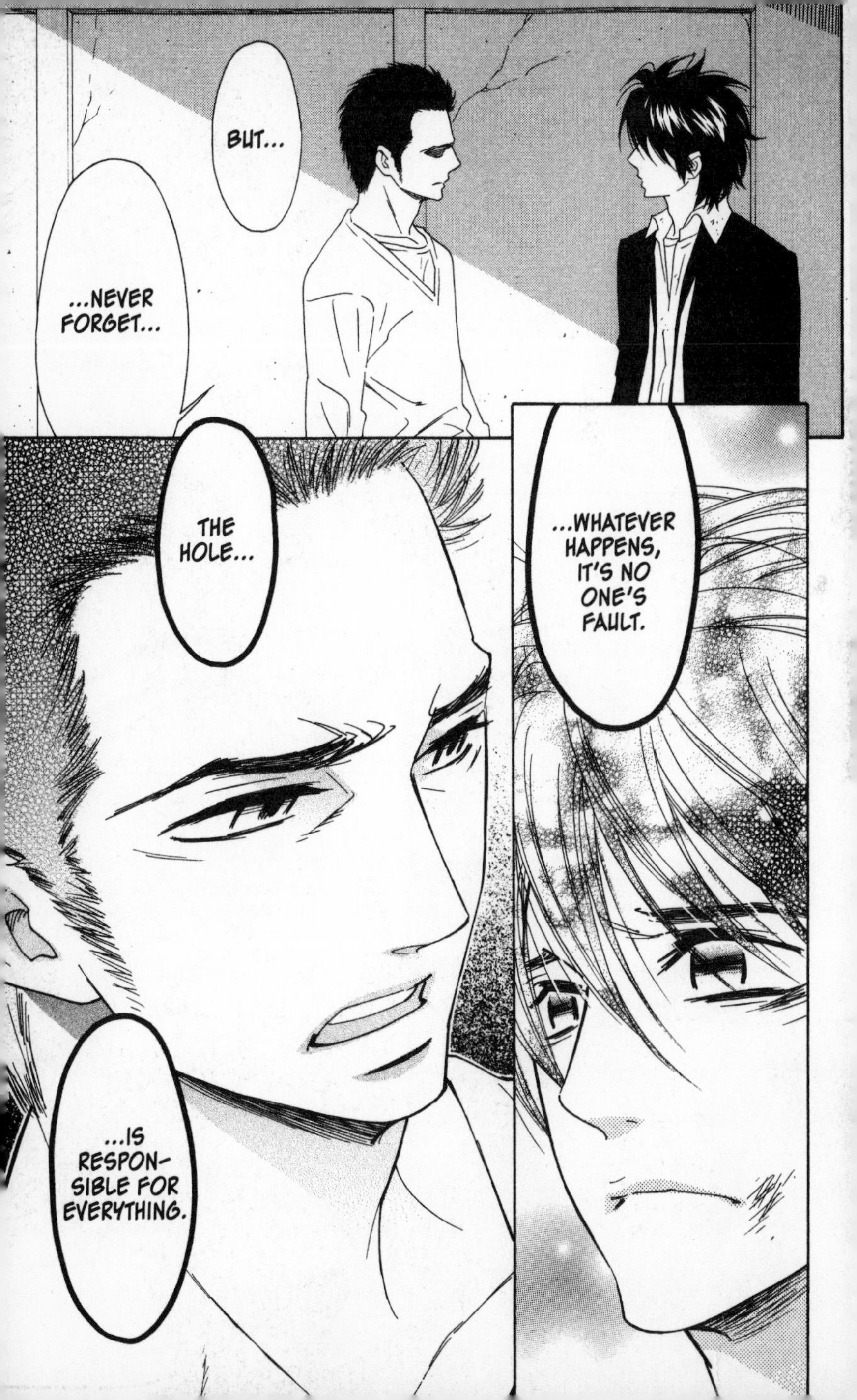
BUT...
...NEVER FORGET...
...WHATEVER HAPPENS, IT'S NO ONE'S FAULT.
THE HOLE...
...IS RESPON-SIBLE FOR EVERYTHING.

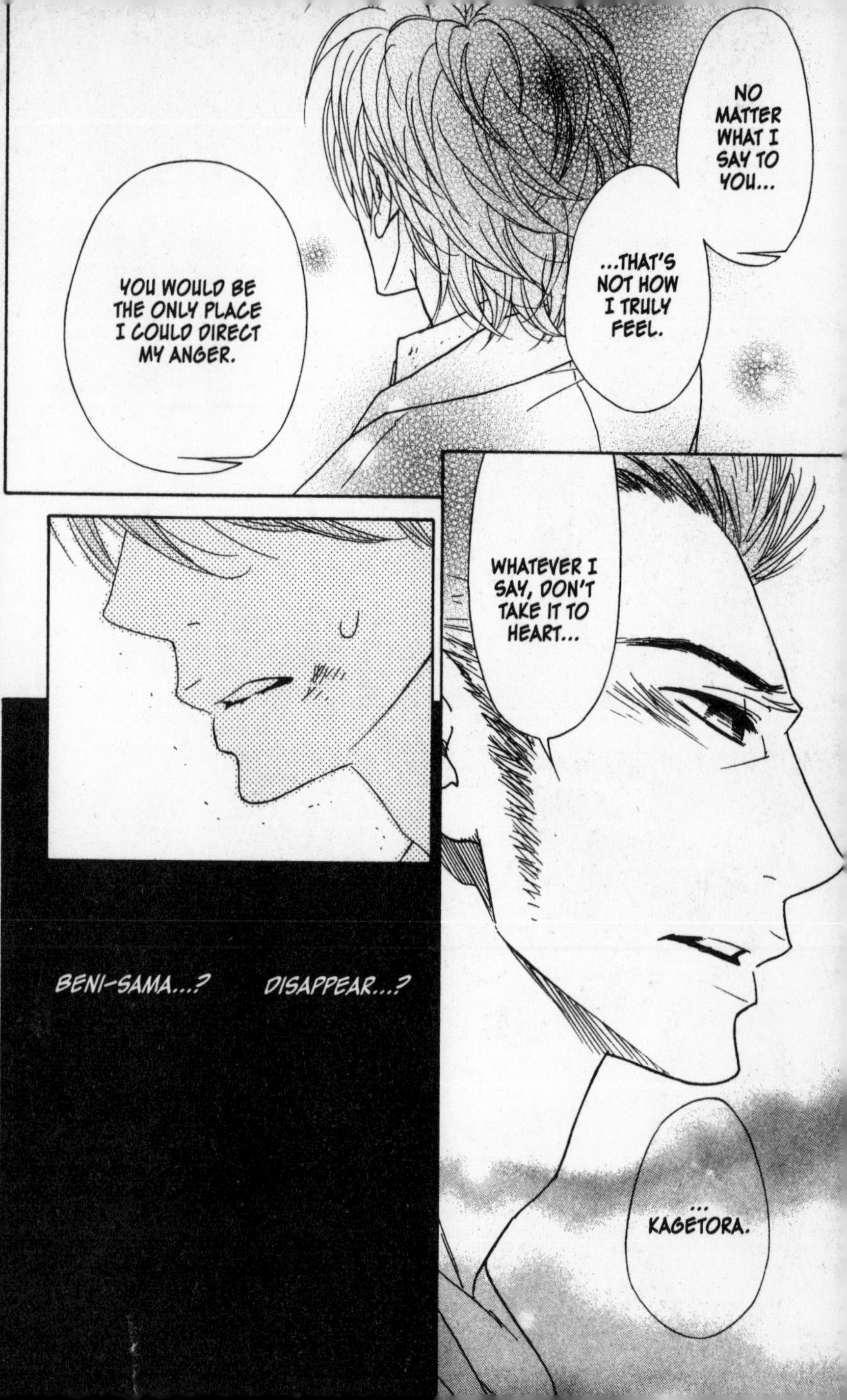
NO MATTER WHAT I SAY TO YOU...
...THAT'S NOT HOW I TRULY FEEL.
YOU WOULD BE THE ONLY PLACE I COULD DIRECT MY ANGER.
WHATEVER I SAY, DON'T TAKE IT TO HEART...
... KAGETORA.
DISAPPEAR...?
BENI-SAMA...?

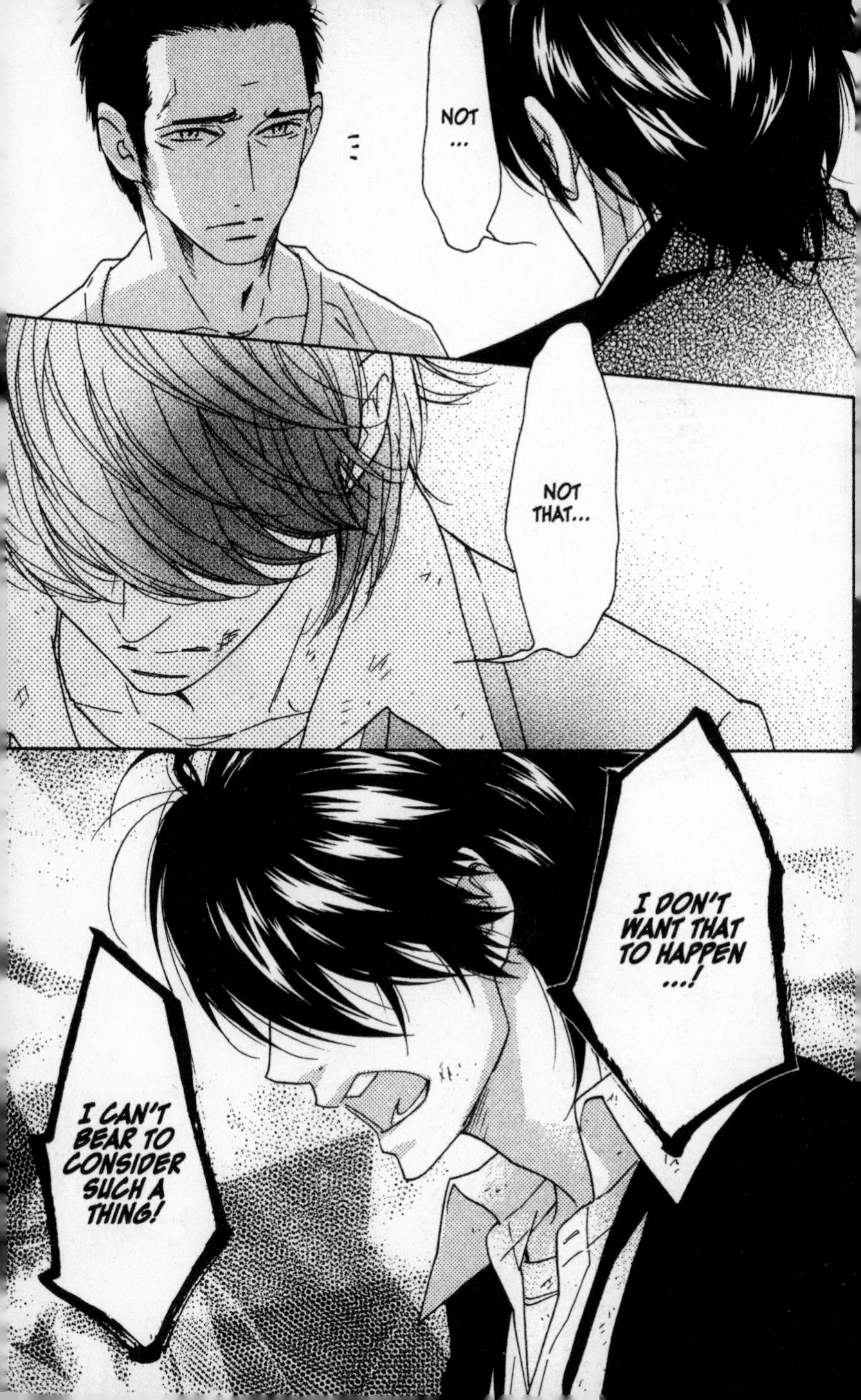
NOT ...
NOT THAT...
I DON'T WANT THAT TO HAPPEN ...!
I CAN'T BEAR TO CONSIDER SUCH A THING!

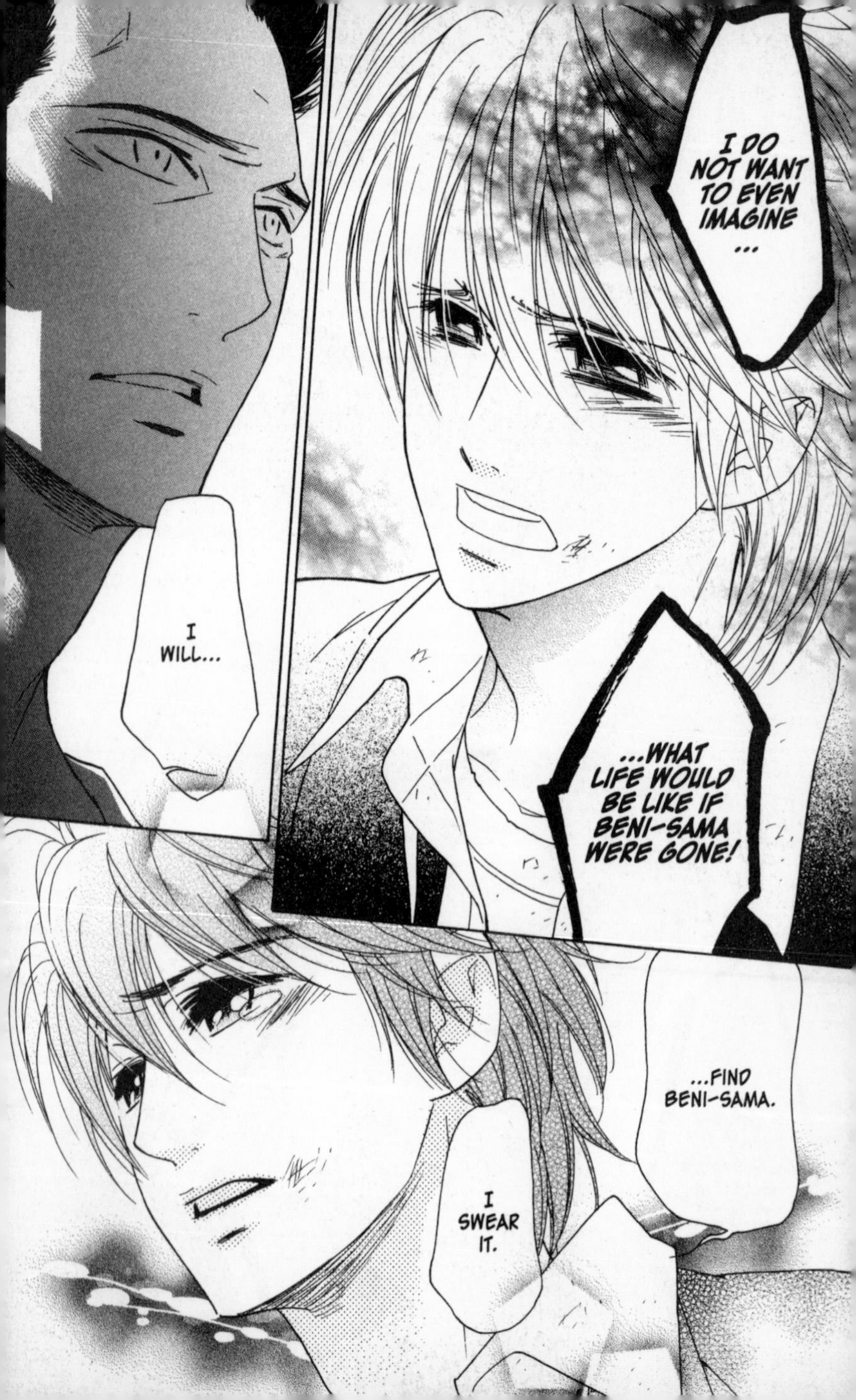
I DO NOT WANT TO EVEN IMAGINE ...
...WHAT LIFE WOULD BE LIKE IF BENI-SAMA WERE GONE!
I WILL...
...FIND BENI-SAMA.
I SWEAR IT.

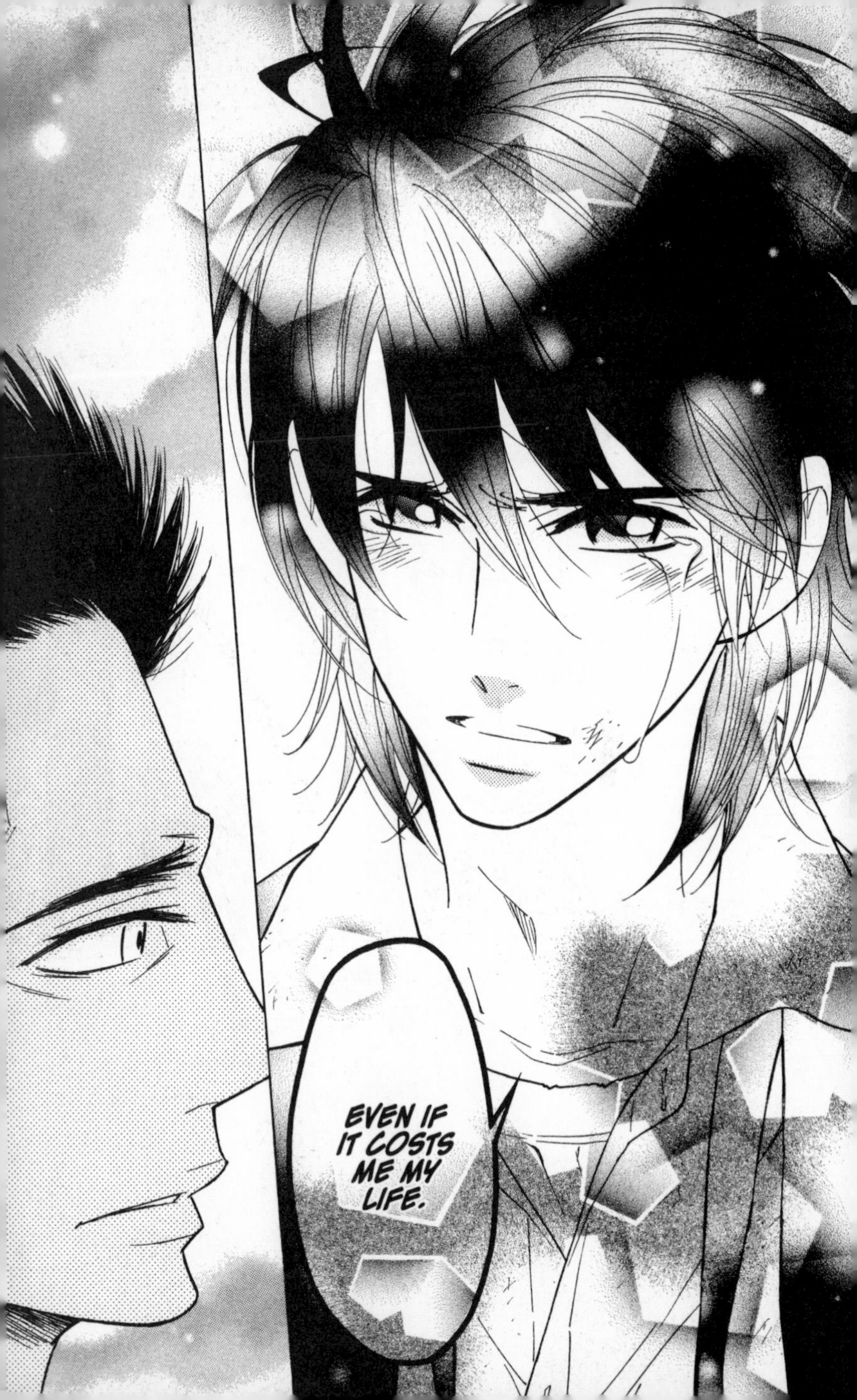
EVEN IF IT COSTS ME MY LIFE.

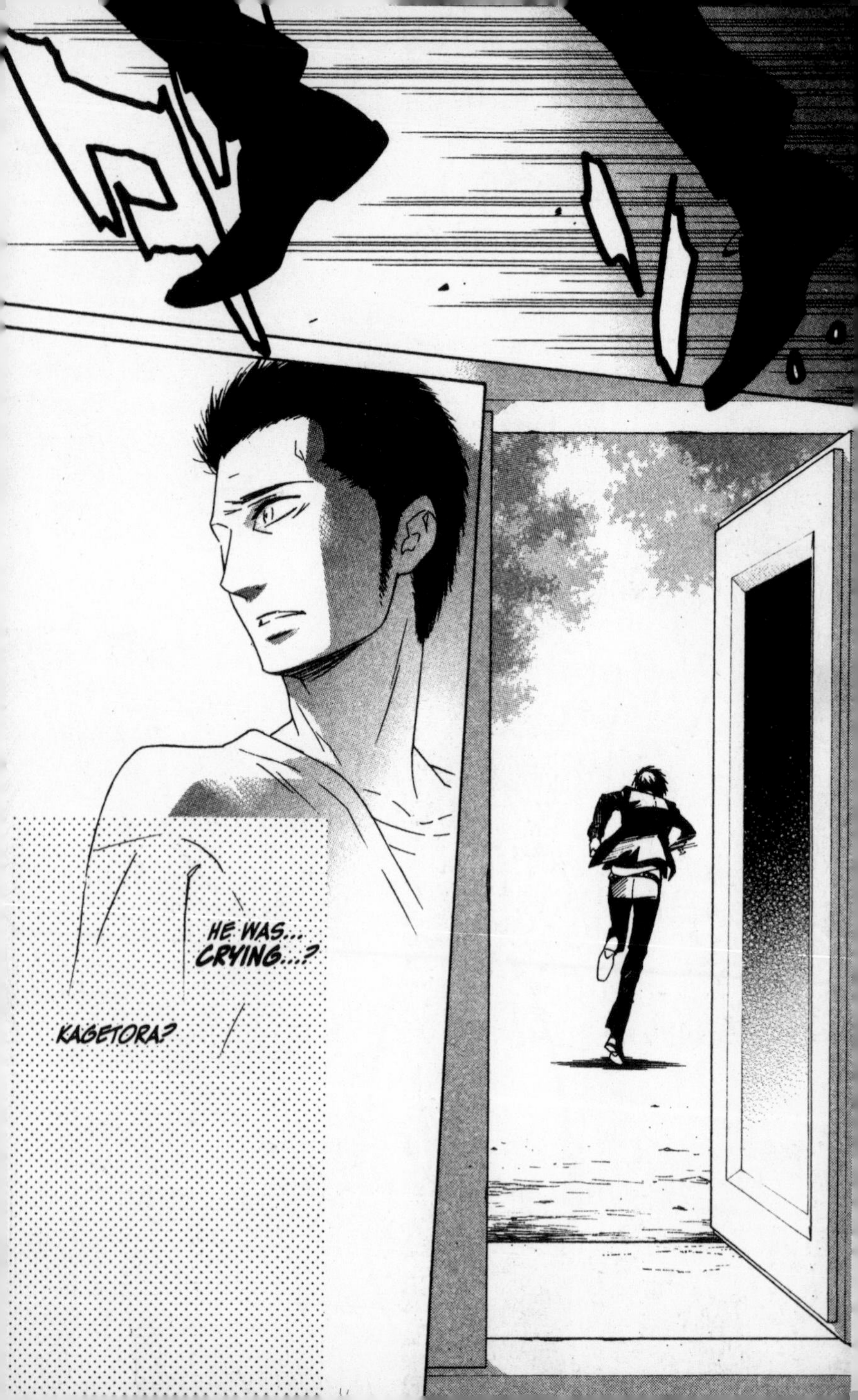
HE WAS... CRYING...?
KAGETORA?

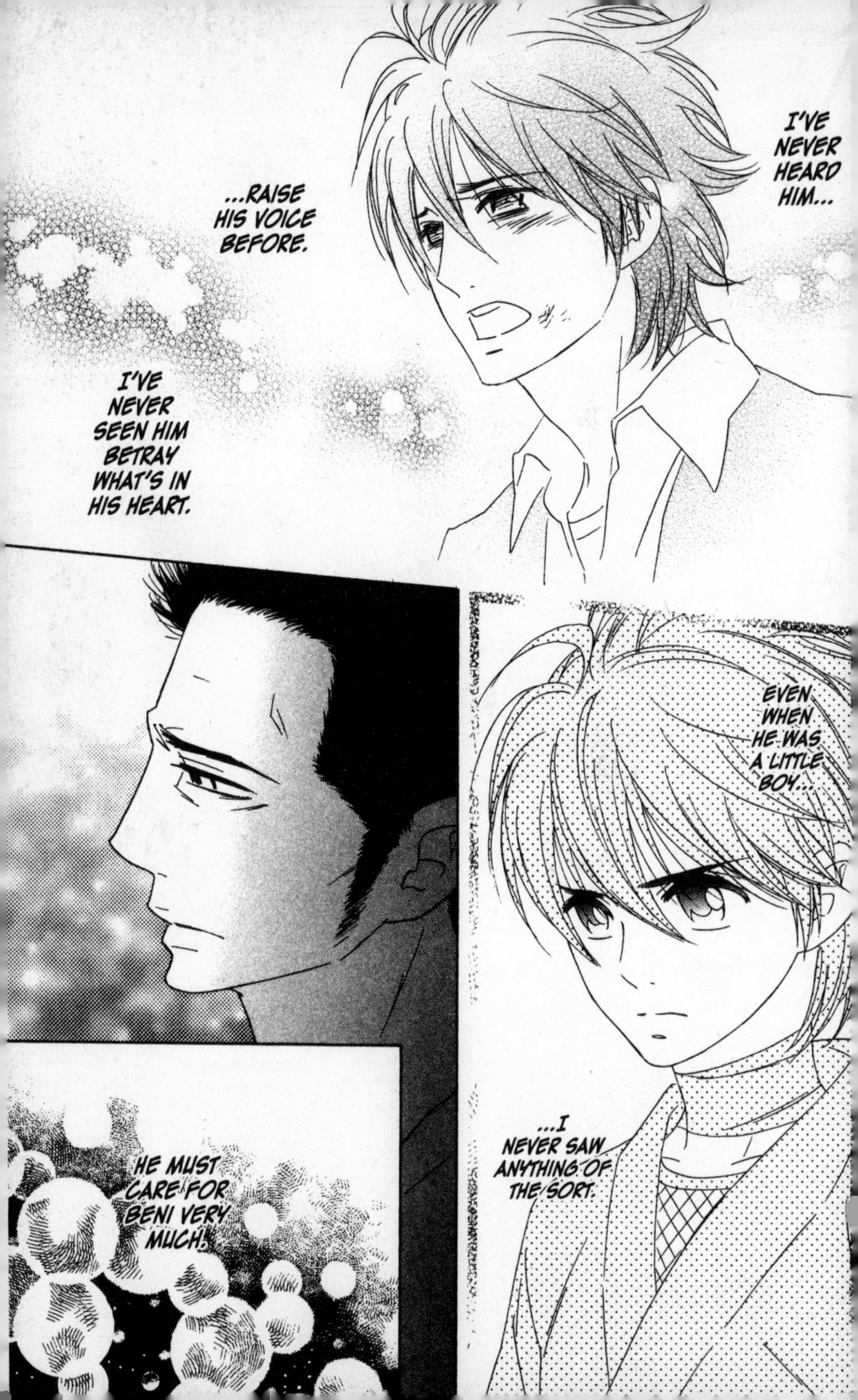
I'VE NEVER HEARD HIM...
...RAISE HIS VOICE BEFORE.
I'VE NEVER SEEN HIM BETRAY WHAT'S IN HIS HEART.
EVEN WHEN HE WAS A LITTLE BOY...
...I NEVER SAW ANYTHING OF THE SORT.
HE MUST CARE FOR BENI VERY MUCH.

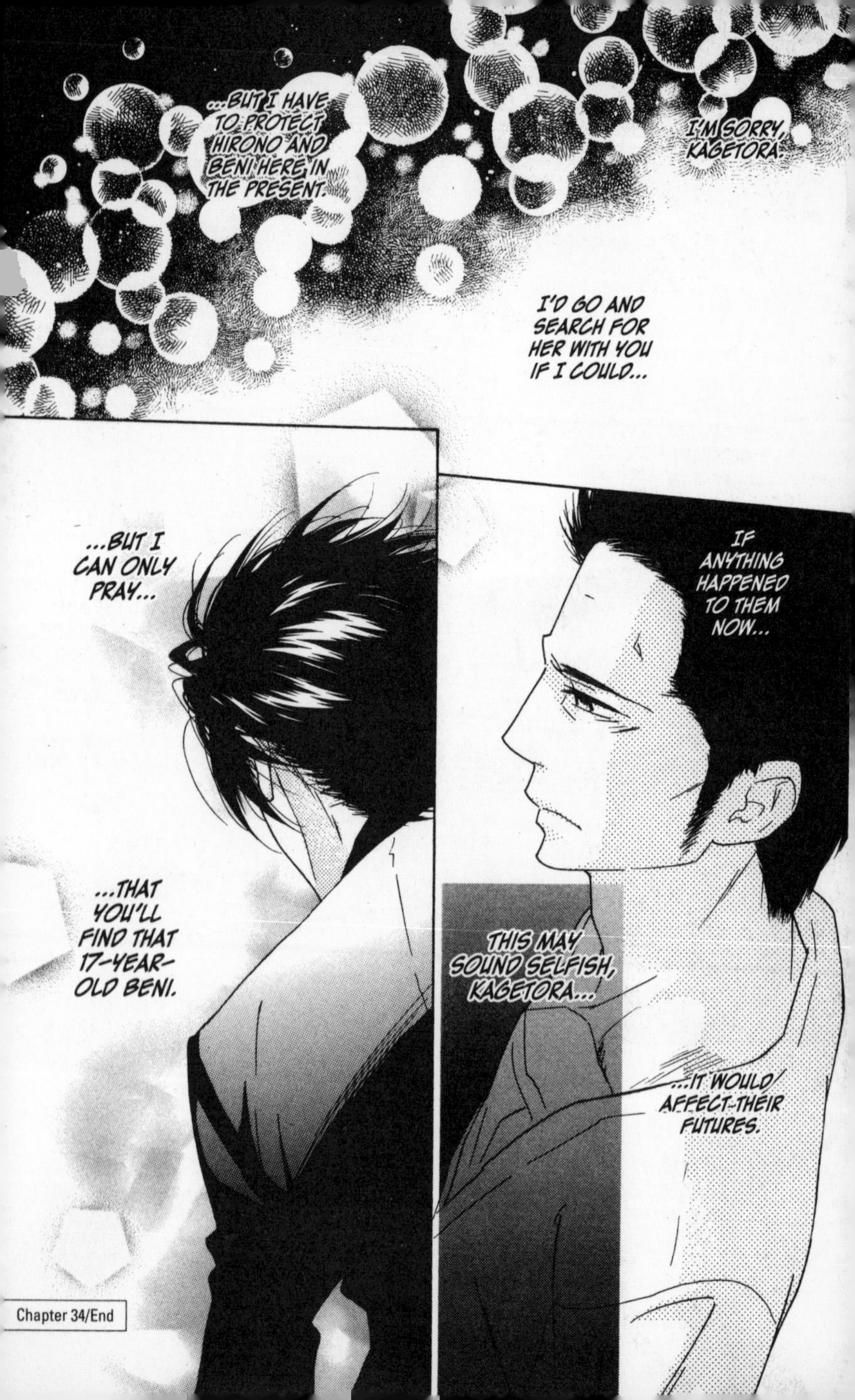
I'M SORRY, KAGETORA.
I'D GO AND SEARCH FOR HER WITH YOU IF I COULD...
...BUT I HAVE TO PROTECT HIRONO AND BENI HERE IN THE PRESENT.
IF ANYTHING HAPPENED TO THEM NOW...
...IT WOULD AFFECT THEIR FUTURES.
THIS MAY SOUND SELFISH, KAGETORA...
...BUT I CAN ONLY PRAY...
...THAT YOU'LL FIND THAT 17-YEAR-OLD BENI.
Chapter 34/End

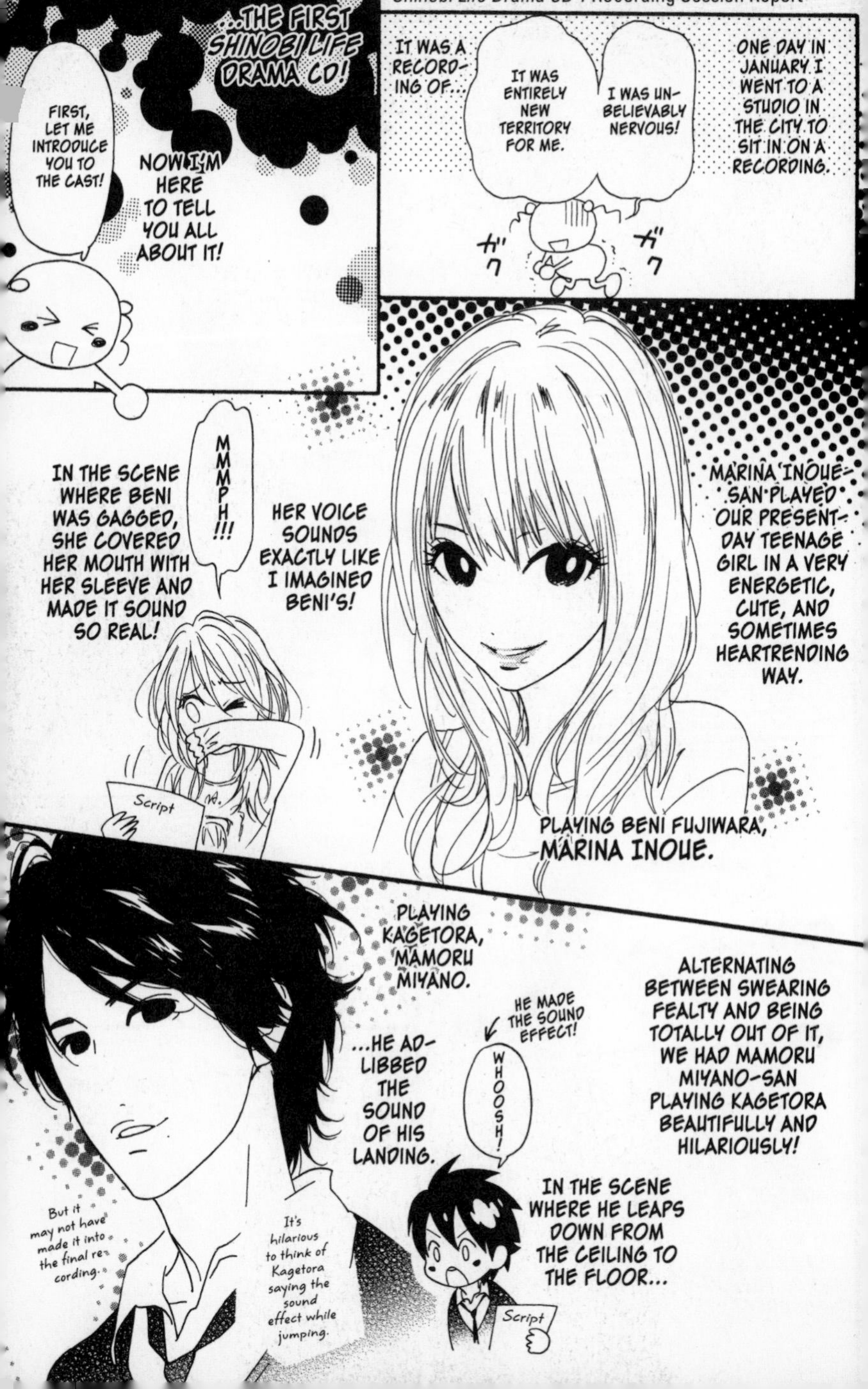
ONE DAY IN JANUARY I WENT TO A STUDIO IN THE CITY TO SIT IN ON A RECORDING.
I WAS UNBELIEVABLY NERVOUS!
IT WAS ENTIRELY NEW TERRITORY FOR ME.
ガク ガク
IT WAS A RECORDING OF...
...THE FIRST SHINOBI LIFE DRAMA CD!
NOW I'M HERE TO TELL YOU ALL ABOUT IT!
FIRST, LET ME INTRODUCE YOU TO THE CAST!
MARINA INOUE-SAN PLAYED OUR PRESENT-DAY TEENAGE GIRL IN A VERY ENERGETIC, CUTE, AND SOMETIMES HEARTRENDING WAY.
PLAYING BENI FUJIWARA, MARINA INOUE.
HER VOICE SOUNDS EXACTLY LIKE I IMAGINED BENI'S!
MMMPH!!!
IN THE SCENE WHERE BENI WAS GAGGED, SHE COVERED HER MOUTH WITH HER SLEEVE AND MADE IT SOUND SO REAL!
Script
ALTERNATING BETWEEN SWEARING FEALTY AND BEING TOTALLY OUT OF IT, WE HAD MAMORU MIYANO-SAN PLAYING KAGETORA BEAUTIFULLY AND HILARIOUSLY!
PLAYING KAGETORA, MAMORU MIYANO.
HE MADE THE SOUND EFFECT!
WHOOSH!
IN THE SCENE WHERE HE LEAPS DOWN FROM THE CEILING TO THE FLOOR...
...HE AD-LIBBED THE SOUND OF HIS LANDING.
Script
It's hilarious to think of Kagetora saying the sound effect while jumping.
But it may not have made it into the final recording.

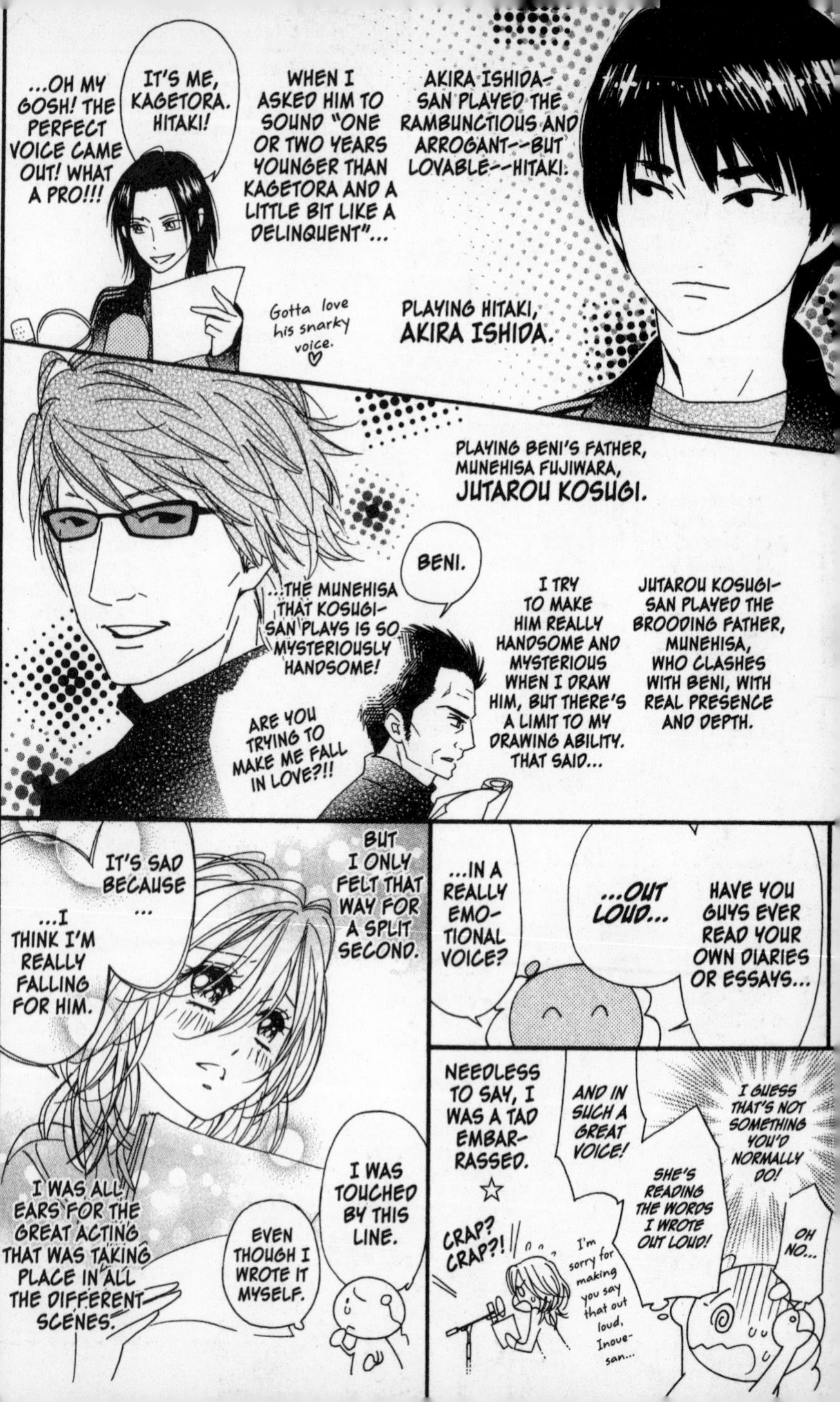
AKIRA ISHIDA-SAN PLAYED THE RAMBUNCTIOUS AND ARROGANT--BUT LOVABLE--HITAKI.
PLAYING HITAKI, AKIRA ISHIDA.
WHEN I ASKED HIM TO SOUND "ONE OR TWO YEARS YOUNGER THAN KAGETORA AND A LITTLE BIT LIKE A DELINQUENT"...
IT'S ME, KAGETORA. HITAKI!
...OH MY GOSH! THE PERFECT VOICE CAME OUT! WHAT A PRO!!!
Gotta love his snarky voice. ♡
PLAYING BENI'S FATHER, MUNEHISA FUJIWARA, JUTAROU KOSUGI.
JUTAROU KOSUGI-SAN PLAYED THE BROODING FATHER, MUNEHISA, WHO CLASHES WITH BENI, WITH REAL PRESENCE AND DEPTH.
I TRY TO MAKE HIM REALLY HANDSOME AND MYSTERIOUS WHEN I DRAW HIM, BUT THERE'S A LIMIT TO MY DRAWING ABILITY. THAT SAID...
BENI.
...THE MUNEHISA THAT KOSUGI-SAN PLAYS IS SO MYSTERIOUSLY HANDSOME!
ARE YOU TRYING TO MAKE ME FALL IN LOVE?!!
HAVE YOU GUYS EVER READ YOUR OWN DIARIES OR ESSAYS...
...OUT LOUD...
...IN A REALLY EMOTIONAL VOICE?
I GUESS THAT'S NOT SOMETHING YOU'D NORMALLY DO!
OH NO...
SHE'S READING THE WORDS I WROTE OUT LOUD!
AND IN SUCH A GREAT VOICE!
NEEDLESS TO SAY, I WAS A TAD EMBARRASSED. ☆
CRAP? CRAP?!
I'm sorry for making you say that out loud, Inoue-san...
BUT I ONLY FELT THAT WAY FOR A SPLIT SECOND.
IT'S SAD BECAUSE...
...I THINK I'M REALLY FALLING FOR HIM.
I WAS TOUCHED BY THIS LINE.
EVEN THOUGH I WROTE IT MYSELF.
I WAS ALL EARS FOR THE GREAT ACTING THAT WAS TAKING PLACE IN ALL THE DIFFERENT SCENES.

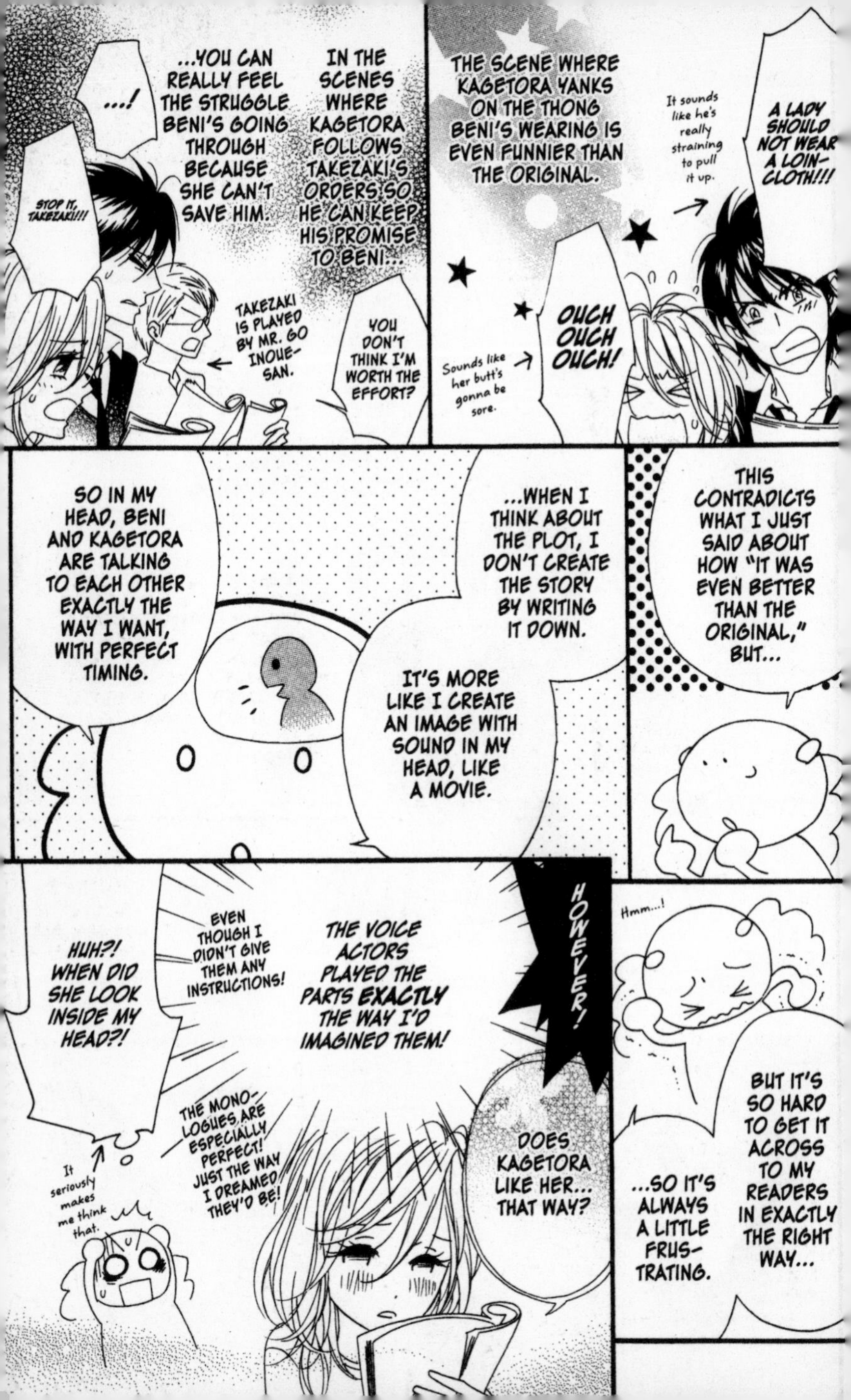
THE SCENE WHERE KAGETORA YANKS ON THE THONG BENI'S WEARING IS EVEN FUNNIER THAN THE ORIGINAL.
A LADY SHOULD NOT WEAR A LOIN-CLOTH!!!
It sounds like he's really straining to pull it up.
OUCH OUCH OUCH!
Sounds like her butt's gonna be sore.
IN THE SCENES WHERE KAGETORA FOLLOWS TAKEZAKI'S ORDERS SO HE CAN KEEP HIS PROMISE TO BENI...
...YOU CAN REALLY FEEL THE STRUGGLE BENI'S GOING THROUGH BECAUSE SHE CAN'T SAVE HIM.
YOU DON'T THINK I'M WORTH THE EFFORT?
...!
TAKEZAKI IS PLAYED BY MR. GO INOUE-SAN.
STOP IT, TAKEZAKI!!!
THIS CONTRADICTS WHAT I JUST SAID ABOUT HOW "IT WAS EVEN BETTER THAN THE ORIGINAL," BUT...
...WHEN I THINK ABOUT THE PLOT, I DON'T CREATE THE STORY BY WRITING IT DOWN.
IT'S MORE LIKE I CREATE AN IMAGE WITH SOUND IN MY HEAD, LIKE A MOVIE.
SO IN MY HEAD, BENI AND KAGETORA ARE TALKING TO EACH OTHER EXACTLY THE WAY I WANT, WITH PERFECT TIMING.
Hmm...!
BUT IT'S SO HARD TO GET IT ACROSS TO MY READERS IN EXACTLY THE RIGHT WAY...
...SO IT'S ALWAYS A LITTLE FRUS-TRATING.
HOWEVER!
THE VOICE ACTORS PLAYED THE PARTS EXACTLY THE WAY I'D IMAGINED THEM!
EVEN THOUGH I DIDN'T GIVE THEM ANY INSTRUCTIONS!
HUH?! WHEN DID SHE LOOK INSIDE MY HEAD?!
DOES KAGETORA LIKE HER... THAT WAY?
THE MONO-LOGUES ARE ESPECIALLY PERFECT! JUST THE WAY I DREAMED THEY'D BE!
It seriously makes me think that.

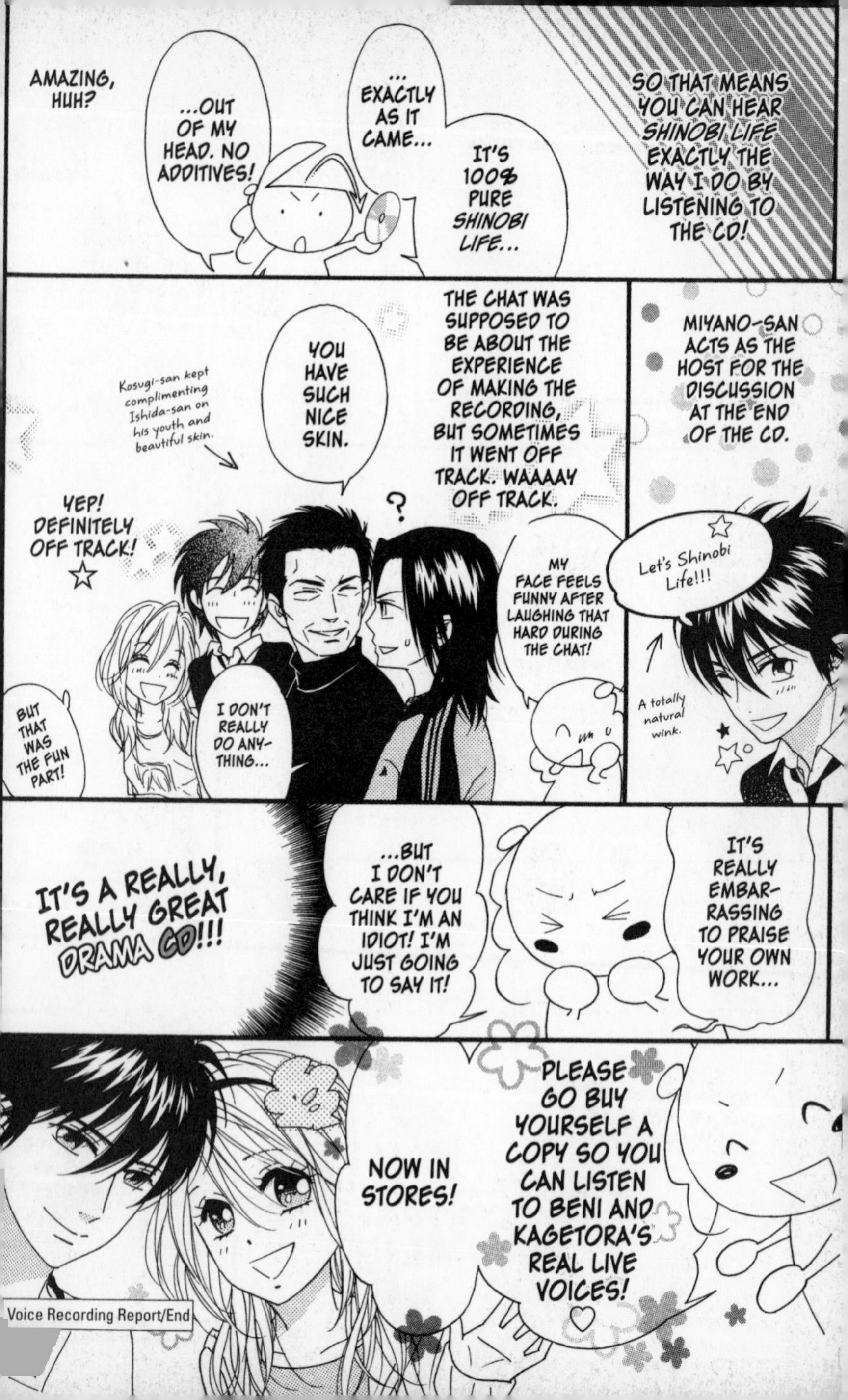
SO THAT MEANS YOU CAN HEAR SHINOBI LIFE EXACTLY THE WAY I DO BY LISTENING TO THE CD!
... EXACTLY AS IT CAME...
IT'S 100% PURE SHINOBI LIFE...
...OUT OF MY HEAD. NO ADDITIVES!
AMAZING, HUH?
MIYANO-SAN ACTS AS THE HOST FOR THE DISCUSSION AT THE END OF THE CD.
Let's Shinobi Life!!!
A totally natural wink.
THE CHAT WAS SUPPOSED TO BE ABOUT THE EXPERIENCE OF MAKING THE RECORDING, BUT SOMETIMES IT WENT OFF TRACK. WAAAAY OFF TRACK.
YOU HAVE SUCH NICE SKIN.
Kosugi-san kept complimenting Ishida-san on his youth and beautiful skin.
?
YEP! DEFINITELY OFF TRACK!
MY FACE FEELS FUNNY AFTER LAUGHING THAT HARD DURING THE CHAT!
I DON'T REALLY DO ANYTHING...
BUT THAT WAS THE FUN PART!
IT'S REALLY EMBARRASSING TO PRAISE YOUR OWN WORK...
...BUT I DON'T CARE IF YOU THINK I'M AN IDIOT! I'M JUST GOING TO SAY IT!
IT'S A REALLY, REALLY GREAT DRAMA CD!!!
PLEASE GO BUY YOURSELF A COPY SO YOU CAN LISTEN TO BENI AND KAGETORA'S REAL LIVE VOICES!
NOW IN STORES!
Voice Recording Report/End

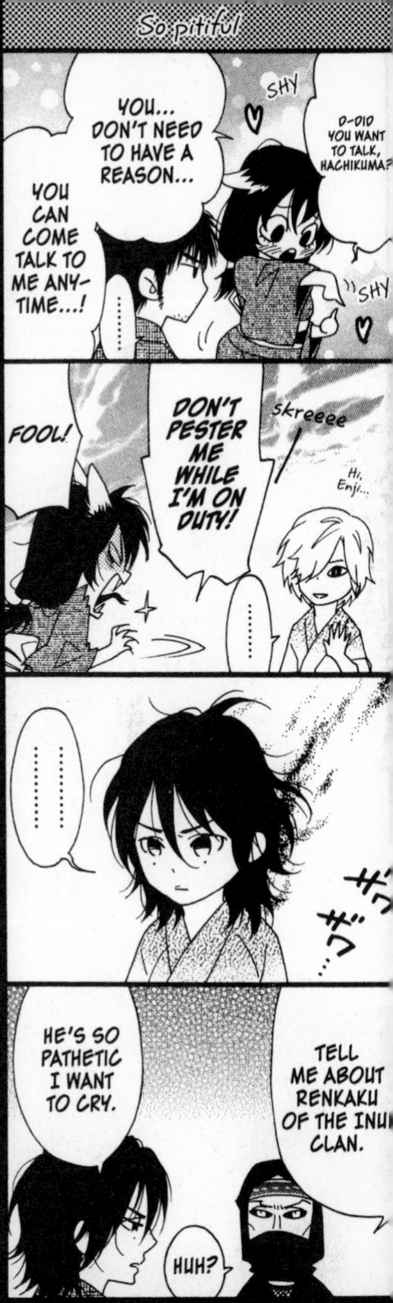
So pitiful
SHY
D-DID YOU WANT TO TALK, HACHIKUMA?
YOU... DON'T NEED TO HAVE A REASON...
YOU CAN COME TALK TO ME ANY-TIME...!
SHY
......
Skreeeee
DON'T PESTER ME WHILE I'M ON DUTY!
FOOL!
Hi, Enji...
......
......
ザワ ザワ...
TELL ME ABOUT RENKAKU OF THE INU CLAN.
HE'S SO PATHETIC I WANT TO CRY.
HUH?

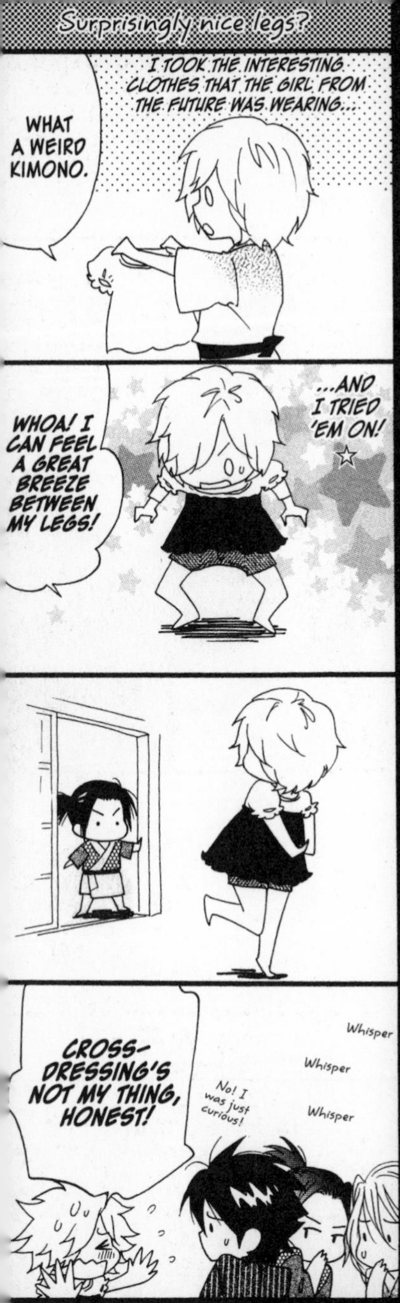
Surprisingly nice legs?
I TOOK THE INTERESTING CLOTHES THAT THE GIRL FROM THE FUTURE WAS WEARING...
WHAT A WEIRD KIMONO.
...AND I TRIED 'EM ON! ☆
WHOA! I CAN FEEL A GREAT BREEZE BETWEEN MY LEGS!
Whisper
Whisper
Whisper
No! I was just curious!
CROSS-DRESSING'S NOT MY THING, HONEST!

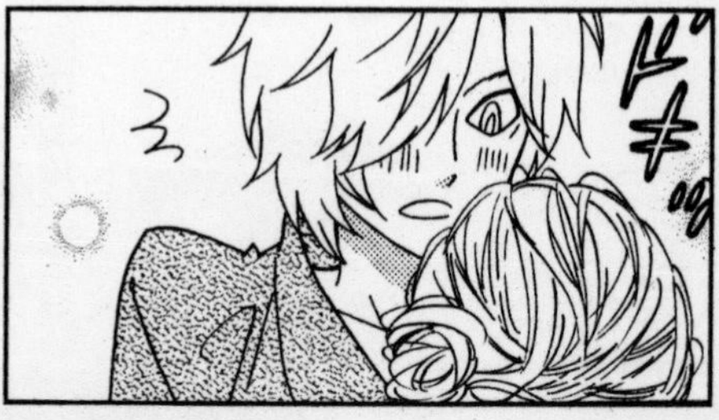
ドキ

IN THE NEXT VOLUME OF

RIHITO MEETS UP WITH OLDER KAGETORA, BACK IN THE PAST, AND THE TWO RESOLVE TO CONTINUE THEIR HUNT FOR BENI. BUT WHAT WILL HAPPEN WHEN "HACHIKUMA" FINALLY MAKES HIS BIG MOVE AGAINST THE INUI CLAN? ESPECIALLY WHEN HIS NEXT TARGET MAY BE BENI HERSELF!

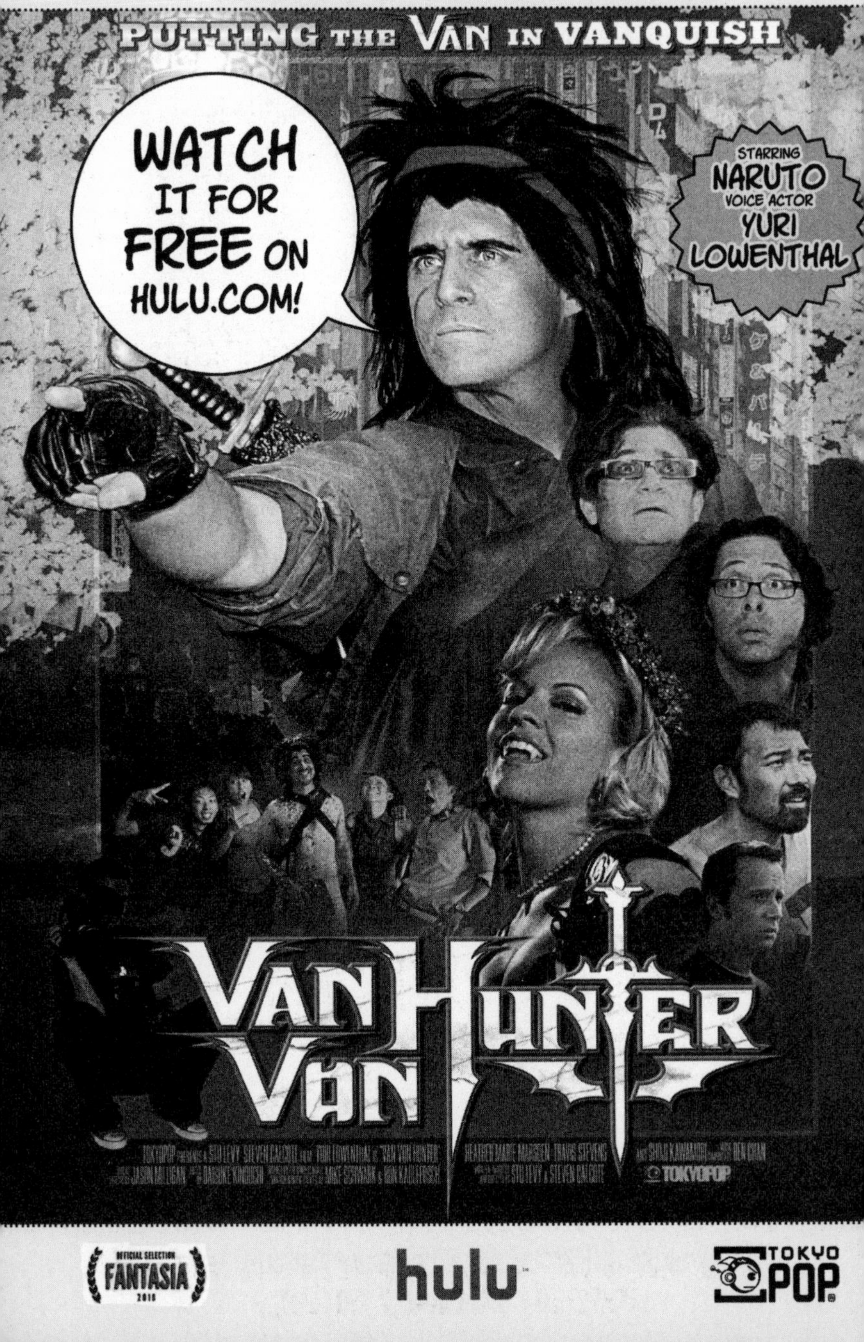
PUTTING THE VAN IN VANQUISH
WATCH IT FOR FREE ON HULU.COM!
STARRING NARUTO VOICE ACTOR YURI LOWENTHAL
VAN VON HUNTER
TOKYOPOP
OFFICIAL SELECTION FANTASIA 2010
hulu
TOKYO POP

EVIL
MERMAIDS
and
MIND-
CONTROLLING
PARASITES
lurk in a
seaside town!

FROM THE
CREATOR OF
chibi-
Vampire

After losing both parents in a car accident, **Tatsuya Tsugawa** tries to fulfill his father's dying wish of becoming an upstanding man. At school, he attempts to save a girl named **Seine** from bullies, but she refuses flat-out and even says that she likes being bullied! What will Tatsuya do when his good will and earnest efforts lead him into a twisted, wicked fantasy world?

© 2009 YUNA KAGESAKI / FUJIMISHOBO.

T
TEEN
AGE 13+

Dead Animals
Need Love Too

RED HOT CHILI SAMURAI
Created By: Yoshitsugu Katagiri

The **HOTTEST** manga in town is about to take a bite out of crime...and the nearest pepper!

Kokaku is the hero and don't you forget it!

As the son of the local lord, his job is to stop evildoers in their tracks. But if he doesn't have a steady flow of the spiciest chili peppers, Kokaku isn't going to stop anything! Can he save his home town from corruption and wrong-doing? Only if you'll pay him in hot sauce!

FOR MORE INFORMATION VISIT: www.TOKYOPOP.com

WARNING:
Nosebleeds Ahead!!!
Karin is back!

laughter, romance and bittersweet
in this must have book for Chibi
ans. Loads of never before seen
sketches, maps and story highlights
nga, anime and novels

A collection of manga stories that follows the
continuing adventures of our favorite vampire
Finally find out what happened to Karin and
her friends in these sweet tales and scary
legends!

CHIBI VAMPIRE
al Fanbook available
January 2011!

CHIBI VAMPIRE: AIRMAIL
available NOW in bookstores
everywhere!

BE SURE TO VISIT WWW.TOKYOPOP.COM/SHOP FOR
EVERYTHING YOU COULD EVER WANT!

Learn From the Best!

Featuring the artists behind *Fruits Basket*, *Vampire Knight*, *Maid Sama* and many more!

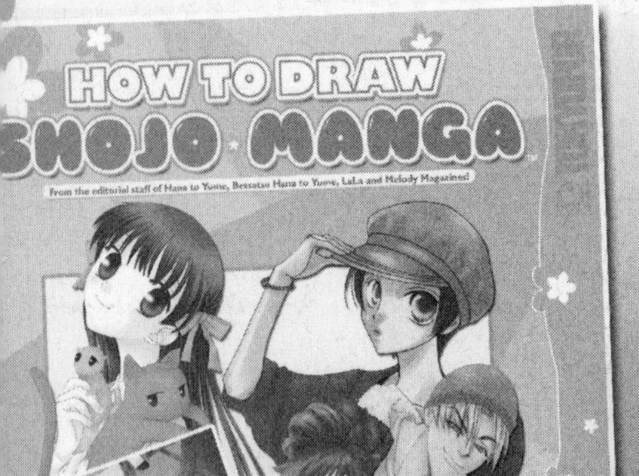
HOW TO DRAW SHOJO MANGA
From the editorial staff of Hana to Yume, Bessatsu Hana to Yume, LaLa and Melody Magazines!
Featuring many of the artists behind today's top shojo series!

Wanna draw your own shojo manga but not quite sure where to start? The editors at Hakusensha Publishing, home of such beloved shojo series as *Fruits Basket*, *Vampire Knight*, *Maid Sama* and *Ouran High School Host Club*, have assembled a book jam-packed with useful tips and practical advice to help you develop your skills and go from beginner to ready for the manga big leagues!

Join aspiring artist Ena as she strives to make her big break drawing manga. Aided by her editor, Sasaki, and some of the best shojo artists in Japan, follow along as Ena creates a short story from start to finish, and gets professional feedback along the way. From page layout and pacing to pencils and perspective, this guide covers the basics, and then challenges you to go to the next level! Does Ena (and you!) have what it takes to go pro? Pick up this book and learn from the best!

ROMANCE

T
TEEN AGE 13+

FOR MORE INFORMATION VISIT: www.TOKYOPOP.com

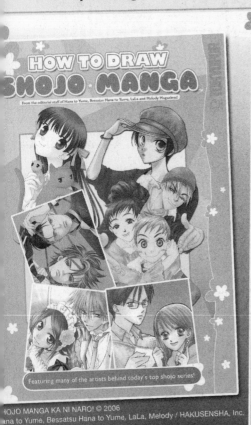

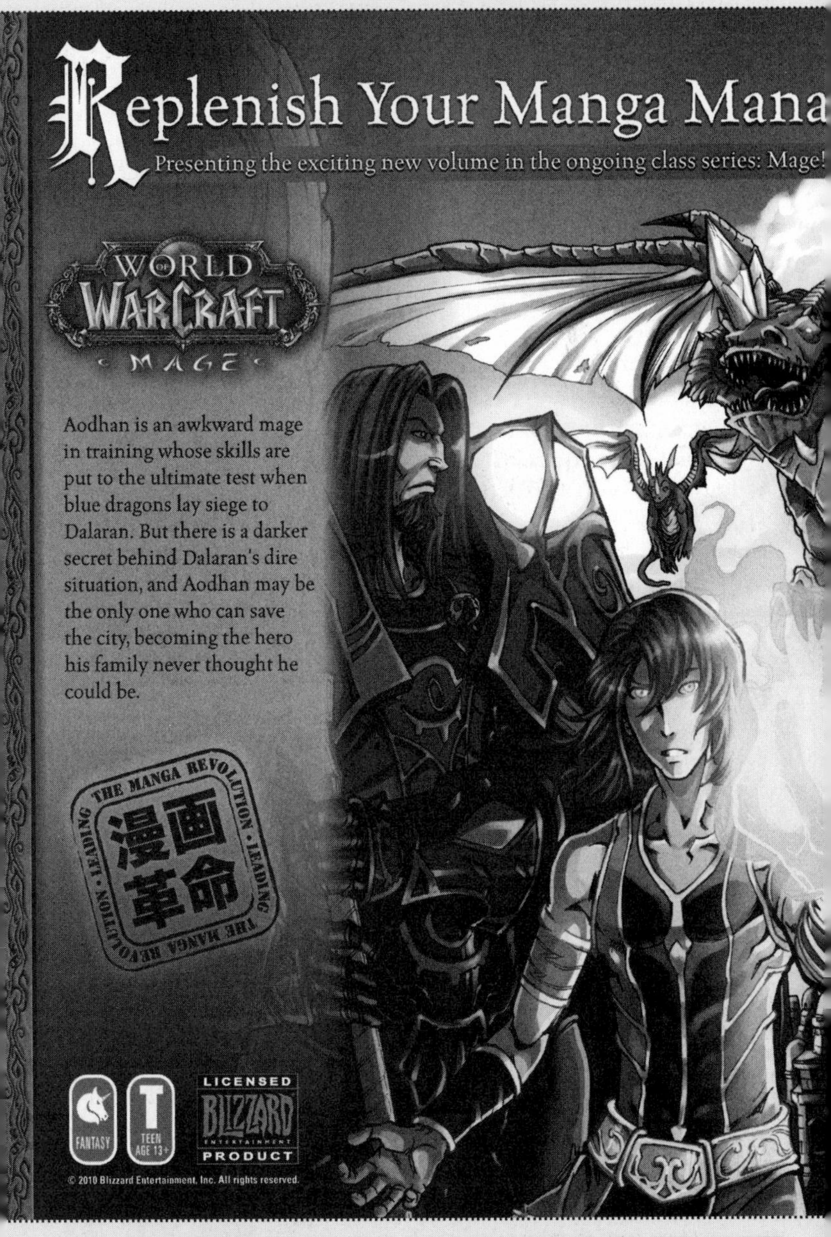
Replenish Your Manga Mana
Presenting the exciting new volume in the ongoing class series: Mage!
WORLD OF WARCRAFT
MAGE
Aodhan is an awkward mage in training whose skills are put to the ultimate test when blue dragons lay siege to Dalaran. But there is a darker secret behind Dalaran's dire situation, and Aodhan may be the only one who can save the city, becoming the hero his family never thought he could be.
THE MANGA REVOLUTION · LEADING
漫画革命
FANTASY
T
TEEN AGE 13+
LICENSED
BLIZZARD ENTERTAINMENT
PRODUCT
© 2010 Blizzard Entertainment, Inc. All rights reserved.

STOP!

This is the back of the book.
You wouldn't want to spoil a great ending!

This book is printed "manga-style," in the authentic Japanese right-to-left format. Since none of the artwork has been flipped or altered, readers get to experience the story just as the creator intended. You've been asking for it, so TOKYOPOP® delivered: authentic, hot-off-the-press, and far more fun!

DIRECTIONS

If this is your first time reading manga-style, here's a quick guide to help you understand how it works.

It's easy... just start in the top right panel and follow the numbers. Have fun, and look for more 100% authentic manga from TOKYOPOP®!